AGAINST JUDICIAL ACTIVISM

Against Judicial Activism

The Decline of Freedom and Democracy in Canada

RORY LEISHMAN

McGill-Queen's University Press
Montreal & Kingston · London · Ithaca

ISBN-13: 978-0-7735-3054-6 ISBN-10: 0-7735-3054-1

Legal deposit second quarter 2006
Bibliothèque nationale du Québec

Printed in Canada on acid-free paper

McGill-Queen's University Press acknowledges the support of the Canada Council for the Arts for our publishing program. We also acknowledge the financial support of the Government of Canada through the Book Publishing Industry Development Program (BPIDP) for our publishing activities.

Library and Archives Canada Cataloguing in Publication

Leishman, Rory, 1942–
Against judicial activism : the decline of freedom and democracy in Canada / Rory Leishman.

Includes bibliographical references and index.
ISBN-13: 978-0-7735-3054-6
ISBN-10: 0-7735-3054-1

1. Political questions and judicial power – Canada.
2. Canada. Supreme Court. 3. Judicial review – Canada. I. Title.

KE8244.L44 2006 347.71′035 C2005-907860-X
KF8764.ZA2L44 2006

Typeset in 10/13 Sabon with Frutiger display by True to Type

Contents

Preface

I owe whatever understanding I have of Canadian constitutional law to several outstanding scholars, beginning with J.A. Corry, the former principal of Queen's University. In an undergraduate course at Queen's in 1961, Corry instilled in me an abiding interest in constitutional issues. As an editorial writer and national affairs columnist for the *London Free Press* in 1981, I was one of the more enthusiastic supporters of the proposed Canadian Charter of Rights and Freedoms. Ian Hunter, a professor in the Faculty of Law at the University of Western Ontario, was no less outspoken in his opposition to the Charter. Consequently, he and I were invited to debate the matter on London's CFPL television station. During this exchange between a bumptious journalist and a learned scholar, I argued that since the Supreme Court of Canada had invalidated only one statute on the ground of incompatibility with the 1960 Canadian Bill of Rights over the previous twenty-two years,[1] there was good reason to believe that the Court would exercise similar restraint in interpreting the similar provisions of the Charter. Hunter predicted that the Court would break with prior restraint and interpret the Charter as a licence to routinely strike down and amend statutes duly enacted by Parliament and the provincial legislatures. Events soon proved that Hunter was right, although it took me several years to admit this in a column in the *Free Press*. When I asked Hunter what he thought about that column, he was kind enough to commend it as one of my more perceptive efforts.

During a conversation in 1992, I told Hunter that I had just come across an illuminating book, *Charter Politics* by Rainer Knopff and F.L.

(Ted) Morton, both professors in the Department of Political Science at the University of Calgary. Hunter observed that it was a sorry commentary on the current state of scholarship in the law faculties of Canada that it took these two professors of political science to write the best and most penetrating account of judicial misinterpretation of the Charter. In 2000 Morton and Knopff produced another insightful study entitled *The Charter Revolution and the Court Party*.

Meanwhile, in 1995 Robert Hawkins and Robert Martin, both professors in the Faculty of Law at the University of Western Ontario, had published an article in the *McGill Law Journal*, "Democracy, Judging and Bertha Wilson," that spells out how activist judges on the Supreme Court of Canada have distorted the original understanding of the Charter. In 2003 Martin followed up with a book, *The Most Dangerous Branch: How the Supreme Court of Canada Has Undermined Our Law and Our Democracy*. One of the features of this aptly titled tome is the foreword by Conservative Senator Anne Cools, a former Liberal whom Prime Minister Trudeau chose for the Senate in 1984. Martin lauds Cools as the Senator Eugene Forsey of our time – a fine tribute inasmuch as Forsey was a formidable constitutional scholar.

If I could choose the next chief justice of Canada, I would have no hesitation in selecting Gwen Landolt, the longstanding national vice president of REAL Women of Canada. She is one of Canada's most experienced constitutional lawyers and perceptive critics of activist judges. Her tract "Project Justice: Changing Canada's Flawed Political and Judicial Systems" is must reading for Canadians who lament the state of our law and democracy.

I used to be no less enthused about Canada's expansive human rights codes than I was about the Charter. On this issue, too, Hunter was right from the start. In a 1983 article in the *McGill Law Journal*, "Liberty and Equality: A Tale of Two Codes," he pointed out that the revised and extended version of the Ontario Human Rights Code, adopted in 1981, "is declaratory in form, comprehensive in scope, and, I venture to assert, totalitarian in its implications." I have learned a lot from this article as well as from Hunter's *Three Faces of the Law: A Christian Perspective*, a succinct and compelling treatise after the manner of John Stuart Mill's *On Liberty*.

I am also indebted to Howard McConnell, emeritus professor in the College of Law at the University of Saskatchewan and the author of a fine biography of Mr Justice William McIntyre of the Supreme Court of Canada. Having kindly read an earlier version of this book's Introduction, he commended the manuscript to Roger Martin, an astute editor at McGill-Queen's University Press. Given that the great majority of legal academics would summarily reject my unconventional thoughts on judicial activism, there could have been fewer more surprised and delighted authors than I on the day that Martin informed me that he had received "two positive reports from two very capable readers." Both of these readers have provided sage advice for improvement of the manuscript. I am most grateful to them and to Martin for their key roles in getting this book into print.

In writing the book, I have drawn upon several of my previously published articles with the kind permission of the publishers: "Robed Dictators," *The Next City*, October 1998; "Our Judges Are Activist Only When It Suits Them," *Policy Options*, September 1999; "Judicial Leaps of Logic," *Policy Options*, October 2003; "The Judicial Imposition of 'Gay Rights,'" in Alphonse de Valk, general editor, *Judicial Activism: A Threat to Democracy and Religion;* and "Mad Court Disease," *Touchstone: A Journal of Mere Christianity*, March 2005.

Of course, the faults in this text are entirely my own. I would be grateful if readers who have suggestions for improvement would send their comments to: mail@roryleishman.com.

Finally, this book is dedicated to my wife, Lientje – my best friend and my best editor. I cannot imagine how I could carry on without her unfailing love.

Rory Leishman,
London, Ontario
June 2005

AGAINST JUDICIAL ACTIVISM

Introduction

Judges ought to remember, that their office is *jus dicere,* and not *jus dare;* to interpret law, and not to make law, or give law.

Sir Francis Bacon, "Of Judicature," *Essays* (1601)

On 17 April 1982 the Canadian Charter of Rights and Freedoms was signed into law. In the meantime, Parliament and the provincial legislatures have also progressively broadened the scope of their respective human rights codes. Together, these radical innovations in the Canadian constitutional order were supposed to safeguard the human rights and fundamental freedoms of Canadians. But have these new laws succeeded? Or have they served as an excuse for human rights tribunals and the courts to undermine freedom, democracy, and the rule of law in Canada?

Prior to the Charter, Parliament and the provincial legislatures were supreme – that is, they had virtually untrammelled authority to make, amend, and revoke laws within their respective spheres of legislative jurisdiction under the division of federal and provincial powers in the Constitution. Today, the Supreme Court of Canada reigns supreme over the legislative as well as the judicial process. Time and again over the past twenty years, unelected judges on this Court have issued guidelines on legislative policy to the democratically elected representatives of the people of Canada in what is supposed to be the legislative branch of government. On occasion, the Court has circumvented the democratic process altogether by changing the law on its own.

Consider, for example, the decision of the Supreme Court of Canada in *Vriend v. Alberta,* 1998 SCC. At issue in this case was a dispute between the administration of King's University College in Edmonton and Delwyn Vriend, an employee of the college who had mocked the school's Christian code of conduct by wearing a T-shirt emblazoned with a homosexual slogan.[1] At the instigation of some indignant students, King's College fired Vriend. He appealed the dismissal, first to the Human Rights Commission of Alberta and then to the courts. Eventually, the case ended up before the Supreme Court of Canada. In a ruling on 2 April 1998, Canada's top court held that in dismissing Vriend for insubordinate behaviour, the college had violated the ban on discrimination on the basis of sexual orientation in the Alberta Human Rights, Citizenship, and Multiculturalism Act.

This was a remarkable ruling inasmuch as there was not, and never had been, any reference to sexual orientation in the Alberta Human Rights Act. Indeed, the Supreme Court of Canada frankly acknowledged in its judgment in *Vriend* that the Alberta Legislature had repeatedly refused to proceed with Opposition demands that a provision on sexual orientation be incorporated into the province's human rights legislation. Likewise, there is not now, and never has been, any mention of sexual orientation in the Canadian Charter of Rights and Freedoms. Like the Alberta Legislature, the Parliament of Canada clearly rejected proposals to include any reference to sexual orientation in the Charter when it was adopted. But has the Supreme Court of Canada paid any heed to such unmistakeable indications of the express will of elected representatives of the people in Parliament and the provincial legislatures? Not at all. First, in *Egan v. Canada,* 1995 SCC, the Court read sexual orientation into the equality rights provisions of section 15 of the Charter, and then, three years later in *Vriend,* the Court cited *Egan* as authority for a decision to flout the Legislature of Alberta by reading a ban on discrimination on the basis of sexual orientation into the Alberta Human Rights Act.

In *M v. H.,* 1999 SCC, the Supreme Court of Canada followed up on *Egan* and *Vriend* by decreeing that the denial of spousal benefits to same-sex couples under the Ontario Family Law Act was inconsistent with the allegedly implicit equality rights of homosexuals in section 15 of the Charter to an extent that could not be demonstrably justified in a free and democratic society. Just five years earlier, the elected representatives of the people of Ontario had debated this same issue at the instigation of Ontario's attorney general, Marion Boyd. On behalf of the New Democratic Party government of Premier Bob Rae, she introduced a bill that proposed to give cohabiting gay and lesbian couples essentially the same rights and responsibilities in provincial law as common law couples.[2] The proposal met with a popular outcry so intense that backbenchers among Boyd's fellow New Democrats were moved to join with the Opposition in defeating the bill. Typically, the Supreme Court of Canada has paid no heed to this clear and deliberate expression of the will of the majority of the elected representatives of the people. However, instead of abruptly amending the law as in

Vriend, the Court condescended in *M. v. H.* to give the Ontario Legislature six months to come up with a series of amendments ensuring that the spousal benefits and obligations of cohabiting same-sex couples are equivalent to those of heterosexual, common law couples in the laws of Ontario. The Legislature promptly complied. Where Boyd failed, the Court succeeded in browbeating the elected legislators of Ontario into expediting passage of an omnibus bill that conferred spousal benefits upon same-sex couples under the Ontario Family Law Act and sixty-six other Ontario statutes. In short order, Parliament and the legislatures of every other province followed suit: They, too, meekly and promptly brought their laws into line with the discovery by the Supreme Court of Canada in *M. v. H.* that the Constitution of Canada mandates equal rights for homosexual and heterosexual couples in common law relationships.

In an attempt to limit the adverse impact of *M. v. H.* on marriage and the natural family, the Canadian Alliance proposed a resolution in the House of Commons on 8 June 1999 declaring: "It is necessary, in light of public debate around recent court decisions, to state that marriage is and should remain the union of one man and one woman to the exclusion of all others, and that Parliament will take all necessary steps within the jurisdiction of the Parliament of Canada to preserve this definition of marriage in Canada." Prime Minister Jean Chrétien supported this Opposition resolution. And so did most of his Liberal Cabinet. In leading off debate for the government on the resolution, Justice Minister Anne McLellan avowed: "Let me state again for the record that the government has no intention of changing the definition of marriage or of legislating same sex marriages." McLellan flatly rejected the contention of gay rights activists that homosexuals have the same right to marry as heterosexuals. She said: "I fundamentally do not believe that it is necessary to change the definition of marriage in order to accommodate the equality issues around same sex partners which now face us as Canadians." She added: "Marriage has fundamental value and importance to Canadians and we do not believe on this side of the House that that importance and value is in any way threatened or undermined by others seeking to have their long term relationships recognized. I support the motion for maintaining the clear legal definition of marriage in Canada as the union of one man and one woman to the exclusion of all others."[3]

With the backing of most Liberal and Progressive Conservative members of Parliament, this Canadian Alliance resolution upholding the historic definition of marriage in the common law of Canada was adopted by the overwhelming margin of 216 to 55. Eight months later, Parliament and the Chrétien government reaffirmed their support for the traditional definition of marriage in the Modernization of Benefits and Obligations Act – the omnibus federal bill that was adopted pursuant to the *M. v. H.* ruling for the purpose of conferring equality rights on same-sex couples in some sixty-eight federal statutes. In an explanatory note, the federal Department of Justice explained that the changes in federal law effected by the Act "will ensure that, in keeping with the Supreme Court of Canada decision in *M. v. H.* (May 1999), same-sex common-law couples have the same obligations and benefits as opposite-sex common-law couples and will provide them with the same access as other Canadian couples to social benefits programs to which they have contributed."[4] A more abject parliamentary capitulation to the legislative will of the Supreme Court of Canada is hard to imagine, yet even in this Act, Parliament made a point of reiterating in section 1.1: "For greater certainty, the amendments made by this Act do not affect the meaning of the word 'marriage,' that is, the lawful union of one man and one woman to the exclusion of all others."

Have the appeal courts of Canada paid any heed to these repeated expressions of parliamentary support for the traditional definition of marriage? Definitely not. On 1 May 2003 the British Columbia Court of Appeal decreed in *Barbeau v. British Columbia (Attorney General)*, 2003 BCCA 406, that the common law bar to same-sex marriage violates the equality rights of homosexuals in section 15 of the Charter. In reasons for the Court, Madame Justice Jo-Ann Prowse said that while she was disposed to reformulate the common law definition of marriage as "the lawful union of two persons to the exclusion of all others," she had decided to suspend this remedy until 12 July 2004 "solely to give the federal and provincial governments time to review and revise legislation to bring it into accord with this decision."

Even this small courtesy to Parliament and the provincial legislatures was too much for the Ontario Court of Appeal. On 10 June 2003 a three-judge panel led by Ontario's chief justice, Roy McMurtry, abruptly declared in *Halpern et al. v. Attorney General of Canada et al.*, 2003 OCA: "We reformulate the common law definition of marriage as 'the voluntary union for life of two persons to the exclusion of all others.'" By this means, the Court immediately granted same-sex couples the unprecedented right to marry in Ontario. Since then, courts in Manitoba, Newfoundland, Nova Scotia, Saskatchewan, Quebec, and the Yukon have done the same: In all of these jurisdictions, activist judges have violated the common law, distorted the Constitution, and defied the express will of Parliament by writing same-sex marriage into law.

In reaction to these illegitimate rulings, Parliament could have invoked its power under the notwithstanding clause of the Constitution to enact a bill reaffirming the traditional definition of marriage. Chrétien rejected this option. He abandoned the formal commitment that he and his Liberal Cabinet colleagues had made just two years earlier to "take all necessary steps within the jurisdiction of the Parliament of Canada to preserve this [traditional] definition of marriage in Canada." Instead, the Chrétien government capitulated to the courts. Scarcely a month after the *Halpern* ruling, Justice Minister Martin Cauchon introduced a bill on behalf of the government that declared: "1. Marriage, for civil purposes, is the lawful union of two persons to the exclusion of all others. 2. Nothing in this Act affects the freedom of officials of religious groups to refuse to perform marriages that are not in accordance with their religious beliefs." Then, in an extraordinary affront to the dignity of Parliament, the Chrétien government referred the bill to the Supreme Court of Canada for approval prior to passage.

Paul Martin took over as prime minister on 12 December 2003. A few weeks later, on 28 January 2004, his government put an additional question to the Supreme Court of Canada, asking if the centuries-old definition of marriage in the common law as the voluntary union for life of a man and a woman is compatible with the Constitution of Canada. In a unanimous ruling on 9 December 2004, the Court ducked this new question while advising that far from violating the Charter, the government's draft bill on same-sex marriage flowed from the section 15 equality rights that the Court had conferred on homosexuals in the 1995 *Egan* judgment.

With this ruling, the Supreme Court of Canada has all but mandated the imposition of same-sex marriage. Earlier, this same Court legalized abortion on demand in *R. v. Morgentaler*, 1988 SCC, and came within one vote of declaring a constitutional right to assisted suicide in *Rodriguez v. British Columbia (Attorney General)*, 1993 SCC. The Supreme Court of Canada has had no compunction about invoking the Charter as justification even for imposing amendments to government acts with major spending implications. This process began in *Schachter v. Canada*, 1992 SCC, when the Court extended postnatal maternity benefits under the Unemployment Insurance Act to fathers. In *Eldridge v. British Columbia*, 1997 SCC, the Court compelled the Government of British Columbia to introduce free sign-language interpretation in all provincial hospitals. In a unanimous judgment in *Hislop et al. v. The Attorney General of Canada*, 2004 OCA, the Ontario Court of Appeal amended both the Modernization of Benefits and Obligations Act and the Canada Pension Plan to make survivors' benefits for same-sex common law couples retroactive to 17 April 17 1985 – the date on which the equality rights provisions of the Charter came into effect. With this ruling, the Court extended survivor's benefits to about 1,500 homosexuals at an estimated cost of $80 million.[5] In *Gosselin v. Quebec (Attorney General)*, 2002 SCC 84, the Supreme Court of Canada came within one vote of ordering the Government of Quebec to hand out extra welfare payments to young Quebecers at an estimated cost to taxpayers of $389 million plus interest.

Ultimately, of course, taxpayers must foot the bills for judicially created entitlements. But that is of no account to our unelected lawmakers in the courts. Time and again, they have ordered governments to spend money on programs that have never been approved by elected representatives of the people in the legislative branch of government. In issuing these orders, these activist judges have repeatedly violated one of the cardinal principles of democracy: no taxation without representation.

With the prominent exception of law professors Michael Mandel of Osgoode Hall Law School[6] and Robert Martin of the Faculty of Law at the University of Western Ontario,[7] the great majority of leftist law professors have joined with left-wing politicians and pundits in applauding the disposition of activist judges on the Supreme Court of Canada to read the agenda of the left into the abstract words of the Charter. However, most of these same leftist intellectuals and politicians were astounded and outraged on 9 June 2005 when the Court handed down one of its rare right-wing decisions in *Chaoulli v. Quebec (Attorney General)*, 2005 SCC 35, which struck down the prohibition on private health insurance in the health and hospital insurance acts of Quebec. With this ruling, the Court signalled that it is prepared to impose two-tiered health care on all Canadians. In reasons for the majority in *Chaoulli*, Chief Justice Beverley McLachlin and Mr Justice John Major stated: "We conclude, based on the evidence, that prohibiting [private] health insurance that would permit ordinary Canadians to access health care, in circumstances where the government is failing to deliver health care in a reasonable manner, thereby increasing the risk of complications and death, interferes with life and security of the person as protected by s. 7 of the Charter." Section 7 of the Charter simply states: "Everyone has the right to life, liberty and security of the person and the right not to be deprived thereof except in accordance with the principles of fundamental justice." Citing this section as justification, McLachlin and Major insist that they and other activist judges on the Supreme Court of Canada have a mandate to impose two-tiered medicare on the people of Canada. Is that correct? Is this a fair reading of the original understanding of section 7?

At least three members of the Supreme Court of Canada think not. In a joint dissent in *Chaoulli*, Justices Ian Binnie, Morris Fish, and

Louis LeBel affirm: "We cannot find in the constitutional law of Canada a 'principle of fundamental justice' dispositive of the problems of waiting lists in the Quebec health system. In our view, the appellants' case does not rest on constitutional law but on their disagreement with the Quebec government on aspects of its social policy. The proper forum to determine the social policy of Quebec in this matter is the National Assembly." Exactly. All Canadians, left and right, should agree on this point: In a genuine parliamentary democracy, political disputes over policy issues like single-versus two-tiered medicare should be resolved by elected representatives of the people, not by nine unelected and unaccountable judges.

Regardless, no matter how much judicial interpretation of the Charter has undermined the democratic process in Canada, it is commonly supposed that enactment of the Charter has at least made Canadians more secure in the enjoyment of their basic human rights and fundamental freedoms. Yet even this assumption is gravely mistaken. Time and again, human rights tribunals and the courts have invoked the Charter to abridge historic rights and fundamental freedoms of all Canadians. That goes even for members of such politically influential organizations as the Vancouver Rape Relief Society, a nationally prominent, nonprofit charitable agency that operates the oldest rape crisis centre in Canada.[8] In a ruling on 17 January 2002, the British Columbia Human Rights Tribunal found that in refusing to admit a transsexual who had undergone male-to-female sex reassignment surgery to a training program for rape crisis counsellors, Rape Relief had contravened the ban on discrimination on the basis of transsexualism that the tribunal held to be implicit in the ban on discrimination on the basis of sex in the British Columbia Human Rights Code and the Canadian Charter of Rights and Freedoms.[9] The tribunal ordered Rape Relief to atone for this judicially contrived offence by paying the transsexual complainant $7,500 as compensation for "the injury to her dignity, feelings and self-respect."

Prior to the enactment of Canada's modern human rights codes and the Charter, such a bizarre legal dispute could not have occurred. Under the venerable rules of the common law, freedom of association was so firmly guaranteed that an organization like Rape Relief had an unimpeachable right in law to accept or reject anyone – homosexual, heterosexual, bisexual, or transsexual – as a voluntary rape crisis counsellor. As it is, thanks to judicial interpretation of the Charter and the British Columbia Human Rights Code, members of Rape Relief have been embroiled for the better part of the past ten years in an expensive legal battle, appealing to the British Columbia Human Rights Tribunal and the courts to uphold the right of a feminist organization to choose only women born as women to serve as rape crisis counsellors.

Rape Relief's plight is not unusual. In a similar case, the Quebec Human Rights Tribunal dealt with a disagreement between Maison des Jeunes, a youth centre in Montreal, and a sexually troubled, male employee who worked with street youths.[10] The conflict started when the male employee showed up for work dressed as a female, pronounced himself a male-to-female transsexual, and requested that his supervisor treat him as a female employee. The management of Maison des Jeunes initially acquiesced to this unusual request, but after the man's contract expired, the agency refused to offer him a renewal. He complained to the Commission des droits de la personne et des droits de la jeunesse (Quebec Human Rights Commission), which readily took up the case. Together, M.L. and the commission asked the Quebec Human Rights Tribunal to declare that in refusing to rehire M.L., Maison des Jeunes had violated the ban on discrimination on the basis of "sex" in Quebec's Charter of Human Rights and Freedoms. In an unprecedented ruling on 2 July 1998, the tribunal agreed with this argument. Tribunal president Michèle Rivet specifically held that Maison des Jeunes had discriminated against M.L. on the basis of transsexualism. There is no mention of transsexualism in the Charter, but this did not inhibit Rivet. She deemed that "transsexualism or the process of unifying disparate sexual criteria is included in the term 'sex' in s. 10. of the Quebec Charter."

It is noteworthy that in bringing this case before the tribunal, the commission designated the complainant M.L. with the male pronoun "il." Regardless, Rivet referred to M.L. throughout her ruling as a female. She explained: "As M.L. presents herself [*sic*] as a woman, she will be designated as such throughout this judgment."[11] In short, Rivet took the view that since the man dressed as a woman and considered himself a woman, he was for the purposes of the law a woman, although he was biologically a male and had not undergone sex reassignment surgery. By this reasoning, she resolved to order the youth centre to pay M.L. $1,750 in compensation for his lost wages and another $4,000 in damages for violating what Rivet called "her [*sic*] right to respect for her [*sic*] dignity."[12]

Over the past twenty years, one freedom-stifling ruling by a human rights tribunal has quickly led to another. Just a few months after the decision of the Quebec Human Rights Commission in *M.L. v. Maison des Jeunes*, the British Columbia Human Rights Tribunal ordered a nightclub in Victoria to pay $2,000 in damages to a cross-dressing man because a club bouncer had refused to allow him to use the women's washroom.[13] Citing *Maison des Jeunes* as a precedent, the British

Columbia tribunal likewise held that a male-to-female transsexual who represents himself as a woman has become a woman for the purposes of human rights legislation, even if he remains physically a man. In arriving at this conclusion, the tribunal paid no heed to the contrary judgment of the Federal Court, General Division, in *Canada v. Owen*, 1994 FCGD. In this case, the appellant was a preoperative, male-to-female transsexual who had lived as a female for more than fifty years and had been "married" to another man during nine of those years. Nonetheless, the Court held that the appellant was not a female within the meaning of the law because he had not undergone sex reassignment surgery, and that he was therefore not entitled to spousal benefits under the Old Age Security Act. Sensible precedents like *Canada v. Owen* mean nothing to activist judges and human rights adjudicators. They prefer to read their own ideological preferences into the law by subjecting the plain words of the text to large, liberal, progressive, and idiosyncratic interpretations.

Avowed homosexuals have often benefited from the unprecedented decisions of Canada's human rights tribunals, but not even members of this now-privileged minority remain secure in the freedoms previously guaranteed to all Canadians by the common law. Former members of the defunct Vancouver Lesbian Connection understand this point all too well. In 1997 they ran afoul of the British Columbia Human Rights Commission for expelling from their sisterhood a man who represented himself as a preoperative male-to-female transsexual.[14] In this instance, the complainant, Susan Amy Mamela, known prior to July 1997 as Eric Friday, testified to the commission that he had developed a strong identity as a lesbian female in November 1995. The following March, he wrote a letter to the Vancouver Lesbian Connection asking for permission to join the organization as a transsexual lesbian. He signed this letter as "Eric (Susan) Friday." At the annual general meeting of the Lesbian Connection in May 1996, the organization resolved after much discussion to open its membership to "self-identified queer, bisexual and transgendered womyn [*sic*]." In October 1996 Mamela duly joined the Lesbian Connection under the name "Susan Friday." But alas for him, his membership did not last long. Five months later, he got into a heated argument with fellow members over an interview he had given to a West Coast homosexual newspaper in which he refused to describe himself as a woman on the ground that the word "woman" is a contemptible construct used by men to put down females. That stance offended the female members of the Lesbian Connection who took pride in their identification as "womyn." They were not mollified by Mamela's explanation that he regarded himself as a lesbian, albeit not a woman. Following a bitter confrontation over his stubborn refusal to identify himself as both a lesbian and a woman, Mamela's associates in the Lesbian Connection denounced him as "aggressive and mannish" and expelled him from their lesbian and feminist fellowship.

Mamela appealed for reinstatement to the British Columbia Human Rights Commission, accusing the Lesbian Connection of unlawfully discriminating against him on the basis of his gender identity as a female. Following several months of investigation and fruitless mediation by the commission, the matter came before the British Columbia Human Rights Tribunal. In a ruling on 8 September 1999, the tribunal held that the Lesbian Connection had indeed discriminated against Mamela on the basis of his sex, ordered the Lesbian Connection to cease discriminating against him and other self-affirming, male-to-female transsexuals, and directed the nonprofit sisterhood to pay Mamela "the sum of $3,000 in compensation for injury to her [*sic*] dignity, feelings and self-respect."

The female members of the Lesbian Connection took exception to the tortured reasoning that had led the tribunal to declare that a man like Mamela qualifies in law as a woman because he self-identifies as a woman, although in all biological respects, he is, and always has been, a man. In protest, the outraged women disbanded the Lesbian Connection. As for Mamela, it seems that he has continued to struggle with his sexual identity: On 20 February 2001, the Canadian Press reported: "Susan Mamela ... has said he will not have surgery to become a woman."[15]

In the Charter era, not even the hitherto most respectable and law-abiding of Canadians remain secure in the historic rights and freedoms formerly guaranteed by the common law and the conventions of the Canadian Constitution. Consider the ordeal of Scott Brockie.[16] He is a Toronto print-shop owner and a devout Evangelical Protestant who became the focus of a precedent-setting judicial confrontation because of his refusal on religious grounds to obey an order by the Ontario Human Rights Tribunal to print letterheads and other materials for an organization that promotes gay, lesbian, and bisexual lifestyles. In a unanimous ruling on 17 June 2002, a three-judge panel of the Ontario Superior Court of Justice ordered Brockie to comply with the tribunal's order. Brockie finally acquiesced. Had he failed to do so, he could have been consigned to jail for contempt of court.

In a similar 1997 dispute, Dianne Haskett, a lawyer and devout Christian then serving as mayor of London, Ontario, was ordered by an Ontario human rights board of inquiry to issue gay pride proclamations.[17] Like Brockie, she refused to comply as a matter of religious principle. Had the complainants in her case pressed the matter, she, too, could have been hauled before the courts and sentenced to jail for standing by her Christian convictions. Even now, the same fate awaits numerous other mayors in cities from Kelowna to Fredericton: They could all end up behind bars if they were to disobey a court order requiring them to heed the directive of a human rights tribunal to issue a gay pride proclamation, regardless of their personal moral convictions and the preferences of their constituents.

Further, the Catholic Church has been singled out for human rights attack. In an ominous development on 10 May 2002, Mr Justice Robert McKinnon of the Ontario Superior Court of Justice issued an interlocutory injunction compelling the Durham Catholic District School Board and the principal of the Monsignor John Pereyma Catholic Secondary School in Oshawa, Ontario, to allow Mark Hall, a seventeen-year-old student, to attend a Grade 12 prom with his twenty-one-year-old homosexual boyfriend as a date.[18] Auxiliary Bishop Anthony Meagher, the supervising Catholic cleric for the Oshawa area, affirmed that permitting a seventeen-year-old boy to take another male to a dance would violate the clear teaching against homosexual behaviour in the definitive Catechism of the Catholic Church. McKinnon presumed to disagree. Notwithstanding the rights conferred on the Catholic schools of Ontario in section 93 of the Constitution Act, 1867, and the ostensible guarantees of freedom of conscience and religion in section 2(a) of the Charter, he took the view that Hall had a constitutional right to attend the prom by virtue of the overriding equality rights conferred on homosexuals in section 15 of the Charter.

Meanwhile, Catholic bishop Fred Henry of Calgary has come under investigation by the Alberta Human Rights Commission for denouncing the Martin government's bill on same-sex marriage.[19] In a pastoral letter issued in January 2005 and in a subsequent column in the *Calgary Sun*, Henry wrote: "Since homosexuality, adultery, prostitution and pornography undermine the foundations of the family, the basis of society, then the State must use its coercive power to proscribe or curtail them in the interests of the common good." In a complaint filed with the Alberta Human Rights Commission, Carol Johnson of Calgary charged that Bishop Henry's letter "is likely to expose homosexuals to hatred or contempt" contrary to section 3 of the Alberta Human Rights, Citizenship, and Multiculturalism Act. Under terms of section 22 of this Act, Marie Riddle, the director of the Alberta Human Rights Commission, could have summarily dismissed the complaint as without merit on the ground that the bishop has an undeniable right to express his views on same-sex marriage by virtue of the guarantees of both freedom of religion and freedom of the press in section 2 of the Charter as well as section 3 of the Alberta Human Rights Act. Instead, she publicly advised that it could take a year for the commission to decide whether to summon Bishop Henry before a human rights panel to answer to the complaints occasioned by his pastoral letter and newspaper column.

Given the judicial distortion of human rights in Canada, it is no longer safe for a Christian or Jew in this country even to draw attention in public to a list of Bible verses that condemn homosexual acts. Hugh Owens, a Regina prison guard, and Lyle Sinkewicz, publisher of the *Saskatoon StarPhoenix*, have first-hand knowledge of the danger. In 2001 a Saskatchewan human rights board of inquiry directed that they must each pay $4,500 in damages to three homosexual complainants who were offended by an advertisement that Owens had placed in the *StarPhoenix*, which simply cited, without quoting, a list of biblical verses condemning homosexual behaviour together with a stick-figure depiction of two hand-holding men superimposed by a circle and slash – the universal symbol for something forbidden. Sinkewicz capitulated to the board's ruling despite having testified to his high regard for freedom of the press.[20] Owens appealed to the Saskatchewan Court of Queen's Bench and lost. He is now taking the case to the Saskatchewan Court of Appeal. If he should end up losing on all appeals, he, too, will face a stark choice: Either pay $4,500 in damages to the homosexuals who objected to his advertisement or go to jail.

The prospect of such a travesty of justice speaks volumes about the sorry state of freedom in Canada. Despite the ostensible guarantees of human rights and fundamental freedoms in the Charter, everyone, from the trendiest gays and lesbians to the most traditional Christians and Jews, could end up in jail for refusing to comply with the freedom-stifling rulings of a human rights tribunal.

What has gone wrong? Is Canada no longer a parliamentary democracy? Are Canadians not still protected by the rule of law? Are not judges and human rights commissioners obligated to uphold the clearly defined legal rules that historically sustained freedom of thought, belief, opinion, and expression as well as all the other basic human rights and fundamental freedoms of Canadians?

Not so long ago, the answer to such questions was indisputable: Our heritage of democracy and freedom under law in Canada was safe from attack. Today, our historic rights and freedoms are in grave jeopardy. Yet most Canadians are oblivious to the danger.

Chief Justice Antonio Lamer of the Supreme Court of Canada has been one of the foremost champions of the Canadian Charter of Rights and Freedoms. In a public tribute to Prime Minister Trudeau, he said: "In my opinion, Pierre Elliott Trudeau did not begin and he did not end the protection of rights and freedoms, because that task is never-ending. But he made an enormous contribution to the implantation of what I call a culture of rights and freedoms of the person in Canada. And I hope that someone will follow up on that, because a charter is not everything. One can do whatever one wants with it. Look what the former Soviet Union did with its charter."[21]

Lamer has a good point: The 1936 Constitution of the Soviet Socialist Republics included an expansive charter of human rights and fundamental freedoms. In article 124 this Soviet document purported to ensure all citizens "freedom of conscience" and "freedom of religious worship," while article 125 affirmed "freedom of speech," "freedom of the press," and "freedom of assembly, including the holdings of mass meetings." Fifty years ago, most intellectuals in western Europe and North America thought that this Stalinist document meant what it said.[22] Today, every authority on the Soviet Union understands that Stalin's 1936 Constitution was a fraud. All the guarantees of human rights and fundamental freedoms in this document were meaningless. Under the cover of a sham constitution, the arch tyrant, Joseph Stalin, conducted a lawless reign of terror that repudiated every basic human right. He proved what Lamer has stated: One can do whatever one wants with a charter. Indeed, a charter can mask the subversion of the very human rights and fundamental freedoms it is supposed to affirm.

George Orwell was one of the first to see through the pretensions of the Soviet Constitution. In *Nineteen Eighty-Four* he projected that a Stalin-like, socialist Big Brother would seize power in England and construct an enormous ministry of truth emblazoned with the slogans: "WAR IS PEACE, FREEDOM IS SLAVERY, IGNORANCE IS STRENGTH."[23] Today, Canadians are living in a quasi-Orwellian nightmare, where freedom often means slavery and ignorance strengthens activist judges. Most Canadians have no conception of how the Supreme Court of Canada has taken advantage of the Canadian Charter of Rights and Freedoms to wrest legislative supremacy from Parliament. Most Canadians do not understand how the Court has subjected the Charter to Orwellian double-think. They believe that the Charter means what it clearly says. They have yet to grasp that, time and again, the Supreme Court of Canada has twisted the original meaning of the Charter out of all recognition.

Take, for example, the purported guarantee of freedom of conscience and religion in section 2(a) of the Charter. Under the guise of upholding this guarantee, the Supreme Court of Canada contrived in *R. v. Big M Drug Mart,* 1985 SCC, to strike down the longstanding Sunday-closing provisions in the federal Lord's Day Act. There is no evidence to indicate that the legislators who adopted the Charter believed that there was any conflict between the Lord's Day Act and the guarantee of freedom of religion as stated in section 2(a) of the Charter. Canada's activist judges came to this novel conclusion entirely on their own.

R. v. Big M Drug Mart was the first of a series of like-minded Charter rulings. In *Three Faces of the Law: A Christian Perspective,* Ian Hunter, emeritus professor of law at the University of Western Ontario, trenchantly observes: "Freedom of religion has been interpreted by the Supreme Court since the landmark decision in *Big M Drug Mart* to mean freedom from religion."[24] Far from upholding freedom of religion and the traditional principles of Judeo-Christian morality as enshrined in judicial precedents, the laws, and the Constitution of Canada, the Supreme Court of Canada has suppressed public expressions of Christianity and imposed unprecedented new laws based on new values that the Court finds appealing. This is why the mayor of a Canadian municipality who refuses as a matter of religious conviction to issue gay pride proclamations is now liable to be consigned by the courts to an indefinite term in jail as a prisoner of conscience.

If such a dire prospect seems far-fetched, consider the precedent-setting case of John Ross Taylor, a former leader of the racist Western Guard Party. He was ordered by a Canadian human rights tribunal in 1979 to cease communicating a series of tape-recorded anti-Semitic opinions by telephone. In the words of Professor Hunter, "Taylor, who was 69 years old, refused to alter either his opinions or his practices. He was then convicted of contempt of court and served one year in jail, thereby becoming Canada's first prisoner of conscience to be jailed for daring to contradict the orthodoxy of human rights."[25]

Until the Canadian Human Rights Act and the Canadian Charter of Rights and Freedoms came into effect, Taylor was free to express his repellent ideas because the laws and the constitutional conventions of Canada granted wide scope to freedom of expression. Within limits clearly defined by law relating to such matters as libel, sedition, fraud, and pornography, most Canadian legislators and judges in the pre-Charter era firmly upheld freedom of expression, including the freedom of all Canadians to express even vile and unpopular opinions on race, gender, and other controversial subjects without interference by the state. It used to be commonplace within the legal profession in Canada to endorse the maxim "I disapprove of everything you say but will defend to the death your right to say it." In marked contrast, most judges, lawyers, and law professors are now less concerned about safeguarding freedom of speech than about preventing Canadians from expressing controversial views.

Until about twenty years ago, it would have been inconceivable for a Canadian court to order a private women's club to admit a male as a member. Likewise, it would have been unimaginable that the Supreme Court of Canada might incarcerate a conscientious Christian solely for the peaceful expression of his or her religious convictions. Today, the once inconceivable in our courts has become commonplace. Linda Gibbons is all too aware of this turn-around. She is a peaceful, diminutive grandmother of four, who, despite the ostensible guarantee of freedom of expression in the Charter, has been repeatedly jailed as a result of a court order obtained in 1994 by Ontario's attorney general, Marion Boyd, that prohibits picketing within fifty feet of several designated abortion clinics.[26] Alan Borovoy, general counsel of the Canadian Civil Liberties Association, has expressed dismay that a government of self-styled progressive New Democrats like Boyd would resort to such "an anti-liberal device."[27] In an aptly entitled book, *The New Anti-Liberals*, Borovoy notes: "The terms of the government's proposed injunction were so broad that they could arguably have prohibited even silent, peaceful, information picketing within easy view of the abortion clinics. A restriction against physical obstruction is one thing; a ban on informational picketing is another thing entirely."[28]

When Boyd obtained the picketing injunction on behalf of Rae's NDP government, Charles Harnick, speaking for the Official Opposition, denounced the measure as an attack on freedom of speech. Yet after taking over from Boyd as attorney general of Ontario in Premier Mike Harris's Progressive Conservative government, Harnick did nothing to get the injunction withdrawn.[29] The infamous court order still remains in effect under the Liberal government of Premier Dalton McGuinty.

Gibbons once had an abortion.[30] She is eager to protect vulnerable young women from making the same grievous error. To this end, she has insisted upon maintaining a peaceful, prayerful, and nonobstructive prolife witness immediately outside Toronto's Scott Street abortion clinic in Toronto in violation of Boyd's freedom-stifling court order. Time and again, Gibbons has been arrested, charged, convicted, and incarcerated. As punishment for her "silent, peaceful, information picketing," she has spent close to four years in an Ontario jail as a prolife prisoner of conscience.[31]

It bears repeating that the distortion of human rights and fundamental freedoms in the Charter era does not relate just to gays, lesbians, prolifers, and traditional Christians. This revolution in the Canadian legal order threatens all Canadians. While theologically orthodox Catholics, Protestants, and Jews are the prime targets for oppression, judges and human rights commissioners have shown that they are prepared to use their enormous powers to harass and coerce any vulnerable minority that defies the orthodoxy of human rights as conceived by these same human rights commissioners and activist judges. Many of the hard-won freedoms of Canadians are fast disappearing. Complacent Canadians should beware. They should remember what happened to complacent Germans in the 1930s. At that time, one of the few Germans who stood up for genuine human rights and fundamental freedoms was Martin Niemoeller, a Lutheran pastor and heroic former First World War U-boat captain. For his defiance of Hitler, Niemoeller was consigned to the Dachau concentration camp. After the war, he is said to have recalled: "In Germany they came first for the Communists, and I didn't speak up because I wasn't a Communist. Then they came for the Jews, and I didn't speak up because I wasn't a Jew. Then they came for the trade unionists, and I didn't speak up because I wasn't a trade unionist. Then they came for the Catholics, and I didn't speak up because I was a Protestant. Then they came for me, and by that time no one was left to speak up."[32]

1

Judicial Activism versus the Rule of Law

The prolonged twisting and turning of the ongoing judicial confrontation pitting Kimberly Nixon and the British Columbia Human Rights Tribunal against the Vancouver Rape Relief Society affords a striking illustration of how human rights commissions and the courts have compromised freedom under law in Canada over the past twenty years. No compassionate person can fail to sympathize with Nixon, the complainant in this case. She has had a troubled life.[1] Although born as a biological male on 7 September 1957 and raised as a male during childhood, she claims that from the age of "around four or five," she started to identify as a female and to act the part of a female in private, while continuing to present herself in public as a male. Nixon says that she kept up this deception throughout her teenage years and continued to do so even after leaving school and finding work as a pilot. According to Nixon's testimony, she used to report for work at an airport dressed outwardly as a man in a pilot's uniform while wearing women's clothing underneath. In an attempt to resolve her confused identity, Nixon began attending the Gender Disorder Clinic at Vancouver General Hospital in 1987. Two years later, she gave up her double life and started living full time as a woman in preparation for sex reassignment surgery, which she underwent in 1990. At the time of her confrontation with Rape Relief before the British Columbia Human Rights Tribunal in 2001, she was living with a man in a heterosexual relationship and coparenting the man's daughter, aged four and a half.[2]

Nixon told the tribunal that during a previous heterosexual relationship in 1992 and 1993, she had endured physical and emotional abuse from a male partner. In distress, she had turned for help to the Battered Women's Support Services of Vancouver, where she underwent eight months of one-on-one professional counselling, followed by an extended period of amateur peer-group counselling with female victims of spousal abuse. Having appreciated the kindness of sympathetic counsellors for battered women, Nixon decided that she, too, would like to help the female victims of spousal abuse, so in 1995 she responded to an advertisement by Rape Relief seeking volunteers to participate in a program to train peer counsellors for victims of male violence. At an interview with a representative of Rape Relief on 22 August 1995, Nixon professed her commitment to the collective's feminist, antiracist, prochoice, and prolesbian beliefs. On this basis, she was accepted into the organization's training program. But when she attended her first training session on 29 August 1995, Danielle Cormier, a facilitator of the training sessions, immediately identified Nixon as a biological male on the basis of her physical appearance, took her aside, and advised her that men were not allowed in the training group. Nixon protested that she was a woman because she had undergone sex reassignment surgery. Cormier was unmoved. According to a summary of evidence by Heather MacNaughton, the human rights adjudicator assigned to this case, Cormier told Nixon "that a woman had to be oppressed since birth to be a volunteer at Rape Relief and that because she had lived as a man she could not participate."[3]

Distraught by Cormier's rejection, Nixon promptly filed a complaint with the British Columbia Council of Human Rights accusing Rape Relief of unlawful discrimination "by refusing me employment, because of my sex contrary to the 1984 British Columbia Human Rights Act."[4] Subsequently, Nixon amended her complaint to include the allegation that Rape Relief had also discriminated by denying her a service customarily available to the public because of her sex.

The council began – and the British Columbia Human Rights Commission, which replaced the council on 1 January 1997, continued – a four-year-long attempt marked by much bureaucratic delay to mediate the dispute between Nixon and Rape Relief. Finally, on 10 September 1999, the commission sought an order from the British Columbia Human Rights Tribunal directing (1) that the Vancouver Rape Relief Society must reverse its decision not to train Nixon as a rape crisis counsellor; (2) that Rape Relief must pay her $10,000 in compensation for the discrimination she had endured; (3) that Rape Relief must post a welcome to cross-dressers, transvestites, and transsexual women on its website; and (4) that Rape Relief must hold a one-day mandatory workshop for its members on the evils of discrimination against transgendered women.[5] On 13 December 1999, with the matter still not resolved, Rape Relief sought a court order prohibiting the tribunal from proceeding with the *Nixon* hearing because the case had already dragged on for too long and because the complaint related to discrimination on the basis of transsexualism, which is not enumerated as a prohibited ground for discrimination in either the 1984 British Columbia Human Rights Act or the succeeding 1996 British Columbia Human Rights Code.

The case came before Mr Justice Barry Davies of the British Columbia Supreme Court. In his judgment in *Vancouver Rape Relief v. B.C. Human Rights,* 2000 BCSC 889, he summarily dismissed the allegation of undue delay on the ground that Rape Relief was continuing to discriminate against women who were not born as women. Next, he addressed Rape Relief's argument that there was no basis for the tribunal to proceed with Nixon's complaint because there had never been a ban on discrimination on the basis of transsexualism in the Code. On the face of it, this argument is compelling. The British Columbia Human Rights Code specifically states in section 8(1): "No person, without a bona fide and reasonable justification, shall (a) deny to a person or class of persons any accommodation, service or facility customarily available to the public ... because of race, colour, ancestry, place of origin, religion, marital status, family status, physical or mental disability or sex or sexual orientation of that person or class of persons." Correspondingly, in section 13, the Code provides that no person shall refuse to employ a person on of any of these same prohibited grounds. In no section of the Code is there any mention of transsexualism.

THE CASE FOR JUDICIAL RESTRAINT

Prior to the 1980s, the plain language of the law was decisive. In the absence of any explicit ban on discrimination on the basis of gender identity or transsexualism in a statute like the British Columbia Human Rights Code, Nixon would have had no legal basis for her claim. Today, the clear and specific wording of a human rights code is no longer determinative, thanks to the proclivity of the Supreme Court of Canada to revise and update the law through interpretation. As justification for this practice, the Court sites the provision in section 15(1) of the 1982 Canadian Charter of Rights and Freedoms: "Every individual is equal before and under the law and has the right to the equal protection and equal benefit of the law without discrimination and, in particular, without discrimination based on race, national or ethnic origin, colour, religion, sex, age or mental or physical disability." Note the vagueness of this designation of equality rights in the Charter. Most of the human rights and fundamental freedoms guaranteed in this document are expressed in similarly broad and ambiguous language. Section 2(a) affirms "freedom of conscience and religion"; section 2(b) "freedom of thought, belief, opinion and expression"; section 2(d) "freedom of association"; section 7 "the right to life, liberty and security of the person and the right not to be deprived thereof except in accordance with the principles of fundamental justice"; section 8 "the right to be secure against unreasonable search or seizure"; and section 11(b) the right "to be tried within a reasonable time."

How should judges apply these general provisions of the Charter to specific issues like the scope of a ban on discrimination on the basis of sex in a human rights code? Professor Peter Hogg, former dean of Osgoode Hall Law School, addressed this question in *Constitutional Law of Canada*. In this textbook, which has often been cited in judgments by the Supreme Court of Canada, Hogg observes that in interpreting the vague phrases denoting human rights and fundamental freedoms in the Charter, "judges will inevitably be influenced by their own social, economic and political values."[6] He adds, "They will also be influenced by their attitudes towards the appropriate relationship between the courts and the other branches of government. An attitude of judicial restraint would be deferential to the decisions of the political branches, resulting in judicial invalidation of political decisions only in clear cases of Charter violations. An attitude of judicial activism would be sympathetic to the expansion of the guaranteed civil liberties, resulting in frequent invalidation of the decisions of the political branches."[7]

During the first hundred years of Confederation, judicial activism, in this precise sense, rarely occurred in Canada.[8] Virtually all Canadian judges practised judicial restraint. In interpreting the law and the Constitution, they were originalists. That is to say, they understood that it was their duty as judges essentially to uphold the plain language of a statute or constitutional law as written and originally understood by members of the legislative branch of government. There was but one major qualification to this general rule of interpretation: Canadian judges have never been reluctant to strike down a federal or provincial statute on the narrow ground that the statute violated the division of powers between Parliament and the provincial legislatures under the Constitution of Canada Act, 1867. Thus, in *Toronto Electric Commission v. Snider*, JCPC 1925, the Judicial Committee of the Privy Council, then the ultimate court of appeal for Canada,[9] addressed the constitutional validity of the federal Industrial Disputes Investigation Act of 1910. In submissions to the court, the Government of Canada argued that the Act came within the exclusive authority over "The Regulation of Trade and Commerce" that was conferred on Parliament in section 91(2) of the original British North America Act, while the Ontario government contended that the federal legislation trespassed upon the general power of the provinces to make laws in relation to "Property and Civil Rights in the Province" as prescribed in section 92(13) of the British North America Act. In this instance, the Judicial Committee sided with the provinces and declared that the federal Act had no force or effect because it was ultra vires – that is, beyond the constitutional powers – of the Parliament of Canada.

In the pre-Charter era, such cases were the exception that proved the rule: Apart from sorting out federal and provincial jurisdictional disputes, Canadian judges almost always exercised judicial restraint. They habitually upheld the plain meaning of the words of a statute or constitutional law. And in so doing, they upheld the separation of legislative, executive, and judicial powers – that most fundamental of constitutional doctrines first propounded by Charles de Secondat, Baron de Montesquieu, in his eighteenth-century classic *De l'esprit des lois (The Spirit of Laws)*. Montesquieu observed: "There is no liberty if the judiciary power be not separated from the legislative and executive. Were it joined with the legislative, the life and liberty of the subject would be exposed to arbitrary control; for the judge would be then the legislator. Were it joined to the executive power, the judge might behave with violence and oppression."[10] Sir William Blackstone, the foremost English constitutional scholar of the eighteenth century, concurred. In his magisterial *Commentaries on the Laws of England* (1765–69), Blackstone likewise warned that liberty "cannot subsist long in any state, unless the administration of common justice be in some degree separated both from the legislative and also from the executive power. Were it joined with the legislative, the life, liberty, and property of the subject would be in the hands of arbitrary judges, whose decisions would be then regulated only by their own opinions, and not by any fundamental principles of law; which, though legislators may depart from, yet judges are bound to observe."[11]

For generations, legal practitioners in England, Australia, Canada, the United States, and every other common law country revered Blackstone as a leading authority on the law and civil liberties. Stanley Katz, a professor of legal history at Princeton University, has described Blackstone's *Commentaries* as "the most important legal treatise ever written in the English language."[12] He points out: "It was the dominant lawbook in England and America in the century after its publication and played a unique role in the development of the fledgling American legal system."[13] The same can be said about the authority of Blackstone's treatise for the legal system of Canada. Up to the 1950s, the *Commentaries* were virtually holy writ for Canadian lawyers, law professors, and judges.

This is not to suggest that the views of Blackstone and Montesquieu were accepted without qualification. On some issues, these two eminent authorities were not in entire agreement. For example, while Montesquieu called for an absolute separation of legislative and executive powers, Blackstone, drawing upon a more intimate knowledge of the English constitution, held only that: "It is highly necessary for preserving the balance of the constitution that the executive power should be a branch, though not the whole, of the legislature. The total union of them ... would be productive of tyranny."[14]

Among today's progressive jurists, it is commonplace to suppose that the judicial power is likewise at least a branch, although not the whole, of the legislature inasmuch as the common law is usually referred to as "judge-made law." Chief Justice Antonio Lamer of the Supreme Court of Canada was given to describing the common law in this way. In *R. v. Swain* 1991 SCC, he characterized the authority of the Crown to submit evidence of insanity during a trial over the objections of an accused as "a common law, judge-made rule." If this description is apt – if judges, indeed, make the rules of the common law – does it not follow that, at least to this extent, judges are legislators?

Sir Francis Bacon would have rejected both the premise and conclusion of this argument. In his seventeenth-century essay "On Judicature," he admonished: "Judges ought to remember that their office is jus dicere, not jus dare, to interpret law, and not to make law, or give law."[15] Bacon scorned judges who impose their own ideas upon the law through "strained inferences." He chided authorities who, under the pretext of upholding the law, are given "to add and alter; and to pronounce that which they do not find; and by show of antiquity, to introduce novelty."[16]

Blackstone, writing almost two centuries after Bacon, was of like mind. He, too, insisted that English judges have a duty not to make, but only to discover, the common law. He held that the rules of the common law reflected "general immemorial custom."[17] In Blackstone's era these common law customs, as distinct from legislative enactments, governed virtually all aspects of the civil law and the criminal law. In a key passage of the *Commentaries*, Blackstone affirmed:

"The only method of proving, that this or that maxim is a rule of the common law, is by showing that it has been always the custom to observe it. But here a very natural, and very material, question arises: How are these customs or maxims to be known, and by whom is their validity to be determined? The answer is, by the judges in the several courts of justice."[18] However, Blackstone emphasized that principled judges do not make or revise the law but seek only to uphold and apply the law as embodied in the judicial decisions of their predecessors. He said:

For it is an established rule to abide by former precedents, where the same points come again in litigation; as well to keep the scale of justice even and steady, and not liable to waver with every new judge's opinion; as also because the law in that case being solemnly declared and determined, what before was uncertain, and perhaps indifferent, is now become a permanent rule, which it is not in the breast of any subsequent judge to alter or vary from, according to his private sentiments: he being sworn to determine, not according to his own private judgment, but according to the known laws and customs of the land; not delegated to pronounce a new law, but to maintain and expound the old one.[19]

The rule that judges of the common law must follow precedents is the doctrine of *stare decisis*, defined in the authoritative *Black's Law Dictionary* as:

To abide by, or adhere, to decided cases. Policy of courts to stand by precedent and not to disturb settled point. Doctrine that, when court has once lain down a principle of law as applicable to a certain state of facts, it will adhere to that principle, and apply it to all future cases, where facts are substantially the same; regardless of whether the parties and property are the same.

Under doctrine a deliberate or solemn decision of court made after argument on question of law fairly arising in the case, and necessary to its determination, is an authority, or binding precedent in the same court, or in other courts of equal or lower rank in subsequent cases where the very point is again in controversy.[20]

Stare decisis is not absolute. Regarding the general obligation to follow precedents, Blackstone said:

Yet this rule admits of exception, where the former determination is most evidently contrary to reason; much more if it be clearly contrary to the divine law. But even in such cases the subsequent judges do not pretend to make a new law, but to vindicate the old one from misrepresentation. For if it be found that the former decision is manifestly absurd or unjust, it is declared, not that such a sentence was bad law, but that it was not law; that is, that it is not the established custom of the realm, as has been erroneously determined. And hence it is that our lawyers are with justice so copious in their encomiums on the reason of the common law, that they tell us, that the law is the perfection of reason, that it always intends to conform thereto, and that what is not reason is not law.[21]

With this passage, Blackstone did not mean to suggest that a judge should have no qualms about changing any customary rule of the common law merely because the rule seems, in the opinion of the judge, to be unreasonable or unjust. To the contrary, Blackstone counselled that a judge should always exercise great caution in changing any rule of the common law because the fact that a rule has stood the test of centuries suggests that the rule embodies wisdom, although this wisdom might not be readily apparent to the contemporary judge. Blackstone stated: "The doctrine of the law then is this: That precedents and rules must be followed, unless flatly absurd or unjust: for though their reason be not obvious at first view, yet we owe such a deference to former times, as not to suppose that they acted wholly without consideration."[22]

In emphasizing the permanence of the common law, Blackstone took little account of the need to adapt legal rules to changing social and economic circumstances. Given the comparative stability of customs and social institutions in England during his lifetime, such a static view of the common law was appropriate. In the modern era of continual social change, a more dynamic view of the common law is clearly required. Mr Justice Benjamin Cardozo of the United States Supreme Court underlined this point in a series of lectures entitled *The Nature of the Judicial Process,* which he delivered at Yale University in 1921. In this famous treatise, Cardozo explained that while immemorial customs and rules of the common law might have been adequate for a simple or homogeneous community, they had to adapt in the industrial age to "the growing complexity of social relations."[23] Yet he stressed: "This work of modification is gradual. It goes on inch by inch. Its effects must be measured by decades and even centuries. Thus measured, they are seen to have behind them the power and the pressure of the moving glacier."[24] Cardozo emphasized that only a gradual, virtually imperceptible process of evolution could enable the law to adapt to social change yet retain the essential qualities of firmness and precision. In his view, judges must uphold the stability and certainty of the law by avoiding any sudden and dramatic breaks with judicial precedents governing either the common law or statute laws.

Like Blackstone and Cardozo, A.V. Dicey also emphasized the vital importance of clarity and stability in the law. In his authoritative nineteenth-century text *Introduction to the Study of the Law of the Constitution*, Dicey affirmed: "When we say the supremacy or the rule of law is a characteristic of the English constitution, we mean, in the first place, that no man is punishable or can be lawfully made to suffer in body or goods except for a distinct breach of law established in the ordinary legal manner before the ordinary Courts of the land. In this sense the rule of law is contrasted with every system of government based on the exercise by persons in authority of wide, arbitrary, or discretionary powers of constraint."[25] Judges, of course, rank with government administrators and police officers as persons in authority. Yet Dicey made no explicit reference in his text to arbitrary judges. Writing in the 1880s, he could not conceive of an arbitrary judge. Like Blackstone and Cardozo, he could not imagine that appeal court judges in a common law country would routinely subvert the rule of law by assuming "wide, arbitrary, or discretionary powers" to impose radical reformulations of the law in accordance with each judge's own personal ideological preferences.

Until about the middle of the twentieth century, the great majority of judges in Canada and other common law countries deferred to the wisdom of Blackstone, Dicey, and Cardozo. These judges shunned discretionary authority. They understood that they had a duty to set aside their personal opinions on the requirements of justice for the purpose of interpreting and applying the law as defined by precedents and spelled out in constitutional laws and statutes enacted by elected representatives of the people in the appropriate section of the legislative branch of government.

Friedrich Hayek underlined the continuing importance of clarity and stability for the rule of law in his penetrating twentieth-century treatise *The Road to Serfdom*. Reflecting upon the depredations of communism and fascism, Hayek wrote: "Nothing distinguishes more clearly conditions in a free country from those in a country under arbitrary government than the observance in the former of the great principles known as the Rule of Law. Stripped of all technicalities, this means that government in all its actions is bound by rules fixed and announced beforehand – rules which make it possible to foresee with fair certainty how the authority will use its coercive powers in given circumstances and to plan one's individual affairs on the basis of this knowledge."[26]

J.A. Corry, professor of political studies at Queen's University and a founder of the Queen's University School of Law, likewise drummed the vital importance of judicial restraint, *stare decisis,* and the stability of the law into the heads of generations of Canadian students of law and politics. In his widely used textbook *Democratic Government and Politics,* Corry compared the structure and functioning of the Governments of Britain, the United States, and Canada.[27] He observed:

> The basic principle of the British constitution is the supremacy of Parliament. Any and every law passed by Parliament is constitutional. It has been said that parliament can do anything except make a man a woman. This is an understatement. If Parliament were to declare that henceforth women were to be treated in all respects as if they were men, the executive and the courts would be obliged so to treat them, even in the face of nature. Women would then have to be called up under the military service law hitherto applicable only to men. Obviously, this means that Parliament can turn absurdities into laws and can work its will on the other two organs of government. It could pass a law dismissing all servants of the Crown and taking into its own hands the entire executive power. It could abolish the judiciary.[28]

Prior to the Charter, much the same was also true of the powers of the Parliament of Canada and the legislatures of the provinces. Corry noted: "Once the distribution of legislative authority imposed by federalism is clearly ascertained, the national Parliament and provincial legislatures each enjoy, within their own area of competence, substantially the same supremacy as the British Parliament."[29] This is not to suggest that Parliament used to have untrammelled power to trample upon civil liberties. In both Britain and Canada elected representatives of the people in the legislative branch of government have always been constrained in the exercise of their legislative powers by customs and conventions of the constitution.[30] While these customs and conventions cannot be enforced by the courts, they are politically binding. They assure that elected legislators will not exercise their supreme legislative powers to commit such dictatorial excesses as abolishing the courts, eradicating habeus corpus, enacting ex post facto laws, or cancelling elections.

Echoing Cardozo, Corry emphasized the overriding importance of stability in the law:

> Law must change when new needs can no longer be denied, but its prime function in any given period is to minister to order and stability. For this purpose, the law must have a fair degree of certainty. The sense of security which is the basis of orderly life depends on knowing what others will do or can be held to in the future. Those who plan for the future must be able to

find out what the law permits and requires ... A law that is always changing is uncertain and defeats its own purpose. Moreover, if it is admitted that the judges can change the law, people lose confidence in it and them. Accordingly, judges are sworn to apply the law as they find it. For the best of reasons, and with complete honesty and considerable truth, the judge insists that he does not make law, but only interprets it.[31]

In conformity with this understanding of the proper role of the judiciary, judges who uphold the rule of law and respect the constitutional separation of legislative and judicial powers do not, in essence, make the law: They only interpret and apply the law to the specific case before the court as the law is found in precedents, statutes, and the Constitution. Blackstone emphasized that in the case of statutes, the guiding rule for interpretation must not be the will of the judge but the will of the legislator. He said: "The fairest and most rational method to interpret the will of the legislator is by exploring his intentions at the time when the law was made, by signs the most natural and probable. And these signs are either the words, the context, the subject matter, the effects and consequence, or the spirit and reason of the law."[32] Blackstone further explained that the words of a statute are not to be given any arcane or idiosyncratic judicial meaning but rather "are generally to be understood in their usual and most known signification; not so much regarding the propriety of grammar, as their general and popular use."[33] While judges are bound to uphold the words of a statute if the meaning is clear, Blackstone allowed: "Where words bear either none, or a very absurd signification, if literally understood, we must a little deviate from the received sense of them ... The most universal and effectual way of discovering the true meaning of a law, when the words are dubious, is by considering the reason and spirit of it; or the cause which moved the legislator to enact it."[34]

Elmer Driedger, a Canadian authority on the interpretation of statutes, followed essentially the same approach as Blackstone. In his text *The Construction of Statutes*, Driedger wrote: "Today there is only one principle or approach, namely, the words of an Act are to be read in their entire context and in their grammatical and ordinary sense harmoniously with the scheme of the Act, the object of the Act, and the intention of Parliament."[35]

A majority of the Supreme Court of Canada took this same view on the proper interpretation of statute laws in *Harrison v. Carswell*, 1976 SCC. In this noteworthy, pre-Charter case, the respondent, Sophie Carswell, worked at a grocery store in the Polo Park Mall in Winnipeg. Together with several union colleagues, she picketed the store during a legal strike. When the owner of the shopping mall ordered her and her fellow pickets to vacate the premises, she refused to comply. Subsequently, she was charged, convicted, and fined $40 under the Manitoba Petty Trespass Act. Carswell appealed, claiming that she had a legal right to picket a grocery store regardless of whether the store was located inside or outside an enclosed shopping mall.

In a similar case five years earlier, *Peters v. the Queen,* 1971 SCC, the Supreme Court of Canada had upheld a trespassing conviction against a person who had picketed a grocery store inside an Ontario mall in support of a grape boycott proclaimed by a farm workers union in California.[36] Given the similar facts of these two cases, the Supreme Court of Canada was bound by the doctrine of *stare decisis* to follow the *Peters* ruling in *Harrison v. Carswell.* Nonetheless, in a dissenting opinion in *Carswell,* Chief Justice Bora Laskin urged the Court to break with the *Peters* precedent on the ground that just as persons engaged in a legal strike have long been free under the law to maintain a peaceful picket on a public sidewalk outside a store on a city street, so, too, does it logically follow that strikers like Carswell should have a corresponding right to picket on a public sidewalk outside a store inside a shopping mall. This was Laskin's personal opinion. He advanced nothing to support his view in either the common law or the Manitoba Petty Trespass Act. Instead, he called upon the Court to change the law through a creative reinterpretation of the common law of trespass and the Manitoba Petty Trespass Act so as to grant strikers the right to picket inside a shopping mall. Given that the then existing law on trespass had been developed prior to the creation of shopping malls, Laskin opined: "It seems to me that the present case involves a search for an appropriate legal framework for new social facts which show up the inaptness of an old doctrine developed upon a completely different social foundation."

Mr Justice Brian Dickson, as he then was, would have none of this argument for having members of the Court abandon precedent, ignore the statute law, and proceed on their own to amend the law on trespass to accord with their personal policy preferences. In a judgment for the majority of the Court in *Carswell,* Dickson held that it is up to the legislative branch of government, not the courts, to change the law to accommodate new social facts. The Court, he insisted, was bound to follow the precedent set in *Peters*:

> Anglo-Canadian jurisprudence has traditionally recognized, as a fundamental freedom, the right of the individual to the enjoyment of property and the right not to be deprived thereof, or any interest therein, save by due process

of law. The legislature of Manitoba has declared in The Petty Trespasses Act that any person who trespasses upon land, the property of another, upon or through which he has been requested by the owner not to enter, is guilty of an offence. If there is to be any change in this statute law, if A is to be given the right to enter and remain on the land of B against the will of B, it would seem to me that such a change must be made by the enacting institution, the legislature, which is representative of the people and designed to manifest the political will, and not by the Court.

In a direct response to Laskin, Dickson added:

The submission that this Court should weigh and determine the respective values to society of the right to property and the right to picket raises important and difficult political and socio-economic issues, the resolution of which must, by their very nature, be arbitrary and embody personal economic and social beliefs. It raises also fundamental questions as to the role of this Court under the Canadian constitution. The duty of the Court, as I envisage it, is to proceed in the discharge of its adjudicative function in a reasoned way from principled decision and established concepts. I do not for a moment doubt the power of the Court to act creatively – it has done so on countless occasions; but manifestly one must ask – what are the limits of the judicial function? There are many and varied answers to this question. Holmes J. said in *Southern Pacific Co. v. Jensen* (1917): "I recognize without hesitation that judges do and must legislate, but they can do it only interstitially; they are confined from molar to molecular actions." Cardozo, *The Nature of the Judicial Process* (1921), p. 141, recognized that the freedom of the judge is not absolute in this expression of his review: "This judge, even when he is free, is still not wholly free. He is not to innovate at pleasure. He is not a knight-errant, roaming at will in pursuit of his own ideal of beauty or of goodness. He is to draw his inspiration from consecrated principles."

With this ruling, Dickson gave a ringing endorsement to judicial restraint. Instead of breaking with the *Peters* precedent, he upheld the doctrine of *stare decisis.* He insisted that the court must adhere to a principle of law established in a previous case when the court is dealing with another case where the facts are substantially the same. Instead of changing the law through a creative reinterpretation of the common law and the Petty Trespass Act as urged by Laskin, he reaffirmed the traditional view that the proper function of the courts is to construe a statute as written and originally understood.

In *Carswell,* Dickson also upheld the principle affirmed by the Supreme Court of Canada in *A.G. Can. v. Hallet & Carey,* 1952 SCC: "Statutes which encroach on the rights of the subject, whether as regards person or property, are subject to a 'strict' construction." This phrase "strict construction" is a technical term denoting the doctrine of the common law that requires a court to construe statutes as conforming with civil liberties unless the wording of the law contains clear and definite language constricting a fundamental freedom or human right.[37] In compliance with this doctrine of strict construction, a judge will deem that a statute does not authorize the violation of a civil liberty unless Parliament or a provincial legislature, as the case might be, has expressly stated or necessarily implied such a violation in the statute. Professor Hogg upholds the continuing validity of strict construction as a means of safeguarding civil liberties from casual statutory encroachment. He has stated: "In my opinion, the principle of strict construction is sound: It is reasonable for the courts to insist that invasion of personal or proprietary rights be clearly authorized by the statutory language."[38]

In a post-Charter case, *R. v. Pare,* 1987 SCC, Madam Justice Bertha Wilson of the Supreme Court of Canada held that strict construction remains an appropriate rule for the interpretation of criminal statutes. She acknowledged:

> The doctrine is one of ancient lineage. It reached its pinnacle of importance in a former age when the death penalty attached to a vast array of offences ... The doctrine was one of many tools employed by the judiciary to soften the impact of the Draconian penal provisions of the time. Over the past two centuries criminal law penalties have become far less severe. Criminal law remains, however, the most dramatic and important incursion that the state makes into individual liberty. Thus, while the original justification for the doctrine has been substantially eroded, the seriousness of imposing criminal penalties of any sort demands that reasonable doubts be resolved in favour of the accused.

Likewise, in *Marcotte v. Deputy Attorney General for Canada,* 1976 SCC, Dickson stated: "It is unnecessary to emphasize the importance of clarity and certainty when freedom is at stake. No authority is needed for the proposition that if real ambiguities are found, or doubts of substance arise, in the construction and application of a statute affecting the liberty of a subject, then that statute should be applied in such a manner as to favour the person against whom it is sought to be enforced. If one is to be incarcerated, one should at least know that some Act of Parliament requires it in express terms, and not, at most, by implication."

Note the consequences of these arguments for human rights statutes. Given the ruling of the Supreme Court of Canada in *Canada*

(Human Rights Commission) v. Taylor, SCC 1990, the case that subjected John Ross Taylor to a year in prison for defying the Canadian Human Rights Tribunal, it is evident that anyone who refuses to obey a court order upholding the directives of a human rights tribunal can be incarcerated. Therefore, it follows, by the reasoning of Wilson and Dickson, that the common law rule of strict construction ought to apply no less to federal and provincial human rights codes than to the Criminal Code.

JUDGE-MADE LAW IN RELATION TO THE *NIXON* CASE

Consider the application of these traditional principles of legal interpretation to the facts of the *Nixon* case. According to the canons of *stare decisis*, strict construction, and the rule of law, the Human Rights Tribunal and the Supreme Court of British Columbia should have had no difficulty in summarily dismissing Kimberly Nixon's complaint against the Vancouver Rape Relief Society on the ground that the British Columbia Human Rights Code contains no clear and definite language that bans discrimination on the basis of either transsexualism or gender identity. Consequently, Rape Relief should have been free under the law to reject a transsexual like Nixon for training and employment as a voluntary rape crisis counsellor.

As it turned out, however, Justice Davies paid no heed to the doctrine of strict construction in his judgment in *Rape Relief*. Nor did he defer to the original understanding of the British Columbia Human Rights Code. Instead, he undertook, in effect, to amend the Code through interpretation by deeming that a ban on discrimination against transsexuals is implicit in the Code.

"Kimberly Nixon is a post-operative male to female transsexual," wrote Davies. "She is medically and legally a woman." To justify this interpretation of the Code, he cited the provision in section 27(1) of the British Columbia Vital Statistics Act, R.S.B.C. 1996: "If a person in respect of whom trans-sexual surgery has been performed is unmarried on the date the person applies under this section, the director [of birth registrations] must, on application made to the director in accordance with subsection (2), change the sex designation on the registration of birth of the person in such a manner that the sex designation is consistent with the intended results of the trans-sexual surgery." Davies noted that this section of the Vital Statistics Act was enacted in 1973, the same year as enactment of the 1973 British Columbia Human Rights Code. On this ground, he maintained: "Section 27 of the Vital Statistics Act establishes that the legislature intended that post operative transsexuals such as Ms. Nixon would be entitled to the same legal status as other members of their post operative sex."

Does the plain wording of section 27 support Davies's sweeping conclusion? Obviously not. This section deals only with changing the sex designation on a birth certificate at the request of an unmarried, post-operative transsexual. Yet, on the sole basis of this provision in the Vital Statistics Act, Davies held: "It is therefore my opinion that in Ms. Nixon's case the discriminatory conduct which she now alleges against the petitioner [Rape Relief] may fairly be characterized as an allegation of discrimination against her as a woman, a complaint over which the Commission and the Tribunal both have jurisdiction just as they have jurisdiction over any complaint of discrimination by any woman based upon appearance."

Note the last phrase: Davies accused Rape Relief of unlawfully discriminating against Nixon because of her "appearance." Yet there is no provision in the British Columbia Human Rights Code that bans discrimination on the basis of a woman's appearance. In British Columbia, as elsewhere in Canada, it is entirely lawful for a man to discriminate against a woman in choosing a date or selecting a bride because he does not like her appearance.

Nonetheless, having decided to his own satisfaction that Nixon's allegation against Rape Relief might fairly be characterized as discrimination on the basis of her sex or appearance, Davies might have concluded his judgment. Instead, he went on to consider what he called "the broader question of whether the prohibition in the 1984 Act and the present Code of discrimination on the basis of sex also includes discrimination on the basis of gender identity or transsexualism." He added: "I recognize that in so doing, my determinations constitute *obiter dicta.*"

Black's Law Dictionary defines *obiter dictum* as "Words of an opinion entirely unnecessary for the decision of the case."[39] In effect, Davies admitted that he was about to proceed in his judgment to express an opinion on the legal status of transsexualism although the issue was irrelevant because he had already concluded that Rape Relief had practised unlawful discrimination against Nixon on the basis of her sex or appearance.

Corry observed in the pre-Charter era that Canadian judges "generally refuse to give gratuitous opinions on the law that are not necessary for the decision in hand."[40] Davies exercised no such restraint. He pronounced a new legal rule of general application that, by his own admission, was not germane to the matter before the court. In thus serving up a gratuitous opinion in *Rape Relief* on the inclusion of discrimination on the basis of transsexualism in the British Columbia Human Rights Code, he acted less like a judge than like an unelected legislator.

The British Columbia Human Rights Commission maintained in its submissions to Davies that a ban on discrimination on the basis of transsexualism is implicit in the ban on discrimination on the basis of sex in the Code. Counsel for Rape Relief opposed the argument on the grounds: (1) that there is no evidence that the Legislature intended that the ban on discrimination on the basis of sex should include discrimination based on gender identity and transsexualism; (2) that the Legislature had failed to act on a recommendation by the British Columbia Human Rights Commission on 19 January 1998 that "gender identity" should be added as a new ground of discrimination in the Code; and (3) that in several previous human rights cases, the courts have refused to interpret the ground "sex" to include sexual orientation and that Davies, therefore, should likewise refuse to interpret the ground "sex" to include transsexualism.

In support of this last argument, Rape Relief cited the judgment of Mr Justice Francis Muldoon of the Federal Court Trial Division in *Nielsen v. Canada (Human Rights Commission)*, 1992 FCTD. In this case, the applicant, Carol Nielsen, was a lesbian who had been living for the previous nine years with another woman and the woman's daughter. Nielsen was an employee of the Canada Employment and Immigration Commission. Under the commission's dental plan, she could claim benefits only on behalf of herself, her dependant children, and a spouse of the opposite sex. Regardless, Nielson applied for dental benefits on behalf of her lesbian partner. The application was rejected, so Nielsen filed a complaint with the Canadian Human Rights Commission accusing the Canada Employment and Immigration Commission of violating the ban on discrimination on the basis of sex, family status, marital status, and sexual orientation in the Canadian Human Rights Act. The Human Rights Commission took the view that in essence, Nielsen was alleging discrimination on the basis of sexual orientation – a ground for discrimination that Parliament had not yet included in the Canadian Human Rights Act. Therefore, the Human Rights Commission suspended the case, pending clarification of the law by the Supreme Court of Canada. Nielsen appealed the suspension to the Federal Court Trial Division, seeking an order requiring the commission to proceed immediately with her complaint.

Justice Muldoon rejected Nielsen's suit out of hand. He noted that her counsel was asking the Court to order the Canadian Human Rights Commission "to enquire into a complaint involving sexual orientation where that matter is not mentioned in the Act. That course of judicial conduct would really amount to the Court's legislating, instead of Parliament. It may be that the Act is under-inclusive, but it does not appear that Parliament so considers it to be." For Muldoon, the will of Parliament, not his own opinion, was the decisive consideration. He explained: "The reality of a democratic society bespeaks rule by the people, and that, where the population is large and the territory extensive, means rule by the majority of the people's elected representatives. For an unelected judge to add what parliament declined to include in legislation is redolent of anti-majoritarian, anti-democratic legislating."

In taking this stance, Muldoon was aware that the Supreme Court of Canada had adopted a decidedly different point of view seven years earlier in *Re B.C. Motor Vehicle Act,* 1985 SCC. This case focused on the proper interpretation of the guarantee in section 7 of the Charter that: "Everyone has the right to life, liberty and security of the person and the right not to be deprived thereof except in accordance with the principles of fundamental justice." In a judgment written by Chief Justice Lamer, the Court held that section 7 confers a broad mandate upon the judiciary to strike down laws that conflict with a judge's perception of sound public policy. Muldoon, a practitioner of judicial restraint, maintained that there is no evidence to indicate that in enacting section 7 or any other section of the Charter, Parliament and the provincial legislatures intended to surrender their law-making powers to the courts. In *Neilsen,* Muldoon asserted: "Society should be governed by laws, not merely judges." He took note of the fact that Canadian society is deeply riven over the morality of homosexual behaviour. He wrote:

> Firmly held attitudes of some consider such sexual orientation to be a sinful abomination and an irredeemable perversity, while to others' attitudes it is morally neutral and normal. To some, it should not be accorded recognition or status by law because that seems to legitimate a foul example for the impressionable young: It is still regarded as one of the obscene seeds of social decadence, even although decriminalized about two decades ago. To others, such sexual orientation liberates expression of sexual preference, if not immutable proclivity; and homosexuals' unions have the same social status for legal protection as do heterosexuals' unions, in effect, normal basic family units of society. To most, Parliament was right to decriminalize homosexual behaviour, but to some it would be wrong to give it equal place with heterosexual behav-

iour ... Simply to recite these notorious facts is to demonstrate that this is an issue for which it would be highly inappropriate for the courts to purport to legislate.

Muldoon then wryly added: "At this time, the fat of courtroom rhetoric is in the Supreme Court's fire. Being constitutionally supreme, it may, in its wisdom, choose to legislate on sexual orientation or not. Until the Supreme Court's judgment be known, this judge prefers to leave the legislating to the legislature, Parliament."

Muldoon's colleagues on the Supreme Court of Canada were not disposed to exercise such restraint. Three years later, they proceeded in *Egan v. Canada,* 1995 SCC, to read "sexual orientation" into section 15(1) of the Charter – the equality rights section. As enacted, this section states: "Every individual is equal before and under the law and has the right to the equal protection and equal benefit of the law without discrimination and, in particular, without discrimination based on race, national or ethnic origin, colour, religion, sex, age or mental or physical disability." There is no reference to sexual orientation in section 15 or any other section of the Charter. The omission was deliberate. During clause-by-clause consideration of the Charter by the Special Joint Committee of the Senate and the House of Commons on the Constitution of Canada on 29 January 1981, New Democratic Party (NDP) Member of Parliament Svend Robinson proposed an amendment to include a ban on discrimination on the basis of sexual orientation in section 15. The committee decisively repudiated Robinson's motion by a vote of twenty-two to two.[41] With this emphatic vote, the great majority of the elected representatives of the people of Canada on this parliamentary committee made clear that they did not want equality rights for homosexuals in the Charter. Regardless, in *Egan,* the Supreme Court of Canada presumed, in Muldoon's phrase, "to legislate on sexual orientation." The Court chose not, in Muldoon's words, "to leave the legislating to the legislature, Parliament." Instead, the Court undertook, in effect, to amend the Charter through interpretation by reading "sexual orientation" into section 15.

Notwithstanding this egregious example of judicial activism by the Supreme Court of Canada in *Egan,* counsel for Rape Relief urged Justice Davies to follow the example of judicial restraint exercised by Justice Muldoon in *Neilsen* by refraining from reading a ban on discrimination on the basis of transsexualism into the ban on discrimination on the basis of sex in the British Columbia Human Rights Code. In the opinion of Rape Relief, such a restrictive interpretation would be consistent not just with the ruling of the Federal Court in *Neilsen,* but also with the holding of the Supreme Court of Canada in *Brooks v. Canada Safeway Ltd.,* 1989 SCC, that sex discrimination constitutes an unjustified refusal of a benefit or the imposition of a burden because one is a man or a woman.

This was a strained argument. In *Brooks* the Supreme Court of Canada not only broke with precedent, but also expanded the legal definition of sex discrimination in the Manitoba Human Rights Code beyond the limits understood by the provincial Legislature. The case was brought before the Supreme Court of Canada by Susan Brooks, a cashier in a Safeway grocery store. Brooks applied for weekly benefits under the company's group insurance plan, claiming a pregnancy related disability. Her application was rejected because the Safeway plan excluded coverage for loss of pay due to pregnancy from the tenth week before birth to the sixth week thereafter. As a result, Brooks had to settle for $133.47 in weekly pregnancy benefits under the Unemployment Insurance Act instead of the $188 weekly that she would have received if the Safeway plan had fully covered pregnancy leave. In a complaint filed with the Manitoba Human Rights Commission, Books argued that the lack of pregnancy benefits for seventeen weeks in the Safeway plan violated the ban on discrimination in employment on the basis of sex in section 6(1) of the Manitoba Human Rights Act.

The Manitoba Human Rights Tribunal dismissed the claim, citing the precedent set by the Supreme Court of Canada in *Bliss v. Attorney General of Canada,* 1979 SCC, a similar pre-Charter case involving a pregnant woman, Stella Bliss, who objected to the denial of basic unemployment benefits to pregnant women in section 46 of the Unemployment Insurance Act. Bliss claimed that such discrimination against pregnant women violated the equality rights of women in section 1 of the 1960 Canadian Bill of Rights, which states: "It is hereby recognized and declared that in Canada there have existed and shall continue to exist without discrimination by reason of race, national origin, colour, religion or sex, the following human rights and fundamental freedoms, namely ... (b) the right of the individual to equality before the law." The Supreme Court of Canada rejected Bliss's claim on the ground that discrimination on the basis of pregnancy does not affect all women on the basis of their sex but only those who are pregnant.

The adjudicator for the Human Rights Tribunal in *Brooks* also observed that courts in England and the United States had ruled that discrimination on the basis of pregnancy is not tantamount to discrimination on the basis of sex. The adjudicator further pointed out that following the *Bliss* ruling, several provinces had amended their human rights codes to include an explicit ban on discrimination on the basis of pregnancy. Given the failure of the Manitoba Legislature to adopt a similar amendment, the adjudicator maintained that he had no authority in law to hold that the treatment of pregnant women in the Safeway group insurance plan violated the Manitoba Human Rights Act.

With the assistance of the federally funded Women's Legal Education and Action Fund (LEAF), Brooks appealed the adjudicator's ruling to the Manitoba Court of Queen's Bench and thereafter to the Manitoba Court of Appeal.[42] Both courts rejected her suit on the same restrained basis as the adjudicator. Brooks then took her case to the Supreme Court of Canada. There she succeeded. In a unanimous ruling on 15 June 1989, the country's top Court held that Safeway's "accident and sickness plan discriminates on the basis of sex by excluding compensation for pregnant women during a seventeen-week period." The Court sent the case back to the adjudicator for determination of an appropriate remedy under the Manitoba Human Rights Act.

The reasons for judgment of the Supreme Court of Canada in *Brooks* were written by Chief Justice Brian Dickson – the same justice who had persuaded the Court in the pre-Charter *Carswell* case that the Court was duty bound not to legislate but to uphold the existing law on trespass. As we have seen, Dickson insisted in *Carswell*: "If there is to be any change in this statute law, it would seem to me that such a change must be made by the enacting institution, the legislature, which is representative of the people and designed to manifest the political will, and not by the Court." In *Brooks,* Dickson flip-flopped. In contradiction of his principled defence of judicial restraint thirteen years earlier, he abandoned precedent in *Brooks* and flouted the separation of powers. "Over ten years have elapsed since the decision in *Bliss,*" Dickson argued. "During that time there have been profound changes in women's labour force participation. With the benefit of a decade of hindsight and ten years of experience with claims of human rights discrimination and jurisprudence arising therefrom, I am prepared to say that *Bliss* was wrongly decided or, in any event, that *Bliss* would not be decided now as it was decided then." With this reasoning, Dickson undermined the rule of stable, predictable law and usurped the legislative authority of the elected legislators of Manitoba by reading a ban on discrimination on the basis of pregnancy into the ban on discrimination on the basis of sex in the province's Human Rights Act.

Brooks is one of many cases over the past twenty years in which the

Supreme Court of Canada has decreed that human rights codes are not subject to ordinary, let alone strict, construction. Justice Davies pointed out in his reasons for judgment in *Rape Relief*: "It is well settled law that human rights legislation is to be approached purposively giving it a fair, large and liberal interpretation with a view to advancing its objects." To support this point, he cited the decision of the Supreme Court of Canada in *Gould v. Yukon Order of Pioneers*, 1996 SCC, a case that dealt with the Yukon Human Rights Act. In reasons for judgment in this case, Mr Justice Frank Iacobucci affirmed that the courts should apply "a true purposive approach" to the interpretation of human rights legislation that "looks at the wording of the statute itself, with a view to discerning and advancing the legislature's intent. Our task is to breathe life, and generously so, into the particular statutory provisions that are before us."

What was the purpose of British Columbia legislators in enacting the Human Rights Code of 1996? Did they intend that the ban on discrimination on the basis of sex in section 8 should include a ban on discrimination on the basis of transsexualism or gender identity? Even the British Columbia Human Rights Commission did not think so. In a report on 19 January 1998, the commission urged the Legislature to amend section 8 to include "gender identity" as a prohibited ground of discrimination. The commission said: "Adding 'gender identity' as a ground for protection would ensure that adequate protection is accorded to all those who fall under the category."[43] The Legislature never acted on the recommendation, but this was of no account to the commission. Despite the lack of any explicit authority in law, the commission arbitrarily accused the Vancouver Rape Relief Society of unlawfully discriminating against Nixon on the basis of her gender identity. In response, Rape Relief urged Davies to quash the charge on the ground that there was no evidence or reason to believe that the Legislature intended to include gender identity in the ban on discrimination on the basis of sex in section 8 of the Code.

Davies rejected the argument. Despite having just cited Iacobucci's contention that human rights legislation should be interpreted "with a view to discerning and advancing the legislature's intent," he held:

> I do not accept the petitioner's premise that by prohibiting discrimination on the basis of sex, the legislature intended to redress only male/female social, economic and political issues. I also do not accept that its failure to amend the 1984 Act or the present Code to specifically include gender identity or transsexualism as enumerated grounds of discrimination should be taken to mean

> that the legislature did not intend that human rights protection on the ground of sex did not extend to transsexuals ...
>
> In my view, unless compelled to do so by specific legislative direction or clear evidence to the contrary, it would be wrong to interpret the prohibition against discrimination on the basis of sex in either the 1984 Act or the present Code as not also prohibiting discrimination against an individual merely because that person or group is not readily identifiable as being either male or female ... I am accordingly of the opinion that the prohibition against discrimination on the basis of "sex" in the 1984 Act and the present Code includes a prohibition against discrimination on the basis of transsexualism.

Note that with this declaration, Davies invoked the authority of the Supreme Court of Canada to reverse the traditional common law doctrine of strict construction: Instead of demanding clear and definite evidence that the Legislature intended to ban discrimination on the basis of transsexualism in the Code, he required "specific legislative direction or clear evidence to the contrary" to prevent him from reading such an unexampled restriction on freedom into the law. As a result, Rape Relief lost its suit. Davies threw out the organization's application for an order prohibiting the Human Rights Tribunal from belatedly proceeding with Nixon's complaint.

RAPE RELIEF'S CONTINUING LEGAL ORDEAL

With the way cleared by the British Columbia Supreme Court, MacNaughton got her tribunal hearings in *Nixon* underway on 11 December 2000. The process proceeded intermittently for twenty-one days ending on 23 February 2001. In support of excluding Nixon from the training program for rape crisis counsellors, Lee Lakeman, a prominent feminist and longstanding leader of Rape Relief, argued before the tribunal that only a woman who was born and raised as a woman can have the sensitivity needed to counsel, comfort, and console the female victims of rape in a sexist society dominated by men. "Kim Nixon lived as a man for 30 years," observed Lakeman. "If Kim Nixon lives until 60 as a woman, I'd be interested in reopening the question of whether he [*sic*] can be a Rape Relief volunteer."[44]

Some feminists have been sorely torn by the *Nixon* case. Judy Rebick, former president of the National Action Committee on the Status of Women, conceded: "There's no question that transgendered people suffer from discrimination. They suffer a great deal. So, of course, [in] your heart as a feminist you want to be on their side in every fight, but you can't be because there is a conflict of rights."[45] In

Rebick's opinion, the dispute between Nixon and Rape Relief pits the rights of male-to-female transsexuals against the rights of women by birth. She pointed out: "The issue at stake is whether a women's group has the right to decide who its members are."[46] In testimony before the tribunal, Rebick made clear that she thinks Rape Relief should be free to exclude male-to-female transsexuals from its membership and programs.

MacNaughton disagreed. After nearly eleven months of deliberation, she handed down her ruling on 18 January 2002. In conformity with the "large and liberal" interpretations of the Charter and human rights codes mandated by activist judges on the Supreme Court of Canada, she concluded that Rape Relief's refusal to accept a transsexual as a volunteer in a training program for rape crisis counsellors violated the provisions of the British Columbia Human Rights Code banning discrimination on the basis of sex in employment and the provision of a public service. To deter further offences, MacNaughton declared: "I order Rape Relief to cease denying, for discriminatory reasons, to transsexual women the opportunity of participating in their training program and the opportunity, on completion of the training, for the same group of women of volunteering at Rape Relief." In addition, MacNaughton directed Rape Relief to "pay to Ms. Nixon the sum of $7,500 as compensation for the injury to her dignity, feelings and self-respect."

This was the largest award for hurt feelings that the tribunal had ever made.[47] Note, also, that MacNaughton did not just confine her ruling to postoperative male-to-female transsexuals like Nixon, but also directed that in training and selecting rape crisis volunteers, Rape Relief must not discriminate against any transsexual women, a category that includes men who identify as women but have yet to undergo sex reassignment surgery. On 24 June 2002 Rape Relief announced that it would appeal the ruling. Speaking on behalf of the voluntary women's group, Suzanne Jay declared: "We are fighting this case as a test case on the protection of women's human rights to women-only organizing. It isn't clear that the Tribunal member understood that every woman's rights, not only Kimberly Nixon's rights, ought to be protected in this situation."[48]

In due course, Rape Relief's appeal came back before the British Columbia Supreme Court, this time with Mr Justice Robert Edwards presiding. Over five days beginning on 18 August 2003, he heard arguments on essentially the same issues that had already been canvassed in lengthy hearings before Justice Davies and Adjudicator MacNaughton. The end result was markedly different: On 19 December 2003 Edwards overturned the tribunal ruling against Rape Relief.[49]

In Edwards's opinion, MacNaughton had misapplied the provision in section 41 of the British Columbia Human Rights Code that a non-profit organization like Rape Relief whose primary purpose is to promote the welfare of an identifiable group defined by sex can discriminate in favour of members of that group without violating the Code. While MacNaughton took the view that Rape Relief was not entitled to a section-41 exemption in relation to transsexuals because the feminist collective had failed to establish that its primary purpose is to promote the interests only of women born as women, Edwards completely disagreed. He said MacNaughton's finding "that s. 41 did not permit Rape Relief to exclude Ms. Nixon from its peer counselling training program was unreasonable."

Edwards also addressed Davies's contention that the change-of-name provision in section 7 of the British Columbia Vital Statistics Act grants postoperative transsexuals "the same legal status as other members of their post operative sex." Edwards pointed out that if this statement of the law were true, it would logically follow that male-to-female transsexuals who were born in British Columbia would be legally entitled by virtue of section 7 of the Vital Statistics Act to compete on the same basis as women from birth in an all-female track tournament. Edwards contended that the Legislature of British Columbia could not have intended to cover all such contingencies through the enactment of section 27 of the Vital Statistics Act. Having noted that this section "does not specifically address the consequences of 'trans-sexual surgery' other than to provide for a change of birth registration," he concluded: "Had the legislature intended to ensure that persons who had undergone 'trans-sexual surgery' were to be treated for all purposes under the law as members of the sex to which they were reassigned, it would have to have reflected that intention by enacting legislation which said so explicitly for all such persons." In short, Edwards upheld the common law doctrine on strict construction in *Nixon* that his colleague Davies had summarily repudiated.

If Edwards were a consistently restrained judge, he would have decided at this point to throw out the case against Rape Relief on the ground that there is no provision in the laws of Canada or British Columbia that clearly and definitely forbids discrimination on the basis of transsexualism. As it is, Edwards agreed with Davies that a ban on discrimination on the basis of transsexualism is implicit in the ban on discrimination on the basis of sex in section 15 of the Charter and sections 8 and 13 of the British Columbia Human Rights Code. MacNaughton took the same view. In her opinion, the case was cut and dried: Given that Rape Relief had refused to allow Nixon to take part in its training program for rape crisis counsellors because she is a transsexual, MacNaughton held: "It is self-evident that this type of exclusion is prima facie discriminatory within the meaning of the Code."

Edwards disagreed. He pointed out that in *Law v. Canada (Minister of Employment and Immigration)*, 1999 SCC 497, the Court has declared that to run afoul of the Charter, differential treatment must "discriminate in a substantive sense, bringing into play the purpose of s. 15(1) of the *Charter* in remedying such ills as prejudice, stereotyping, and historical disadvantage." Referring to discriminatory legislation, the Court stated: "The more severe and localized the consequences of the legislation for the affected group the more likely that the differential treatment responsible for these consequences is discriminatory within the meaning of s. 15(1)."[50] While MacNaughton ruled that the discrimination practised by Rape Relief against transsexuals was so severe as to satisfy the *Law* criteria, Edwards, once again, disagreed. He wrote: "Rape Relief provides access to only a tiny part of the economic, social and cultural life of the province." Given the small number of members of the Rape Relief agency, he held that "exclusion from its programs is quite evidently exclusion from a backwater, not from the mainstream of the economic, social and cultural life of the province."

In the end, Edwards quashed the tribunal orders that Rape Relief cease discriminating against transsexuals and pay $7,500 in damages to Nixon for alleged injury to her dignity, feelings, and self-respect. As a leader of Rape Relief, Jay could not have been happy with Edward's denigration of her organization as an inconsequential backwater in the cultural life of the province, but she hailed his decision: "Other women's groups felt intimidated by the threat of human rights complaints for organizing exactly as we are entitled to organize," she said. "Women are a historically disadvantaged group and there is provision in the Charter of Rights and Freedoms and in the Human Rights Code for us to group independently to address these experiences of inequality."[51]

Jay's jubilation might have been premature. Nixon's lawyer, barbara findlay, a lesbian feminist who affects to spell her name without capital letters, has vowed to take the *Nixon* case all the way, if necessary, to the Supreme Court of Canada. [52] Unlike many feminists, findlay resents Edwards's contention that Nixon's exclusion from the Rape Relief training program was a trifling matter. "Women's organizations [are] a vital and important part of the political life of British Columbia," said findlay. "It's insulting to the women's movement to characterize this as a small, private fight. The women's movement matters; exclusion from the women's movement matters."[53]

Findlay also underlined the significance of the disagreement between MacNaughton and Edwards over the proper application of the *Law* criteria to the British Columbia Human Rights Code. While MacNaughton took the view in Rape Relief that it is necessary for a complainant to show only that he or she was treated differently to establish a contravention of a ban on discrimination in the Code, Edwards contended that the complainant must also establish that the differential treatment has had severe consequences for his or her dignity and self-respect. In findlay's opinion, Edwards's interpretation eviscerates the Code. She accuses him of having handed down a "transphobic" ruling in *Nixon* that has compromised the rights of all equality-seeking groups in Canada.[54]

Clearly, there is no end in sight to litigation in the *Nixon* case. She filed her initial, human rights complaint against Rape Relief on 30 August 1995. So far, this case has gone through a prolonged investigation, one lengthy tribunal hearing, and two trials. The expense to the taxpayers of British Columbia for legal fees and court costs has run into hundreds of thousands of dollars. To what end? So that the British Columbia Human Rights Tribunal can affirm the right of a biological male who identifies as a female to join a training program run by an avowedly prolesbian and profeminist organization.

Prior to enactment of human rights codes and the Charter, members of a woman's group like Rape Relief had an unimpeachable right to freedom of association. Under the common law of Canada, they could not have been forced by any human rights tribunal or court to admit transsexuals to their voluntary, feminist fellowship except in accordance with the clear and definite language of a statute that had been duly enacted into law by elected representatives of the people in the appropriate section of the legislative branch of government. Today, as the *Nixon* case attests, Canadians can no longer take for granted the rule of law. We are no longer strictly governed, as Hayek put it in *The Road to Serfdom*, "by rules fixed and announced beforehand – rules which make it possible to foresee with fair certainty how the authority will use its coercive powers in given circumstances and to plan one's individual affairs on the basis of this knowledge."[55] Instead of upholding the law as it exists, the British Columbia Human Rights Tribunal and two judges on the British Columbia Supreme Court have undertaken in the *Nixon* case to "amend" the law through interpretation by reading a ban on discrimination on the basis of transsexualism into the British Columbia Human Rights Code. But having done so, the judges and the adjudicator could not agree on how this new law of their own devising applies to the dispute between Nixon and the Vancouver Rape Relief Society. Such confusion is not at all surprising. It is inherent to judicial activism. There can be no clarity and stability in the law when judges indulge in the "wide, arbitrary and discretionary powers of constraint" that Dicey denounced in *The Law of the Constitution* as incompatible with the rule of law.

2

Gay Rights Trump Freedom of Religion

On 7 October 1997 an Ontario human rights board of inquiry delivered an unprecedented blow to the historic rights of Canadians to freedom of expression by ruling that Mayor Dianne Haskett of London, Ontario, must issue a gay pride proclamation at the request of the Homophile Association of London Ontario (HALO).[1] In the opinion of the board, Haskett's refusal on principle to issue such a proclamation violated the ban on discrimination on the basis of sexual orientation in the Ontario Human Rights Code. Like Rape Relief in the *Nixon* case, Haskett stoutly resisted this oppressive ruling. Instead of bowing down to the board of inquiry, she resolved as mayor to uphold her personal beliefs as a Christian that she must not only manifest loving care for homosexuals, but also respect the traditional teaching of the church that all sexual intercourse outside of marriage is wrong and sinful.

Haskett told the board of inquiry that upon taking office as mayor in 1995, she had established as her settled policy that she would not issue any mayoral proclamations relating to abortion, sexuality, or any other issue that "would cause serious controversy in the community" or "would incite hatred towards any group." In conformity with this determination, she refused to proclaim a Chastity Week for the city of London in the spring of 1995. In a letter to the group that requested this proclamation, she advised: "During my term of office as Mayor, I will not be making any proclamation with respect to sexuality, whether it be heterosexuality, homosexuality or celibacy." Less than a week later, Haskett received a letter from a representative of HALO requesting a gay pride proclamation. Haskett replied: "In response to your letter of April 7, 1995, please be advised that it is the policy of my office to decline requests for proclamations that relate to sexuality, whether it be heterosexuality, homosexuality or celibacy. A previous request of this sort has already been denied by my office." Richard Hudler, president of HALO, sent the mayor another letter, asking her to reconsider. She declined to do so. In yet another letter on the subject, Hudler and Clarence Crossman, another influential HALO member, suggested to the mayor that in view of her religious objections to homosexual behaviour, she might declare a conflict of interest on HALO's request and delegate her sole discretion to make proclamations to the then deputy mayor, Grant Hopcroft, or to a vote of City Council. "We agree," wrote Hudler and Crossman, "that it is not fair to force you to make a proclamation about something you believe to be wrong."

In a responding letter, the mayor reiterated: "My position with regard to your request for a proclamation has been made clear. If London City Council should choose to deal with this issue differently, and make a proclamation on its own behalf, it is within its power to do so." Subsequently, City Council considered the proposal and refused HALO's request by a vote of fifteen to four, with Haskett abstaining. At this point, having had HALO's request for a pride proclamation turned down not just by the mayor, but also by the Board of Control and City Council as a whole, Hudler appealed to the Ontario Human Rights Commission. In a complaint filed on 11 October 1995, he charged the mayor and City Council with contravening the Ontario Human Rights Code by refusing to recognize in public the contributions and achievements of HALO. Hudler stated: "I am a gay man and I believe that my right to equal treatment with respect to services, goods and facilities, without discrimination because of sexual orientation has been infringed in contravention of ss. 1 and 9 of the Ontario Human Rights Code."

Section 1 of the Code states: "Every person has a right to equal treatment with respect to services, goods and facilities, without discrimination because of race, ancestry, place of origin, colour, ethnic origin, citizenship, creed, sex, sexual orientation, age, marital status, same-sex partnership status, family status or handicap." Section 9 provides: "No person shall infringe or do, directly or indirectly, anything that infringes a right under this Part." The Code includes no definition of "services," apart from a stipulation that the term "services does not include a levy, fee, tax or periodic payment imposed by law." There is no clear and definite language in the Code relating to mayoral proclamations. Indeed, the Code contains no mention whatsoever of mayoral proclamations. Therefore, according to the doctrine of strict construction for freedom-constricting statutes, the mayor should have been free under the Ontario Human Rights Code to accept or reject any proclamation request.

However, in *Ontario Human Rights Commission v. Simpson Sears Ltd.*, 1985 SCC, the Supreme Court of Canada ordained that the doctrine of strict construction shall not apply to restrictions on freedom imposed by a human rights code. Mr Justice William McIntyre, one of the most restrained judges to sit on the Supreme Court in the Charter era, stated in his reasons for judgment in this case:

> It is not in my view a sound approach to say that according to established rules of construction no broader meaning can be given to the [Ontario Human Rights] Code than the narrowest interpretation of the words employed. The accepted rules of construction are flexible enough to enable the Court to recognize in the construction of a human rights code the special nature and purpose of the enactment ... and give to it an interpretation which will advance its broad purposes. Legislation of this type is of a special nature, not quite constitutional but certainly more than the ordinary – and it is for the courts to seek out its purpose and give it effect. The Code aims at the removal of discrimination.

Similarly, in *Ontario Human Rights Commission v. Zurich Insurance Company*, 1992 SCC, Mr Justice John Sopinka said: "In approaching the interpretation of a human rights statute, certain special principles must be respected. Human rights legislation is amongst the most pre-eminent category of legislation. It has been described as having a 'special nature, not quite constitutional but certainly more than the ordinary.' One of the reasons such legislation has been so described is that it is often the final refuge of the disadvantaged and the disenfranchised. As the last protection of the most vulnerable members of society, exceptions to such legislation should be narrowly construed."

Prompted by these instructions from the Supreme Court of Canada to subject human rights codes to large and liberal interpretations, Elizabeth Beckett held in an unprecedented ruling for an Ontario human rights board of inquiry on 6 March 1995 that Mayor Bob Morrow of Hamilton had violated the ban on discrimination on the basis of sexual orientation in the Ontario Human Rights Code by refusing to proclaim a Lesbian and Gay Pride Week in Hamilton at the request of the city's Gay and Lesbian Alliance.[2] In support of this finding, Beckett argued that mayoral proclamations constitute a service within the meaning of the Ontario Human Rights Code. Echoing the Supreme Court of Canada, she said: "The Code does not qualify the term 'service' and because the Code is remedial legislation, the word 'service' must be given a broad and liberal interpretation ... Issuing a proclamation is a service because it is generally perceived in the community as being a benefit to the groups that seek it and therefore it should be seen as a legitimate privilege to which citizens have access without fear of discrimination."[3]

Unlike Haskett, Morrow did not profess to have religious objections to issuing gay pride proclamations. In a letter to the Gay and Lesbian Alliance, he explained that he was unwilling to proclaim a Gay and Lesbian Pride Week in the city "because it would be so overwhelmingly opposed by the members of our community." Beckett was unmoved by this argument. She paid no heed to the mayor's perception of the preferences of the majority of the people. She ordered him to pay $5,000 in damages to the complainant and to issue a lesbian and gay pride proclamation upon request. Morrow complied.

In the Haskett case, the Ontario Human Rights Commission likewise summoned London City Council to issue a gay pride proclamation at HALO's request. Council refused to comply, so the commission referred the matter to a board of inquiry. On behalf of Hudler, the commission asked for:

> a. a declaration that the Mayor's refusal to proclaim 'Pride Weekend' constitutes unlawful discrimination on the basis of sexual orientation; b. that the City of London proclaim Pride Day/Weekend and recognize the service provided to the London community by HALO, if so requested by HALO or any other 'Pride' organizing committee; c. that the City of London and London City Council make a statement of recognition that the Lesbian and Gay and Bisexual Communities are integral and important communities within the City of London and that they make a commitment to investigate ways of fostering a positive relationship between the City of London and the Gay, Lesbian and Bisexual communities.

Note that Hudler and the commission formally requested that the board enjoin the City of London, not the mayor, to proclaim a Pride Day/Weekend. This was in accord with Hudler's submission to the mayor that it would not be fair to force her to make a proclamation about something that she conscientiously believes to be wrong. By this reasoning, however, how could it be fair to force other members of London City Council to do the same? The mayor was not the only elected representative of the people on the council who had moral objections to issuing a gay pride proclamation. Counsellors Anne Marie Decicco, a Roman Catholic, and Ab Chabhar, a Muslim, indicated that they, too, were conscientiously opposed to proclaiming gay pride. In a genuine democracy, would a human rights tribunal have the power to order city councillors like Decicco and Chabhar to approve proclamations about any matter that they believe on religious grounds to be wrong? The Ontario Human Rights Commission thinks so. It urged Mary Anne McKellar, the board of inquiry adjudicator assigned to the Haskett case, to order members of London City Council to issue a gay pride proclamation upon request. McKellar had ample authority to make such an extraordinary order under the provisions of section 41 of the Code, which state that:

> (1) Where the board of inquiry, after a hearing, finds that a right of the complainant under Part I has been infringed and that the infringement is a contravention of s. 9 by a party to the proceeding, the board may, by order, (a) direct the party to do anything that, in the opinion of the board, the party ought to do to achieve compliance with this Act, both in respect of the complaint and in respect of future practices; and (b) direct the party to make restitution, including monetary compensation, for loss arising out of the infringement, and, where the infringement has been engaged in wilfully or recklessly, monetary compensation may include an award, not exceeding $10,000, for mental anguish.[4]

McKellar held hearings in London between 6 and 22 August 1997. The highlight of the proceedings came during emotional testimony by Mayor Haskett on 21 August. While averring that she has always advocated care and compassion for homosexuals, Haskett maintained that she could not issue the pride proclamation requested by HALO because the public would interpret the concession as her personal endorsement of gay, lesbian, and bisexual lifestyles. To the suggestion that she should separate her religious convictions from the performance of her duties as mayor, Haskett, her voice cracking with emotion, responded:

> My life, my spiritual life is tied up in my relationship with God and to at some point in time say I'm going to separate myself from that ... I can't conceive of how to do it. I think at the very least a person who separates themselves from their deeply held beliefs, at the very least, they are a hypocrite and at the very worst, they are turning their back on God and I can't do that ... I think that the people of London have the right to expect that I'm going to be consistent with what I am in what I say and in what I do and if I cease to be consistent with what I am, then I don't know what they have to depend on. I also believe that every privilege and every opportunity that's been given to me in my life, I give the credit to God for that and if I were to turn my back on God, that is the moment that I would lose my authority as the Mayor of the City of London.[5]

In an extensive brief filed with the board of inquiry, Scott Ritchie and Kathryn McKerlie, Haskett's legal counsel, argued that an order forcing the mayor to issue the pride proclamation requested by HALO would contravene the guarantees in section 2 of the Canadian Charter of Rights and Freedoms that: "Everyone has the following fundamental freedoms: (a) freedom of conscience and religion (b) freedom of thought, belief, opinion and expression, including freedom of the press and other means of communication." In a separate brief, James Barber, the city's legal counsel, contended: "Council and the Mayor do not function like a bulletin board or hydro pole to which people affix their signs, banners and proclamations. The ability of politicians to debate issues of public policy freely and to express their views is a right enshrined in the Constitution. Compelling speech by the Mayor or Council is 'to put a particular message in their mouths' and is a violation of constitutional rights and freedoms."[6]

In support of these arguments, Barber, Ritchie, and McKerlie cited several judgments by the Supreme Court of Canada about freedom of expression, beginning with the pre-Charter judgment from the 1930s in the *Alberta Press* case.[7] At issue in this instance was the constitutional validity of an Alberta statute entitled "An Act to Ensure the Publication of Accurate News and Information," which compelled newspapers to publish government statements responding to criticisms of government policy. In declaring this bill beyond the lawful powers of the Alberta Legislature, Chief Justice Sir Lyman Duff stated:

> The right of public discussion is, of course, subject to legal restrictions; those based upon considerations of decency and public order, and others conceived for the protection of various private and public interests with which, for example, the laws of defamation and sedition are concerned. In a word, freedom of discussion means, to quote the words of Lord Wright in *James v. Commonwealth,* (1936), "freedom governed by law."
>
> Even within its legal limits, it is liable to abuse and grave abuse, and such abuse is constantly exemplified before our eyes; but it is axiomatic that the practice of this right of free public discussion of public affairs, notwithstanding its incidental mischiefs, is the breath of life for parliamentary institutions.

In a post-Charter decision, *Irwin Toy v. Quebec,* 1989 SCC, Chief Justice Dickson expressed an even broader view:

> Freedom of expression was entrenched in our Constitution and is guaranteed in the Quebec Charter so as to ensure that everyone can manifest their [*sic*] thoughts, opinions, beliefs, indeed all expressions of the heart and mind, however unpopular, distasteful or contrary to the mainstream. Such protec-

tion is, in the words of both the Canadian and Quebec Charters, "fundamental" because in a free, pluralistic and democratic society we prize a diversity of ideas and opinions for their inherent value both to the community and to the individual ...

We cannot, then, exclude human activity from the scope of guaranteed free expression on the basis of the content or meaning being conveyed. Indeed, if the activity conveys or attempts to convey a meaning, it has expressive content and prima facie falls within the scope of the guarantee.

Note that with this judgment, Dickson affirmed that the guarantee of freedom of expression in section 2 of the Charter encompasses any activity that even attempts to convey a meaning. That would include not just mayoral proclamations, but even the vilest pornography. Correspondingly, in *Edmonton Journal v. Alberta,* 1989 SCC, Mr Justice Peter Cory stated: "It is difficult to imagine a guaranteed right more important to a democratic society than freedom of expression. Indeed a democracy cannot exist without that freedom to express new ideas and to put forward opinions about the functioning of public institutions. The concept of free and uninhibited speech permeates all truly democratic societies and institutions. The vital importance of the concept cannot be over-emphasized."

Granted, Haskett's refusal to issue a gay pride proclamation involved not so much the freedom to speak as the right to remain silent. However, the freedom to speak and the freedom to remain silent are essentially two sides of the same legal coin. In *Slaight Communications Inc. v. Davidson,* 1989 SCC, Chief Justice Lamer stated: "There is no denying that freedom of expression necessarily entails the right to say nothing or the right not to say certain things." In *Gay Alliance Toward Equality v. Vancouver Sun,* 1979 SCC, the Court dealt with freedom of expression specifically in relation to gay rights. This case arose from the refusal of the newspaper to publish a classified advertisement at the request of Gay Alliance Toward Equality. For this snub, the gay rights organization accused the *Vancouver Sun* of violating a provision in the British Columbia Human Rights Code that prohibited a company from refusing to provide a service to a person "unless reasonable cause exists." In a ruling for the Supreme Court of Canada, Mr Justice Brian Martland rejected this argument. He stated: "The law has recognized the freedom of the press to propagate its views and ideas on any issue and to select the material which it publishes. As a corollary to that, a newspaper also has the right to refuse to publish material which runs contrary to the views it expresses." Counsel for Mayor Haskett argued before the board of inquiry that if a newspaper has a constitutional right to reject an advertisement from a gay organization, it surely follows that an elected mayor and city council are no less entitled to refuse to issue a gay pride proclamation.

In addition to the general scope of freedom of expression, Haskett's case addressed the constitutional propriety of having a quasi-judicial agency compel someone to issue a statement that he or she does not believe to be true. The Supreme Court of Canada dealt with this issue in *National Bank of Canada v. Retail Clerks' International Union,* 1984 SCC. In reasons for the Court, Mr Justice Jean Beetz denounced an order by the Canada Labour Relations Board that required the employer to read a letter to the bank's employees stating that the firm approved of unionization. In the judgment of Beetz:

> This type of penalty is totalitarian, and as such alien to the tradition of free nations like Canada, even for the repression of the most serious crimes. I cannot be persuaded that the Parliament of Canada intended to confer on the Canada Labour Relations Board the power to impose such extreme measures, even assuming that it could confer such a power bearing in mind the Canadian Charter of Rights and Freedoms, which guarantees freedom of thought, belief, opinion and expression. These freedoms guarantee to every person the right to express the opinions he may have: *a fortiori* they must prohibit compelling anyone to utter opinions that are not his own.

McKellar reserved just one day of her hearing for counsel to sum up their arguments with regard to all the Supreme Court rulings and other complicated legal and constitutional issues pertinent to the Haskett case. The session developed into a marathon that began in the morning, broke for lunch, and dragged on without a break for supper until late into the evening. Then, just ten days later, McKellar handed down her decision. The political timing could hardly have been more dramatic, with the decision coming scarcely a month before the 1997 municipal election in which Haskett was seeking a second term as mayor.

As expected, McKellar found, in line with the Morrow precedent, "that the Respondents have discriminated against the Complainant with respect to services on the basis of sexual orientation contrary to ss. 1 and 9 of the Code." While conceding "that the right to freedom of expression guaranteed in s. 2(b) of the Charter also includes the right not to speak, and the right not to be made to say things one does not wish to say," McKellar contended that requiring Haskett to issue gay pride proclamations would not encroach upon the mayor's Charter right to freedom of expression. How can that be? McKellar argued: "Interpreting 'services' to require that in municipalities where statements of the civic recognition of special days are available, they be made available on [a] non-discriminatory basis does not directly prohibit or compel speech. To so interpret 'services' does not trench on s. 2(b) rights at all."

Can anyone other than a human rights adjudicator make sense out of this argument? By this reasoning, McKellar deduced that a human rights tribunal can order a mayor to say, or not to say, something without trenching upon the mayor's constitutional right to freedom of expression. Furthermore, McKellar concluded that in refusing to issue a gay pride proclamation at the request of Hudler, Haskett had unlawfully discriminated against him on the basis of his sexual orientation. To compensate Hudler for "the loss of the right to be free from discrimination, and for mental anguish caused by the infringement of that right," McKellar held Haskett and the city jointly responsible for paying him $10,000 in damages. McKellar also directed that the City of London must (1) "make a statement of recognition that the Lesbian and Gay and Bisexual Communities are integral and important communities within the City of London" and (2) "proclaim Pride Day/Weekend and recognize the service provided to the London community by HALO, if so requested by HALO or any other 'Pride' organizing committee." Finally, McKellar ruled "that HALO may seek its requested proclamation and recognition from either of the respondents."

Note that with this last statement, McKellar empowered HALO to insist upon having the mayor issue a gay pride proclamation and statement of appreciation for HALO, notwithstanding the fact that Hudler and the Human Rights Commission had explicitly requested proclamations only from "the City of London and London City Council." If HALO had taken advantage of this ruling by once again asking Haskett to issue a pride proclamation, she would have been obligated to acquiesce or face the consequences of defying a direct order by a human rights board of inquiry.

All Canadians, whatever their views on the morality of homosexuality, should be alarmed and incensed by this ruling. With it, McKellar implied that regardless of the guarantee of freedom of expression in the Charter, a so-called human rights tribunal can force citizens who are performing a public service to make statements that run contrary to their most profound moral convictions. Journalists and preachers who are prone to express controversial opinions should beware: What opinions might a board of inquiry ban or prescribe next? Who would have thought a few years ago that a human rights tribunal in Canada might subject anyone, let alone the elected mayor of a city, to a hefty fine for refusing to proclaim support for the lifestyles and behaviours of sexually active gays, lesbians, bisexuals, and transsexuals?

Would the Supreme Court of Canada have gone along with McKellar's paradoxical suggestion that compelling the mayor or City Council to issue a gay pride proclamation is compatible with the guarantee of freedom of expression in section 2 of the Charter? Even McKellar entertained some doubts on this point. In a second line of argument in her reasons for judgment in *Hudler*, she contended that while her order "could be viewed as an incidental infringement" of freedom of expression, it is justifiable because the rights and freedoms guaranteed in the Charter are not absolute but sometimes conflict and need to be appropriately balanced out, one against another.

That Charter rights collide is incontestable. For example, if journalists were allowed to exercise their right to freedom of expression under section 2 of the Charter by publishing full details of all the evidence revealed during the preliminary hearing of a sensational murder trial, the resulting publicity could gravely compromise the right of an accused under section 11(d) of the Charter "to be presumed innocent until proven guilty according to law in a fair and public hearing by an independent and impartial tribunal." For this reason, Parliament has decided that publication of information revealed at a preliminary hearing in Canada shall be prohibited by law, despite the incidental conflict between this ban on publication and the guarantee of freedom of expression in section 2 of the Charter. In this way, our legislators have undertaken to strike an appropriate balance between legal rights and expression rights.

Correspondingly, McKellar argued that even if her order requiring either the mayor or City Council to issue a gay pride proclamation might incidentally infringe upon the Charter rights of the mayor and other city councillors to freedom of expression, the order would be justified by the overriding need to ban the kind of discrimination forbidden in the Ontario Human Rights Code. In McKellar's words: "An order compelling the respondents, or either of them, to speak constitutes a prima facie infringement of s. 2(b) of the Charter, which guarantees the freedom to remain silent. In the circumstances of this case, however, such an order withstands scrutiny under s. 1." Section 1 of the Charter provides that the rights and freedoms guaranteed in the Charter are subject to "such reasonable limits prescribed by law as can be demonstrably justified in a free and democratic society." In McKellar's opinion, her order was a demonstrably justifiable means of remedying a direct infringement of the Ontario Human Rights Code by Haskett and City Council in refusing to issue gay pride proclamations. "Here the infringement was occasioned by a failure to speak," McKellar argued. "Logically, then, the remedy is to compel speech that ought to have been made. This is particularly the case here where public acknowledgement of sexual identity is the uniquely appropriate means of overcoming the historical discrimination suffered by gays and lesbians."

To bolster this argument, McKellar pointed out that the Supreme Court of Canada held in *Slaight Communications* that although an order by a labour code arbitrator requiring an employer to provide a specified letter of recommendation on behalf of a wrongfully dismissed employee was an infringement of freedom of expression in section 2, the order was constitutionally justified under section 1. Yet how could the court have squared this ruling with its previous declaration in *National Bank* that no agency of the state could compel someone to utter an opinion not one's own? McKellar explained that in making this turnaround,

> the Court was influenced by the fact that the letter of recommendation [in Slaight Communications] contained only a recitation of objective facts, and not any statements of opinion. The compelled statement of opinions not one's own had previously been found to offend s. 2(b) of the Charter and not be justified under s. 1 in Re National Bank of Canada and Retail Clerks International Union, 1984 SCC. The upshot of Slaight and National Bank is that ordering of compelled speech will run afoul of s. 1 where it requires the uttering of opinions that are not those of the speaker. The statements that I am asked to compel do not contain opinion, with the possible exception of the word "important" in Paragraph 77(c).[8]

What can be said for this argument? A gay pride proclamation is not a statement of mere facts but an expression of opinion. Hudler and Crossman acknowledged in their letter on behalf of HALO to the mayor "that it is not fair to force you to make a proclamation about something you believe to be wrong." The mayor agreed. Like Hudler and Crossman, she had good reason to surmise that the public would interpret a gay pride proclamation as an expression of her support for the lifestyles of sexually active lesbians, gays, and bisexuals. Consequently, it was ludicrous for McKellar to argue that her order compelling Haskett and City Council to issue gay pride proclamations was tantamount to obligating these elected officials to state an incontestable truth as authorized by the Supreme Court of Canada in *Slaight Communications.*

"Counsel for the Mayor tried to convince me that proclamations were a form of political speech and entitled to a great deal of deference," wrote McKellar in her judgment. "I have reviewed the draft proclamations in question again. In my view, they are devoid of political content, and they are not made political merely because uttered by a politician. The Mayor expressed concern that they would be viewed as her endorsement of a political agenda for gay and lesbian rights." Once again, McKellar's argument is far-fetched. The mayor had sound reason to apprehend that the issuing of a gay pride proclamation would have political ramifications. And she was not alone in holding this view: Hudler concurred. In testimony before the board, he acknowledged that his complaint against Haskett was part of the political action mandate undertaken by HALO to promote gay, lesbian, and bisexual rights.[9] McKellar ignored this testimony. In defiance of all reason and evidence, she insisted: "The proclamation words simply do not express what the Mayor referred to as 'support for homosexuality as a preferred lifestyle.'"

MAYOR HASKETT STANDS HER GROUND

The ruling of the board of inquiry in *Hudler* dropped on the City of London like a political bombshell. In a public statement on 8 October 1997, the mayor pointed out: "If this ruling is left unchallenged, any Canadian can be forced to say what they don't believe ... The implications are so staggering it should be a matter for legal review."[10] Other members of City Council saw matters differently. With Haskett abstaining, they voted unanimously on 20 October 1997 not to appeal the ruling. Instead, council resolved to pay the $10,000 penalty as directed by McKellar; to open discussions with members of HALO on how to improve relations with the city's lesbian, gay, and bisexual communities; and to determine whether HALO might still want the city to issue a pride proclamation.[11]

Meanwhile, Haskett stood her ground. Reading from a prepared statement at City Hall, she deplored the decision of City Council not to appeal the board of inquiry ruling. Drawing upon her varied experiences as the Mayor of London, a lawyer, and a human rights activist, she declared:

> I am very disappointed, because the Council knows that this case was unfairly decided and is wrong in fact and in law. It takes away fundamental freedoms that are meant to be protected by our Constitution in the Canadian Charter of Rights and Freedoms.
>
> I stand on my right as a Canadian to freedom of expression – and that means choosing what I will say and what I will not say. I never advocated discrimination and I never discriminated. I had a policy that allowed me to remain silent on issues of deep personal conviction, so that I would neither force those values on the community nor be forced to compromise them.[12]

Haskett opined that the majority of Londoners supported her policy on mayoral proclamations. She underlined:

> I have never advocated discrimination against gays and lesbians, many of whom have been my clients, my tenants, my colleagues and my friends. I do not judge or condemn. And I am not angry or bitter at HALO or any members of it for what I have had to go through to maintain my right to choose what I will say and what I will not say. I have never interfered with the activities of this group, as evidenced by the Pride celebrations that go on very openly each year.
>
> But at the same time, I am not prepared to be, now or in the future, the advocate for this organization or its agenda. I will not bow down to the ruling of the Human Rights Commission and I am willing to bear any consequences of that. I will not offer any proclamations, either presently, or in the future. In fact, let me make it clear that I intend to cease from making any proclamations of any kind hereafter.[13]

Nonetheless, Haskett said that she hoped to conciliate the gays and lesbians of London after the election. "I respect their right to live out their lives as they see fit and I look for their respect to allow me to be true to what I believe," she said. "I am truly sorry for the hurt that all this has caused. I like Richard Hudler, and as a fellow human being, I wouldn't want to hurt him for all the world. It's just that caring for someone and being forced to say that what they [*sic*] are doing is to be celebrated are two very different things."[14]

In an attempt to move the City beyond the unpleasantness generated by the confrontation with the Ontario Human Rights Commission, Haskett disclosed that instead of appealing McKellar's ruling, she had decided to take an immediate three-week unpaid leave of absence pending the upcoming municipal election with a view to having the city use the money saved from her salary to pay her share of the $10,000 fine levied by the human rights tribunal. While avowing that she was "in perfect health and in very good spirits," Haskett said she hoped that the people of London would reelect her for a second term. In closing, she announced that she would do no more campaigning before the vote so as not to place her principal rival in the mayoral contest, Deputy Mayor Hopcroft, at a competitive disadvantage inasmuch as he would be saddled with the additional duties of acting mayor for the balance of the election campaign.

As usual, the mayor was true to her word: During the final three weeks of the election campaign, she did not make a single public appearance. In a lead editorial on 22 October 1997, the *London Free Press* denounced this decision, saying: "When London taxpayers chose

Dianne Haskett to be Mayor it was with the expectation they were electing a leader. But leaders don't stay home when times are tough ... This is a difficult issue for Haskett who says it was not her intention to hurt anyone in the gay community. But this wouldn't even be an issue if she hadn't decided to make it one."[15] In a *Free Press* column, Jane Bradley charged: "Haskett cannot have it all ways at once: She cannot portray herself as a broad-minded, inclusive individual while at the same time rejecting a sizeable part of the population as simply being morally wrong."[16]

These views were typical. The great majority of editorial comments by print and broadcast journalists in the London area were relentlessly critical of the mayor. The same was true of outpourings by local academics. Herman Goodden was a conspicuous dissenter. In a freelance article in the *London Free Press*, he drew a parallel between Haskett's unwillingness to "turn her back on God" and the reluctance of Sir Thomas More to sign an oath as Lord Chancellor of England sanctioning the divorce and remarriage of King Henry VIII.[17] Under pain of consignment to the Tower of London and execution, More absolutely refused to subordinate his private conscience to the king's understanding of More's public duty. In *A Man for All Seasons*, Robert Bolt depicts a confrontation between More and his persecutors in which More declares: "I am a dead man. You have your desire of me. What you have hunted me for is not my actions, but the thoughts of my heart. It is a long road you have opened. For first men will disclaim their hearts and presently they will have no hearts. God help the people whose statesmen walk your road."[18]

The human rights board of inquiry tried to force Mayor Haskett to walk the same road. Goodden expressed confidence that "ultimately, the truth will out. Almost 500 years ago a beloved public figure was put to death because a lecherous monarch resented the compelling strength of his religious convictions. With any luck Mayor Haskett should be allowed to keep her head. Otherwise, I believe we're seeing the same sort of persecution today."[19]

Robert Butcher, a professor of philosophy at Brescia College, a nominally Roman Catholic affiliate of the University of Western Ontario, took strong issue with Goodden's defence of the mayor. In an article published in the *London Free Press* on 28 October 1997, Butcher argued: "Politicians have a special set of moral obligations which they must accept as a condition of public office. Part of that obligation is found in our human rights codes. Our public officials have a moral obligation to do their business in accordance with Canadian moral values of tolerance and non-discrimination. This ought not to cause a problem, for those moral values ought to be held as a matter of course and should not need enforcement by a tribunal."[20] To illustrate how the moral obligations of a politician can sometimes clash with personal convictions, Professor Butcher cited the agonizing dilemma confronted by Prime Minister Sir Winston Churchill during the Second World War when British intelligence found out about an impending air raid on the City of Coventry. The information forced Churchill to choose between: (a) ordering the preparation of antiaircraft defences to protect the hitherto undefended city or (b) allowing Coventry to be bombed for fear of tipping off the enemy that Britain had broken Germany's secret military code. Churchill decided to leave the city undefended.

What does this tragic decision have to do with Haskett? Professor Butcher contended: "The Haskett drama does not have the ingredients of tragedy – it operates more on the level of farce – but the principles are the same. Public life entails moral obligations. In the unhappy event these obligations clash with personal convictions, the morality required by elected office must defeat personal interests. These conflicts are sad, but not surprising. Our moral lives are complex affairs and require constant attention and decision. Public life has its rewards, but also its demands. At the risk of sounding clichéd, those who cannot stand the moral heat should stay out of the political kitchen."[21]

This argument rests on the premise that in making the difficult decision not to alert the Coventry defences, Churchill put his sense of public duty ahead of his personal moral convictions. But surely this was not the case. It stands to reason that it was, in fact, in the light of his personal moral convictions that Churchill decided that he had a public duty under the circumstances to conceal the vital fact that Britain had cracked Germany's secret military code. A fair reading of the historical record of Churchill's behaviour as prime minister would suggest that he completely agreed with More's assertion: "When statesmen forsake their own private conscience for the sake of their public duties, they lead their country to chaos."[22]

Professor Butcher is not alone among contemporary academics in upholding the authoritarian doctrine that all Canadians, including their elected representatives, have a duty to subordinate their personal moral convictions to the state approved canons of progressive morality decreed by the courts and human rights tribunals. In a column published by the *Free Press* on 3 November 1997, Bruce Feldthusen, a professor in the Faculty of Law at the University of Western Ontario, wrote: "Human rights legislation does restrict what some might claim as their freedom – the freedom to be sexist, racist, ageist and homophobic." He warned: "A party is not simply free to ignore or disobey a lawful order of a human rights board that has not been overturned on appeal. Persons who do so can and should be disciplined for contempt in a superior court. That so many people, including some lawyers, believe that obeying human rights legislation is a matter of personal preference rather than a basic civil obligation indicates how far away from a truly non-discriminatory society we remain."[23]

Haskett is a lawyer. She did not need any gratuitous lessons from Professor Feldthusen on the importance of upholding justice and the rule of law. Before entering politics, she headed her own law firm and actively promoted respect for fundamental human rights within the City of London. Professor Feldthusen overlooked in his patronizing *Free Press* column that Haskett rejected McKellar's ruling as illegal and unconstitutional. In Haskett's opinion, McKellar had no authority to order her to make a public proclamation that violated her cherished religious beliefs.

Some of the most vitriolic attacks on Haskett came from an ad hoc group styling itself People Opposing Principled Bigotry. In a news release, the group charged that while the mayor had been lauded for integrity despite her discriminatory behaviour, "her actions have fostered an environment where homophobia and gay and lesbian bashing have become acceptable, even respectable, attitudes and behaviours. They have encouraged hatred and rejection of people who are already marginalized in our society."[24] At a City Hall rally for Hopcroft three days before the election, twenty speakers denounced the mayor before a crowd of close to 300. Former London mayor Jane Bigelow said: "London doesn't need division. London needs a stable, diverse community where people respect each other." Haskett's immediate predecessor as mayor, Tom Gosnell, said: "We must not allow one individual's agenda to tear our community apart." Joan Smith, a Liberal activist and former Ontario solicitor general, alleged that the turmoil at City Hall generated by Haskett's stance on gay pride proclamations was making London such an unattractive place for new business that Londoners would have to face higher taxes and cuts in services. Smith warned: "It is the price you will pay for prejudice and disunity at city hall. We can't stand another three years of going backwards." Rev. Marcie Wexler, pastor of the Holy Fellowship Metropolitan Community Church in London, declaimed: "It is time we put down homophobic religion. No homophobic religion."[25]

People Opposing Principled Bigotry followed up the rally with a half-page advertisement in the *London Free Press* listing 286 Hopcroft supporters. Among the prominent local residents on this list were former Ontario attorney general Marion Boyd; Clarence Peterson, father of former Ontario Liberal premier David Peterson; and Mark

Handelman, one of the leading Progressive Conservative activists in London. Two of the city's more outspoken clergymen, Rev. Dr Barry Moore of the United Church of Canada and Rev. Doug Mackenzie of the Anglican Church of Canada, appended their names to the advertisement, as did J. Allyn Taylor, former chairman of Canada Trust and one of London's most prominent philanthropists. Styling themselves Citizens for Grant Hopcroft, this group claimed that "Grant Hopcroft's honest approach and work ethic is [*sic*] vital to restore London's reputation as a stable community that welcomes economic development and new jobs."[26]

Two days later, on 10 November 1997, the balloting took place. To the astonishment of many, Haskett won in a landslide. She received more votes than Hopcroft by a margin greater than two to one. The postelection commentators who appeared on the two local television stations that night looked stunned: Hardly anyone outside the Haskett reelection team had anticipated such a huge victory for the mayor. It was a singular triumph, coming scarcely a month after Haskett had been rebuked by the human rights board of inquiry, pilloried by a host of prominent local citizens, and derided by almost everyone in the local media for refusing on principle to issue a gay pride proclamation. While Deputy Mayor Hopcroft campaigned vigorously during the last three weeks of the campaign, Haskett withdrew from public life. Yet when the people of London got a chance to express their viewpoint at the polls, they gave overwhelming support to their principled mayor. It was, indeed, a stunning victory.

To an enthusiastic rally of supporters on the night of her decisive reelection, Mayor Haskett exulted: "I want to begin by giving the glory to God for the outcome this evening. He gave to us the courage and the strength and the hope in what have been some very dark days ... Power and money did not take back the city tonight; the people did."[27] Haskett blamed the Ontario Human Rights Commission for the bitterness of the election campaign. She said: "The HALO issue should never have been a focal point of this election. But the Human Rights Commission chose to interfere in the political process in the City of London, by dropping its decision into our laps without the benefit of proper deliberation or the application of appropriate legal principles. We did not choose this timing. We regret this timing and the impact it has had."[28]

The mayor then called upon everyone in the community to help end the bitterness and bind up the city's wounds:

> For us to walk down the path of the good things ahead, we must resolve here and now to stop the spewing forth of negativity that this community has

witnessed in recent days. The unrelenting assault by the media must stop. And the mean-spirited attacks coming from many sectors of the community must cease. Let me make one thing very clear. All Londoners are deserving of fair treatment and respect. That includes me and it includes Richard Hudler and all the members of the gay and lesbian community, as well as everyone else. I believe each Londoner is precious in God's eyes and we need to treat one another as we would treat our own family.

The mayor insisted that there is no place for hatred or ill-will in the City of London. She concluded: "I have been horrified at some of the gay bashing that has recently gone on, because I care very much for Londoners who are gay or lesbian. My three week leave of absence, my marathon of silence, was never a protest against the gay community. I only sought to maintain my constitutional right as a Canadian to freedom of expression. Until our Canadian Charter of Rights and Freedoms is overthrown, we as Canadians still have the right to choose what we will say and what we will not say. And no Human Rights Commission, acting outside the law, can take that right away from us."

MAYOR GRAY VERSUS THE RAINBOW COALITION

Do human rights commissioners care about such clear expressions of the popular will? Evidently not. Since Haskett's extraordinary reelection, human rights tribunals have carried on as usual, ordering mayors from one end of the country to another to issue gay pride proclamations regardless of the preferences of ordinary citizens. One of the first victims was Mayor Walter Gray of Kelowna, British Columbia. He came under fire from the British Columbia Human Rights Commission for issuing a proclamation stating: "WHEREAS the Corporation of the City of Kelowna is committed to working in partnership with the community to pursue shared goals, encourage a sense of community pride, promote social equity and justice, and build a healthy and vibrant community for the future; NOW THEREFORE I, Walter Gray, Mayor of the City of Kelowna, do hereby proclaim June 28, 1997 as 'LESBIAN AND GAY DAY.'"[29]

The noticeable absence of the word "pride" in the proclamation of "Lesbian and Gay Day" angered members of the Okanagan Rainbow Coalition. They had asked Mayor Gray to proclaim a "Lesbian and Gay Pride Day." In a complaint filed with the British Columbia Human Rights Commission, a representative of the coalition argued that the mayor's insistence on proclaiming a "Lesbian and Gay Day" violated the provision in section 8(1) of the British Columbia Human Rights

Code that no one must deny a public service to any class of persons because of their sexual orientation.

Gray denied the accusation. After more than two years of dithering by the commission, the matter came before Carol Roberts of the British Columbia Human Rights Tribunal. In a ruling on 21 March 2000, she described the Okanagan Rainbow Coalition as "an informal organization of people promoting the rights of lesbians, gays, bisexual and transgendered people in the Okanagan Valley." Gray stated in his testimony before the tribunal that he did not share the moral outlook of this group and recalled that the citizens of Kelowna had reacted very negatively to the "gay pride day" proclaimed by his predecessor in 1996. In her summary of Gray's testimony, Roberts observed: "Although he did not dislike or object to homosexuals and wanted to help the lesbian and gay community, he did not approve of homosexual behaviour and did not want to appear to be supporting, approving or endorsing a homosexual lifestyle. It was his evidence that he changed the proclamation to wording he felt comfortable with and that would also be politically acceptable. He said that he wanted to show support to the homosexual community without violating his personal convictions, and he thought he had arrived at a compromise."

Roberts allowed Dr Becki Ross, an associate professor of women's studies and anthropology/sociology at the University of British Columbia, to testify as an expert on lesbian and gay studies. Ross stated: "Lesbians, gay men, bisexual and transgendered people have been constructed variously in Canadian history as unnatural, criminal, undesirable, mentally ill, indecent and threatening to the 'traditional family.'" She said: "Even though Canada boasts a reputation for tolerance, diversity and inclusion in both formal and substantive terms, queer people have been refused equal protection of the law, equal rights in employment, parenting, social status, partnership rights and marriage." Ross further testified that: "Lesbian and Gay Pride Days serve several functions, which include providing a safe public space for the celebration of sexual identities and communities that do not conform to heterosexual norms, providing an opportunity for queers to talk about being queer, for enhancing racial, cultural and gender diversity, for providing an opportunity to effect social change within the local context, and for providing parents, families and friends of queer people [an opportunity] to show their commitment to public acceptance of homosexuality." In winding up her testimony, Ross excoriated Mayor Gray. She said: "By eliminating inclusion of 'Pride' the Mayor resurrects the shadow of shame and humiliation that has kept homosexuals fearful, closeted, and unacknowledged. In my view, Gray's stance is tantamount to a public insult, one which is mean spirited, short sighted, and damaging to positive, respectful relations between people of all sexualities in and outside Kelowna."

Who could have doubted the outcome of this case? Roberts sided with the Okanagan Rainbow Coalition and the British Columbia Human Rights Commission. She concluded: "Mayor Gray's decision to alter the wording of both the preamble as well as the actual proclamation requested was not only unprecedented; it changed the meaning of the phrase, which is used in celebration of lesbian and gay pride throughout the world. Furthermore, his decision negatively affected many members of the lesbian and gay community in Kelowna, including those who appeared before the Tribunal. The evidence is that the lesbian and gay community felt that the educational and social advances accomplished as a result of the proclamation of the previous year had been eliminated."

Gray had testified that in refusing to issue a controversial gay pride proclamation, he had intended not to discriminate against the homosexuals of Kelowna but only to help them avoid public controversy. Counsel for the Okanagan Rainbow Coalition did not dispute this claim. However, Gray's good intentions were of no account to Roberts. She pointed out: "Although Mayor Gray contends that he had no intention of discriminating against the Complainant, it is well-established in human rights jurisprudence that intention is irrelevant to a finding of a contravention." As authority, Roberts cited section 2 of the British Columbia Human Rights Code, which states: "Discrimination in contravention of this Code does not require an intention to contravene this Code." Correspondingly, in *Andrews v. Law Society of British Columbia,* 1989 SCC, the Supreme Court of Canada declared that within the context of section 15 of the Canadian Charter of Rights and Freedoms, "discrimination is a distinction which, whether intentional or not but based on grounds relating to personal characteristics of the individual or group, has an effect which imposes disadvantages not imposed upon others or which withholds or limits access to advantages available to other members of society." Consequently, while lack of mens rea, or evil intent, is usually a sufficient defence against a charge in a criminal court, it is irrelevant to the proceedings of a human rights tribunal, where even a person acting from the purest and best motives can be found guilty of violating one of the multivarious grounds of discrimination prohibited in both the human rights codes of Canada and the Canadian Charter of Rights and Freedoms.

Roberts put the matter clearly. She said: "The Mayor's personal views, no matter how well intentioned, do not constitute a *bona fide* exception under s. 8(1) of the *Code.*" She added:

A *bona fide* justification defence requires proof both of a subjective element (good faith) and an objective element (related to the provision of the service) ... The Complainant did not dispute the Mayor's assertion that he acted in a sincere and honest manner. Nevertheless, in my opinion, it cannot be said, on the evidence, that the Mayor's refusal to issue a proclamation in the manner requested by the Complainant solely on the grounds of the sexual orientation of the members, was, in an objective sense, related to any duty or obligation the Mayor has to the general public. Therefore, I cannot conclude that the Respondents [Mayor Gray and the City of Kelowna] have established a *bona fide* justification.

In essence, Roberts contended that regardless of what the mayor of Kelowna and the great majority of the citizens of his city might prefer, he had no right under the Charter to refuse to issue a gay pride proclamation. She noted that Gray believed that "the proclamation of lesbian and gay pride day would send the community the message that he endorsed homosexuality, a message that was not compatible with his personal convictions." She also observed: "He contends that his decision not to send a false message about his personal convictions was *bona fide* and reasonable." Roberts rejected all these considerations as irrelevant on the ground that an order requiring the mayor not to discriminate against homosexuals in the issuing of public proclamations would place no more than a reasonable and demonstrably justifiable restriction on his rights to freedom of thought, belief, and expression as guaranteed in section 2 of the Charter. In conclusion, Roberts found that "the Mayor of Kelowna and the City of Kelowna have contravened s. 8 of the [British Columbia Human Rights] Code by treating the Complainant's request for a proclamation differently from other requests, in whole or in part, on the basis of the sexual orientation of the members of the Complainant. Pursuant to s. 37(2)a) [of the Code], I order that the Respondents cease the contravention and refrain from committing the same or a similar contravention."

In response to the ruling, Mayor Gray vowed to refrain from issuing proclamations altogether. He said: "I mean, next time, it may be the Rainbow Coalition again, and I would still have to take the same position I did two years ago, or it may be some race hatred organization."[30] Barbara findlay, the lawyer who represented the Okanagan Rainbow Coalition before the tribunal, was incensed. She charged that Gray's no-proclamations pledge "further increases intolerance against lesbians, gay men, bisexual and transgendered people." She warned that if he persists in refusing to issue all proclamations, including the declaration of a gay pride day for Kelowna, he could be targeted once again with a human rights complaint of discrimination on the basis of sexual orientation.[31]

Mayor Gray was not intimidated. He stood his ground in refusing to issue all proclamations. And in doing so, he retained the support of the great majority of the citizens of Kelowna. Scarcely five months after Roberts handed down her decision, he was reelected as mayor with over 95 per cent of the vote. Meanwhile, neither findlay nor the Okanogan Rainbow Coalition has acted upon the threat to haul him back before the British Columbia Human Rights Tribunal for refusing to issue gay pride proclamations.

3

Trust Not in the Charter

In an article published in the *London Free Press* shortly after the ruling by the Ontario human rights board of inquiry in the Haskett case, Professor Bruce Feldthusen contended that the purpose of human rights tribunals is not to imprison, fine, or otherwise punish malefactors but to remedy discrimination. He wrote:

> Human rights hearings are quite different from criminal trials. There is no Crown attorney, no charge and no accused. There is no finding of guilt and no power to fine or imprison. The purpose of human rights law is remedial, not punitive. If the adjudicators uphold the complaint, they are empowered to order the respondent to make a compensatory payment, just as a judge in a civil suit could order one party who assaulted another to pay damages. Damages in human rights matters tend to be insignificant compared to personal injury damages awarded in the courts. The adjudicator is also empowered to order steps taken to prevent the violation from continuing.[1]

Should Canadians draw comfort from this portrait of the limited powers of a human rights tribunal? Hardly. Feldthusen's assertion that an Ontario human rights board of inquiry has no power to levy fines or imprison offenders is technically correct but fundamentally misleading. Who but a lawyer can find any substantial difference between a fine and a "compensatory payment"? In this same article, Feldthusen held that anyone who refuses to obey a lawful order of a human rights board "can and should be disciplined for contempt in a superior court." But what is the ultimate penalty for contempt of court? Jail. It may be, as Feldthusen says, that the purpose of human rights law is remedial, not punitive. Nonetheless, a person who persistently disobeys a court order upholding the ruling of a human rights tribunal is liable to be consigned to jail for contempt of court.

Scott Brockie is familiar with the draconian powers of a board of inquiry under the Ontario Human Rights Act. He is the president of Imaging Excellence, a family-owned print shop in downtown Toronto. In April 1996 Ray Brillinger, the president of the Canadian Lesbian and Gay Archives, entered Brockie's print shop and asked him to print some letterheads, envelopes, and business cards for the archives.[2] The stated aim of the archives is to "help lesbian and gay men live free, proud and positive lives."[3] Without inquiring about the purposes of the organization, Brockie reasonably concluded from the group's very name, Lesbian and Gay Archives, that it is an organization for gay and lesbian activists. Brockie is a conscientious Evangelical Christian. In good conscience, he could not print materials for the group, so he declined Brillinger's print order. Brillinger accused Brockie of violating the human rights of homosexuals and left the print shop.

At this point, Brillinger might easily have taken his business to any one of a number of other print shops in downtown Toronto that would have had no qualms about printing materials for gay activists. Instead, he chose to escalate his dispute with Brockie by filing a complaint with the Ontario Human Rights Commission. In short order, the commission accused Brockie of denying commercial printing services to Brillinger on the basis of Brillinger's sexual orientation – one of fourteen prohibited grounds for discrimination in section 1 of the Ontario Human Rights Code. The commission summoned Brockie to atone for this offence by apologizing to Brillinger, paying him $5,000 in damages, and pledging never again to refuse on principle to accept print orders from the archives or any other gay activist organization. Brockie refused to comply.

In an article commenting on Brockie's plight in the *London Free Press* on 8 October 1998, Michael Coren wrote: "The Ontario Human Rights Commission has, in its wisdom, decided this case is so serious that it will go to a full board inquiry. If Brockie is found 'guilty,' he will be fined and if he refuses to pay the fine he could, and probably will, go to prison. His family and friends would, naturally, be devastated."[4] In a rebuttal published in the *London Free Press* on 15 October 1998, Chief Commissioner Keith Norton of the Ontario Human Rights Commission stated: "I want to make it clear there is nothing in the process under the Ontario Human Rights Code that provides for a person going to prison. That could only happen in a subsequent proceeding if the individual were found to be in contempt of court. I know of no case in the 36-year history of human rights legislation where that has happened."[5]

In making this statement, Norton overlooked the precedent set by John Ross Taylor, who served a year in jail for defying the Canadian Human Rights Commission. After this fact was drawn to Norton's attention, he wrote another letter to the editor of the *London Free Press*, stating: "I wish to apologize for any misunderstanding that might have been created by my earlier letter ... While I was aware of the case of John Ross Taylor, the '36-year history of the human rights legislation' to which I referred was the Ontario Human Rights Code, first passed in 1962. Taylor's case was dealt with under the Canadian Human Rights Act, which this Commission does not administer. My wording could have been more precise. Sorry."[6] In essence, Norton conceded that Coren was right to point out that if Brockie were found "guilty" by a human rights tribunal, he could be fined and, ultimately, jailed for contempt.

The same fate awaits anyone who steadfastly defies the order of a federal or provincial human rights tribunal. In the case of Mayor Haskett, London City Council agreed to issue the pride proclamation requested by the Homophile Association of London Ontario (HALO). Neither Richard Hudler nor the Ontario Human Rights Commission petitioned the Ontario Superior Court of Justice for an order requiring Haskett also to issue a pride proclamation as directed by Adjudicator McKellar. What, however, might have been the outcome if either party had obtained such a court order against Haskett? Under such duress, would she have bowed down in humility before the Ontario Human Rights Commission? This is inconceivable. Haskett has a reputation for absolute integrity: She would prefer to languish in jail rather than make a statement that conflicts with her Christian convictions.

However, Haskett did not think that her resolve would be put to the test. She was confident that upon appeal, the courts would strike down the board's ruling as a clear violation of her historic rights as a Canadian to the freedoms of conscience, religion, thought, belief, opinion, and expression as guaranteed in section 2 of the Charter. Was this confidence in the courts well placed? That is doubtful, especially in view of the Brockie case.

Like Haskett, Brockie is not a homophobe. Prior to the confrontation with Brillinger, he had printed materials for other customers serving the homosexual community, including a manufacturer of underwear for gay men. Why, then, did he refuse to print materials for the Lesbian and Gay Archives? Brockie has explained: "I don't want my name associated with printing material that is for an organization that has as its primary motive to promote the cause of the gay community." He added: "We have gay clients. That's not an issue to me. People who are gay can come in and bring their work, the same as anybody else, and I'll print their general commercial printing work for them. But I'm not going to produce material for a cause that so strongly contradicts what the Bible teaches – what I believe."[7]

The Ontario Human Rights Commission spent three years trying to settle the Brockie case through mediation, before finally referring the dispute to an Ontario human rights board of inquiry. Heather MacNaughton, the same lawyer who presided over *Nixon v. Rape Relief* for the British Columbia Human Rights Tribunal, was assigned to the case. In testimony before the board, Brockie avowed that he tries to live his life according to biblical principles and teaching, including the admonition in Leviticus 18:22: "Do not lie with a man as one lies with a woman; that is detestable." Consequently, he argued that the commission's order requiring him to print material for the archives violated his constitutional right to freedom of conscience and religion as guaranteed in section 2(a) of the Canadian Charter of Rights and Freedoms.

On this point, there was no dispute. In her ruling in *Brockie* on 24 February 2000, MacNaughton noted: "Both Counsel for the Commission and Counsel for the Complainants acknowledge that the orders they seek would infringe Brockie's constitutional rights by compelling him to provide a service to members of the lesbian and gay community, and to their organizations. They accept that Brockie believes that such a compulsion would cause him to act against his religious convictions and his understanding of the teachings of the Christian Bible."

Having conceded this point, MacNaughton observed that the rights and freedoms guaranteed in the Charter are subject in section 1 "to such reasonable limits prescribed by law as can be demonstrably justified in a free and democratic society." In her opinion, the central legal issue in the Brockie case is the nature and extent of reasonable limits to freedom of conscience and religion in a democracy. While Brockie contended that the commission's order constituted an unreasonable violation of his rights to freedom of conscience, religion, and expression under section 2 of the Charter, counsel for the Ontario Human Rights Commission and Brillinger took the view that the order constituted a justifiable restriction of the freedoms guaranteed in section 2 for the purpose of upholding the overriding equality rights of homosexuals under both section 15 of the Charter and section 1 of the Ontario Human Rights Code.

In considering these arguments, MacNaughton dealt first with what she called "the issue of the scope of the individual right to religious and conscientious [*sic*] freedom and the limitation on that freedom that may be appropriate under s. 1." She noted that in *Ross v. New Brunswick School District No. 15*, 1996 SCC, Mr Justice Gerard La Forest of the Supreme Court of Canada declared: "Freedom of religion ensures that every individual must be free to hold and to manifest without State interference those beliefs and opinions dictated by one's conscience." Taken alone, this statement would have settled the matter. The Ontario Human Rights Commission is an instrument of the state; the commission violated Brockie's right to freedom of religion by ordering him to print materials in violation of his religious beliefs; therefore, the commission's order violates the guarantee of freedom of religion in section 2 of the Charter. But, of course, the rights and freedoms guaranteed in the Charter are not absolute. La Forest went on in his reasons for judgment in *Ross* to state: "Freedom of religion is subject to such limitations as are necessary to protect public safety, order, health or morals and the fundamental rights and freedoms of others. This said, a broad interpretation of the right has been preferred, leaving competing rights to be reconciled under the s. 1 analysis elaborated in *R. v. Oakes*, 1986 SCC."

THE *OAKES* DISASTER

In *Oakes*, the Supreme Court of Canada created one of the most disastrous precedents in the history of Canadian jurisprudence. The respondent in this case, David Edwin Oakes, was charged with unlawful possession of a narcotic for the purpose of trafficking, contrary to section 4(2) of the Narcotic Control Act. Under the terms of this law, the Crown was required to prove beyond a reasonable doubt that the accused was guilty of unlawful possession of a narcotic. If the Crown succeeded in this undertaking at trial, the onus shifted to the accused to establish that he had not been engaged in narcotic trafficking. In the words of section 8 of the Act: "If the accused fails to establish that he was not in possession of the narcotic for the purpose of trafficking, he shall be convicted of the offence as charged and sentenced accordingly."

At trial in *Oakes*, the Crown presented conclusive evidence that the accused had been in unlawful possession of a narcotic. At this point, instead of trying to establish that Oakes had not been in possession of the narcotic for the purpose of trafficking, his defence counsel called upon the trial judge to throw out the trafficking charge on the ground that the imposition of a reverse onus of proof upon the accused in section 8 of the Narcotic Control Act violated the guarantee in section 11(d) of the Charter that: "Any person charged with an offence has the right ... to be presumed innocent until proven guilty."

In a similar pre-Charter case, *R. v. Appleby,* 1972 SCC, the Supreme Court of Canada had considered the legitimacy of the reverse onus of proof in relation to impaired driving in section 224A(1)(a), now section 258(1)(a), of the Criminal Code. In this instance, the law provides that "where it is proved that the accused occupied the seat or position ordinarily occupied by a person who operates a motor vehicle ... the accused shall be deemed to have had the care and control of the vehicle ... unless the accused establishes that the accused did not occupy that seat or position for the purpose of setting the vehicle ... in motion." Counsel for the defence in *Appleby* argued that this reverse onus of proof in the context of impaired driving violates the provision in section 2(f) of the 1960 Canadian Bill of Rights that no law shall "deprive a person charged with a criminal offence of the right to be presumed innocent until proved guilty." The Supreme Court of Canada rejected this argument. In a judgment written by Mr Justice Roland Ritchie, the Court held that once the Crown proves beyond a reasonable doubt that an accused had been slumped over the wheel of an automobile while impaired, the accused might reasonably be required by law to establish his innocence on a charge of having had care and control of the vehicle while impaired by proving on a balance of probabilities that he had not intended to drive the vehicle. Ritchie said: "It seems to me the words 'presumed innocent until proved guilty according to law' as they appear in s. 2(f) of the Bill of Rights, must be taken to envisage a law which recognizes the existence of statutory exceptions reversing the onus of proof with respect to one or more ingredients of an offence in cases where certain specific facts have been proved by the Crown in relation to such ingredients."

With this ruling in *Appleby,* the Supreme Court of Canada exercised the kind of judicial restraint typical of the pre-Charter era. The Court did not presume to second-guess the wisdom of Parliament in deciding that a reverse onus of proof in the context of the law on impaired driving is a reasonable means of safeguarding the lives of Canadians from drunk drivers. What, however, did the Supreme Court of Canada do in *Oakes*? Did it defer to the judgment of Parliament that the inclusion of a reverse onus of proof in section 8 of the Narcotic Control Act was a reasonable means of curtailing the menace of drug trafficking? Did the Court in *Oakes* follow its own precedent in *Appleby*, which had established that a reverse onus of proof in relation to an offence where certain specific facts relating to that offence have been proved by the Crown is compatible with the guarantee that everyone has the right "to be presumed innocent until proven guilty"? No. In *Oakes* the Court struck down section 8. Chief Justice Dickson declared: "I am in no doubt whatsoever that it violates s. 11(d) of the Charter by requiring the accused to prove on a balance of probabilities that he was not in possession of the narcotic for the purpose of trafficking."

Dickson virtually admitted that this ruling contradicted the decision of the Supreme Court of Canada just a few years earlier in *Appleby*. He said: "Although there are important lessons to be learned from the Canadian Bill of Rights jurisprudence, it does not constitute binding authority in relation to the constitutional interpretation of the Charter." Why not? In support of the Court's wilful abandonment of precedents set in the interpretation of the Canadian Bill of Rights, Dickson cited nothing other than his own judgment just a few months earlier in *R. v. Big M Drug Mart Ltd.*, 1985 SCC. In this case, the respondent, a Big M Drug Mart in Calgary, had been charged with carrying on the sale of goods on Sunday in violation of the Lord's Day Act. Mr Justice Brian Stevenson of the Provincial Court of Alberta threw out the charge on the ground that the Sunday-closing provisions of the Lord's Day Act were no longer valid enactments under the power over criminal law assigned to Parliament by section 91(27) of the Constitution Act, 1867. In affirming this conclusion, Stevenson flouted a long line of precedents from *Attorney-General for Ontario v. Hamilton Street Railway Co.*, 1903 JCPC, to *Robertson and Rosetanni v. The Queen*, 1963 SCC, that regarded Sunday observance legislation as falling within the power of Parliament over "criminal law in its widest sense." Stephenson ruled that these precedents were no longer binding because, in his opinion, changed social conditions and attitudes in Canada have virtually eliminated the influence of Christianity on the criminal law.

Upon appeal by the attorney general of Alberta, a five-judge panel of the Alberta Court of Appeal unanimously repudiated Stevenson's finding that Parliament no longer has jurisdiction over Sunday-closing legislation. In an opinion that was joined by Chief Justice William McGillivray, Mr Justice R.H. Belzil described Stevenson's assertion that "in light of today's social conditions," the Lord's Day Act no longer comes under the criminal power of Parliament as "a startling departure from settled authority" and "a novel but erroneous proposition in law." Belzil and McGillivray held that the validity of federal or provincial legislation under the distribution of powers in the Constitution "is determined as at the date of the passing of the legislation, and does not thereafter fluctuate with social change." In the opinion of Belzil and McGillivray, unelected judges have no right to change the law to suit their perception of changed social conditions.

Belzil and McGillivray also affirmed that the Court was bound to follow the precedent set by the Supreme Court of Canada in *Robertson and Rosetanni* that the Lord's Day Act is compatible with the guarantee of "freedom of religion" in section 1 (c) of the Canadian Bill of Rights. As in *Appleby,* the judgment for the Court in *Robertson* was written by Justice Ritchie. Referring to the Lord's Day Act, he said:

> I can see nothing in that statute which in any way affects the liberty of religious thought and practice of any citizen of this country. Nor is the "untrammelled affirmations of religious belief and its propagation" in any way curtailed.
>
> The practical result of this law on those whose religion requires them to observe a day of rest other than Sunday, is a purely secular and financial one in that they are required to refrain from carrying on or conducting their business on Sunday as well as on their own day of rest. In some cases this is no doubt a business inconvenience, but it is neither an abrogation nor an abridgment nor an infringement of religious freedom, and the fact that it has been brought about by reason of the existence of a statute enacted for the purpose of preserving the sanctity of Sunday, cannot, in my view, be construed as attaching some religious significance to an effect which is purely secular in so far as non-Christians are concerned.

In conformity with this judgment, Belzil wrote:

> The Charter does not purport to change the meaning of words and in particular the meaning of "freedom of conscience and religion" as traditionally and universally understood and earlier defined as the birthright of every human being. The "freedom of religion" declared and secured by the Canadian Bill of Rights in 1960 and considered by the Supreme Court of Canada in *Robertson* has the same meaning as the "freedom of conscience and religion" guaranteed by the Charter of Rights in 1981 [*sic*]. The effect of the Lord's Day Act upon that same freedom of conscience and religion has been decided in *Robertson.* While it may be technically true that this court is not bound in this case by *Robertson* because the two cases deal with different documents, yet the interpretation by the Supreme Court of Canada of the same provision of the Lord's Day Act and the same fundamental right of freedom of conscience and religion is compelling.

With this judgment, Chief Justice McGillivray and Justice Belzil upheld the rule of law. They followed the legally binding precedent set by the Supreme Court of Canada in *Robertson* on the compatibility of the Lord's Day Act with freedom of religion. McGillivray and Belzil did not presume, in the light of their personal understanding of the requirements of changed social conditions and attitudes, to lay down a new definition of freedom of religion for the Charter. Neither did they strike down the Sunday-closing provisions in the Lord's Day Act. These two distinguished appeal court judges exercised judicial restraint. They insisted that there is nothing in the Charter that authorizes appointed judges to usurp the authority of elected representatives of the people in the legislative branch of government to determine that changed social circumstances warrant the repeal or amendment of a statute law relating to Sunday closing or any other matter.

This proper and restrained approach to Charter interpretation was rejected by a majority of the Alberta Court of Appeal. Of the five judges who heard the *Big M* case, the remaining three upheld the trial judge's acquittal of the company on the ground that the Act violated the guarantee of freedom of conscience and religion in the Charter to an extent that cannot be demonstrably justified in a free and democratic society. Upon further appeal, the Supreme Court of Canada did the same. Like McGillivray and Belzil, all the judges of Canada's top court could have chosen to interpret the vague guarantees of rights and freedoms in the Charter in accordance with prior legislative enactments and judicial precedents. In doing so, these judges would also have respected the fundamental separation of legislative and judicial powers in a democracy as described and advocated by Montesquieu, Blackstone, Dicey, Corry, Hodgetts, and all other traditional authorities on parliamentary democracy and the common law. Instead, our self-appointed Solons on the Supreme Court of Canada have wilfully undermined both democracy and the rule of law by invoking the Charter as a licence to abandon judicial precedents, overturn statute laws, and amend the Constitution through interpretation.

In an attempt to justify the repudiation of the *Rosetanni* precedent, Chief Justice Dickson noted in his reasons for judgment in *Big M* that the Canadian Bill of Rights proclaims in section 1: "It is hereby recognized and declared that in Canada there have existed and shall continue to exist ... the following human rights and fundamental freedoms, namely, ... (*c*) freedom of religion." Dickson alleged that the guarantee of rights in the Charter is inherently different. He said:

> The language of the Charter is imperative. It avoids any reference to existing or continuing rights but rather proclaims in the ringing terms of s. 2 that: 2. Everyone has the following fundamental freedoms: (a) Freedom of conscience and religion.
>
> I agree with the submission of the respondent that the Charter is intended to set a standard upon which present as well as future legislation is to be tested. Therefore the meaning of the concept of freedom of conscience and religion

is not to be determined solely by the degree to which that right was enjoyed by Canadians prior to the proclamation of the Charter. For this reason, *Robertson and Rosetanni*, supra, cannot be determinative of the meaning of "freedom of conscience and religion" under the Charter.

Can this argument stand up to examination? According to Blackstone and Driedger, the words of a statute "are generally to be understood in their usual and most known signification." By this standard, the freedom of religion proclaimed in the bill of rights is the same freedom of religion affirmed in the Charter. When the Charter states that "everyone has the following fundamental freedoms: (a) Freedom of conscience and religion," it is simply reiterating the declaration in the Bill of Rights that freedom of religion has existed, and shall continue to exist, in Canada. Dickson observed that "the Charter is intended to set a standard upon which present as well as future legislation is to be tested." But the same also goes for the Bill of Rights, which states in section 2: "Every law of Canada shall, unless it is expressly declared by an Act of the Parliament of Canada that it shall operate notwithstanding the Canadian Bill of Rights, be so construed and applied as not to abrogate, abridge or infringe or to authorize the abrogation, abridgment or infringement of any of the rights or freedoms herein recognized and declared." In these respects, the Charter and the Bill of Rights are essentially identical. Dickson advanced no reasonable basis for claiming that the Charter has conferred a mandate upon the Supreme Court of Canada to flout the original understanding of the provisions of the Charter and to ignore judicial precedents defining the historic rights and freedoms proclaimed in the Charter. Activist judges on the Supreme Court of Canada have assumed entirely on their own authority to read whatever they want into the Charter. As a result, many of the historic rights and freedoms proclaimed in this document have taken on entirely new meanings of the Court's own devising.

Thus in 1963 the Supreme Court of Canada declared in *Robertson and Rosetanni* that it could see nothing in the Lord's Day Act that "in any way affects the liberty of religious thought and practice of any citizen of this country." Yet just twelve years later in *Big M Drug Mart*, Chief Justice Dickson struck down this same Lord's Day Act on the ground that it infringes upon the freedom of conscience and religion of Canadians to an extent that cannot be demonstrably justified in any free and democratic society. With this pronouncement, Dickson and the Court repudiated not only the Court's own precedent, but also the understanding of freedom of religion held by the majority of the elected representatives of the people of Canada in Parliament, who had adopted the Charter. Majority rule – that most basic of democratic concepts – means little to the Supreme Court of Canada in the Charter era. In *Big M Drug* Mart, Dickson openly disparaged the majoritarian principle. "The Charter," he said, "safeguards religious minorities from the threat of 'the tyranny of the majority.'" But how does the Supreme Court of Canada decide cases? By majority vote, of course. Who will protects us from the tyranny of nine unelected judges who routinely presume to revise and overturn laws that have been duly enacted by elected representatives of the people in complete conformity with the Constitution as originally understood?

In *Oakes*, Dickson cited his unprecedented ruling in *Big M Drug Mart,* which repudiated the precedent set in *Rosetanni,* as his justification for proceeding in *Oakes* to disregard the precedent set in *Appleby,* which upheld a reverse onus of proof as compatible with the guarantee of a fair trial. By such reasoning, Dickson concluded that the reverse onus of proof in section 8 of the Narcotic Control Act violated the right of an accused to be presumed innocent until proven guilty according to law in section 11(d) of the Charter. He then considered whether this purported violation of the right to a fair trial could be justified by the overriding need to curb the menace of drug trafficking. Note that in taking it upon himself to decide this issue, he was dealing not with a justiciable principle of law but with a prudential question of public policy. Parliament had twice debated the wisdom of including a reverse onus of proof in the Narcotic Control Act, first in 1952 and again in 1970. After due deliberation on both occasions, a majority of the elected representatives of the Canadian people in Parliament had resolved to enact this provision into law. In their considered opinion, this reverse onus of proof placed no more than a reasonable and demonstrably justified limit upon the historic right of Canadians to be presumed innocent until proven guilty according to law.

Prior to enactment of the Charter, judges on the Supreme Court of Canada habitually deferred to the judgment of Parliament on such policy issues. As appointed officials, judges understood that they had no right to overturn the policies adopted by the elected representatives of the people no matter how distasteful those policies might be. Thus in *Bryden v. Union Colliery,* 1899 JCPC, the Judicial Committee of the Privy Council upheld the blatantly racist British Columbia Coal Mines Regulation Amendment Act of 1890 that prohibited "Chinamen" from working underground. Speaking for the Judicial Committee, Lord Watson stated: "In so far as they possess legislative jurisdiction, the discretion committed to the parliaments, whether of the Dominion or of the provinces, is unfettered. It is the proper function of a court of law to determine what are the limits of the jurisdiction committed to them; but, when that point has been settled, courts of law have no right whatever to inquire whether their jurisdiction has been exercised wisely or not." Having made this point, Lord Watson struck down this repellent British Columbia law, but he did so only on the narrow, technical, and entirely justifiable ground that the provincial enactment trespassed in pith and substance upon the exclusive authority of Parliament under section 91(25) of the original British North America (BNA) Act to make laws in relation to Naturalization and Aliens.

In *Quong-Wing v. the King,* 1914 SCC, the Supreme Court of Canada dealt with a no-less-egregious enactment by the Saskatchewan Legislature forbidding Chinese Canadians from employing a white woman. In reasons for judgment in *Quong-Wing,* Mr Justice L.H. Davies of the Supreme Court of Canada disavowed any personal support for this odious measure. Yet he upheld the law. In a classic expression of judicial restraint, he observed: "The question on this appeal is not one as to the policy or justice of the Act in question, but solely as to the power of the provincial legislature to pass it." Davies all but invited critics of the racist Act to take their complaint to the responsible policy-making authority: the Saskatchewan Legislature. But as for Davies and a majority of his colleagues on the Supreme Court of Canada, they upheld the repellent law on the ground that it came within the jurisdiction of the Saskatchewan Legislature over "Property and Civil Rights in the Province" as provided by section 92(13) of the BNA Act. Sir Lyman Duff, one of the most esteemed members of the Supreme Court of Canada prior to the Charter, was among the majority of judges who supported this ruling in *Quong-Wing.*[8]

Such restraint used to be typical of the judiciary. The great majority of Canadian judges understood that the courts do not have any right in a democracy to pass judgment on the prudence, wisdom, or fairness of a statute or constitutional law. As late as 1976, Chief Justice Laskin expressed approval for the ruling in *Quong-Wing* on the ground that "however distasteful such legislation was," the racist Saskatchewan law was a valid constitutional enactment within the legislative jurisdiction of the province.[9] At least in this instance, even Laskin acknowledged that in a democracy, responsibility for changing or rescinding a repugnant statute law belongs to elected legislators, not unelected judges.

In *Oakes* the Supreme Court of Canada rejected this basic tenet of the proper role of the judiciary. In his judgment for the Court in *Oakes,* Chief Justice Dickson quashed the legislative supremacy of Parliament and the provincial legislatures. In effect, he held that in the Charter era, the Supreme Court of Canada has primary responsibility for judging the compatibility of statute laws with the basic rights and fundamental freedoms of Canadians. In interpreting the Charter, he said: "The Court must be guided by the values and principles essential to a free and democratic society which I believe embody, to name but a few, respect for the inherent dignity of the human person, commitment to social justice and equality, accommodation of a wide variety of beliefs, respect for cultural and group identity, and faith in social and political institutions which enhance the participation of individuals and groups in society."

Notably missing from this list is any reference to the specific moral precepts and legal principles elaborated upon and enshrined in myriad provisions of the common law, statute laws, and judicial precedents that had hitherto governed Canada as a free and democratic society. Dickson also decreed in *Oakes* that: "The onus of proving that a limit on a right or freedom guaranteed by the Charter is reasonable and demonstrably justified in a free and democratic society rests upon the party seeking to uphold the limitation." And he stipulated that the standard of proof "must be high in order to ensure that objectives which are trivial or discordant with the principles integral to a free and democratic society do not gain s. 1 protection. It is necessary, at a minimum, that an objective relate to concerns which are pressing and substantial in a free and democratic society before it can be characterized as sufficiently important." Finally, Dickson specified that a legislatively enacted limit on a Charter right or freedom must comply with a strict proportionality test based on the following criteria: "First, the measures adopted must be carefully designed to achieve the objective in question. They must not be arbitrary, unfair or based on irrational considerations. In short, they must be rationally connected to the objective. Second, the means, even if rationally connected to the objective in this first sense, should impair 'as little as possible' the right or freedom in question ... Third, there must be a proportionality between the effects of the measures which are responsible for limiting the Charter right or freedom, and the objective which has been identified as of 'sufficient importance.'"

With the imposition of these subjective standards for the application of section 1 of the Charter in *Oakes*, the Court worked a veritable revolution in Canadian constitutional law: In essence, it arrogated to itself supreme power over legislation as well as adjudication. Was this the intention of Parliament and the provincial legislatures in enacting the Charter? Were the stringent criteria laid down by Dickson in *Oakes* for evaluating the compatibility of laws with the Charter consistent with the scheme of the Act and the object of the Act and the plain words of the Charter in the context of the Constitution of Canada? Justice

McLachlin is typical of the judicial activists on the Supreme Court of Canada who would answer these questions in the affirmative. She fully supports the *Oakes* judgment. In her reasons for the majority in *RJR-MacDonald Inc. v. Canada (Attorney General),* 1995 SCC, she wrote: "I find no conflict between the words of s. 1 and the jurisprudence founded upon *R. v. Oakes.*" She then applied the *Oakes* test to the ban on tobacco advertising in the 1988 Tobacco Products Control Act and decided to strike down the ban based on the conclusion that Parliament was wrong to suppose that forbidding tobacco advertising constituted no more than a reasonable and demonstrably justifiable restriction on the guarantee of freedom of expression in section 2 of the Charter.

While such use of the *Oakes* test to overturn the policy decisions of Parliament is typical of the Supreme Court of Canada, it has met with strong objections from several learned appellate court judges. Mr Justice William Marshall, Mr Justice Denis Roberts, and Mr Justice Geoffrey Steele of the Newfoundland Court of Appeal rank among the more outspoken dissenters. In *Newfoundland Assn. of Public Employees v. R.*, 2002 NLCA 72, a judgment that was written by Marshall and joined by Roberts and Steele, the trio recalled that the doctrine of the separation of powers "emerged from bloody revolutions in the 17th and 18th centuries," and they warned that the judicial subversion of this doctrine under the guise of interpreting the Charter could lead to more civil unrest. Marshall wrote: "The lessons of history accentuate the perils of re-vesting ultimate decisions over policy in institutions controlled by persons without elective mandates to make such decisions. It is safe to assume the Charter would have been framed in full alertness to this peril, and without any intent to distort or disrupt the deeply ingrained structural Separation of Powers." On this basis, these three judges urged the Supreme Court of Canada "to revisit" the three gateways to proportionality in the *Oakes* test and, "if not to completely reframe them, at least to oil their hinges to assure they swing in harmony with the separation of powers."

Earlier, in an unusually frank dissent in *Blainey v. Ontario Hockey Association,* 1986 OCA, Mr Justice George Finlayson of the Ontario Court of Appeal repudiated the *Oakes* criteria for determining the compliance of a statute with section 1 of the Charter. Finlayson stated: "With great deference, I can think of no statute enacted by an elected legislature or Parliament whose objectives can be stigmatized by the epithets 'trivial', 'unfair', or 'arbitrary' [as envisioned in *Oakes*]. Hopefully such legislation will never be passed and if it is, I question respectfully if it can be struck down on that account simply because a court takes this view of it."

With this judgment, Finlayson upheld the traditional separation of powers under the Constitution between the legislative and judicial branches of government. Like his three colleagues on the Newfoundland Court of Appeal, he recognized that the *Oakes* test represents a power grab by the Supreme Court of Canada that has no warrant in the language or history of the Charter. Nonetheless, Finlayson conceded: "I must apply the *Oakes* test." Finlayson had no choice. In the Charter era, he and all other judges on the provincial courts of appeal are no less bound than ordinary citizens to obey the decrees of the Supreme Court of Canada.

BE YE HEARERS OF THE WORD ONLY: THE *BROCKIE* CASE

In using the *Oakes* criteria to determine if the violation of Brockie's rights to freedom of conscience and religion in the order sought by the Ontario Human Rights Commission could be justified under section 1 of the Charter, adjudicator MacNaughton began by considering the objectives of the Ontario Human Rights Code. She wrote: "Its stated purpose, as set out in the Preamble, is to recognize 'the inherent dignity and worth of every person' and to provide for 'equal rights and opportunities without discrimination.' Further, it is to create a 'climate of understanding and mutual respect for the dignity and worth of each person.'"

Brockie might reasonably have assumed that the Code obligates the Ontario Human Rights Commission to recognize his inalienable rights as a person to freedom of conscience and religion, while fostering "a climate of understanding and mutual respect" for his dignity and worth as a Christian. MacNaughton took an opposing view. In applying the three-fold *Oakes* test, she concluded: First, that the restriction of Brockie's right to freedom of religion sought by the Commission served a pressing and substantial objective, namely "to eradicate discrimination on the basis of sexual orientation." Second, she held that ordering Brockie to print materials for all lesbian and gay organizations in the same way that he would for other groups is rationally connected to this objective. "The more troubling assessment," she acknowledged, "is whether the orders sought would impair Brockie's rights 'as little as possible' in proportion to the objective sought to be achieved" as required by the third branch of the *Oakes* test. Counsel for Brockie argued that in balancing his religious rights against the equality rights of Brillinger and the Lesbian and Gay Archives, MacNaughton should take into account that Brockie's refusal to print materials for Brillinger and the archives caused only a small inconvenience to the complainants because there must be thirty top-quality printers who could have done the job for Brillinger within a ten-minute walk of Brockie's downtown office. For Brockie, however, the order sought by the Commission was a matter of overriding significance in that it constituted a direct attack on his core religious beliefs. In the opinion of Brockie's counsel, facilitating the provision of "a non-life-essential service" to one or other of the groups singled out for special treatment in the Ontario Human Rights Code cannot justify a gross violation of the fundamental right to freedom of religion.

In rebuttal, counsel for Brillinger, the archives, and the commission maintained that Brockie's denial of service to gay activist groups amounted to more than a trivial inconvenience for gays and lesbians. Testimony in support of this argument was presented by three supposedly expert witnesses: Kathleen Lahey, a law professor at Queen's University; Barry Adam, a sociology professor at the University of Windsor;[10] and Rev. Dr Bruce McLeod, former moderator of the United Church of Canada. Professor Lahey testified that lesbians and gays experience heavy pressure to conceal their identity to avoid discrimination. Professor Adam argued that concealment of their sexuality has had "deleterious psychological and emotional effects on lesbians and gays." And Rev. Dr McLeod recounted how his church has renounced discrimination against lesbians and gays. According to MacNaughton's summary: "Dr McLeod testified that the United Church, after a lengthy and divisive debate, declined to introduce a discriminatory practice into its Church policy that would have excluded lesbians and gays from ordination. He said that those in the Church who disagreed with this decision were welcome to remain members of the Church and that the Church respected their right to continue to hold beliefs opposite to those of Church policy. They were not, however, able to impose those opposite beliefs on Church policy, or behaviour, in a manner that would harm lesbians and gays."

The suggestion that the United Church had declined after a lengthy and divisive debate "to introduce a discriminatory practice into its Church policy that would have excluded lesbians and gays from ordination" is plainly incorrect. The homosexuality debate that erupted within the United Church in the 1980s was not over the introduction, but over the termination, of the church's policy barring from ordination anyone who refuses to uphold the historic teaching of the Christian church on the sinfulness of homosexual acts. As recently as 1960, the ruling General Council of the United Church deplored homosexual conduct as "a moral problem in four ways: It violates the will of God as an offence against the proper expression of sexuality in monogamous marriage; by misuse of natural functions, homosexual activity is a sin against the self; since it involves at least one other person of the same sex, with or without his consent, homosexual activity is unedifying and destructive of 'neighbour love'; it tends to undermine the foundations of stable society based on heterosexual marriage and family responsibility."[11]

The sexual revolution of the 1960s created turmoil within the United Church, as liberal clerics conformed their thinking to this latest pattern of the secular world. In 1980 the church's Division of Mission in Canada released *In God's Image ... Male and Female: A Study on Human Sexuality,* which suggested that fidelity within marriage includes "openness to secondary relationships of emotional intimacy and potential genital expression."[12] This same study also stated: "There is no reason in principle why mature, self-accepting homosexuals, any more than mature, self-accepting heterosexuals, should not be ordained or commissioned."[13] With this equivocal statement, the study stopped just short of repudiating the primeval teaching of the church that all people, homosexual and heterosexual, must remain celibate outside the bond of marriage between a man and a woman. However, a 1984 draft statement on human sexuality published by the Division of Mission in Canada asserted: "The church has too readily accepted marriage as the norm for society and so has not valued single persons for themselves or ... allowed them the opportunity of sexual fulfilment."[14] Four years later, the General Council of the United Church affirmed that "all persons, regardless of sexual orientation, who profess Jesus Christ and are obedient to Him, ... are eligible to be considered for the Ordered Ministry."[15] Finally, in 2000, following yet another tumultuous sexuality debate, the General Council adopted resolutions that renounced the 1960 statement that homosexuality is a sin; affirmed that "lesbian, gay, bisexual and transgendered as well as heterosexual orientations are gifts from God, part of the marvellous diversity of creation"; and called upon the church to "affirm lesbian and gay partnerships, recognize them in church documentation and services of blessing, and actively work for their civil recognition."[16] In 2003 the General Council overwhelming approved a motion urging the federal government to legalize same-sex marriages.[17]

Since the 1970s many Anglicans, Presbyterians, and Lutherans have also embraced the gay rights agenda. In contrast, Scott Brockie, Dianne Haskett, and numerous other Protestants and Catholics have continued to uphold the hitherto universal and constant teaching of the Christian church that sodomy is no less sinful and wrong than fornication and adultery. In support of this viewpoint, these Christians cite authoritative texts of the Bible such as the explicit reference to the sinfulness of homosexual acts by the Apostle Paul in Romans 1. Referring to people who had "exchanged the truth of God for a lie," Paul wrote:

God gave them up to dishonourable passions. Their women exchanged natural relations for unnatural, and the men likewise gave up natural relations with women and were consumed with passion for one another, men committing shameless acts with men and receiving in their own persons the due penalty for their error ... They were filled with all manner of wickedness, evil, covetousness, malice. Full of envy, murder, strife, deceit, malignity, they are gossips, slanderers, haters of God, insolent, haughty, boastful, inventors of evil, disobedient to parents, foolish, faithless, heartless, ruthless. Though they know God's decree that those who do such things deserve to die, they not only do them but approve those who practice them.[18]

In commentaries on this passage, some liberal theologians have argued that Paul was alluding only to homosexual prostitution and pederasty, while others have claimed that Paul meant only to recall that homosexual acts were banned in the Holiness Code in Leviticus.[19] This same code also forbade eating pork, interbreeding cattle, and wearing clothes made with two kinds of cloth.[20] It is argued that Paul held that none of these antiquated rules is still binding on Christians.

None of these revisionist arguments in support of homosexuality have stood up to rigorous biblical analysis. In *Straight and Narrow? Compassion and Clarity in the Homosexuality Debate*, Professor Thomas E. Schmidt, a Protestant specialist in New Testament ethics, has demonstrated on the basis of a close textual analysis of the original Hebraic and Greek passages in the Bible that bear upon sexual ethics that both Jesus and Paul regarded all homosexual acts as sinful. In summary, Schmidt states: "The Bible views same-sex relations as a violation of the created good of marital union between male and female ... When any same-sex act – with angels, with prostitutes, with boys, with mutually consenting adults – is evaluated in relation to the marital union of male and female, it falls short of the plan of God present from creation. As revisionists have rightly pointed out, it is inappropriate for Christians to call such an act impure or disgusting. But as revisionists have failed to recognize, Christians who give the Bible primary and final authority must still call such an act wrong."[21]

While the Gospels record no clear and specific references by Jesus to homosexual acts, it is evident that he did not condone sodomy because it is inconceivable that such a sensational break with centuries of Jewish teaching could have gone unreported in the New Testament. Consequently, instead of trying to argue that Jesus condoned loving homosexual acts, some biblical revisionists now contend that Jesus, like all his rabbinical contemporaries, was a homophobe. The Rev. Dr Gary Comstock is one of the more prominent exponents of this viewpoint. He is a sexually active gay man and a chaplain at Wesleyan University in Connecticut, serves as an ordained minister in the United Church of Christ, and holds a PhD from the liberal Union Theological Seminary in New York City. In *Gay Theology without Apology*, Rev. Comstock confides: "As part of a lingering desire to regard the Bible as a parental authority from which I wanted and needed approval and permission, I have tended to compromise it and myself. I have been more willing to apologize for it than to criticize it; and I have been slow to admit or accept the Bible's bias against homosexuality."[22] Having thrown off this childish complex, Comstock explains that he now approaches the Bible and Christianity "not with the purpose of fitting in or finding a place in them, but of fitting them into and changing them according to the particular experiences of lesbian/bisexual/gay people. Christian Scriptures and tradition are not authorities from which I seek approval; rather they are resources from which I seek guidance and learn lessons as well as institutions that I seek to interpret, shape and change."[23] Likewise, Rev. Comstock no longer regards Jesus as an infallible guide on all questions of faith and morality: "We perhaps have regarded Jesus too exclusively as a hero and not permitted him the status of a friend who would value our criticism and contributions," Rev. Comstock contends.[24] "It is Jesus the master who says, 'Don't look to me for answers; you're on your own ... I'm not the boss, simply a friend who's soon dead and gone. Goodbye'."[25]

With these candid arguments, Rev. Comstock has demonstrated that the dispute over same-sex relations within the Christian church goes to the essence of Christology: Who was this man Jesus? Was he just an ordinary, fallible mortal corrupted by the homophobic prejudices of his time? Or was he the very Son of God, who is and shall forever remain a sure and certain guide on all questions of faith and morality? Wolfhart Pannenberg, a distinguished Lutheran theologian, warns:

> Here lies the boundary of a Christian church that knows itself to be bound by the authority of Scripture. Those who urge the church to change the norm of its teaching on this matter must know that they are promoting schism. If a church were to let itself be pushed to the point where it ceased to treat homosexual activity as a departure from the biblical norm, and recognized homosexual unions as a personal partnership of love equivalent to marriage, such a church would stand no longer on biblical ground but against the unequivocal witness of Scripture. A church that took this step would cease to be the one, holy, catholic and apostolic church.[26]

Popes Benedict XVI and John Paul II have expressed the same view. In the authoritative Catechism of the Catholic Church, they observed: "Sacred Scripture ... presents homosexual acts as acts of grave depravity."

The Catechism also teaches that: "Tradition has always declared that 'homosexual acts are intrinsically disordered.' They are contrary to the natural law. They close the sexual act to the gift of life. They do not proceed from a genuine affective and sexual complementarity. Under no circumstances can they be approved." [27]

Within Judaism, there is no less division on the moral status of homosexual activity than among the various denominations of Christianity. While most Reform Jews have embraced gay rights, Orthodox Jews uphold the traditional teaching of the Hebrew Bible, which condemns all homosexual acts. Albert Vorspan, senior vice president emeritus of the Union of American Hebrew Congregations, has stated: "Orthodox Jewish leaders ... charge that radical changes such as ... support for gay/lesbian rabbis and congregations have cast Reform beyond the pale of Jewish authenticity."[28]

On at least one point in the controversy over homosexuality, virtually all Catholics, Protestants, and Jews are agreed: Any expression of violence or animosity toward homosexuals is illegitimate and deplorable. Strange and incredible as it might seem to the secular mind, theologically orthodox Christians and Jews who are true to their faith not only believe that homosexual behaviour is sinful, but also care for homosexuals as persons and would not presume to pass judgment on them. Prior to addressing the morality of homosexual acts in *Straight and Narrow? Compassion and Clarity in the Homosexuality Debate*, Schmidt confessed:

> In terms of sexuality, I represent that class of people responsible for the vast majority of sexual wrongdoing in the world today: male heterosexuals. I have contributed more than my share of wrongdoing, and I need the forgiveness and grace of God every day to become the sexual being God desires. I have never desired sexual intimacy with another male, nor have I ever been propositioned or treated with anything but respect by gay men I have known.
>
> Apart from the natural concern that some extremist might threaten me or my family in retaliation for the public expression of my views, I do not think I have any reason to fear gay and lesbian people. Without exception in my experience, gay men and lesbians have been among the most intelligent, talented and thoughtful people I have known. Their sexual desires and practices differ from mine, but they do not particularly repulse or threaten me. I simply disapprove, as I do of some heterosexual desires and practices.[29]

In the conclusion to his book, Schmidt writes: "Finally, and by no means least important, Christians should be known for the kind of hands-on help that characterized the ministry of our Lord. People with AIDS, in particular, are the lepers of our day ... They often need errands run, basic housekeeping and home-cooked meals. In areas where no hospice care is available, they may need money or a place to stay. More than anything, they need simple human companionship. As relationships of trust develop, they may open up to spiritual help. But there is no guarantee of this, and we should not make it a condition of service."[30]

Apart from Christians and Jews, many Canadians of other religions, and no religion, agree that all people should have a compassionate concern for the health and wellbeing of practising homosexuals. In *Homosexuality and the Politics of Truth*, Dr Jeffrey Satinover has graphically demonstrated that there is grave reason for concern over the health risks assumed by anyone who takes up a homosexual lifestyle. Dr Satinover is an authority on this subject, having been a fellow in psychiatry and child psychiatry at Yale University as well as a William James Lecturer in psychology and religion at Harvard. He advises that it is a commonplace observation among psychoanalysts that men and women, homosexual and heterosexual, who indulge in "the so-called 'perverse' forms of sexual expression" are apt to become sexually compulsive.[31] Dr Satinover states: "This observation is consistent with the enormously greater promiscuity that is typical of the gay lifestyle." He notes that in a recent survey of sexual behaviour in the United States, heterosexuals reported a lifetime average of four sexual partners, whereas homosexuals estimated a lifetime average of fifty.[32] Dr Satinover warns that in addition to AIDS, sexually promiscuous homosexual men incur a significantly increased risk of contracting infectious hepatitis and rectal cancer;[33] they have "a much higher than usual incidence of suicide";[34] and overall, they incur "a 25 to 30-year decrease in life expectancy."[35] A recent study of gay and bisexual men in Canada focused on AIDS mortality. The authors report: "In a major Canadian centre, life expectancy at age 20 years for gay and bisexual men is 8 to 20 years less than for all men. If the same pattern of mortality were to continue, we estimate that nearly half of gay and bisexual men currently aged 20 years will not reach their 65th birthday. Under even the most liberal assumptions, gay and bisexual men in this urban centre are now experiencing a life expectancy similar to that experienced by all men in Canada in the year 1871."[36]

Given all the heartache and morbidity caused by promiscuous homosexual behaviour, one might reasonably expect that educators, religious leaders, and public officials would do whatever they can to warn young people about the perils of taking up a gay or lesbian lifestyle. At the least, the merits of homosexual practices should be a legitimate subject for public debate. Yet what do we find in Canada? With the complicity of provincial governments and legislatures from one end of the country to another, human rights commissions have arrogated to themselves the power to force elected mayors like Dianne Haskett and ordinary citizens like Scott Brockie to promote homosexual behaviour. No one is free from these dictatorial edicts, not even the religiously devout who deplore homophobia and have a sincere regard for the moral, spiritual, and physical welfare of homosexuals.

How can any reasonable person justify such severe restrictions on freedom of religion and expression in the name of democracy and human rights? MacNaughton contended in her *Brockie* ruling that it is a matter of affirming the overriding rights of gays. In her opinion, the equality rights of homosexuals take precedence over freedom of conscience, freedom of religion, and freedom of expression for all other people, including Christians and Jews who have the most serious and high-minded objections to abetting the practice of homosexuality. To the surprise of no one acquainted with Ontario human rights tribunals, she ended up siding with the homosexual complainants in the Brockie case. She wrote: "Having considered all of the evidence before me and in balancing the competing rights, I have concluded that it is reasonable to limit Brockie's freedom of religion in order to prevent the very real harm to members of the lesbian and gay community, and their organizations, by the denial of services because of their sexual orientation."

To the contention that Brockie had only mildly inconvenienced Brillinger and the archives by refusing to perform a "non-essential" service, MacNaughton rejoined that this argument failed to appreciate "the seriousness of the impact on the Complainants of this refusal in the context of historical and continuing discrimination. Such a focus devalues their experience of discrimination and the endeavour the Archives is involved in to allow lesbians and gays to live open and proud lives. As Dr Robin Brownlie testified during the first phase of these proceedings, 'each new incident (of denial) reopens the wound of that discrimination and harm.'"[37]

MacNaughton also disputed the suggestion that gay activists could easily get their materials printed by someone other than Brockie. She wrote: "While other services are currently available to the lesbian and gay community in Toronto, a large metropolitan center, this will not necessarily be the case in smaller centers. Further, even in Toronto, allowing Brockie to rely on his religious freedom to deny a service could result in an erosion of other services that are currently available to lesbians and gays." Note that in making these observations, MacNaughton was not addressing the specific dispute before the tribunal in accordance with established law. Rather, she was making the case for her promulgation of a new legal rule requiring all Christian service providers to perform willy-nilly even a "non-essential" service for a homosexual group, even where the group has ready access to an alternative service provider.

What does an order requiring a conscientious Christian like Brockie to print materials for gay activist groups say about the current state of freedom of conscience and religion in Canada? MacNaughton argued:

> While it may be difficult to see any 'balance' in an imposition of a penalty against Brockie and Imaging Excellence, in fact nothing in my order will prevent Brockie from continuing to hold, and practice, his religious beliefs. Brockie remains free to hold his religious beliefs and to practice them in his home, and in his Christian community. He is free to espouse those beliefs and to educate others as to them. He remains free to try to persuade elected representatives, through his involvement in the democratic process, that the Code protections currently granted to the lesbian and gay community are wrong.
>
> What he is not free to do, when he enters the public marketplace and offers services to the public in Ontario, is to practice those beliefs in a manner that discriminates against lesbians and gays by denying them a service available to everyone else. He must respect the publicly-arrived-at community standards embodied in the Code. My order does not restrict Brockie's right to believe as he does, just the manner in which he may practice those beliefs.

The apostle James admonished Christians: "Be ye doers of the word and not hearers only."[38] MacNaughton insists that Christians in Canada who provide a service to the public must be hearers of the word only: They must not act upon the word of God in the Bible by refusing to provide their services to any individual or group for the purpose of promoting the practice of homosexuality. To drive this point home, MacNaughton stated in her conclusion:

> I therefore order Brockie and Imaging Excellence to provide the printing services that they provide to others, to lesbians and gays and to organizations in existence for their benefit.
>
> I further order that Brockie and Imaging Excellence pay damages in the amount of $5,000 to Brillinger and the Archives. It is only through an award of damages of this magnitude that I am able to indicate the seriousness of the breach that occurred here. Counsel for the Respondents in this case repeatedly referred to the issues in this case as being ones of "political correctness". While it is apparent to me that nothing in this decision will persuade Brockie of the serious impact of his discriminatory act, I am hopeful that others will be informed by it.

Brockie appealed MacNaughton's ruling to the Ontario Superior Court of Justice. There, he lost again. In a unanimous ruling on 17 June 2002, a three-judge panel of the Court upheld MacNaughton's order subject only to the provision that it "shall not require Mr. Brockie or Imaging Excellence to print material of a nature which could reasonably be considered to be in direct conflict with the core elements of his religious beliefs or creed." Brockie insisted that printing even letterheads and stationery for the Lesbian and Gay Archives would bring him into direct conflict with his core religious beliefs. The Court held that in taking this position, Brockie was unreasonable. And on this basis, the Court obligated him to pay $5,000 in damages to Brillinger and never again to refuse on principle to print letterheads and other similar materials for gay rights groups like the archives.

In a statement to family and friends on 4 July 2002, Brockie disclosed: "After much thought, prayer, and discussions with many lawyers, we have decided not to appeal the court's ruling, as the grounds for appeal are fairly thin, and we risk losing the gains that we have made." Was this a sound conclusion? Did the expert counsel advising Brockie have reason to believe that the supporters of gay rights on the Supreme Court of Canada would be all too likely to reinstate MacNaughton's full order requiring him to print virtually anything at the request of a homosexual organization, even if the material could reasonably be considered to be in direct conflict with the core elements of his beliefs as a Christian?

Such a travesty of justice would be inconceivable if the time-honoured rules of the common law were still in effect in Canada. As it is, Canadians can no longer rely on the historic precepts of the common law that used to safeguard freedom of conscience, freedom of religion, and freedom of association in this country. To an alarming extent, unelected, activist judges on the Supreme Court of Canada have become a law unto themselves. While purporting to uphold the Canadian Charter of Rights and Freedoms, they routinely rewrite or ignore the common law, statute laws, and constitutional laws of Canada. In view of this record, Brockie had good reason to apprehend that by appealing further, he might well have lost what little he had gained from the Ontario Superior Court of Justice.

JUDICIAL ATTACK ON THE BIBLE: THE *OWENS* CASE

Meanwhile, Hugh Owens is continuing his struggle in the courts to overturn a ruling by a Saskatchewan human rights board of inquiry that bars him from publicly citing verses of the Bible. In the controversial advertisement that he placed in the *Saskatoon StarPhoenix* on 30 June 1997, Owens merely listed four Bible passages – Romans 1, Leviticus 18:22, Leviticus 20:13, and 1 Corinthians 6:9–19 – together with a pictograph of two men holding hands superimposed with a circle and slash, the universal symbol for something forbidden. Underneath these depictions, the advertisement advised: "This message is available in bumper sticker form. Please call 306-584-2611." While the advertisement listed only the chapter and verse numbers for the Bible passages without the text, the gist of the message was clear: The Bible forbids homosexual behaviour.

Some gay rights activists in Saskatoon were outraged, especially as the advertisement appeared in the *StarPhoenix* during the city's Gay Pride Week. About seventy-five people mounted a protest demonstration outside the newspaper's building.[39] Owens was undaunted: He resolutely insisted upon his right to proclaim in public what the Bible teaches about homosexuality. In contrast, Lyle Sinkewicz, chief operating officer of the *StarPhoenix*, was cowed: He expressed regret that the advertisement had been perceived as an attack on gay people and promised that the newspaper would never again publish such an offensive message.

Nonetheless, three homosexual men residing in Saskatoon – Jeff Dodds, Jason Roy, and Gens Hellquist – filed identical complaints with the Saskatchewan Human Rights Commission against both Owens and the *StarPhoenix*, charging that publication of the advertisement violated the ban in section 14(1) of the Saskatchewan Human Rights Code on the publication of "any notice, sign, symbol, emblem, article, statement or other representation ... which exposes or tends to expose to hatred, ridicules, belittles or otherwise affronts the dignity of any person or class of persons on the basis of a prohibited ground." Originally, there were seven prohibited grounds of discrimination in the Saskatchewan Human Rights Code: race, religion, colour, sex, nationality, ancestry, and place of origin. Today, there are fourteen, including age, creed, marital status, family status, disability, receipt of public assistance, and sexual orientation. Like similar provisions in other provincial human rights codes, section 14(1) of the Saskatchewan version is a veritable bear trap of a law. According to the plain words of this section, it is unlawful to tell a Newfie joke, to chide a Scot on his alleged parsimony, or to make any other ethnic crack that "ridicules, belittles or otherwise affronts the dignity" of a person or a class of persons on the basis of their place of origin. It is also an offence under section 14(1) to affront anyone's dignity by suggesting that he or she suffers from "a disorder of thought, perception, feelings or behaviour that impairs a person's judgment." Taken literally, this provision would bar the *StarPhoenix* from expressing the mildest editorial criticism of any crook, businessman, or politician.

Granted, the ethnic jokers and editorial writers in Saskatchewan have little reason to fear. The Saskatchewan Human Rights Commission is unlikely to go after them for ridiculing Newfoundlanders or belittling the thought processes of a politician. Beware, however, the person who challenges the orthodoxy of gay rights by quoting the Bible. He or she could end up in jail. Ironically, Owens was one of the first to recognize the danger. Following the addition of "sexual orientation" to the Saskatchewan Human Rights Code in 1993, he wrote a note to the province's Human Rights Commission listing sixteen passages of the Bible that condemn homosexual sexual relations, including the four passages that he later listed in the *StarPhoenix* advertisement.[40] Owens asked the Commission for assurance that the ban on discrimination on the basis of sexual orientation in the Code did not outlaw these biblical passages. In reply, Bill Rafoss, chief human rights officer for the commission, not only assured Owens that the Bible did not conflict with the Code, but also averred that Christians and Jews are protected by sections 4, 5, and 6 of the Code, which explicitly reaffirm the freedoms of belief, expression, and association. Nonetheless, Rafoss could not refrain from serving up a gratuitous lecture to Owens on the understanding of Scripture: "Different individuals and religions interpret the Bible in different ways," wrote Rafoss. "Some interpret the Bible quite literally, while others seek symbolic truths from its teachings. You are entitled to your interpretation of what the Bible says. But others may disagree as to how these complex passages should be read or what meaning should be ascribed [to them]."[41]

Owens was not altogether reassured by Rafoss. For greater certainty, he asked the Court of Queen's Bench in Regina in September 1993 for a declaration that the Bible as a whole, and the specific passages that condemn homosexual sexual relations in particular, are exempt from section 14(1) of the Code. He also asked the Court for a guarantee that the people of Saskatchewan remain free to affirm in public the biblical strictures against sodomy. In December 1995, Ross Macnab, the Crown Counsel assigned to the case, told *Report Magazine* that Owens had nothing to fear: "I'm not worried about his concerns," Macnab said. "The (Code) and the Charter guarantee him freedom of expression and religion. I'm not fearful that Christians will ever be persecuted in Saskatchewan."[42]

Given all these assurances, Owens might well have felt free and safe under the law to list Bible verses opposed to homosexuality in his advertisement in the *StarPhoenix*. Instead, he was dismayed to find that the Saskatchewan Human Rights Commission promptly condemned the advertisement as a violation of the Saskatchewan Human Rights Code and summoned both him and the *StarPhoenix* to pay $2,000 in damages to each of the three complainants as compensation for their hurt feelings. In addition, the commission directed Owens to refrain from publishing or distributing his bumper stickers ever again and ordered him to attend an education seminar on human rights.[43]

Owens and the *StarPhoenix* refused to comply, so the commission referred the dispute to a Saskatchewan human rights board of inquiry. Typically, the complainants were represented at public expense by a lawyer employed by the commission, while the respondents were left to arrange and pay for their own defence. Hiring lawyers to help mount such a defence does not come cheap. Brockie ran up a legal bill of close to $100,000, before surrendering to the Ontario Human Rights Commission and the Lesbian and Gay Archives.[44] Owens is a modestly paid guard at the Regina Correctional Centre. He simply could not afford such a huge legal bill, so he chose to defend himself before the board of inquiry without the benefit of legal counsel.

Valerie Watson, a young lawyer who adjudicates for the board, got the hearings underway in August 1999. One of the featured witnesses for the Commission was Rev. Brent Hawkes, pastor of the Metropolitan Community Church in Toronto. Watson accepted Rev. Hawkes as "an expert in homosexual issues particularly in spiritual and theological issues." In his testimony, Rev. Hawkes asserted that the biblical passages cited by Owens condemn only pedophilia.[45] Rabbi Steve Kaplan of the Saskatoon Jewish Centre took strong issue with this interpretation of the Hebrew texts. In testimony before the board on behalf of Owens and the *StarPhoenix*, Kaplan contended that the Hebrew Bible and rabbinical commentaries unequivocally condemn the gay lifestyle, although not gay people.[46] Kaplan stated: "The Bible is the Bible, is the Bible: It cannot be changed." In response to the suggestion by a lawyer for the Human Rights Commission that the passages of the Hebrew Bible cited by Owens might be open to the alternative interpretations advanced by Rev. Hawkes, Kaplan insisted that the injunction "Do not lie with a man as one lies with a woman; that is detestable" (Leviticus 18:22) means exactly what it says: The Hebrew Bible unequivocally repudiates all homosexual sexual relations.

Kaplan also took issue with the testimony of Rev. Canon Colin Clay, an Anglican chaplain at the University of Saskatchewan, who told the board that the publication of a list of Bible verses on gay sex without any context created an environment in which people would be hurt and, therefore, transgressed the limits of freedom of religion and speech.[47] In Kaplan's opinion, banning the publication of a mere list of Bible verses would deal a devastating blow to freedom of religion and freedom of speech in Canada. He vowed to fight any human rights ruling that constricts the right of Canadians to state their opposition to homosexuality. He declared: "No one can tell me I can't express the tenets of my faith."[48] Father Paul Donlevy, a Roman Catholic priest, concurred. He told the board that Owens's plight reminded him of several Saskatoon priests working in Africa who have been attacked by African governments for missionary work. Donlevy wondered how far suppression of freedom of religion might also go in Canada.[49] Rev. Erwin Buck, a professor of the New Testament at the Lutheran Theological Seminary affiliated with the University of Saskatchewan, took a more nuanced position: He testified that all people should be allowed to express even hurtful religious views on homosexuality provided the message is conveyed with compassion.[50]

Owens is a fundamentalist. In testimony before the board, he said he believes the Criminal Code should prescribe the death penalty for sodomy because Leviticus 20:13 states: "If a man lies with a male as with a woman, both of them have committed an abomination; they shall be put to death, their blood is upon them." It happens that in this same chapter of Leviticus, the death penalty is also prescribed for adultery, incest, bestiality, and the cursing of one's parents.[51] Owens told the board that he thinks that the commission of any of these sins should be a capital offence under the Criminal Code of Canada.

Needless to say, the overwhelming majority of Christians and Jews would reject such a literal application of the Holiness Code in Leviticus to the laws of Canada. As for Owens, he has explained:

> I believe in God's word as it pertains to the issue of homosexuality. I also believe in God's word as it pertains to the issue of the death penalty: the death penalty for all instances, not one sin to the exclusion of the others, but all sins. If you are not going to employ the death penalty, say, for murder and for rape and for adultery and for everything else for which God commands the death penalty, you do not do it for homosexuality either. You either apply it universally as God has given it, or you don't. These commandments were given by God to the King and his judiciary. In our time, it would be to Chrétien and his governing party, but they refuse to apply it. It's not my job as a Christian to start executing murderers because God condemns murder, even to the death penalty; and the same with rape and adultery and bestiality and child molestation. It is not my job. It's the government's job. If they refuse, then all I can do is fight for better laws.[52]

Asked if he had ever condoned lawless violence against homosexuals, Owens responded: "No, never. It's the biblical absolutes of love and forgiveness. People can change. I know. I've been there." He explained that before converting to Christianity, he had had serious problems with alcohol, drugs, and sex. He says these afflictions were his own fault: "No matter how drunk or stoned I was, I was still in charge, I still surrendered my will to the alcohol and to the drugs. I decided one day to take it back and to give it to God and it was as if it never happened."[53] Owens is convinced that people caught up in an unhealthy and self-destructive gay lifestyle can experience this same liberation: "I believe that you come to a point where you surrender your will to sin, whatever sin that might be, and that applies to the homosexual as well. I know there is a way out for them, because God says there's a way out."[54]

Asked about the maxim "hate the sin, but love the sinner," Owens said he thinks that this slogan has become "kind of trite, because of overuse by the secular media; but the bottom line is it's true. God does make that separation, and thank God He does, because if He didn't, even Billy Graham who is one of the most respected Christian preachers in the world would be lost. If he is lost, then we truly all are lost."[55]

Like Owens, Sinkewicz denied any evil intent in publishing Owens's advertisement. "I didn't see anything wrong with it," Sinkewicz told the board. "It was calling attention to certain passages in the Bible. In that the Bible is the best-selling book in the world and it is generally not thought to be hate literature, I thought it was OK to run the ad."[56] Sinkewicz described freedom of speech in his testimony as the "most precious" right in a democracy. He told Watson: "Homosexual rights and matters pertaining to homosexual rights are public issues. We have a responsibility to provide a forum to the public for public discussion."[57] He related that in addition to running advertisements by organizations promoting Gay Pride Week and by individuals seeking same-sex romances, his newspaper had published many articles, letters to the editor, and opinion pieces expressing various views on gay issues.

THE DECISION OF THE BOARD

Watson was unmoved by the arguments of either Owens or Sinkewicz. She pointed out that the lack of evil intent is not a defence against a charge of violating the ban on the expression of discriminatory statements in the Saskatchewan Human Rights Code. Citing the judgment by the Supreme Court of Canada in *Canada (Human Rights Commission) v. Taylor,* 1990 SCC, she said: "The Board must use an objective test in determining whether or not the advertisement is in breach of Section 14(1) [of the Saskatchewan Code]. This means that the intention of Mr. Owens in placing the advertisement and to a degree the intention of the newspaper in publishing it are not determinative of whether or not the advertisement had the effect that is being alleged." In her opinion, the advertisement objectively violated the Code. While allowing that the depiction of a circle and slash over two stick men holding hands might not in itself have communicated hatred, she said: "When combined with the passages from the Bible, the Board finds that the advertisement would expose or tend to expose homosexuals to hatred or ridicule, or may otherwise affront their dignity on the basis of their sexual orientation. It is the combination of both the symbol and the biblical references that have lead [*sic*] to this conclusion." Watson made clear that she found the Bible verses especially offensive. In her opinion, the use of the circle and slash indicates "that the advertisement is intended to make the group depicted appear to be inferior or not wanted at best. When combined with the Biblical quotations, the advertisement may result in a far stronger meaning. It is obvious that certain of the Biblical quotations suggest more dire consequences and there can be no question that the advertisement can objectively be seen as exposing homosexuals to hatred or ridicule." She concluded that Owens and the *StarPhoenix* had violated section 14(1) of the Saskatchewan Human Rights Code by publishing an advertisement that "ridicules, belittles or otherwise affronts the dignity of any person or class of persons" on the basis of their sexual orientation.

Watson next turned to subsection 2 of section 14 of the Code, which states: "Nothing in subsection (1) restricts the right to freedom of speech under the law upon any subject." Note the Orwellian nature of section 14. While subsection 1 affirms that no one is allowed to publish anything that ridicules, belittles, or otherwise affronts the dignity of any person on the basis of fourteen prohibited grounds, including sexual orientation, subsection 2 purports to guarantee freedom of speech upon any subject. Taken together, these two subsections are antithetical. Section 14 as a whole can make no sense, except perhaps to a practitioner of Orwellian double-think – that is, someone adept at simultaneously holding two contradictory ideas in the mind and believing both to be true.

Yet all provinces, except Quebec, have similar, contradictory provisions in their human rights codes. Chief Justice Dickson alluded to this anomaly in an aside in his judgment in *Taylor*. "Though not wishing to disparage legislative efforts to bolster the guarantee of free expression, for several reasons I think it mistaken to place too great an emphasis upon the explicit protection of expressive activity in a human rights statute," he said. "Having decided that there exists an objective in restricting hate propaganda of sufficient importance to warrant placing some limits upon the freedom of expression, it would be incongruous to require that [the law] exempt all activity falling under the rubric of 'expression'." What, then, is the point of the ostensible guarantee of freedom of speech in section 14(2) of the Saskatchewan Code? Dickson opined: "Perhaps the so-called exemptions found in many human rights statutes are best seen as indicating to human rights tribunals the necessity of balancing the objective of eradicating discrimination with the need to protect free expression."

In the case of the Saskatchewan Human Rights Code, section 14(2) is not the only provision that purports to uphold "the right to freedom of speech under the law upon any subject." Section 5 of the Code states: "Every person and every class of person shall, under the law, enjoy the right to freedom of expression through all means of communication, including, without limiting the generality of the foregoing, the arts, speech, the press or radio television or any other broadcasting device." Likewise, section 4 of the Code states: "Every person and every class of persons shall enjoy the right to freedom of conscience, opinion and belief and freedom of religious association, teaching, practice and worship." In her ruling in the *Owens* case, Watson acknowledged: "There is no question that Mr. Owens believed that he was publicly expressing his honestly held religious belief as it related to his interpretation of the Bible and its discussion of homosexuality." But did Watson draw the logical conclusion that Owens is legally entitled to publish his advertisement by virtue of the ostensibly unequivocal guarantees of freedom of conscience and expression in sections 4, 5, and 14(2) of the Saskatchewan Human Rights Code?

No, she did not. Instead, she noted that in *Taylor*, Chief Justice Dickson had upheld the ban on hate messages in section 13(1) of the Canadian Human Rights Act as a reasonable and demonstrably justifiable limit on the guarantee of freedom of conscience and expression in section 2 of the Charter. She also observed that in *Saskatchewan (Human Rights Commission) v. Bell,* 1994 SCA, Mr Justice Nicholas Sherstobitoff of the Saskatchewan Court of Appeal had maintained that the ban in section 14(1) of the Saskatchewan Human Rights Code on the publication of any statement that "tends to expose to hatred, ridicules, belittles or otherwise affronts the dignity of any person or class of persons" on the basis of fourteen different grounds constitutes no more than a reasonable and demonstrably justifiable limit on the guarantees of freedom of expression in both the Code and the Charter. In summary, Watson wrote: "The Board has concluded that the complainants, Jeff Dodds, Jason Roy, and Gens Hellquist, have been discriminated against with respect to the advertisement placed in the Saskatoon Star Phoenix [*sic*] on June 30, 1997, and as a result, were exposed to hatred, ridicule and their dignity was affronted on the basis of their sexual orientation. Based on the evidence given by the complainants, the Board finds that the complainants suffered in respect of their feelings and self-respect as a result of the contravention."

For this offence, Watson directed that Owens and the *StarPhoenix* must each pay each of the complainants $1,500 in damages, prohibited the newspaper from ever again publishing Owens's advertisement, and directed that Owens must refrain from further publishing or displaying his bumper stickers in any newspaper or other medium. Watson stopped short of requiring Owens to attend an education seminar on human rights as requested by the Saskatchewan Human Rights Commission, although such an order was clearly within her powers under the Saskatchewan Human Rights Code. And the same goes for human rights adjudicators in other provinces. Suppose, for example, that Owens had taken out his Bible-quoting advertisement in an Ontario newspaper. As we have seen, section 41 of the Ontario Human Rights Code provides that where the Ontario Human Rights Tribunal finds that a party has violated a right of a complainant under the Code, the tribunal may, by order, "direct the party to do anything that, in the opinion of the Tribunal, the party ought to do to achieve compliance with this Act, both in respect of the complaint and in respect of future practices." Such draconian provisions are typical of Canadian human rights laws. How can this be? Chairman Mao would have relished the unbridled power conferred upon Canada's so-called human rights tribunals.

In response to Watson's judgment, Sinkewicz caved in. Rather than appeal her freedom-stifling decision, he directed the *StarPhoenix* to pay $1,500 in damages to each of the three homosexual complainants in the case and pledged that the *StarPhoenix* would never again publish an advertisement like Owens's. Such was the behaviour of a publisher who testified under oath to his belief in freedom of speech as the most precious right in a democracy.

Owens is made of tougher stuff. He did not capitulate to Watson. He appealed to the Saskatchewan Court of Queen's Bench. Appearing once again without the benefit of legal counsel, he repeated to the Court essentially the same arguments that he had used before the board and got the same result. In a ruling on 11 December 2002, Mr Justice Ron Barclay stated: "In my view the Board was correct in concluding that the advertisement can objectively be seen as exposing homosexuals to hatred or ridicule. When the use of the circle and slash is combined with the passages of the Bible, it exposes homosexuals to detestation, vilification and disgrace. In other words, the Biblical passage which suggest[s] that if a man lies with a man they must be put to death exposes homosexuals to hatred." Barclay also agreed with

Watson on the application of the Charter. Following the reasoning of the Supreme Court of Canada in *Ross v. New Brunswick School District No. 15*, 1996 SCC, he stated: "In my view, s. 14(1) of the Code is a reasonable restriction on the appellant's right to freedom of expression and religion as contemplated by s. 2(a) of the Charter." And on the basis of this reasoning, Barclay upheld Watson's ruling in every respect.

Owens has launched a further appeal to the Saskatchewan Court of Appeal and vows to take his case, if necessary, all the way to the Supreme Court of Canada.[58] If he loses on all appeals, he will face court orders to pay $4,500 in damages to the complainants and to refrain from further publishing or otherwise displaying his bumper stickers. If Owens were to refuse to comply, he, like John Ross Taylor, could be charged with contempt of court and incarcerated.

BILL WHATCOTT COURTS IMPRISONMENT

William G. (Bill) Whatcott, a registered practical nurse in Saskatoon, is no less likely than Owens to end up in jail. On 2 May 2002 the Saskatchewan Human Rights Tribunal ruled that Whatcott had violated section 14(1) of the Saskatchewan Human Rights Code by writing and distributing a series of flyers that denounced homosexuality as sinful and harmful to health.[59] In support of this finding, Anil Pandila, a Prince Albert lawyer who was selected to chair the tribunal, noted that the flyers included statements like the following: "Sodomites are 430 times more likely to acquire Aids and 3 times more likely to sexually abuse children!" "Born Gay? No Way! Homosexual sex is about risky and addictive behaviour!" In testimony before the tribunal, Whatcott insisted that these assertions are all true. As authority, he cited the evidence provided by Dr Satinover in *Homosexuality and the Politics of Truth.* Pandila rejected this argument on the ground that the Saskatchewan Human Rights Code does not make any provision for truth as a defence against a charge of expressing an idea that ridicules, belittles, or affronts the dignity of homosexuals. This omission is typical of Canada's human rights codes. While many Canadians might suppose that a human rights statute that suppresses the free expression of truthful statements is plainly incompatible with the guarantees of freedom of expression in section 2 of the Charter, the Supreme Court of Canada has decided otherwise. In *Taylor,* Chief Justice Dickson declared that the ban on expressions of hatred or contempt for protected groups in the Canadian Human Rights Code does not constitute an excessive restriction on the guarantee of freedom of expression in section 2 of the Charter, even if the ban "operates to suppress statements which are either truthful or intended to be truthful, as it is not necessary that truthful statements be used for such ends."

Rev. Irwin Pudrycky, a retired minister of the Lutheran Church of Canada, appeared before the tribunal as an expert witness on behalf of Whatcott. Pudrycky noted in his testimony that the ruling synod of his church had adopted a resolution in 1993 affirming: "Homosexuality is a distortion of God's intention for the human race and homosexual thoughts, desires, words and deeds are contrary to God's will." This same resolution also stated: "A self-declared and practicing homosexual person is not to be approved for ordination and, if already ordained, is not to be recommended for call." Pudrycky told the tribunal that in his opinion, the views expressed in Whatcott's flyers were entirely consistent with the position of the Lutheran Church of Canada on the sinfulness of homosexuality.

Whatcott used some strong language in the flyers. Referring to sex education in public schools, he wrote: "Now the homosexuals want to share their filth and propaganda with Saskatchewan's children ... Our children will pay the price in disease, death, abuse ... if we do not say no to the sodomite desire to socialize your [*sic*] children into accepting something that is clearly wrong." While conceding that many members of the church "would be reluctant to be as blunt and forthright as Whatcott," Pudrycky commended him "for speaking out on and drawing attention to matters relating to homosexuality that needed to be exposed."[60] Pudrycky insisted that Whatcott's flyers were not hateful. He contended that they were "simply relating true facts and then indicating that the solution was to seek forgiveness of the sins through Christ."

Whatcott has first-hand knowledge of the seamier side of the gay lifestyle. He was a homosexual prostitute and drug abuser before converting to Christianity at age eighteen.[61] He acknowledged his homosexual past to the tribunal and professed that the Lord had set him free. Pandila, in his reasons for judgment, did not question Whatcott's sincerity. Neither did he challenge Pudrycky's testimony that Whatcott's flyers reflect the doctrinal teaching of the Lutheran Church of Canada. Following the precedents set in *Taylor, Bell,* and *Owens,* Pandila held that the intentions of Whatcott in spreading the flyers were no less irrelevant than the truthfulness of the statements in the flyers. Notwithstanding the ostensible guarantees of freedom of conscience, religion, speech, and expression in section 2 of the Charter, Pandila ruled that Whatcott had no right to express truthful statements or honestly held religious convictions that expose homosexuals to hatred, ridicule, or contempt. In conclusion, he ordered Whatcott to pay $17,500 in damages to four homosexual complainants and directed that he must never again distribute the flyers at issue in this case "or any similar material which promotes hatred against individuals because of their sexual orientation."

Whatcott is not easily daunted. In media interviews following the ruling, he announced that he would appeal Pandila's "sick and draconian" decision.[62] He also said that he could not and would not pay the $17,500 in damages. "My entire life assets are substantially less than that. If I had a million dollars I still wouldn't pay it," he said.[63] "Let's be very clear," Whatcott declared. "I believe homosexual activity is a sin. I really believe that and to give me a $17,500 fine and say I can't say that is quite frankly garbage and is not something I am going to abide by. If I have to sit in jail for the rest of my life, I am not going to be quiet." Within two weeks, Whatcott and fellow members of a group called the Christian Truth Activists followed up on his words by stuffing Saskatoon mailboxes with 1,000 "new and improved" flyers entitled "Sodomites and the Saskatchewan Human Rights Commission."

Whatcott understands that he is courting martyrdom. He knows that if he loses on appeal and refuses to obey a court order upholding Pandila's directives, he could, and probably would, be charged with contempt of court and consigned to jail. And there he could remain as a Christian prisoner of conscience as long as he refuses to renounce the publication of any more flyers that Pandila and homosexual complainants might consider offensive.

Prior to the Charter, there was hardly any peacetime political censorship in Canada. Most Canadian legislators subscribed to the traditional democratic view that it is safer to allow even genuine hatemongers to engage in open public debate with decent citizens than to empower the state to suppress freedom of speech. In *On Liberty*, a classic statement of the case for freedom of expression, John Stuart Mill argued:

> If all mankind minus one, were of one opinion, and only one person were of the contrary opinion, mankind would be no more justified in silencing that one person, than he, if he had the power, would be justified in silencing mankind. Were an opinion a personal possession of no value except to the owner; if to be obstructed in the enjoyment of it were simply a private injury, it would make some difference whether the injury was inflicted only on a few persons or on many. But the peculiar evil of silencing the expression of an opinion is, that it is robbing the human race; posterity as well as the existing generation; those who dissent from the opinion, still more than those who hold it. If the opinion is right, they are deprived of the opportunity of exchanging error for truth: if wrong, they lose, what is almost as great a

benefit, the clearer perception and livelier impression of truth, produced by its collision with error.

Over the past thirty years, most of our elected representatives in Parliament and the provincial legislatures have abandoned this robust understanding of freedom of expression. They think that it is reasonable to try to stamp out all invidious discrimination in Canada. To this end, they have conferred sweeping powers on human rights tribunals and the courts. Most Canadians are not alert to the danger. They think that the familiar words of the Charter and our human rights codes – freedom of conscience, freedom of religion, freedom of speech, freedom of association – mean what they say. They have yet to comprehend how human rights tribunals and the courts have invoked the Canadian Charter of Rights and Freedoms to suppress some of the very historic rights and freedoms that the Charter was supposed to safeguard and enhance.

If only hate-mongering anti-Semites like Taylor had reason to fear the freedom-suppressing powers of our human rights tribunals and the courts in the Charter era, most Canadians could relax. As it is, Canadians urgently need to wake up to the reality that the judicial perversion of human rights in Canada threatens the freedom of virtually everyone, from lesbians to traditional Christians who insist upon the peaceful expression of their inalienable rights to freedom of thought, belief, opinion, and association.

4

How Human Rights Commissions Suppress Our Freedoms

The people of the United States are hardly less threatened than Canadians by the sweeping powers of contemporary human rights tribunals. Consider the experience of the Seattle Employees Association for Gays and Lesbians (SEAGL). In 1990 members of this city-sponsored group barred Philip Irvin, a fellow city employee, from attending their meetings because he is a Christian activist opposed to equality rights for homosexuals.[1] Irvin filed a complaint with the Seattle Office for Civil Rights[2] claiming that SEAGL was violating the city's Human Rights Code by discriminating against him on the basis of his religious and political beliefs. Following more than six years of investigation and litigation, the Office for Civil Rights upheld Irvin's complaint.[3] Germaine Covington, the director of the office, explained: "City policy has to be applied fairly, and if there is a law that mandates certain behaviour, then we, the city, have to follow it like everyone else."[4] Consequently, she ruled that the city should pay Irvin $1,000 in damages, cover part of his lawyer's expenses, and train SEAGL members not to discriminate against Christians.[5]

Irvin was not satisfied because he believed that the Office of Civil Rights was incapable of providing appropriate antidiscrimination training.[6] In a letter to the editor of the *Seattle Times*, he explained: "Under city ordinance, you can't be discriminated against merely because you believe, as I do, that homosexuality is morally wrong. If we are really interested in reducing discrimination, we should eliminate Seattle's Office for Civil Rights. We need to eliminate Seattle's gay rights law and others like it that are enforced in an overtly discriminatory manner."[7]

The same goes for the human rights codes of Canada. We need to eliminate the Canadian Human Rights Act and other laws like it that are enforced in an overtly discriminatory manner. Worse, these so-called human rights codes have stifled the historic rights and freedoms of Canadians. What more striking evidence of the loss of freedom of association in Canada could we have than the 1999 ruling of the British Columbia Human Rights Tribunal that ordered the owners of a licensed video lounge catering to gays and lesbians in the basement of the Carlton Plaza Hotel in Victoria, British Columbia, to pay $2,000 in compensation to a cross-dressing man for refusing to allow him to use the women's washroom.[8] Anyone who thinks this ruling might have been an aberration should consider *Ferris v. Office and Technical Employees Union, Local 15*, 1999 BCHRT. This case arose out of a dispute between Leslie Ferris, a biologically male transsexual employed by Black Top Cabs in Vancouver, and members of a union local representing the company's employees. Betty Lambert, a shop steward for the union, objected to Ferris's use of the women's washroom at the cab company. In testimony before the tribunal, Ferris said that a friend had told him that Lambert was telling everyone at work that there was a grievance concerning his use of the women's washroom. Nitya Iyer, the tribunal adjudicator assigned to the case, noted in her reasons for decision that the union "objected to this evidence as hearsay. I admitted it." This is typical. While the submission of hearsay evidence is forbidden in a criminal court, it is acceptable in proceedings before a human rights tribunal. This is not the only difference in evidentiary rules. In the *Ferris* case, the union called for dismissal of the complaint because counsel for Ferris had tabled no direct evidence to establish that the union had treated him worse than others because he is a transsexual. Iyer dismissed this argument on the ground that in proceedings before a human rights tribunal, "direct evidence is not necessary to establish a prima facie case or to find a complaint justified." To support this assertion, she cited a 1993 ruling of the British Columbia Council on Human Rights that "discrimination often does not occur through direct, unequivocal acts, but must be inferred from circumstantial evidence. Accordingly ... it is often relatively easy for a complainant to make out a *prima facie* case, i.e., persuade the Tribunal that the respondent has engaged in conduct that requires an explanation."[9]

What has happened to the common law rules of evidence that evolved over centuries to protect the innocent? In several key respects, these historic safeguards for freedom under law have been abandoned by our equality-seeking Canadian human rights tribunals. The respondent in a human rights case can end up in jail on the basis of little or no direct evidence to back up the claims of the complainant.

Despite the lack of any direct evidence of differential treatment in the *Ferris* case, Iyer concluded that Lambert and the union had unlawfully discriminated against Ferris. She stated: "I find the complaint justified. Section 37(2)(a) of the *Code* requires me to order the Respondent Union to cease its contravention of the *Code* and to refrain from committing the same or a similar contravention. I so order." In plain language, Iyer directed the union to allow Ferris or any other cross-dressing man who identifies himself as a female to use the women's washroom at Black Top Cabs. Furthermore, she ordered the union "to pay to the Complainant the sum of $1,000.80 in compensation for lost wages and the sum of $5,000 in compensation for the injury it has done to her [*sic*] dignity, feelings and self-respect."

Shortly after this ruling, the Canadian Human Rights Act Review Panel, a body chaired by former Justice La Forest of the Supreme Court of Canada, issued a report to Parliament. Among the many recommendations in this report was the suggestion that Parliament should adopt an amendment to section 2 of the Canadian Human Rights Act that would "specifically prohibit discrimination against transgendered individuals," defined as "persons who have undergone or will undergo treatment and surgery to bring their physical gender in line with their psychological gender."[10] What, it might be wondered, was the point of this recommendation? Why did the panel want members of Parliament to go through the motions of amending the Canadian Human Rights Act to confer rights on transsexuals when it was apparent that our judicial legislators could be counted upon to make this change in the law on their own?

In fact, it did not take long for the Canadian Human Rights Tribunal and the Federal Court to preempt Parliament on this issue. In a ruling on 31 August 2001 in *Kavanagh v. Attorney General of Canada*, 2001 CHRT, a three-member panel of the Canadian Human Rights Tribunal unanimously declared: "There is no dispute that discrimination on the basis of Transsexualism constitutes sex discrimination as well as discrimination on the basis of a disability." As authority for this statement, the tribunal cited no provision of the Canadian Human Rights Act or any other federal or provincial legislative enactment: It relied entirely upon the unilateral affirmation of transsexual rights in prior rulings by the Quebec and British Columbia Human Rights Tribunals.[11] Thanks to the large and liberal redefinition of sex discrimination by the unelected members of these tribunals, cross-dressing men who identify as females have gained the right to use women's washrooms on Parliament Hill, in Victoria's B.J.'s Lounge, in the offices of Black Top Cabs in Vancouver, and, it seems, in virtually all other buildings open to the public throughout Canada.

Synthia Kavanagh, the complainant in the case that prompted the Canadian Human Rights Tribunal to read transsexual rights into the Canadian Human Rights Act, is a convicted murderer and transsexual, who was incarcerated in a male penitentiary for the 1989 hammer-killing of her best friend, a Toronto transvestite.[12] Kavanagh asked Correctional Service Canada (CSC) to allow her to undergo hormone therapy and sex reassignment surgery while in custody. She also insisted that as a male-to-female transsexual, she should be transferred to a female correctional facility. CSC refused these requests. In 1993 Kavanagh complained to the Canadian Human Rights Commission that the CSC was engaging in unlawful discrimination on the basis of transsexualism. Following six years of vacillation, the CSC reached a voluntary settlement with Kavanagh in November 1999, as a result of which she underwent sex reassignment surgery at a private clinic in Montreal and was thereafter transferred to the Joliette Institution for women in Joliette, Quebec. Kavanagh's lawyer, barbara findlay, hailed the settlement as "a great victory for all transgendered people, inside and outside the prison system."[13] As for Kavanagh, soon after settling in at the Joliette Institution, she established a consensual sexual relationship with another female inmate. It seems, however, that neither sex reassignment surgery nor a transfer to Joliette ended her anguishing psychiatric problems: Federal Court records indicate that "While at Joliette, Ms. Kavanagh self-mutilated, which precipitated her voluntary placement at the Philippe Pinel Institute, a psychiatric hospital."[14]

Meanwhile, the Canadian Human Rights Tribunal proceeded to consider the complaints against the CSC that Kavanagh had filed with the Canadian Human Rights Commission in 1993. The tribunal acknowledged at the outset of its ruling that "Ms. Kavanagh's individual complaints against CSC have been settled." Therefore, by the tribunal's admission, there was no longer any live issue to adjudicate between Kavanagh and the CSC. In deciding, nonetheless, to proceed with the case, the tribunal evidently undertook not to adjudicate the dispute between Kavanagh and the CSC but to engage in the essentially legislative process of rewriting the law in relation to the rights of transsexual inmates.

For medical guidance in the case, the tribunal relied on the testimony of three psychiatrists and a psychologist: Dr Robert Dickey, the Head of the Gender Identity Clinic at the Centre for Addiction and Mental Health (Clarke Division) in Toronto; Dr Stephen Hucker, a professor of psychiatry and academic head of the Forensic Psychiatry Division of the Department of Psychiatry and Behavioural Neurosciences at McMaster University; Dr Diane Watson, a cofounder and former director of the Gender Dysphoria Clinic at the Vancouver Hospital; and Maxine Petersen, a psychologist, described by the tribunal "as one of the relatively few experts in the field who is herself a transsexual." Relying on the testimony of these four experts, the tribunal concluded that: "Sex reassignment surgery is a recognized and appropriate treatment for properly screened candidates."

Jane Laishes, senior project manager for Mental Health at the CSC, told the tribunal that in response to Kavanagh's request for permission to undergo sex reassignment surgery, she had asked Watson and Dickey to evaluate Kavanagh for the procedure. Watson gave her approval, but Dickey, drawing upon an interview that he had conducted with Kavanagh in the Don Jail some ten years earlier, rejected her as a suitable candidate for sex reassignment surgery. Laishes then sought a third opinion from Hucker. Following an interview with Kavanagh at the Mission Institution, a medium-security penitentiary for men in British Columbia, he agreed with Dickey that Kavanagh should not undergo sex reassignment surgery. Laishes testified that it was the inability of these experts to agree on Kavanagh's suitability for sex reassignment surgery that prompted the CSC to reject her request for the procedure and to adopt as a general policy that: "Sex reassignment surgery will not be considered during [any] inmate's incarceration."

In support of this policy, Laishes suggested to the tribunal that providing sex reassignment surgery to inmates at CSC's expense, when this procedure is not always available to law-abiding citizens in the community at public expense, "could create some incentive for people to commit crimes."[15] She noted that prisoners in the United States, the United Kingdom, Australia, and New Zealand are not allowed to undergo sex reassignment surgery unless the procedure has been court ordered or will be paid for by the inmate. Nonetheless, despite all these considerations, she said that the CSC had left open "the possibility that sex reassignment surgery could be permitted in exceptional cases, where it qualified as an essential service." In applying this policy to Kavanagh, the CSC initially refused her request for sex reassignment surgery, subsequently approved her for the procedure as a special case, enabled her to undergo the surgery at the Menard Clinic in Montreal, and thereafter transferred her to the Joliette Institution for female offenders.

The tribunal weighed all the arguments advanced by the CSC for generally refusing to consider sex reassignment surgery for inmates and rejected them. Notwithstanding that sex reassignment surgery is not provided in any public hospital in Canada, the tribunal held that if physicians at a recognized gender identity clinic have approved a transsexual inmate for sex reassignment surgery as an essential service prior to incarceration, it follows that the surgery "should be paid for by CSC, as would any other essential medical service." Ultimately, of course, the taxpayers of Canada will have to pick up the not-inconsiderable costs. In a position paper on transsexualism, the Ontario Public Health Association describes sex reassignment surgery as a "costly procedure, which ranges anywhere from $12,000 to $65,000 and up."[16] The variation in cost depends on the extent of the treatment. While some male-to-female transsexuals settle for the minimum of penis amputation and vaginaplasty, others also undergo such related surgeries as breast enlargement and shaving of the Adam's apple. In the case of inmates, there is the additional expense of guarding the prisoner before and after surgery. Kavanagh's lawyer, barbara findlay, estimates that sex reassignment surgery for a male prisoner "could cost up to $100,000."[17]

On appeal, the CSC argued that the tribunal exceeded its jurisdiction in ruling that the CSC must pay for sex reassignment surgery at the direction of nongovernmental physicians inasmuch as these physicians are accountable neither to Parliament nor to taxpayers for the expenditure of public funds. Madam Justice Carolyn Layden-Stevenson of the Federal Court disagreed. She said: "I do not take issue with the conclusion that the role of the court is limited when reviewing policy-based determinations by officials who are accountable for public funds. However, the right of government to allocate resources as it sees fit is not unlimited."[18] As authority, Layden-Stevenson cited *Canada v. Kelso,* 1981 SCC, in which the Supreme Court of Canada held: "The government's right to allocate resources cannot override a statute such as the Canadian Human Rights Act."

On the second issue raised by the Kavanagh case – the right of a male-to-female transsexual to seek placement in a prison for women – the expert witnesses were also divided in their testimony before the tribunal. Dickey, Hucker, and Peterson expressed grave concern about incarcerating a preoperative male-to-female transsexual in a women's prison on the ground that a male prisoner could still be capable of raping a female prisoner even if he were undergoing hormone therapy in preparation for a sex-change operation. In contrast, Watson advised the tribunal that a male transsexual inmate in an advanced stage of hormone therapy would pose no especial threat to female prisoners and should be placed in a female institution so that he can have a real-life experience among females. For similar reasons, Watson said that she would place a female inmate preparing for sex reassignment surgery in a male penitentiary. Specifically, Watson stated that

Kavanagh did not pose any risk of indulging in "sexualized behaviour" with female inmates prior to her operation, because she was "exclusively oriented towards men sexually." Informed by the tribunal that Kavanagh had admitted to having, "in fact, had a sexual liaison with a female prisoner while incarcerated at Joliette Institution," Watson allowed that it was possible that Kavanagh is bisexual.

As for the CSC, it contended that its policy of refusing to place preoperative male-to-female transsexuals in a female penitentiary constituted no more than a demonstrably justifiable restriction of their equality rights because incarcerating an anatomically male transsexual who had yet to undergo sex reassignment surgery in a women's penitentiary would require such extraordinary measures for the protection of female prisoners as to constitute an undue hardship on the CSC. In rebuttal, the Canadian Human Rights Commission told the tribunal that the CSC has a responsibility to deal with all assaults in a penitentiary, be they committed by males on males in a male penitentiary, by females on females in a female penitentiary, or by preoperative transsexual males incarcerated with females in a joint male-female institution. Citing the judgment of the British Columbia Human Rights Tribunal in *Sheridan,* the commission contended that preoperative male-to-female transsexuals are females for the purposes of the law and, therefore, are legally entitled to be incarcerated in a prison for women.

The tribunal in *Kavanagh* rejected the commission's argument on this point, claiming that the *Sheridan* precedent was not germane to preoperative transsexual prisoners because it dealt only with the refusal of a bar to admit a cross-dressing man to a women's washroom. While acknowledging that "there may well be situations where it is appropriate to treat pre-operative transsexuals as members of the target gender," the tribunal held that incarcerating a preoperative male transsexual in an institution for female prisoners would be inappropriate. Referring to anatomically female prisoners, the tribunal said: "It appears from the evidence that many of these women are psychologically damaged, as a consequence of the physical, psychological and sexual abuse they have suffered at the hands of men. Like transsexuals, female inmates are a vulnerable group, who are entitled to have their needs recognized and respected." Recall, however, that the Vancouver Rape Relief Society advanced much the same argument in *Nixon,* claiming that women who have suffered physical, psychological, and sexual abuse at the hands of men should not be required by the British Columbia Human Rights Commission to undergo rape crisis counselling at the hands of a male-to-female transsexual. Even though the British

Columbia Human Rights Tribunal had rejected this argument in *Nixon* and directed that Rape Relief must allow both pre- and post-operative transsexuals to counsel the female victims of male violence, the Canadian Human Rights Tribunal held in *Kavanagh* that vulnerable female prisoners have a right not to associate in prison with preoperative male-to-female transsexuals.

According to Laishes, there were only ten preoperative transsexuals in the federal prison system in November 2000. For the potential benefit of these ten felons, a three-person tribunal held nine days of hearings in Vancouver and another two days in Joliette. Was this an appropriate use of taxpayers' funds? Should the Canadian Human Rights Commission have interfered in a dispute over sex reassignment surgery between a convicted murderer and the CSC? Who should have ultimate responsibility for setting policy for transsexual prisoners – the minister of correctional services, who has access to the collective wisdom of the public service and is accountable to Parliament, or the Canadian Human Rights Tribunal, which acts independently of Parliament and has demonstrated little understanding of the complexities of guarding, treating, and safeguarding transsexual prisoners?

It might be supposed that regardless of the impact on female prisoners, at least preoperative male-to-female transsexuals in the prison system have benefited from the tribunal's ruling in *Kavanagh*. However, even this assumption is questionable. While the three psychiatrists and the psychologist who testified before the tribunal agreed with the tribunal's finding that sex reassignment surgery is "a recognized and appropriate treatment for properly screened candidates," there is no consensus within the medical community on the issue. To the contrary, the appropriateness of sex reassignment surgery is a matter of intense medical controversy. One of the most prominent critics of this surgery is Dr John McHugh, University Distinguished Service Professor of Psychiatry at the Johns Hopkins University School of Medicine in Baltimore. It was the Johns Hopkins psychiatry department that originally proposed sex reassignment surgery as an appropriate treatment for transsexuals. Upon taking over as psychiatrist in chief at Johns Hopkins in 1975, McHugh directed a colleague, Dr Jon Meyer, to proceed with research on the psychiatric effects of sex reassignment surgery. Meyer found that men who had undergone the treatment at John Hopkins did not improve psychologically. McHugh relates: "They had much the same problems with relationships, work, and emotions as before. The hope that they would emerge now from their emotional difficulties to flourish psychologically had not been fulfilled."[19]

For this reason, the Johns Hopkins psychiatry department ceased to prescribe sex reassignment surgery. Almost all hospitals in North America have done the same. In McHugh's opinion, the experiment with sex reassignment surgery has been a tragic failure in the treatment of transsexuals. Speaking on behalf of his fellow psychiatrists, he confesses: "We have wasted scientific and technical resources and damaged our professional credibility by collaborating with madness rather than trying to study, cure, and ultimately prevent it."[20]

Regardless of this controversy over the appropriateness of sex reassignment surgery, the Canadian Human Rights Tribunal has ordered the CSC to make the procedure available at taxpayers' expense for all qualifying inmates in federal penitentiaries. The panel that made this decision consisted of two lawyers and a government bureaucrat: respectively, Anne Mactavish, then chair of the Canadian Human Rights Tribunal; Grant Sinclair, the current chair; and Sarah Goldstein, a part-time member of the tribunal. They asserted: "All of the experts agree that sex reassignment surgery is a legitimate, medically recognized treatment for Transsexualism, in properly selected individuals." Evidently, none of these tribunal panellists was aware of the devastating criticisms of sex reassignment surgery expressed by Dr McHugh and other well-informed authorities.

Like human rights adjudicators and judges, politicians and bureaucrats can also make ill-informed decisions with potentially tragic consequences. The difference is that politicians and bureaucrats can readily change their policies, as did the Government of Ontario in 1998 when it reversed a decision made in 1969 to list sex reassignment surgery as a medical service covered by the Ontario Health Insurance Plan (OHIP). The Canadian Human Rights Tribunal does not have the same flexibility: It cannot say: "Sorry, we made a mistake in *Kavanagh*. In the light of new research by leading psychiatrists that demonstrates the tragic failure of sex reassignment surgery to benefit transsexuals, we hereby reverse our ruling that Correctional Services Canada must make this surgery available at taxpayers' expense to all qualifying transsexual inmates in federal custody."

As it is, the delisting of sex reassignment surgery has become a hot political issue in Ontario. Egale Canada, a federally subsidized lobby that styles itself as "a national organization that advances equality and justice for lesbian, gay, bisexual, and trans-identified people and their families across Canada," has launched a campaign to restore funding for sex reassignment surgery under OHIP.[21] Marilyn Churley, deputy leader of the Ontario New Democratic Party, has lent her support to the cause. She says that the McGuinty Liberal government gave members of the homosexual community the impression that these medical procedures would be reinstated under OHIP. Therefore, she says: "The government should restore funding immediately."[22]

What, however, is the point of having the Ontario Legislature reexamine this issue? On 30 April 1999 Michelle Josef, a male-to-female transsexual, filed a "notice of constitutional question" with the Ontario Superior Court of Justice challenging the constitutional validity of the 1998 government regulation under the Ontario Health Insurance Act that delisted sex reassignment surgery on the ground that it discriminates on the basis of sex, disability, and/or gender identity in violation of the equality rights of transsexuals as guaranteed in section 15 of the Charter.[23] Meanwhile, four transsexuals have also filed complaints with the Ontario Human Rights Commission, variously charging that the delisting of sex reassignment surgery violates their rights to freedom from discrimination on the basis of sex and/or disability in section 1 of the Ontario Human Rights Code. On 16 December 2002 the commission brought the matter before the Human Rights Tribunal of Ontario. What will happen if, after years of the usual delay in these cases, the tribunal and the courts decree that the Government of Ontario is obligated by the Ontario Human Rights Code and the Charter to resume funding for sex reassignment surgery under OHIP? Regardless of all the other pressing priorities for medicare, the Ontario government and the Legislature will be compelled to obey this judicial edict unless they are willing to invoke the notwithstanding clause of the Constitution as a means of reasserting the ultimate authority of the Legislature to determine which services qualify for coverage under OHIP.

Premier McGuinty and his fellow Liberals have sworn that they will never invoke the notwithstanding clause of the Constitution. In doing so, they have effectively surrendered to unelected and unaccountable judges the ultimate authority formerly exercised by elected representatives of the people in the Ontario Legislature to determine public policy and spending decisions. Such is the sorry state of democracy in Ontario.

PERMISSIBLE AND IMPERMISSIBLE DISCRIMINATION

Within the tangled web of Canadian human rights laws, members of some favoured groups are allowed to practise the kind of discrimination that is forbidden to everyone else. For example, in section 14(1), the Ontario Human Rights Code provides that the bans on fourteen different kinds of discrimination in part 1 of the Code do not apply to any "special program designed to relieve hardship or economic disadvantage or to assist disadvantaged persons or groups to achieve or attempt to achieve equal opportunity or that is likely to contribute to the elimination of the infringement of rights under Part 1." Section 15(2) of the Canadian Charter of Rights and Freedoms likewise stipulates that the wide-ranging ban on discrimination in section 15(1) "does not preclude any law, program or activity that has as its object the amelioration of conditions of disadvantaged individuals or groups including those that are disadvantaged because of race, national or ethnic origin, colour, religion, sex, age, or mental or physical disability."

Consider the application of these provisions to the strange case of Justine Blainey. As a ten year old, she had enough talent as a hockey player to compete with the boys in the Metro Toronto Hockey League but was not allowed to join one of the boys' teams because of a league rule barring female players. Blainey's mother complained to the Ontario Human Rights Commission, accusing the league of practising unfair sex discrimination.[24] Initially, the commission rejected the complaint, citing section 19(2) of the 1981 Ontario Human Rights Code, which stipulated that membership in an athletic organization or competition could be limited to persons of the same sex, notwithstanding the ban on sex discrimination in section 1 of the Code. During deliberations on the 1981 Code in the Ontario Legislature, representatives of several organizations, including the School of Physical and Health Education of the University of Toronto, submitted briefs opposing sex segregation in sports. Judith Keene notes in *Human Rights in Ontario*: "In the light of these efforts, s. 19(2) of the 1981 Code was obviously a firm legislative policy in support of sex-segregated athletics in Ontario."[25]

Regardless, lawyers for Blainey went to court, arguing that section 19(2) violated the equality rights of female hockey players under section 15(1) of the Charter. In a turnaround, counsel for the commission now agreed with this argument. Fran Rider of the Ontario Women's Hockey Association was incensed. She defended the section 19(2) exemption for all-male sport leagues on the ground that forcing the Ontario Hockey Association to admit female athletes would ruin her league. She argued: "With uncontrolled emigration of girls to boys' teams, girls' teams will fold, and many girls unwilling or unable to compete with boys will have no chance to play. This is equality?"[26]

The Ontario Court of Appeal rejected Rider's argument and overturned the considered judgment of the Ontario Legislature by resolving in *Blainey v. Ontario Hockey Association*, 1986 OCA, to strike down section 19(2) on the ground that maintenance of an all-male hockey league violates the equality rights of female athletes to an extent that cannot be demonstrably justified in a free and democratic society. Subsequently, the Supreme Court of Canada refused leave to appeal the ruling, but this did not put an end to sexual discrimination in sport. Within a few months of the *Blainey* decision, an Ontario human rights board of inquiry held that although the Ontario Hockey Association must admit qualified female athletes, the Ontario Women's Hockey Association can go on barring qualified male athletes because female hockey players are a disadvantaged group that is legally permitted to discriminate against males under terms of section 14(1) of the Ontario Human Rights Code.[27]

As a result of these rulings, Blainey was free to play hockey with the boys within the Ontario Hockey Association. Later, when she could no longer compete with the boys, she switched to the all-female Mississauga Chiefs, a Senior AAA team within the Ontario Women's Hockey Association. Her case reflects the current state of the law in Ontario: Regardless of the express will of the elected representatives of the people in the Ontario Legislature, a provincial board of inquiry and the courts have decreed that females have a right to play in all-male leagues but that boys have no right to play in all-female leagues.

The Supreme Court of Canada has been no less zealous to uphold special rights for women. In *Action Travail des Femmes v. Canadian National Railway Co.*, 1987 SCC, the Court ruled that an affirmative action program that discriminates in favour of women at the expense of men is permitted by section 15 of the Charter. This judgment has had a wide-ranging impact. While few males have suffered from sex discrimination by all-female athletic teams, a great many men have become prime targets for reverse discrimination in education, employment, and numerous other areas under Canadian human rights laws.[28] In November 1993 the Ontario Management Board Secretariat went so far as to place an advertisement in *Jobmart*, an official publication of the Ontario government, advising that the board was conducting a competition for a position as director of information technology that was open to everyone except able-bodied white males. The advertisement stated: "As a positive initiative under the Ontario Public Service employment equity program and consistent with the Ontario Human Rights Code, this competition is limited to the following employment equity designated groups: aboriginal peoples, francophones, persons with disabilities, racial minorities and women."[29] Such blatant discrimination by a government agency provoked an uproar in the Legislature and a reversal of policy by the province's New Democratic Party government. Premier Bob Rae told the Legislature: "An ad which says that someone cannot even apply is wrong. That's wrong and we should not hesitate to say that on the basis of the experience and on the basis of the very clear message that we're getting from the people of the province ... We have to make it very clear that that will not happen again and that indeed the policy that led to that advertisement needs to be reviewed."[30] Rae followed up on this commitment: He not only reviewed, but also abolished, the offensive policy.

Meanwhile, on the federal level, successive Progressive Conservative and Liberal governments have routinely practised overt discrimination against able-bodied white males in hiring and promotion. Such policies did not sit well with Danny Pruden, a freelance editorial cartoonist for the *Winnipeg Sun*. On 12 July 2001, he provoked a national uproar with a cartoon depicting a man applying to Winnipeg mayor Glen Murray for a job, saying: "I'm uneducated. I'm illiterate. I have no experience but I'm a visible minority." Murray is portrayed as responding: "Welcome aboard!" Louis Ifill of the Workers of Colour Support Network in Winnipeg denounced the cartoon as racist.[31] Pruden, who is a Cree, rejected the charge.

The federal Department of Human Resources Development gave a striking demonstration of its understanding of equality rights under the Charter in an advertisement inviting applications for the position of "team leader" within the department's "visible minority recruitment program."[32] The advertisement stated: "Human Resources Development Canada, as an equal opportunity employer, is committed to achieving a skilled workforce that reflects the diversity of the Canadian population. In support of attaining such a workforce, this opportunity is limited to those persons belonging to a visible minority group. Applicants must clearly self-identify as belonging to such a group." Note the irony: The department avows that it is "an equal opportunity employer" yet advised that no white man or white woman was eligible for this advertised position. In fact, not even an Aboriginal like Pruden could have applied for this job because the Public Service Commission of Canada, which does hiring for the federal government, defines a member of a "visible minority group" as "someone, other than an Aboriginal person, who is non-white in colour/race, regardless of his/her place of birth."[33] For greater certainty, the commission currently lists more than twenty subgroups within the category of visible minorities, including "indigenous persons from Central and South America."[34] As a result, Aboriginal immigrants from Latin America can apply for a government job that is denied to Canadian-born status Indians, non-status Indians, and Métis. And this is the policy of a government that prides itself as "an equal-opportunity employer."

Granted, the Public Service Commission routinely lists other jobs within the federal public service that are open only to Canadian Aboriginals. But this policy has created conundrums of its own: When is an Aboriginal not an Aboriginal? How much Native blood does a person need to have running through his or her veins to qualify as a Métis?

Unlike Premier Rae, who declared on behalf of his Ontario New Democratic Party more than ten years ago that "an ad which says that someone cannot even apply is wrong," the Liberal, New Democratic, and Bloc Quebecois parties on the federal level still maintain that there is nothing wrong with discriminating against some groups of people for the benefit of others in government employment. Note that in the past, the targets of unfair discrimination were mainly Jews, Orientals, and blacks. Today, the prime victims are heterosexual, able-bodied, white males. Even the poorest and most disadvantaged of white men are not allowed to apply for many plum posts in the federal public sector, yet these posts are open to privileged individuals from well-off families who happen to be female, black, gay, or a member of some other group designated for preferential treatment.

Ruth Gruhn, professor emerita of anthropology at the University of Alberta, Edmonton, has observed that people who suffer the most from affirmative action are sometimes members of the groups that these policies are supposed to benefit. She notes: "Many university departments now have an explicit policy of hiring a man only if he is 'significantly' or 'demonstrably' superior to any available woman candidate; obviously if a man is hired, he must look damned good as compared to a woman."[35] Thanks to a distinguished publishing record, Gruhn has a well-established international reputation for academic excellence. Unlike most females, blacks, Aboriginals, gays, and members of other groups designated for preferential treatment on and off campus, she has not had to live down the suspicion that she owed her position to discrimination against better qualified individuals. In agreement with such prominent African Americans as Professor Stephen L. Carter of the Yale Law School,[36] Professor Thomas Sowell, an economist and philosopher at Stanford University,[37] and Mr Justice Clarence Thomas of the United States Supreme Court,[38] she insists that employment equity and affirmative action are wrong. She rejects all government-enforced discrimination in hiring, promotion, and the provision of public services as unfair, unjust, divisive, and harmful to all concerned.

As the cases of Haskett, Owens, and Whatcott make clear, Canadians are no longer secure even in their basic rights to freedom of expression. In this respect, the people of Ontario should especially beware: Section 13(1) of the Ontario Human Rights Act prohibits anyone from publishing or displaying before the public "any notice, sign, symbol, emblem, or other similar representation that indicates the intention of the person to infringe a right under Part 1 or that is intended by the person to incite the infringement of a right under Part 1." (Part 1 is the section of the Code that bans discrimination on the basis of any of fourteen different grounds.) Note that it is an offence under section 13(1) merely to announce one's intention to violate the equal treatment provisions of part 1, regardless of whether this intention is carried into action. Thus Mayor Diane Haskett of London and Mayor Bob Morrow of Hamilton had broken the law simply by disclosing that they did not intend to issue gay pride proclamations. Professor Ian Hunter comments: "Although a refined sense of ethics or morality might condemn intention standing alone, the law has always required an overt act. Indeed, the requirement that intention manifests itself in criminal behaviour is one point of distinction between the rule of law and totalitarian legal systems. [Section 13(1)], apparently, tends to eliminate the distinction, and assigns liability on the basis of a declared intention alone. By so doing, it lends credence to those critics who consider that human rights commissions have become the 'thought police' of contemporary society."[39]

Note also that section 13(1) bans the incitement of an infringement of part 1. It follows that anyone who publicly supports the determination of a mayor not to issue a gay pride proclamation could be summoned before an Ontario human rights tribunal and ordered to apologize for offending gays. And those who refuse to obey such an order could end up in jail on a charge of contempt of court.

Despite the unprecedented restrictions on freedom of expression imposed in section 13(1) of the Ontario Human Rights Code, section 13(2) of this same Code states that "Subsection (1) shall not interfere with freedom of expression of opinion." In view of the Owens case, no one should be taken in by this sham guarantee of freedom of expression. Robert Martin, a professor of constitutional law at the University of Western Ontario, warns: "In its crusade to free us from discrimination, the Human Rights Commission has shown little respect for other rights. Free expression, or so the Commission believes, can be used to perpetuate discrimination. So freedom of expression must give way.[40]

Even the rule of law must give way to the determination of human rights commissions to stamp out prohibited forms of discrimination. Prior to enactment of the Canadian Charter of Rights and Freedoms and the corresponding federal and provincial human rights laws, Canadians could foresee with fair certainty what the law requires under the great majority of circumstances. Today, there is no such certainty. The rule of law has, to an alarming extent, given way to the arbitrary rule of human rights adjudicators and judges. All too often, the most conscientious and law-abiding citizen cannot know what the vague and sweeping provisions of these laws require in a particular circumstance until a human rights tribunal and the courts come up with a ruling. Recall the plight of the Vancouver Rape Relief Society. After more than nine years of litigation and a series of contradictory rulings by the British Columbia Human Rights Tribunal and the courts, it is still not clear whether the members of this voluntary association are legally obligated by the British Columbia Human Rights Code and the Canadian Charter of Rights and Freedoms to allow a transsexual man to train and serve as a voluntary rape crisis counsellor for their feminist group. Likewise, given the proclivity of human rights tribunals and the courts to create new rights for transsexuals, the leaders of a battered women's shelter in Ontario can have no way of knowing whether, or to what extent, they remain free under the law to refuse to accommodate a preoperative male-to-female transsexual in a shelter for women.

Not even powerful corporate managers are immune from the legal turmoil engendered by expansive human rights laws. Consider the treatment meted out to Imperial Oil Ltd. by the Ontario Human Rights Commission in a dispute over the company's policies on alcohol and drug abuse.[41] Imperial Oil had been prompted to revise these policies by a number of industrial accidents in the oil industry, including the Exxon Valdez disaster in 1989, which saw an oil-laden tanker under the control of an allegedly inebriated captain run aground in Alaska. To avoid such a calamity in Ontario, Imperial Oil introduced a comprehensive policy on alcohol and drug abuse on 1 January 1992, which required an employee in a safety-sensitive position in one of the company's Ontario plants to disclose any current or past "substance abuse problem." The policy stipulated that upon disclosure of such a problem, the employee shall be transferred to a nonsafety-sensitive position and can only be reinstated in a safety-sensitive job after completing a two-year rehabilitation program and five years of abstinence from alcohol and drug abuse.

In response to the adoption of this policy, Martin Entrop, a senior control board operator at Imperial Oil's Sarnia refinery, told management that he was a recovered alcoholic who had been sober continuously for the past seven years. Imperial Oil immediately reassigned him to a nonsafety-sensitive job with the same pay. Entrop found the new job to be less desirable than his previous one, so he filed a complaint with the Ontario Human Rights Commission on 16 January 1992 alleging that Imperial Oil had violated "his right to equal treatment in employment without discrimination ... because of my handicap and perceived handicap contrary to s. 5(1) of the Ontario Human Rights Code (1990)." Imperial Oil promptly arranged for a thorough medical evaluation of Entrop, which established that he no longer had a problem with alcohol abuse. On 26 May 1992 the company reinstated him in his old job, notwithstanding the announced policy of requiring employees to forgo a safety-sensitive job for several years following disclosure of an alcohol or drug abuse problem.

Despite Entrop's reinstatement, the Ontario Human Rights Commission referred his complaint to an Ontario human rights board of inquiry. The case was assigned to Constance Backhouse, then a law professor at the University of Western Ontario.[42] She began her hearings in August 1994 and proceeded over the next two years to issue no fewer than eight interim decisions before winding up the case with a final ruling on 12 September 1996.

In the sixth of these interim decisions on 23 June 1995, Backhouse dealt specifically with Entrop's complaint that Imperial Oil had discriminated against him on the basis of his handicap as an alcoholic, contrary to section 5(1) of the Ontario Human Rights Code. Imperial Oil argued that alcoholism is not a handicap within the meaning of section 10(1)(a) of the Code, which defines "handicap" as "any degree of physical disability, infirmity, malformation or disfigurement that is caused by bodily injury, birth defect or illness and, without limiting the generality of the foregoing, includes diabetes mellitus, epilepsy, any degree of paralysis, amputation, lack of physical co-ordination, blindness or visual impediment, deafness or hearing impediment, muteness or speech impediment, or physical reliance on a guide dog or other animal or on a wheelchair or other remedial appliance or device."

There is no mention of alcohol in section 10 or in any other section of the Ontario Human Rights Code. Naturally, this was of no account to Backhouse. She held that alcohol abuse constitutes a handicap within the large and liberal meaning that she attributed to section 5(1). She further found that in removing Entrop from his safety-sensitive position, Imperial Oil had unlawfully discriminated against him on the basis of his alcohol handicap because the company could not establish that alcoholism had adversely affected his performance on the job. She also found that Imperial Oil managers had retaliated against Entrop for complaining to the Ontario Human Rights Commission. As compensation, she awarded him \$10,000 in general damages, \$10,000 for mental anguish, and \$1,214.93 for lost overtime pay in his reassigned job.

Part way through the *Entrop* hearings, Backhouse announced that in addition to dealing with Entrop's specific complaints, she would evaluate the legality of a provision in Imperial Oil's policy that required employees in safety-sensitive positions to undergo random tests for illegal drugs. This issue had nothing to do with the *Entrop* case: He had not made any complaint about the drug testing. Regardless, Backhouse went on in her eighth interim decision in *Entrop* to rule that drug abuse, like alcohol abuse, is a handicap under the Code and that Imperial Oil could not lawfully fire an employee in a safety-sensitive position for failing a urinalysis test for an illegal substance because the test cannot prove that the drug abuser was impaired while on the job.

Did this decision conform with the rule of law? To paraphrase Hayek, did Backhouse's ruling affirm rules fixed and announced beforehand? Obviously not. Imperial Oil could not have foreseen with fair certainty that the board of inquiry would use its coercive powers to prevent management from transferring an employee from a safety-sensitive position because the employee tests positive for an illicit drug, the unauthorized possession of which was a criminal offence under the existing Narcotic Control Act.[43]

Just a few months prior to Backhouse's ruling that prohibited random drug testing in *Entrop,* a three-person panel of the Canadian Human Rights Tribunal headed by Keith Norton, currently chief commissioner of the Ontario Human Rights Commission, had unanimously approved random drug testing in *Canadian Civil Liberties Association v. Toronto Dominion Bank,* 1994 CHRT. In the judgment of Norton's panel, a federally regulated company could lawfully fire an employee who persistently tests positive for an illicit drug even if the employee is not in a safety-sensitive position. The federal tribunal arrived at this determination despite the explicit ban on discrimination on the basis of a "previous or existing dependence on alcohol or a drug" in the Canadian Human Rights Act. Norton and Backhouse are two of the country's most experienced human rights adjudicators. Yet they could not agree on the application of human rights law to random drug testing in the workplace. Under these circumstances, it is obvious that Imperial Oil could not have known with any certainty that aspects of its drug policy were illegal. The company had no reason to suppose that it could not test employees in safety-sensitive positions for illicit drugs until Backhouse handed down her rulings in *Entrop.*

In an attempt to clear up the confusion over the legality of random drug testing, Imperial Oil appealed Backhouse's *Entrop* rulings first to the Ontario Court of Justice (General Division) and then to the Ontario Court of Appeal. Like the Canadian and Ontario human rights tribunals, these two courts also could not agree on the legality of drug testing in relation to the Ontario Human Rights Code. While the Ontario Divisional Court sided with Backhouse on all points, the Court of Appeal impugned her decision to broaden the inquiry into the drug issue. In a judgment written by Mr Justice John Laskin, a three-judge panel of the Appeal Court held that Backhouse "lacked a proper factual underpinning" to rule on drug testing because Entrop had never been tested for drugs and had no history of drug abuse.[44] Laskin observed: "The courts have, with good reason, been wary about resolving disputes that do not have a proper factual or evidentiary foundation." Quite so. Just a few years ago, Canadian judges were constrained by the rules of the common law to confine their rulings to live matters of dispute before the court. Today, activist judges know no such restraint. In *Entrop,* Laskin argued: "The Board had no jurisdiction to inquire into drug testing. That said, because both the Board and the Divisional Court have considered whether the drug testing provisions of the Policy violate the Code, practically I see no alternative but to do so as well."

Is this not astounding? Despite having acknowledged that neither the board of inquiry, the Divisional Court, nor the Court of Appeal had any proper factual, evidentiary, or jurisdictional foundation for ruling on the legality of Imperial Oil's drug testing policy, Laskin plunged blindly into these same uncharted legal waters. First, he observed: "Common sense and experience suggest that an accident at a refinery can have catastrophic results for employees, the public and the environment. Promoting workplace safety by minimizing the possibility employees will be impaired by either alcohol or drugs while working is a legitimate objective." Laskin also noted that the board had found "that drug testing programs have not been shown to be effective in reducing drug use, work accidents or work performance problems." He then concluded: "On these findings, random drug testing for employees in safety-sensitive positions cannot be justified as reasonably necessary to accomplish Imperial Oil's legitimate goal of a safe workplace free of impairment."

Consider the implications of this ruling. Without any proper factual or evidentiary basis, the Ontario Court of Appeal upheld the board of inquiry in imposing a ban on drug testing for employees in safety-sensitive positions. Subsequently, in a two-to-one ruling on 23 July 1998, the Federal Court of Appeal overturned the decision of the Canadian Human Rights Tribunal in *Canadian Civil Liberties Association v. Toronto Dominion Bank,* which upheld the policy of the bank to fire an employee who either refuses to undergo a test for illicit drugs or fails the test three times.[45] And on 10 July 2002 the Canadian Human Rights Commission announced a new drug policy that bans random drug testing of all employees, including those in safety-sensitive positions.[46] One can only hope that these ill-considered acts of judicial legislation by our human rights commissions, human rights tribunals, and the courts will not result in a catastrophic industrial accident.

EQUALITY OF RESULTS TRUMPS FREEDOM

In proceedings before a human rights tribunal, the deck is stacked against the respondent. While the complainant typically enjoys free legal representation provided by the prosecuting human rights commission at taxpayers' expense, the respondent can easily get stuck with more than $100,000 in legal bills if the case ends up in the courts. For many small businesses, voluntary associations, and private individuals, this is a daunting prospect. Faced with the unjust demands of a human rights commission, less-than-wealthy respondents can hardly be faulted for not attempting to defend themselves. Sometimes, even the best, most expensive counsel can be of little benefit to an innocent party appearing before a human rights tribunal. Under the peculiar rules of procedure and evidence governing these tribunals, the complainant and prosecuting human rights commission are allowed to introduce hearsay evidence and rely entirely on indirect evidence to build their case. They are under no obligation even to establish that the respondent acted with a guilty intent or with reckless disregard for the law. Anyone who is summoned before a human rights tribunal for allegedly violating one of the vague and imprecise provisions of a human rights code can lose the case even if he or she has been entirely innocent of any intentional wrongdoing.

Worse, the respondent in a human rights proceeding can have no confidence of receiving a fair hearing before an independent and impartial adjudicator. Professor Martin warns that in a typical case: "The hearing will be conducted by someone who does this sort of thing part-time, often to supplement the income gained from a well-paid full-time job. It is likely this person will also be sympathetic to the Commission and has a proven record of resolving hearings in favour of complainants."[47] Moreover, this person has extraordinary powers. He or she can order the respondent to apologize to the complainant, to pay substantial damages to the complainant, and to accommodate the needs of the complainant by all means short of "undue hardship." Should the respondent refuse to abide by a court order upholding the ruling of a human rights tribunal, he or she can be incarcerated for contempt of court.

What is the purpose of the enormous and arbitrary powers that the various federal and provincial human rights codes have conferred upon human rights tribunals? With reference to the Ontario version, Justice McIntyre of the Supreme Court of Canada put the matter succinctly: "The Code aims at the removal of discrimination."[48] Surely, such a utopian goal is incompatible with freedom under law. Not even the most brutal dictatorship could come close to stamping out all forms of discrimination.

Certainly, Canada's human rights commissions have shown that they are not up to the task. They have all demonstrated an inability to make timely decisions on the admittedly huge number of complaints that they receive of unfair discrimination. For example, the Ontario Human Rights Commission disclosed in its *Annual Report: 2003–2004* that it had accumulated an active caseload of 2,549 on 31 March 2005, up from 2,137 a year earlier.[49] The report also indicated that it had taken an average of 10.8 months to complete cases closed in the previous year. On the federal level, the Canadian Human Rights Commission reported that it had an active caseload of 955 in 2004 but was taking "just over 12 months" to complete a case.[50]

The great majority of human rights cases are settled between the parties without the need for adjudication. Disputes that end up before a board of inquiry can take years to resolve. The epic conflict between Mike Naraine and the Ford Motor Company of Canada is all too common.[51] Naraine, who self-identifies as an East Indian, was born in Guyana in 1943, immigrated to Canada in 1967, and began to work for Ford in 1976 as an electrician at a company plant in Windsor. Between 1982 and 1985, he was cited for five disciplinary incidents and accumulated thirty-one days of suspension. On 19 August 1985 Ford fired him for injuring a fellow worker in a fight at the plant.

On 24 May 1985 and again on 24 October 1985, Naraine filed complaints with the Ontario Human Rights Commission alleging that Ford and certain Ford employees had infringed his right to equal treatment with respect to employment because of his race, colour, place of origin, and ethnic origin, contrary to sections 4(1), 4(2), 7, 8, and 10 of the 1981 Ontario Human Rights Code. Naraine also grieved his dismissal through his union, the Canadian Auto Workers (CAW). In February 1986 an independent arbitrator appointed under the Labour Relations Act ruled that the company had been justified in firing Naraine because he had struck and injured a fellow worker.

In the spring of 1987 Naraine went to work for General Motors. Two years later, General Motors also fired him for an alleged physical confrontation with a supervisor. Naraine filed yet another complaint with the Ontario Human Rights Commission, accusing General Motors of racial discrimination. Rather than dispute the allegation, General Motors settled with Naraine for $15,000.

Meanwhile, the Ontario Human Rights Commission continued to back Naraine's complaints against Ford, and the company refused to capitulate. After almost eight years of plodding investigation and delay, the commission referred the matter to a human rights board of inquiry in February 1993. In a ruling on 25 July 1996, Constance Backhouse, the board chair, found that the Ford plant was rife with racism although she conceded that in the fight that led to Naraine's dismissal, his antagonist was an immigrant from Ecuador "who appears to have been designated as 'non-white' according to the workers in the plant." Regardless, Backhouse concluded: "On the facts before me, I find that there is a causal connection between the poisoned working environment and the discipline and ultimate termination meted out to Mr. Naraine ... The real reason for his termination was not the altercation with a fellow worker, but the underlying factors of racial discrimination and harassment. By disciplining an employee in such circumstances, an employer is condoning the discriminatory conduct." Finally, on 9 December 1996 Backhouse directed that Ford must reinstate Naraine, provide him with retraining and employment-assistance counselling, restore his seniority, compensate him for the income and benefits that he would have received between his firing in August 1985 and hiring at General Motors in the spring of 1987, and pay him an additional $30,000 plus prejudgment interest for mental anguish, the infringement of his rights, and "his experiences of victimization."

Ford appealed to the Divisional Court. On 23 June 1999 the Court sided with Backhouse. Ford took the case to the Ontario Court of Appeal. In a ruling on 14 December 2001 the Court of Appeal sustained Backhouse in all respects but one: The Appeal Court held that Ford was not obligated to rehire Naraine on the ground that the company's liability to him had terminated when he obtained a comparable job at General Motors. Thus ended this dispute, more than sixteen years after Naraine had filed his original complaint against Ford with the Ontario Human Rights Commission. The company must have squandered hundreds of thousands of dollars on legal bills alone for all the litigation in this case. In comparison, the $15,000 settlement paid by General Motors to Naraine was a bargain.

In her ruling on 25 July 1996, Backhouse took note of the delay in settling the *Naraine* dispute. She said: "The adjudication phase of this complaint added more than three years to the almost eight years that can be laid at the foot of the Commission. No one's interests are served by this sort of record, which is all too reminiscent of Charles Dickens' 'Bleak House.'" Quite so. Proceedings before the Ontario Human Rights Tribunal resemble nothing so much as the interminable chancery suit of Jarndyce v. Jarndyce depicted in *Bleak House.* It could have been an encounter with a Canadian human rights tribunal that prompted the exclamation of Mr Bumble: "The law is a ass – a idiot."

In her *Naraine* ruling, Backhouse underlined:

> The systemic practices which lie at the root of these delays urgently require alteration ... Studies such as the Cornish Task Force Report: Ontario Human Rights Code Review Task Force, Achieving Equality: A Report on Human Rights Reform (Toronto: Ontario Ministry of Citizenship, 1992), which diagnose some of the ills of human rights procedures and recommend significant changes, lie gathering dust. It bears repeating that due to the Supreme Court of Canada's ruling in *Bhadauria*,[52] human rights disputes in Ontario presently have no where else to go but through this torturous route. Those who find themselves to be involved with violations of the Human Rights Code cannot resort to the civil courts directly. That an administrative process which is theoretically supposed to offer speed, flexibility and efficiency offers so little to its litigants is cause for urgent and significant response.[53]

The Cornish Task Force alluded to by Backhouse was appointed in 1991 by the Rae government to find solutions for the chronic delays afflicting the human rights process in Ontario. Mary Cornish, a prominent human rights lawyer, headed the inquiry. Together with two other human rights activists, Rick Miles and Ratna Omidvar, she was mandated to "review the process for the enforcement of human rights" and "examine the features of the current procedures which may limit fair and timely results."[54] In the final report of the Task Force, Cornish and her colleagues asserted:

> The Task Force is not naïve. It realizes that the job of ending discrimination in this province is a massive one and will not happen overnight ...
>
> The Task Force believes that the success of an enforcement system can ultimately be measured by one test – did the system lead to measurable and real reduction in the discrimination faced by its citizens who are protected by the Code.
>
> The Task Force believes that the current system fails this test. Persons and groups who experience discrimination are denied proper justice in the human rights enforcement system. The Task Force heard the frustration, anger, and impatience of people and groups who experience discrimination.[55]

Cornish and her colleagues rejected the option of turning human rights cases over to the civil courts because the judicial process is too slow and expensive. The Task Force said: "Specialized Equality Rights

Tribunals were set up precisely because the courts demonstrated a lack of knowledge and understanding of human rights."[56] In a research report for the Task Force, Robert Reid, a retired judge, averred: "Judges as a group have traditionally been drawn from social classes unsympathetic to social change. This has been perceived as clouding their judgement by inclining them to decide against the change the legislation seeks to achieve. Judges have been perceived as unsympathetic to the problems of the 'common man.'"[57]

If it is true that judges have been perceived as unsympathetic to the problems of the "common man," one wonders why criminal cases are not also turned over to human rights tribunals. Be that as it may, the Task Force concluded that "the courts are not expert in the subject matter of human rights and should not hear human rights cases."[58] Likewise, the Task Force held that enforcement of human rights laws through the criminal courts would be inappropriate because a prime aim of the Ontario Human Rights Code is to eliminate not just planned and deliberate discrimination, but also inadvertent, systemic discrimination in the form of rules and procedures that create barriers to equality for groups protected by the Code. For example, a police department might engage in systemic discrimination against women by adopting standards of strength and height for recruits that are tougher than what the job requires with the result that most female candidates fail to qualify. If systemic discrimination were a crime, the police supervisors who adopted such unduly stringent recruitment standards could not be successfully prosecuted unless the Crown could prove that the officers intended to discriminate against women. The Task Force explained: "In order to win a criminal case in the courts, it is necessary to prove beyond a reasonable doubt that a person intentionally carried out a criminal act. The Canadian Charter of Rights and Freedoms sets out a number of protections to ensure that an accused person's right to be presumed innocent is not infringed. The stress in a criminal case is on individual intent and guilt. The criminal process places a heavy burden on claimants, and criminal penalties are not conducive to seeking or imposing systemic remedies."[59]

Given a choice between protecting the rights of the innocent or eliminating discrimination, Cornish and her fellow Task Force members chose to slight the rights of the innocent. What the Province of Ontario needs, the Task Force concluded, is a powerful new Equality Rights Tribunal that can briskly stamp out discrimination, unencumbered by legal niceties. Consider some of the more striking recommendations of the Task Force:

- The Tribunal should be required to base its decision upon the real merits and justice of the case. It will not be bound to follow strict legal precedent but shall give a full opportunity for a hearing.[60]
- The Tribunal adjudicator shall have the power to order a Tribunal Officer to conduct any necessary investigation in order to ensure that the case is heard on its real merits or in order to delegate to the Officer the hearing of any evidence. A warrant should not be required.[61]
- The Tribunal should be able to accept any evidence which it believes is reliable and relevant whether it is allowed as evidence in court or not.[62]
- The Tribunal should have the exclusive jurisdiction to exercise its power to determine all questions of fact or law that arise in any matter before it.[63]
- In light of [the] informality of the process, and the elimination of a full appeal right, there should be no requirement to record evidence.[64]
- The $10,000 limit for an award for mental anguish should be removed, allowing the amount of the award to depend on the facts of the case.[65]
- The Tribunal should have the power to reconsider any decision and to vary, revoke, or substitute a new decision.[66]
- Apart from the power to reconsider, the Tribunal's decision should be final and protected from review by the courts except where the decision is patently unreasonable.[67]
- The Code should provide that orders of the Tribunal, when filed with the Ontario Court of Justice (General Division), have the same force and effect as an order of that Court and therefore can result in fines and/or a jail term for non-compliance.[68]
- The Code should be amended to increase the fines for obstruction of the Tribunal process or failure to comply with a Tribunal order to ... a minimum fine of $2,000 and a maximum fine of $200,000.[69]

What could be more ironical: To enhance the efficiency of the Ontario Human Rights Commission, the Cornish Task Force called upon the Ontario Legislature to quash some of the most basic human rights and fundamental freedoms of the people of Ontario. As envisioned by the Task Force, the Ontario Equality Rights Tribunal would have had greater arbitrary powers than any comparable agency in the history of parliamentary government in Canada. Indeed, it would have been more potent than any quasi-judicial body to arise in any common law country since the Long Parliament of England abolished the Star Chamber in 1641. In Iraq, Saddam Hussein authorized his police officers to seize evidence without a warrant; mandated his hand-picked judges to base their decisions entirely on hearsay evidence in unrecorded trials; and gave Iraqi defendants no right of appeal to an independent and impartial court on questions of fact or law. Is it not alarming that an official Task Force of the Ontario government recommended that essentially these same dictatorial procedures should apply in the province's so-called human rights tribunals?

If British Columbia had adopted the draconian rules recommended by the Cornish Task Force, members of the Vancouver Rape Relief Society would have been liable to a maximum fine of $200,000 and/or a jail term for refusing to train and employ a male-to-female transsexual as a rape crisis counsellor, yet Rape Relief would have had virtually no right of appeal to the courts, not even on an issue of Charter interpretation. The Cornish Task Force stated: "The power to decide all questions of law or fact will ensure the Tribunal can consider Charter issues relevant to its jurisdiction."[70] In this way, tribunal adjudicators, not the courts, would, in essence, have had the final say on the application of the Charter to all human rights cases.

Bob Rae's New Democratic Party government in Ontario declined to adopt the repressive measures recommended by the Cornish Task Force. Nonetheless, in 1992 the government rewarded Richard Miles for his service on the Cornish Task Force by appointing him to the Ontario Human Rights Commission. Ontario New Democrats deemed Miles well qualified to uphold the province's human rights act.

There is no disputing at least one finding of the Cornish Task Force: The Ontario Human Rights Code is wholly inadequate to the task of both "ending discrimination" and eradicating what the Task Force called the "blight of inequality." These twin objectives are incompatible. Suppose that all forms of discrimination were eradicated in Canada and the United States? Would whites enjoy proportionally equal representation to blacks in the National Basketball Association? Would Jews no longer be overrepresented in most law schools or Asians in most engineering faculties? Obviously not. Eliminating the so-called blight of inequality in these cases would require not a decrease, but an increase, in discrimination against blacks, Jews, and Asians for the benefit, mainly, of white Christians. The idea is appalling. Besides, it would not work. No government or police agency, no matter how powerful, can eradicate inequality. Lenin, Stalin, Mao, and Pol Pot all vainly tried to achieve an egalitarian utopia in their respective societies. Why should members of the Ontario Human Rights Commission think that with more power, they could succeed where these ruthless tyrants failed?

To mark the thirty-fifth anniversary of the Ontario Human Rights Commission, Chief Commissioner Norton wrote: "The search for equal treatment has led to something of a 'backlash' against human rights in the last few years. Books and articles decrying diversity or tolerance have fuelled not only an increase in the respectability of hate groups but they have generated a mini-industry of 'rights critics' who characterize progressive laws as threats and who see multiculturalism as a concession to 'special interests.'"[71]

Professor Sowell is one of those critics who does not share Norton's peculiar conception of human rights. In *Civil Rights: Rhetoric or Reality?* Sowell points out that preferential treatment for blacks serves mainly to benefit a relatively well-off minority of blacks like himself at the expense of disadvantaged blacks. He explains: "Affirmative action hiring pressures make it costly to have no minority employees, but continuing affirmative action pressures at the promotion and discharge phases also make it costly to have minority employees who do not work out well. The net effect is to increase the demand for highly qualified minority employees while decreasing the demand for less qualified minority employees or for those without a sufficient track record to reassure employers."[72]

Despite the failures of preferential treatment to help the neediest, proponents of employment equity and affirmative action for blacks keep pushing these unfair policies at the expense of mounting resentment against all blacks. Sowell observes that in the United States: "These resentments are increasingly expressed in hate groups like the Ku Klux Klan and the Nazis, which are gaining members not only among ignorant southern rednecks but also in more middle class and educated classes across the nation – in short, in places where they never had a foothold before. Earmarked benefits for blacks provide some of these hate groups' strongest appeals to whites, however little these earmarked policies actually help blacks, either absolutely or compared to more general social benefits that would not have the same potential for racial polarization."[73]

Sowell has documented case after case in which attempts to benefit disadvantaged women and minorities through hiring quotas and other forms of politically enforced preferential treatment have bred resentments and hatred. He has cited such failures of affirmative action not just in the United States, but in numerous other countries, ranging from India and Malaysia to Uganda and South Africa. Canada is no exception. In *The Pursuit of Division: Race, Gender, and Preferential Hiring in Canada,* Martin Loney has likewise shown how two decades of government-enforced preferential hiring policies in Canada has saddled the country with "an increasingly destructive agenda whose outcome is not unity, equality or fairness but division."[74]

Sowell and Loney champion equality of opportunity as traditionally understood. It is not academics like them who are fuelling hate groups but human rights zealots like Norton who are wedded to the vain pursuit of equality of results through the imposition of unfair, reverse discrimination for women, blacks, Aboriginals, gays, and other politically favoured groups at the expense, mainly, of white males and the disadvantaged.

The attempt to remove discrimination through the enforcement of human rights codes is not just Quixotic: It is wrong in principle because eliminating discrimination is incompatible with the preservation of freedom under law. Sowell has put the matter well: "If you are free only when others think you are right, then you are not free at all."[75] Sowell contends that the government of a well-ordered democracy should refrain from unfair discrimination in its own activities but safeguard the freedom of citizens in nongovernmental settings to "make their own decisions, without being second-guessed by political or legal authorities as to whether those decisions are wise or foolish, noble or mean ... The scope of those boundaries of immunity from public authority are the scope of people's rights. This is a process conception of rights – the legal ability of people to carry on a certain process without regard to the desirability of the particular results, as judged by others."[76]

In this precise sense, the people of Canada no longer have rights. Speaking in the British Columbia Legislature on 23 October 2002, Attorney General Geoff Plant denounced the province's system for enforcing human rights as "unreasonably complex, structurally flawed, burdensomely expensive and unnecessarily adversarial."[77] In an attempt to streamline and improve the system, he persuaded the Legislature to abolish the British Columbia Human Rights Commission while retaining the province's human rights tribunal.[78] This was an egregious error. In conformity with the process conception of human rights, the Legislature should have abolished the tribunal. And the same goes for Parliament and the legislatures: They should see to it that every human rights tribunal in Canada, federal and provincial, is eliminated. If human rights commissions are to be retained, they should have only educational and advisory powers. They should have no authority to stifle the freedom of Canadians, including the freedom to err. As Sowell persuasively argues, freedom of association is meaningless unless it includes freedom for Jews to establish all-Jewish businesses, freedom for blacks to form all-black schools, freedom for lesbians to associate only with lesbians, and freedom for boys to play hockey only with boys. Within broad limits clearly defined by law, freedom of association should even include freedom for bigots to associate peacefully only with bigots. Likewise, within similar limits, freedom of speech should include freedom for bigots to say bigoted things. Democracy postulates that freedom, including the freedom to err, is better than tyranny. Thomas Jefferson observed: "Sometimes it is said that man cannot be trusted with the government of himself. Can he, then, be trusted with the government of others? Or have we found angels in the forms of kings to govern him? Let history answer this question."[79]

Canada's supreme court judges and human rights commissioners are no angels, yet they have taken to changing the laws and governing the rest of us. Is this appropriate? In conformity with the principle that governments derive their just powers from the consent of the governed, should we, in Canada, not insist that our elected legislators curb the law-making powers assumed by our unelected and unaccountable judges? This is not a politically partisan question. Professor Robert Martin is a former candidate for the New Democratic Party in a federal election. Professor Ian Hunter is a conservative. Together, they and others like them spanning the political spectrum maintain that democracy and the rule of law are preferable to the autocratic and arbitrary rule of judicial legislators and human rights adjudicators.

As it is, few federal or provincial politicians have been willing to criticize the courts and human rights tribunals for even the most blatant encroachments upon the powers of the legislative branch of government. Mike Harris is no exception. In evaluating his performance as premier of Ontario in 1997, Martin said of this allegedly conservative politician that he "seems to be afraid to touch the Human Rights Commission. He has inflicted savage spending cuts on health care and social services, but the Commission has hardly been touched. Its annual operating budget was $13.2 million in 1994. For 1997–98 the actual operating budget has only slipped to $10.6 million. That's about $10.6 million more than it should be."[80]

What has gone wrong? Why have our elected legislators consistently acquiesced over the past twenty-five years to the freedom-stifling decisions of activist judges and human rights adjudicators? Hunter suggests that part of the answer lies in the observation of Alexis de Tocqueville that: "Democratic communities have a natural taste for freedom: left to themselves, they will seek it, cherish it, and view any privation of it with regret. But for equality, their passion is ardent, insatiable, incessant, invincible: they call for equality in freedom; and if they cannot obtain that, they still call for equality in slavery."[81]

Hunter adds:

> The rest of the answer, I venture to suggest, lies in the essentially theological nature of human rights legislation. To a secular society the quest for equality fulfils the same yearning as, in centuries past, did once the quest for God. The religious vision of heaven, a land beyond time and mortality and very far off,

has been replaced by a utopian vision of an egalitarian society, to be attained through Charters of Rights, Human Rights Codes, and affirmative action. To criticize human rights legislation and its premises is regarded as antediluvian, if not blasphemous. Because such statutes come clothed in the mantle of "human rights," with much reassuring talk of brotherhood and compassion, we are disinclined to reflect on the cost in human freedom which our relentless pursuit of equality exacts.[82]

5

How Our Judges Have Become Politicians

To secure freedom under law in Canada, it will be necessary to curb the usurpation of legislative powers by the courts as well as by human rights tribunals. Prior to enactment of the Canadian Charter of Rights and Freedoms, it would have been inconceivable for the courts to change the law and the Constitution so that someone like Scott Brockie, Bill Whatcott, or Mayor Dianne Haskett could end up in jail for expressing their views on the lifestyles of sexually active homosexuals. Today, such a breakdown of freedom under law is all too likely. Since the Canadian Charter of Rights and Freedoms was incorporated into the Constitution in 1982, the Supreme Court of Canada has abandoned judicial restraint. Instead of upholding the law and the Constitution as enacted by the legislative branch of government and defined in judicial precedents, the judges on Canada's top court have taken to imposing their personal political preferences from the bench. They have routinely struck down some laws and amended others on grounds of public policy. On occasion, they have ignored the law altogether. They have not shrunk from telling legislators what laws to enact and when to enact them on pain of having existing laws declared null and void. Prior to the Charter, such high-handed encroachments by unelected judges upon the law-making authority of elected legislators were unthinkable. Today, the inconceivable has become routine.

ARBITRARILY STRIKING DOWN LAWS: THE *MORGENTALER* CASE

Over the past thirty-five years, few political issues have been more controversial than the 1969 decision of the Parliament of Canada to relax the restrictions on abortion in the Criminal Code. The issue came before the Court in a pre-Charter case, *Morgentaler v. the Queen,* 1976 SCC. In this instance, Dr Henry Morgentaler summoned the Court to remove all remaining restrictions on abortion in the Criminal Code on the ground that they violated the substantive rights of women under section 1 of the 1960 Canadian Bill of Rights "to life, liberty, security of the person and enjoyment of property, and the right not to be deprived thereof except by due process of law." Chief Justice Bora Laskin rejected the argument out of hand. He declared: "How foreign to our constitutional traditions, to our constitutional law and to our conceptions of judicial review was any interference by a Court with the substantive content of legislation."

In 1983 Morgentaler was charged again with violating the abortion provisions in the Criminal Code. Once more, he appealed to the Supreme Court of Canada. This time, his counsel contended that the law on abortion violated the substantive rights of women in section 7 of the Canadian Charter of Rights and Freedoms "to life, liberty and security of the person and the right not to be deprived thereof except in accordance with the principles of fundamental justice." In a complete turnaround, a majority of the Court now agreed with this argument. In striking contrast to *Morgentaler,* 1976 SCC, the Court considered the substantive content of the abortion law in *R. v. Morgentaler,* 1988 SCC, decided that the law was ill advised, and struck it down.

As we have seen, the Supreme Court of Canada likewise cited section 7 of the Charter as authority for imposing two-tiered health care on Quebecers. But is there reason to believe that Parliament intended with the enactment of section 7 of the Charter to confer upon the Court a wide-ranging mandate to strike down or amend crucial legislation like the Canada Health Act or the law on abortion because a majority of judges on the Court disagrees with the substantive content of the law? Not at all. In *Re B.C. Motor Vehicle Act,* 1985 SCC, even Chief Justice Antonio Lamer conceded that there is compelling evidence to the contrary. To begin with, Lamer recalled that in 1981, Barry Strayer, then a senior official in the Justice Ministry and now a judge of the Federal Court of Appeal, had advised the Special Joint Committee of the Senate and the House of Commons on the Constitution that the drafters of the Charter intended the term "fundamental justice" in section 7 to allow less scope for judicial review than the corresponding term "due process of law" in section 1 of the Canadian Bill of Rights. Strayer stated: "Mr. Chairman, it was our belief that the words 'fundamental justice' would cover the same thing as what is called procedural due process – that is the meaning of due process in relation to requiring fair procedure. However, it in our view does not cover the concept of what is called substantive due process, which would impose substantive requirements as to policy of the law in question."

The distinction between "substantive" and "procedural" due process has been a subject of intense debate among constitutional authorities in the United States. At issue is the proper interpretation of the provision in the Fifth and Fourteenth Amendments to the United States Constitution that: "No person shall be ... deprived of life, liberty or property without due process of law." As originally understood, the due process clause referred only to civil rights, political rights, and the principles of procedural fairness codified in the common law.[1] The first to attribute a substantive dimension to the due process clause was Chief Justice Roger Taney of the United States Supreme Court. In his notorious judgment in *Dred Scott v. Sandford*, 1857 USSC, he struck down a Congressional ban on slavery in the northern territories of the United States on the ground that slave owners have a substantive right by virtue of the due process clause to hold slaves throughout the country.

Oliver Wendell Holmes, Jr, took strong exception to such judicial activism. He insisted that judges should not resort to creative interpretations of the Constitution as a pretence for encroaching upon legislative authority. Writing in dissent in *Tyson & Brother v. Banton*, 1927 USSC, a case that dealt with a statute regulating the resale of theatre tickets, Holmes said: "I think the proper course is to recognize that a state legislature can do whatever it sees fit to do unless it is restrained by some express prohibition in the Constitution of the United States or of the State, and that Courts should be careful not to extend such prohibitions beyond their obvious meaning by reading into them conceptions of public policy that the particular Court may happen to entertain." Likewise, in *Adkins v. Children's Hospital*, 1923 USSC, he admonished his fellow judges to consider: "The criterion of constitutionality is not whether we believe the law to be for the public good."

As recently as *Ferguson v. Skrupa*, 1963 USSC, a majority of the United States Supreme Court stated: "The doctrine that prevailed in Lochner, Coppage, Adkins, Burns, and like cases – that due process authorizes courts to hold laws unconstitutional when they believe the legislature has acted unwisely – has long since been discarded. We have returned to the original constitutional proposition that courts do not substitute their social and economic beliefs for the judgment of legislative bodies, who are elected to pass laws. As this Court stated in a unanimous opinion in 1941: 'We are not concerned ... with the wisdom, need, or appropriateness of the legislation.'"[2]

With this statement, the United States Supreme Court exercised judicial restraint. It upheld the rule of law. It reaffirmed the separation of legislative and judicial powers under the United States Constitution. But this reversion to orthodox judicial behaviour did not long endure. Just two years later in *Griswold v. Connecticut*, 1963 USSC, the Court arbitrarily struck down a Connecticut statute banning the sale of contraceptives on the ground that the law violated a purported right to privacy implicit in the due process clause. Ten years later, the Court followed up with its egregious ruling in *Roe v. Wade*, 1973 USSC, which discovered a substantive right to abortion throughout a pregnancy within this same alleged zone of privacy guaranteed by the due process clause. *Roe* was totally unprecedented. It had no basis in law. By means of this unvarnished act of judicial legislation, the Court peremptorily invalidated the abortion laws of forty-six states.

The legislators who enacted the Canadian Charter of Rights and Freedoms were very much aware of *Griswold*, *Roe v. Wade*, and numerous other cases in which the United States Supreme Court had used a substantive interpretation of the due process clause to usurp legislative powers. To deter such excesses by the Supreme Court of Canada, the drafters of the Charter substituted the phrase "principles of fundamental justice" in section 7 for the United States' term "due process of law." In testimony on this point before the Joint Committee on the Constitution, Strayer explained: "The term due process has been given the broader concept of meaning both the procedure and substance. Natural justice or fundamental justice in our view does not go beyond the procedural requirements of fairness." Jean Chrétien took the same view in his testimony to the committee as minister of justice. And on the basis of these assurances, the Joint Committee approved the wording of section 7, as did Parliament and the provincial legislatures.

In submissions to the Supreme Court of Canada in *Re B.C. Motor Vehicle Act*, the attorneys general for British Columbia and Ontario urged the Court to uphold section 7 as intended. The Court declined to do so. Lamer maintained:

> There has prevailed in certain quarters an assumption that all but a narrow construction of s. 7 will inexorably lead the courts to "question the wisdom of enactments," to adjudicate upon the merits of public policy.
>
> From this have sprung warnings of the dangers of a judicial "super-legislature" beyond the reach of Parliament, the provincial legislatures and the elec-

torate. The Attorney General for Ontario, in his written argument, stated that,

> ... the judiciary is neither representative of, nor responsive to the electorate on whose behalf, and under whose authority policies are selected and given effect in the laws of the land.

This is an argument which was heard countless times prior to the entrenchment of the *Charter* but which has in truth, for better or for worse, been settled by the very coming into force of the Constitution Act, 1982. It ought not to be forgotten that the historic decision to entrench the *Charter* in our Constitution was taken not by the courts but by the elected representatives of the people of Canada. It was those representatives who extended the scope of constitutional adjudication and entrusted the courts with this new and onerous responsibility. Adjudication under the *Charter* must be approached free of any lingering doubts as to its legitimacy.

With this argument, Lamer stood truth on its head. Despite compelling evidence that the legislators who enacted the Charter intended section 7 to serve only as a narrow guarantee of procedural fairness, he wilfully construed the section as a broad guarantee of both procedural and substantive fairness. In *Chaoulli,* Chief Justice McLachlin took the same view. In so doing, Lamer, McLachlin, and most other judges on the Supreme Court of Canada have conferred upon the Court the status of a judicial super-legislature. Instead of upholding the plain language of legislative enactments as originally understood and intended, these activist judges have taken to changing the law as they see fit. Granted, in *Re B.C. Motor Vehicle Act,* Lamer denied that the Court would interpret section 7 arbitrarily. He said: "Rather the proper approach to the determination of the principles of fundamental justice is quite simply one in which ... 'future growth will be based on historical roots.'"[3]

Activist judges like Lamer and McLachlin cannot have it both ways: They cannot ignore judicial precedents and the original understanding of the laws and the Constitution while pretending to restrain themselves by upholding the historic roots of legislation. Certainly, no such restraint was evident in the opinions of the judges who supported the ruling of the Supreme Court of Canada in the 1988 *Morgentaler* ruling. In this instance, a majority of the Court not only ignored the long history of legal constraints on abortion in Canada, but also flouted the express intentions of Parliament in enacting section 7 of the Charter. On 27 November 1981 Prime Minister Pierre Trudeau had specifically assured the Commons that section 7 would have no impact on the law on abortion. He stressed: "The Charter is absolutely neutral on this matter." Likewise, Chrétien told the Special Joint Committee on the Constitution:

> If you write down the words "due process of law" here, the advice I am receiving is the court could go behind our decision and say that their decision on abortion was not the right one, their decision on capital punishment was not the right one, and it is a danger, according to legal advice I am receiving, that it will very much limit the scope of the power of legislation by the Parliament and we do not want that; and it is why we do not want the words "due process of law." These are the two main examples that we should keep in mind.
>
> You can keep speculating on all the things that have never been touched, but these are two very sensitive areas that we have to cope with as legislators and my view is that Parliament has decided a certain law on abortion and a certain law on capital punishment, and it should prevail and we do not want the courts to say that the judgment of Parliament was wrong in using the constitution.[4]

In *Morgentaler,* 1988, the Supreme Court of Canada paid no attention to the legislative history of either the Charter or the restrictions on abortion in the Criminal Code. Like their counterparts in the United States, activist judges on Canada's highest court imposed their personal views on abortion. *Morgentaler,* 1988, was a legally unprincipled ruling in which a majority of the judges decided for a variety of conflicting reasons that the minimal restrictions on abortion that Parliament had enacted at Trudeau's behest in 1969 violated the guarantee of life, liberty, and security of the person in section 7 of the Charter to an extent that could not be justified. For example, Justice Wilson argued that the law restricting abortion was too sweeping because it purported to protect the lives of the unborn throughout a pregnancy. In her reasons for judgment in *Morgentaler,* she wrote: "It would be my view that the value to be placed on the fetus as potential life is directly related to the stage of its development during gestation." She then considered the stage in a pregnancy at which the state might justifiably intervene to protect the life of an unborn child. She opined: "It seems to me that it might fall somewhere in the second trimester." In an apt response to Wilson, Professors Rainer Knopff and F.L. Morton of the University of Calgary acidly comment: "Justice Wilson is admirably frank in admitting that this is only 'my view,' which raises the troublesome issue of why 'her view' should be preferred to the collective view of Parliament."[5]

Mr Justice William McIntyre raised this same point in a dissenting opinion in *Morgentaler,* 1988. He did not challenge Wilson's views on the evolving value of life in the womb. Neither did he express any opinion on the morality of abortion. Instead, he pointed out that the Charter did not mandate the courts to decide upon an appropriate abortion law for Canadians. He underlined: "The solution to this question in this country must be left to Parliament. It is for Parliament to pronounce on, and to direct, social policy. This is not because Parliament can claim all wisdom and knowledge but simply because Parliament is elected for that purpose in a free democracy and, in addition, has the facilities – the exposure to public opinion and information – as well as the political power to make effective its decisions."

AMENDING LAWS FROM THE BENCH

While the courts have always played a role in adapting the law and the Constitution to changing social and economic circumstances, the overriding aim of Canadian judges prior to the Charter was to uphold the essential purposes and principles of the common law, statute laws, and the Constitution in accordance with judicial precedent. Certainly, no judge in the pre-Charter era would have presumed to add new spending provisions to a statute law. Today, even this cardinal rule of judicial restraint no longer applies. In an unprecedented ruling in *Schachter v. Canada,* 1990 FCA, the Federal Court of Appeal initiated the process of increasing government benefits from the bench. At issue in *Schachter* were diverse rules governing payments to adoptive and natural parents under the Unemployment Insurance Act, 1971. Section 30 of the Act specified that either parent of a newly adopted child could claim benefits for up to fifteen weeks while staying at home to care for the child; but in the case of natural parents, only the mother would qualify for such benefits. Shalom Schachter, a natural father of a newborn child, complained that the law unfairly discriminated against natural parents, contrary to the equality rights guaranteed in section 15 of the Charter. Restrained judges would have invited a complainant like Schachter to take his grievance to his elected representatives in Parliament, who alone have constitutional authority to change the law. Instead, the Federal Court of Appeal not only agreed in *Schachter* that the law unfairly discriminated against natural parents, but also remedied the alleged defect by unilaterally amending the Act to extend the offer of parental benefits on an equal basis to natural fathers and mothers.

In *Schachter v. Canada,* 1992 SCC, the Supreme Court of Canada endorsed this audacious ruling. Moreover, instead of sticking to the facts of the *Schachter* case, the Court concocted a number of rules of general application relating to the authority of the courts to read new spending provisions into a statute law for the purpose of upholding the Charter. Among these rules is the requirement that the new entitlement must "not involve an intrusion into legislative budgetary decisions so substantial as to change the nature of the legislative scheme in question." What is this limitation supposed to mean?

In *Eldridge v. British Columbia,* 1997 SCC, the Supreme Court of Canada gave the government of British Columbia six months to change regulations under the province's Hospital Insurance Act to provide free sign-language interpretation for the deaf at all provincial hospitals. In the judgment of the Court, the BC government's failure to provide this translation service in publicly funded hospitals violated equality rights for the deaf as guaranteed in the Charter to an extent that is not reasonably justifiable in a free and democratic society. Both the British Columbia Supreme Court and the British Columbia Court of Appeal had come to the opposite conclusion: The Solons of the Supreme Court of Canada acted entirely on their own when they directed that the provinces must give priority of sign-language interpretation over reducing lengthy waiting lists for hip replacement surgery, magnetic resonance imaging, and other important medical procedures.[6] In a commentary on this judgment, Iain Benson and Bradley Miller of the Centre for Cultural Renewal pointedly ask: "Is it the place of the Supreme Court of Canada to be overturning policy decisions of an elected legislature in matters such as the allocation of funds in an overburdened health care system?"[7]

DICTATING LAWS TO PARLIAMENT: THE *FEENEY* CASE

With *R. v. Feeney,* 1997 SCC, the Supreme Court of Canada took judicial legislation to yet another new extreme. The accused in this case, Michael Feeney, had brutally bludgeoned an eighty-five-year-old man to death in Likely, British Columbia. Within hours of the murder, a police officer tracked Feeney down to a house trailer, called out "police," entered the dwelling, found Feeney in bed, and arrested him while he was still dressed in a T-shirt splattered with the victim's blood. On the basis of this evidence, a jury found Feeney guilty of second-degree murder. The British Columbia Court of Appeal unanimously concurred in the verdict. But on further appeal, the Supreme Court of Canada overturned Feeney's conviction. In a five-to-four ruling written by Mr Justice John Sopinka, the Court held that in entering Feeney's dwelling without a warrant, the police had violated Feeney's right "to be secure against unreasonable search or seizure" as guaranteed in section 8 of the Charter. With this finding, Sopinka overturned a common law rule, going back hundreds of years, that authorized a police officer to enter a private dwelling by force without a warrant for the purpose of making an arrest provided the officer has reasonable grounds to believe that the suspect has committed an indictable offence. Scarcely ten years prior to *Feeney*, the Supreme Court of Canada had deemed in *R. v. Landry*, 1986 SCC, that this same, venerable common law rule was fully compatible with the guarantee of "life, liberty [and] security of the person" in section 1(a) of the Canadian Bill of Rights.

In *Feeney* the Supreme Court of Canada did not make the kind of marginal change that is often necessary to adjust a longstanding rule of the common law to new circumstances: The Court changed the law altogether. It imposed an entirely new law requiring police to obtain a warrant prior to entering a private dwelling for the purpose of arresting a criminal. Next, the Court found that the police officer who arrested Feeney had violated this new judge-made law by entering Feeney's trailer without a warrant. And on this basis, the Court not only quashed Feeney's conviction, but also ruled that in any new trial for Feeney, the Crown could not submit into evidence the bloody T-shirt and other incriminating items that the police had obtained by illegally entering Feeney's dwelling.

Chief Justice Beverley McLachlin, Mr Justice Charles Gonthier, and Madam Justice Claire L'Heureux-Dubé took strong issue with the decision of the majority in *Feeney*. In a joint dissent written by L'Heureux-Dubé, they pointed out that Sopinka's rule obligating the police to obtain a warrant prior to entering a private dwelling to arrest a criminal would seriously impede police investigations. Sopinka rejected this argument on the ground that the police could easily have kept watch on Feeney's trailer while waiting to obtain a warrant. L'Heureux-Dubé rejoined:

> The suggestion that the police could have simply watched the trailer while waiting for a warrant fails to recognize that the nearest police station was over one hour's drive away. Even assuming that it would have been possible to see a Justice of the Peace and obtain a warrant at that time, the entire procedure of communicating with the station, conveying the necessary information and arranging for another officer to obtain a warrant and drive to Likely, would probably have taken, at a minimum, close to two hours. This would have given the appellant ample time to destroy evidence. In addition ... this delay would have had even greater significance if in actuality the police had been incorrect about the appellant's whereabouts or his involvement in the crime. In that case, the delay likely would have allowed for the offender to escape.

In summation, L'Heureux-Dubé held that in apprehending Feeney, the police had acted in conformity with all of the demanding conditions required by the common law for arrests without a warrant in a private dwelling. She added:

Before concluding, I feel compelled to address some of the statements made by my colleague Sopinka J. in his reasons. Reading his assessment of the conduct of the investigation in this case, one might draw the conclusion that the police officers were operating as lawless vigilantes, flagrantly and deliberately violating the Charter at every turn. Frankly, I could not disagree more ... The police were in the process of investigating a serious crime, one which had recently been committed and involved a savage, physical beating inflicted on a helpless victim for no apparent reason. Given the brutality of the murder scene and the seeming randomness of the act, there is little doubt that the police felt obliged to act quickly in order to prevent any further violence of that nature in the community. For this foresight, they should be commended, not rebuked.

I would dismiss the appeal.

In addition, L'Heureux-Dubé underlined her fundamental disagreement with the ruling of the majority on the meaning of section 8 of the Charter. Together with Gonthier and McLachlin, she concluded that where police face the kind of urgent circumstances manifested in the *Feeney* case, "the common law authorizing entries onto private premises constitutes a 'reasonable' entry for the purposes of s. 8 of the Charter." She also held that even if the police had acted illegally in seizing the bloody shirt and other incriminating materials in Feeney's trailer, she would have allowed the Crown to submit this evidence in a new trial as required by section 24(2) of the Charter, which provides that illegally obtained evidence can be excluded only if, "having regard to all the circumstances, the admission of it in the proceedings would bring the administration of justice into disrepute." L'Heureux-Dubé held that given the circumstances of the *Feeney* case, the opposite was likely to be true. She concurred with the findings of the trial judge and the Court of Appeal "that considering the exigent circumstances and seriousness of the crime, excluding this evidence would clearly bring the administration of justice into disrepute, particularly since this result would likely preclude the appellant, who was convicted by a jury, of being brought to justice." However, not even this dire prospect moved the Supreme Court majority. Sopinka blithely contended: "If the exclusion of this evidence is likely to result in an acquittal of the accused, ... then the Crown is deprived of a conviction based on illegally obtained evidence. Any price to society occasioned by the loss of such a conviction is fully justified in a free and democratic society which is governed by the rule of law."

Note the irony. Far from affirming the rule of law, Sopinka abandoned it in *Feeney*. Instead of upholding the common law rule on arrests without a warrant, he and his like-minded colleagues on the Supreme Court imposed a new law of their own devising. To compound this affront to the legislative process, the Court gave Parliament six months in *Feeney* to enact a new law on arrest warrants that would be acceptable to the Court, failing which the courts would release thousands of other criminals on the ground that they, like Feeney, had been arrested contrary to the new legal requirements imposed by the Supreme Court of Canada.

At the behest of Prime Minister Trudeau, Senator Anne Cools was appointed to the Senate as a Liberal in 1984.[8] She bristles at judicial abuse of the Charter to blackmail the legislative branch of government. During debate on the bill introduced by the Chrétien government as required by the Feeney ruling, she observed:

> Supreme Court Justice John Sopinka has ruled in the Feeney case that a novel and additional warrant, not previously required, never previously legislated, would now be required to make an arrest in a dwelling house. The fact that Canada's Criminal Code did not require or legislate this additional warrant was inconsequential to him, as was the fact that the enactment of statute law, the Criminal Code, is the singular and exclusive jurisdiction of the Parliament of Canada ...
>
> That Justice Sopinka has reviewed Parliament's wish to pass or not pass a statute, and has made an order that effects a command to Parliament to enact a statute by his deadline as ordered; that Justice Sopinka could come to this Chamber to give Royal Assent to this same Bill C-16, is an exercise of power unknown to Canada's constitutional Monarchy and, more important, unknown to Canadian Parliamentary history and practice.[9]

On these points, Senator Gerald-A. Beaudoin, one of Canada's most prominent constitutional authorities, disagreed with Cools. In response to her remarks, he said:

> Honourable senators, I see nothing in opposition to the Canadian constitutional system in the fact that the Supreme Court has made a decision and laid down a time line ... I do not see how the Canadian Parliament ceases to be sovereign on the legislative level. In our system, what is sovereign is the Constitution. Who interprets the Constitution? The Supreme Court.
>
> The Canadian Parliament is also sovereign in its field. It cannot be prevented from passing legislation. If, however, it passes legislation and goes against the division of powers, or if it passes legislation and goes against the Canadian Charter of Rights, the Supreme Court can declare the legislation invalid. This is very clear; there is absolutely no debate about it. On the purely legislative level, the Supreme Court does not intervene in the process of passing legislation. It is perfectly entitled to say, as it did in Feeney, that a six-month deadline is set for passing legislation.[10]

With these remarks, Beaudoin missed Cools's main point: Neither she nor any other reasonably informed critic of activist judges disputes that Parliament and the provincial legislatures have always been subject to the Constitution. Her concern is that on the basis of a misconstruction of the provisions on the Charter in the Constitution, the Supreme Court of Canada has taken to dictating the laws that Parliament must enact. Such high-handed judicial behaviour is both arrogant and undemocratic.

REVISING THE CONSTITUTION: THE JUDICIAL PAY REFERENCE

In *Manitoba Provincial Judges Assn. v. Manitoba (Minister of Justice)*, 1997 SCC, the Supreme Court of Canada went so far as to concoct a constitutional provision giving the judges of Canada unprecedented authority to determine their own pay. This extraordinary exercise in judicial law making was prompted by the decisions of the Governments of Prince Edward Island, Manitoba, and Alberta to reduce the salaries of judges in line with general public-sector wage and salary rollbacks adopted during the recession at the beginning of the 1990s. The size of the reductions in judicial salaries ranged from 3.8 per cent in Manitoba to 7.5 per cent in Prince Edward Island. Counsel for persons brought before the provincial courts in these provinces claimed that the unilateral imposition of salary cutbacks by the governments of these provinces undermined the independence of the judiciary to an extent that fatally compromised the guarantee in section 11(d) of the Charter that: "Any person charged with an offence has the right ... to be presumed innocent until proven guilty according to law in a fair and public hearing by an independent and impartial tribunal." On behalf of the Supreme Court of Canada, Chief Justice Antonio Lamer agreed with this fanciful argument. In his reasons for judgment in the judicial compensation reference, he enacted an unprecedented constitutional law by declaring that

> any changes to or freezes in judicial remuneration require prior recourse to a special process, which is independent, effective, and objective, for determining judicial remuneration, to avoid the possibility of, or the appearance of, political interference through economic manipulation. What judicial independence requires is an independent body, along the lines of the bodies that exist in many provinces and at the federal level to set or recommend the levels of judicial remuneration. Those bodies are often referred to as commissions ... Governments are constitutionally bound to go through the Commission process. The recommendations of the Commission would not be binding on

the executive or the legislature. Nevertheless, though those recommendations are non-binding, they should not be set aside lightly, and, if the executive or the legislature chooses to depart from them, it has to justify its decision – if need be, in a court of law.

Professor Martin Friedland of the Faculty of Law of the University of Toronto has noted that as a result of this extraordinary ruling, judges are "in a real sense determining their own compensation, particularly with respect to federally appointed judges. Provincial court judges can at least say that the determination is ultimately being made by a different court. In other situations, permitting a person to be a judge in his or her own cause would be a ground for reversing a judgment."[11] Indeed. Besides, Lamer's ruling in the judicial compensation reference is incompatible with the plain words of section 100 of the Constitution Act, 1867, which provides: "The Salaries, Allowances, and Pensions of the Judges of the Superior, District, and County Courts ... shall be fixed and provided by the Parliament of Canada." There is no provision in this or any other section of the Constitution requiring Parliament or the provincial legislatures to establish independent judicial compensation commissions. In *Valente v. The Queen,* 1985 SCC, the first ruling by the Supreme Court of Canada on the meaning of the guarantee of judicial independence and impartiality in section 11(d), Mr Justice Gerald Le Dain stated that he did "not consider the existence of such a committee to be essential to security of salary for purposes of s. 11(d)." Lamer noted this statement by Le Dain, only to dismiss it as nonbinding obiter dicta. Lamer claimed that

> the express provisions of the Constitution should be understood as elaborations of the underlying, unwritten, and organizing principles found in the preamble to the Constitution Act, 1867. Even though s. 11(d) is found in the newer part of our Constitution, the Charter, it can be understood in this way, since the Constitution is to be read as a unified whole ...
>
> Judicial independence is an unwritten norm, recognized and affirmed by the preamble to the Constitution Act, 1867. In fact, it is in that preamble, which serves as the grand entrance hall to the castle of the Constitution, that the true source of our commitment to this foundational principle is located.

Is this right? The preamble to the Constitution Act, 1867, states that Canada is to have a Constitution "similar in Principle to that of the United Kingdom." From this phrase, Lamer and the Court majority derived the strained inference that the Constitution requires the federal and provincial governments to establish independent compensation commissions to decide upon changes to judicial pay.

At the direction of the Court, Justice Minister McLellan duly introduced an amendment to the Judges Act for the creation of an independent Judicial Compensation and Benefits Commission consisting of three persons, one nominated by the judiciary, another by the minister of justice, and a third chosen by the previous two, who serves as chairperson. The Act also granted federally appointed judges an 8.3 per cent salary increase, to be phased in over two years beginning 1 April 1997.

On 31 May 2000 the commission submitted its first report to the government, recommending a salary increase of 11.2 per cent retroactive to 1 April 2000. Under terms of 26(7) of the 1998 Judges Act, the minister of justice is obligated to respond to a report of the commission within six months of receiving it. In this instance, the deadline fell on 30 November 2000. McLellan failed to meet this deadline. On the following day, Chief Justice McLachlin sent McLellan a personal note indicating that she had violated the law by failing to respond on time to the commission's report.[12] What are the citizens of Canada to make of this most extraordinary action? If McLellan's response to the commission had become a matter of litigation before the Supreme Court of Canada, how could McLachlin suppose that any reasonable person would retain confidence in the impartiality of the Court?

As it is, less than two weeks after receiving McLachlin's note, McLellan officially disclosed that the Chrétien government had accepted the commission's recommendation of a salary hike for judges of 11.2 per cent.[13] McLachlin had good reason to be pleased: The agreement provided her with a hefty retroactive salary increase that brought her annual pay to $254,000, up from $230,200. Correspondingly, the salaries of her Supreme Court colleagues rose to $235,700 from $213,000.

Not everyone was supportive of the deal. During parliamentary debate on the issue, Canadian Alliance Member of Parliament Kevin Sorenson suggested that a judicial pay hike of 11.2 per cent on top of a recent 8.3 per cent increase was excessive. "It is important to note," he said, "that while the government considers this raise reasonable, the official opposition views it as extremely generous considering senior public servants have received raises of no more than 5.7 per cent. As well, the pay of public servants is not indexed, while the pay and salaries of judges are. We on this side of the House, therefore, are opposed to Bill C-12."[14]

Let us suppose that Parliament as a whole had opposed the salary hikes recommended by the Judicial Compensation and Benefits Commission. What would the Supreme Court of Canada have done – summon members of Parliament before the Court to defend their decision to oppose the recommendation of the commission? This outcome would accord with Lamer's ruling that "if ... the legislature chooses to depart from [the Commission's recommendations], it has to justify its decision – if need be, in a court of law." If the Supreme Court had still felt after this hearing that the decision of Parliament was not justified, would the Court have directed Parliament to comply with the commission's recommendations? And if Parliament had disobeyed such a direct order, would Chief Justice McLachlin have issued a bench warrant for the arrest of honourable members?

Justice La Forest was a lone dissenter in the judicial compensation reference. He wrote:

> I have had the advantage of reading the reasons of the Chief Justice who sets forth the facts and history of the litigation. Although I agree with substantial portions of his reasons, I cannot concur with his conclusion that s. 11(d) forbids governments from changing judges' salaries without first having recourse to the "judicial compensation commissions" he describes. Furthermore, I do not believe that s. 11(d) prohibits salary discussions between governments and judges. In my view, reading these requirements into s. 11(d) represents both an unjustified departure from established precedents and a partial usurpation of the provinces' power to set the salaries of inferior court judges pursuant to ss. 92(4) ["The Appointment and Payment of Provincial Officers"] and 92(14) ["The Administration of Justice in the Province"] of the Constitution Act, 1867.

La Forest also rebuked Lamer for citing the preamble to the Constitution in his reasons for the majority. Given that only minimal reference had been made to this provision by counsel before the Court, La Forest said: "I am, therefore, deeply concerned that the Court is entering into a debate on this issue without the benefit of substantial argument. I am all the more troubled since the question involves the proper relationship between the political branches of government and the judicial branch, an issue on which judges can hardly be seen to be indifferent, especially as it concerns their own remuneration. In such circumstances, it is absolutely critical for the Court to tread carefully and avoid making far-reaching conclusions that are not necessary to decide the case before it."

La Forest demonstrated that the declaration in the preamble that Canada shall have "a Constitution similar in Principle to that of the United Kingdom" could not reasonably be construed as mandating independent judicial compensation commissions. "Unlike Canada, Great Britain does not have a written constitution," he noted. "Under accepted British legal theory, Parliament is supreme. By this I mean that there are no limitations upon its legislative competence." In support of this view, he cited Dicey's explanation that Parliament has "under the English constitution, the right to make or unmake any law whatever; and, further, that no person or body is recognised by the law of England as having a right to override or set aside the legislation of Parliament."[15] Dicey specifically asserted "the non-existence of any judicial or other authority having the right to nullify an Act of Parliament, or to treat it as void or unconstitutional."[16]

La Forest noted that in the early 1930s, Viscount Buckmaster, the Lord Chancellor,[17] expressed strong objection on behalf of the judiciary to an order in council that reduced the salaries of judges, along with the pay of civil servants, by 20 per cent as a means of coping with a crisis in government finances brought on by the Great Depression. However, like Dicey, Buckmaster conceded that the British Parliament was supreme and therefore had full constitutional authority not just to enact a rollback in judicial salaries, but also to repeal, if it chose to do so, the Act of Settlement of 1701 that established the independence of the judiciary. In view of this precedent, La Forest argued: "The idea that there were enforceable limits on the power of the British Parliament to interfere with the judiciary at the time of Confederation, then, is an historical fallacy. By expressing a desire to have a Constitution 'similar in Principle to that of the United Kingdom', the framers of the Constitution Act, 1867 did not give courts the power to strike down legislation violating the principle of judicial independence."

La Forest held that the sole guarantees of judicial independence in the Constitution of Canada are in sections 96–100 of the Constitution Act, 1867, and in section 11(d) of the Charter. He said:

> While these provisions have been interpreted to provide guarantees of independence that are not immediately manifest in their language, this has been accomplished through the usual mechanisms of constitutional interpretation, not through recourse to the preamble. The legitimacy of this interpretive exercise stems from its grounding in an expression of democratic will, not from a dubious theory of an implicit constitutional structure. The express provisions of the Constitution are not, as the Chief Justice contends "elaborations of the underlying, unwritten, and organizing principles found in the preamble to the Constitution Act, 1867." On the contrary, they are the Constitution. To assert otherwise is to subvert the democratic foundation of judicial review.

Law professor Robert Martin has been one of the most outspoken critics of the Lamer Court, yet even he was astonished by La Forest's frank charge that the Court had subverted democracy. "It is amazing that a Supreme Court judge would say that about a majority opinion of his court," Martin commented. "That's worse than anything I've ever said."[18] And this is not all that La Forest had to say. He reminded his errant colleagues that judicial review "is politically legitimate only insofar as it involves the interpretation of an authoritative constitutional instrument. In this sense, it is akin to statutory interpretation. In each case, the court's role is to divine the intent or purpose of the text as it has been expressed by the people through the mechanism of the democratic process." Exactly. This is a fine restatement of the proper and legitimate role of the judiciary in a parliamentary democracy. Why, however, did La Forest not apply this same basic principle of democratic judicial interpretation to the law in the judgment he wrote for the Court in *Egan*? Had he done so – had he upheld the intent or purpose of the Charter as it has been expressed by the people through the mechanism of the democratic process – he would have concluded that sexual orientation is not analogous to the enumerated grounds of protection in section 15. And in so doing, he might have diverted the Supreme Court of Canada from the string of illegitimate gay rights judgments that led to the ultimate subversion of the democratic foundations of judicial review in the *Halpern* ruling on same-sex marriage.

Be that as it may, La Forest at least struck a belated blow for parliamentary democracy and the rule of law with his lone dissent in the judicial compensation reference. The ruling came on 18 September 1997. Twelve days later, he resigned from the Supreme Court of Canada. Truly, nothing in his career as a judge became him like the leaving of it.

INEPT JUDICIAL POLICY MAKING: THE *RESSAM* SCANDAL

Time and again, the Supreme Court of Canada has intruded into the legislative process, even though, with rare exceptions, judges lack both the skills and information necessary to determine sound public policies. Few judges have any training in economics or public administration. Most judges have no experience in crafting the political compromises that are often necessary to mobilize popular support for effective public policies. Besides, judges cannot pretend to uphold the rule of law while making major alterations in the law in quick response to changing social and political circumstances.

Consider the legislative incompetence of judges in relation to Bill C-36, the 171-page Anti-Terrorism Act that Justice Minister McLellan introduced into the Commons scarcely a month after the attack by Islamist terrorists on the United States on 11 September 2001. The purpose of the legislation was to strengthen the capacity of Canada to investigate, suppress, and incapacitate terrorist activity.[19] No fewer than thirty Justice Ministry officials worked on the bill.[20] They divided themselves into six drafting teams, put in long hours, and laboured through the weekends with a mandate to produce a bill for combating terrorism that is compatible with the Charter. The entire drafting process was closely monitored by the National Security Committee of the Cabinet, headed by Foreign Affairs Minister John Manley. Together, Cabinet ministers and experts from the public service came up with a bill that included some extraordinary measures, including a provision for preventive detention that authorizes a police officer to arrest and detain a suspected terrorist without a warrant if the officer has reasonable grounds to believe that the measures are necessary to prevent the commission of an imminent terrorist offence. To safeguard the rights of the detainee, the Act stipulates that the suspect must be brought before a judge within twenty-four hours of arrest. To protect the public, the Act authorizes the judge to impose limitations upon the suspect's movements or associations as conditions for release. If the suspect refuses to accept the conditions, the judge can impose a jail term of up to twelve months. In addition, the Anti-Terrorism Act includes a section on investigative hearings that authorizes a judge to require a material witness to disclose information relating to terrorism without a formal trial. To avoid self-incrimination, the Act provides that evidence obtained in these hearings cannot be used against the witness at a subsequent trial. However, anyone who refuses a judicial order to testify at a pre-trial investigative hearing on terrorism can be sentenced to jail for contempt of court.

While the provisions of the Anti-Terrorism Act were under consideration in the Commons, the Senate was giving close consideration to antiterrorism measures in Bill C-11, the Immigration and Refugee Protection Act. On 17 September 2001 Immigration Minister Elinor Caplan told the Commons: "Bill C-11 gives us important new tools to ensure that we are able to do things such as up-front security screening and to bar access to the refugee determination system for anyone that we believe poses a security threat to Canada." Thus section 64(1) of the Act provides: "No appeal [of a deportation order] may be made to the Immigration Appeal Division by a foreign national or their sponsor or by a permanent resident if the foreign national or permanent resident has been found to be inadmissible on grounds of security." In section 115 the Act stipulates that a refugee applicant who is inadmissible to Canada on grounds of serious criminality or national security can be deported to his country of origin even if he would be at risk in that country of torture or cruel and unusual punishment.

The Cabinet ministers and security experts who drafted these extraordinary provisions for the protection of Canadians in the Anti-Terrorism Act and the Immigration and Refugee Protection Act were no doubt mindful of the Islamist terrorist Ahmed Ressam.[21] On 24 February 1994 he was caught trying to enter Canada at Montreal's Mirabel airport with a false French passport. Ten years earlier, he could have been immediately detained under such circumstances and summarily deported. In 1994 the Immigration Department no longer had such powers, and Ressam knew it. Among would-be migrants in his home country, Algeria, it is generally known that virtually anyone can foil the Canadian immigration system by applying for refugee status on Canadian soil. Thus Ressam readily admitted to suspicious immigration officials at Mirabel that he had a phoney passport. To avoid deportation, he promptly applied for refugee status, claiming that he feared political persecution in his native Algeria. To lend credence to this claim, he told immigration officials that he had escaped from Algeria after having been arrested and tortured by Algerian police on a false charge of selling firearms to a terrorist. There was no truth to this story, but the ploy worked. Ressam was admitted to Canada as a refugee. Within a few days, he was living with a fellow Algerian in an apartment in Montreal and collecting $550 a month in welfare payments.

At the time of his admission at Mirabel, Ressam was told that he must show up for a further immigration hearing in Montreal on March 28. He failed to keep the appointment. Subsequently, he was arrested, photographed, and fingerprinted for this offence, but as he claimed that he had simply forgotten about the appointment, he was released on condition that he show up for a new hearing. Soon thereafter, Ressam began to supplement his welfare income with the proceeds of petty theft. On 30 January 1995 he was arrested again, this time on a charge of shoplifting from a store in downtown Montreal. At trial, he was convicted, fined $100, placed on probation for two years, and ordered to leave Canada by 23 July 1995. Ressam flouted this order and went underground. Immigration officials did not bother to track him down because they were overwhelmed at the time with a backlog of about 100,000 deportation orders that was growing at a rate of about 10,000 a year.

What had gone wrong? Why was the Canadian immigration system not working? The answer is incontrovertible: The inability of Canadian authorities to summarily deport fraudulent refugee claimants and criminals like Ressam is due to the ill-considered decision of the Supreme Court of Canada in *Singh v. the Queen*, 1985. In this case, the Court held that anyone who lands on Canadian soil is entitled to all the rights and freedoms guaranteed to Canadian citizens in the Canadian Charter of Rights and Freedoms. This *Singh* ruling was an act of judicial legislation. It had no basis in law, precedent, or the wording and history of the Charter. Regardless, as a result of this unprincipled Supreme Court judgment, everyone who arrives on Canadian soil now has a Charter right to appeal a deportation order through the courts – a process that not infrequently takes years of litigation to complete.

Take the case of Manickavasagam Suresh, a citizen of Sri Lanka.[22] Like Ressam, he entered Canada as a phoney refugee claimant in October 1990. Suresh concocted a story of political persecution in Sri Lanka. The Immigration and Refugee Board granted him refugee status in April 1991. Four years later, the Canadian Security and Intelligence Service found out that he was actually a member and fundraiser for the Liberation Tigers of Tamil Eelam (LTTE), a terrorist organization that is rebelling against the democratically elected government of Sri Lanka. On 17 October 1995 the minister of immigration filed a certificate under section 40.1 of the Immigration Act designating Suresh a security risk subject to deportation. The next day, he was placed in detention. He appealed to the Federal Court Trial Division, which held fifty days of hearings in the case before deciding in August 1997 to uphold the security certificate. This ruling cleared the way for a deportation hearing. On 17 September 1997 the adjudicator in the case held that Suresh should be deported on grounds of membership in a terrorist organization. Suresh appealed the ruling. This appeal was denied by an immigration officer who held that "to allow Mr. Suresh to remain in this country and continue his activities runs counter to Canada's international commitments in the fight against terrorism." On 6 January 1998 the minister of immigration declared that Suresh constitutes a danger to the security of Canada and shall be deported. Suresh went back to the Federal Court, this time claiming that the deportation procedures in his case had violated his rights to freedom of expression and freedom of security as guaranteed in sections 2 and 7 of the Charter. In 1999 the Federal Court rejected this appeal. Suresh took the case to the Federal Court of Appeal, which also rejected his appeal. He then resorted to the Supreme Court of Canada. In a ruling on 11 January 2002 Canada's top court reversed both lower courts, upheld the appeal, and directed that Suresh was entitled to yet another deportation hearing. The case is still ongoing.

At least, during all these appeals, Suresh has been held in secure confinement as a terrorist threat. After Ressam was arrested in 1995, he was allowed to go free because the Canadian Security and Intelligence Service (CSIS) had not yet learned that he was getting much of his income by stealing credit cards, passports, and other forms of identification for sale to an Islamist terrorist, Fateh Kamel, a Montreal man who had fought in Afghanistan and Bosnia. In October 1996 Ressam was arrested for a third time, on this occasion for the theft of $300 from a tourist in downtown Montreal. The judge fined him $500, placed him on another two years probation, and once more set him free, although he was supposed to have left the country three months earlier. Moreover, by this time, CSIS had learned that Ressam was associating with known Islamist terrorists in Montreal. Still, he remained at large. Shortly thereafter, he stole a Quebec birth certificate and obtained a Canadian passport. In March 1998 he flew out of the country to Pakistan, made his way from there to an Al Qaeda camp in Afghanistan, and spent the rest of the year undergoing terrorist training. Early in 1999 he flew back to Montreal and got started on plans to mark the millennium in the United States by setting off a massive bomb inside the Los Angeles International Airport. The plot was foiled thanks only to the alertness of a United States Customs Agent at Port Angeles, Washington, who pulled Ressam over for questioning on 14 December 1999 as he was trying to enter the United States on a ferry from Vancouver. An inspection of his car revealed a hidden cache of high explosives and triggering devices. Following a short chase, Ressam was arrested and detained. In March 2001 he was convicted in the United States on charges of plotting to blow up the Los Angeles International Airport. Then, in an evident attempt to win a reduced sentence, he started cooperating with United States security officials by making a full confession and testifying against other Islamist terrorists in the United States and Canada.[23]

Let us turn the clock back to 1999 and suppose that agents of the Canadian Security and Intelligence Service had got wind of Ressam's plot to blow up the Los Angeles Airport and that the provisions of the Anti-Terrorism and Immigration Acts of 2001 were already in effect. Under these circumstances, CSIS agents could have arrested and detained Ressam without a warrant, a judge could have required him on pain of imprisonment to testify against his Islamist coconspirators, and immigration officials might have summarily deported him back to Algeria, despite the risk that Algerian authorities might subject him to torture and execution. Are such extraordinary powers justifiable? Given the grave threat posed by Islamist terrorists, do the exceptional security provisions in the Anti-Terrorism and Immigration Acts constitute no more than reasonable and demonstrably justified restrictions on the guarantees of "life, liberty and security of the person" in section 7 of the Charter and of the right in section 11(d) "to be presumed innocent until proven guilty according to law in a fair and public hearing by an independent and impartial tribunal"?

Parliament took considerable care to assure that the Anti-Terrorism and Immigration Acts of 2001 are compatible with the Charter. During detailed, clause-by-clause consideration of the legislation in committees of the Commons and Senate, members of Parliament informed themselves on the vitally important issues at stake by eliciting testimony from the head of CSIS, the chief commissioner of the Royal Canadian Mounted Police, and other senior officials within several government ministries. Committees of the Commons and Senate also heard testimony from an array of outside experts. Yet in the end, despite all this care and consideration by both government and Parliament, the Supreme Court of Canada might decide to strike down crucial parts of these bills – without having taken part in the debates in Parliament or having heard any direct testimony from experts on policing, intelligence, and defence. In evaluating the wisdom of the security provisions in the Immigration and Anti-Terrorism Acts, the Court would have to rely mainly on the submissions of lawyers, who, like the judges themselves, typically lack any expertise in national security.

All of these considerations are excellent reasons for judges to practise restraint in second-guessing the wisdom of Parliament in enacting laws, especially insofar as these laws bear upon national security. But alas, the Supreme Court of Canada is filled with activist judges who know no such restraint. They are all too likely to repeat disasters like the 1985 *Singh* ruling that crippled the Canadian refugee-processing system and nearly led to a catastrophic millennial bombing at the Los Angeles airport.

JUDICIAL INTRUSIONS INTO THE PATRIATION CONTROVERSY

Activist judges on the Supreme Court of Canada are not loath to overturn the policy decisions of Parliament and the provincial legislatures on even the most sensitive issues of constitutional reform. Consider in this respect the egregious intrusion of the Supreme Court of Canada into the political negotiations that led to the Constitution of Canada Act, 1982. The need for a constitutional settlement became critical following the Quebec referendum on 20 May 1980, when a solid majority of Quebecers voted "no" to a proposal that would have mandated the Government of Quebec to negotiate "sovereignty-association" with Canada. During the referendum campaign, Prime Minister Pierre Trudeau had promised that if the outcome favoured national unity, he would work to renew Canadian federalism. True to his word, he immediately initiated an intensive round of talks with the provincial premiers in the summer of 1980 on a federal plan for "patriating" the Constitution.[24] At the time, formal amendments to the British North America Act, as the Constitution of Canada was then known, could be adopted only by the British Parliament at Westminster. Trudeau's plan for ending this quasi-colonial practice included a number of controversial constitutional amendments, including the introduction of a Canadian Charter of Rights and Freedoms. At a crucial meeting in

Ottawa in September 1980, the nation's first ministers failed to reach agreement on this federal proposal, so Trudeau announced on 2 October 1980 that his government would proceed without provincial consent to ask both houses of the Parliament of Canada to enact resolutions requesting the Parliament at Westminster to enact into law a set of proposals for patriating the Constitution of Canada.

While the premiers of Ontario and New Brunswick supported the unilateral federal initiative, the premiers of British Columbia, Alberta, Manitoba, Quebec, Prince Edward Island, and Newfoundland were adamantly opposed. Together, this "gang of six" premiers asked the courts of appeal in Manitoba, Quebec, and Newfoundland for a ruling that the Parliament of Canada was bound by both law and convention to obtain the approval of the provinces before requesting that the Parliament at Westminster enact an amendment to the Canadian Constitution. To Trudeau's consternation, the Newfoundland Court of Appeal sided with the "gang of six" on this issue. It was then up to the Supreme Court of Canada to provide a definitive ruling.

On 28 September 1981 the Supreme Court of Canada handed down its judgment in the *Patriation Reference*.[25] The ruling was a legal shambles. On the key issue of the legality of Parliament acting without provincial consent to obtain a constitutional amendment affecting provincial powers, the Court was clear: Seven of the judges who took part in the case, including Laskin and Dickson, held that there is nothing "that casts any doubt in law as to the undiminished authority of the Parliament of the United Kingdom over the British North America Act." This same majority also concluded that "the law knows nothing of any requirement of provincial consent, either to a resolution of the federal Houses or as a condition of the exercise of United Kingdom legislative power."

Having settled these points of law, the Court next considered the political question raised by the dissenting provinces: Was the federal government bound by a convention of the Constitution to obtain provincial consent for amendments affecting the provinces? Citing Hogg, *Constitutional Law of Canada*, the Court affirmed that a constitutional convention is not a law but "a rule which is regarded as obligatory by the officials to whom it applies." To illustrate the difference between a law and a convention, the Court observed that the Queen is empowered by law to refuse to give royal assent to any bill, although she is bound by convention not to withhold her consent because of disagreement with the policy of the bill. If the Queen were to break this convention, she would provoke a storm of political controversy, but the courts would have no recourse in law to provide a remedy.

Note that by the Court's own definition of a constitutional convention, there could not have been any convention requiring provincial consent to constitutional amendments affecting provincial powers because the federal officials to whom this alleged rule applied denied its existence. Despite this fact, six judges of the Supreme Court of Canada, including Dickson but excluding Laskin, held that there was a convention that required a "substantial degree" of provincial consent to constitutional amendments affecting provincial powers. Just what constituted this substantial degree of consent the Court would not say, beyond stipulating that it consisted of more than two but fewer than ten provinces. In defence of this vague formulation, the majority argued: "It would not be appropriate for the Court to devise in the abstract a specific formula which would indicate in positive terms what measure of provincial agreement is required for the convention to be complied with. Conventions by their nature develop in the political field and it will be for the political actors, not this Court, to determine the degree of provincial consent required."

One might wonder: If it was up to the political actors, not the Court, to determine the degree of provincial consent required, why was it not also up to political actors, rather than the Court, also to determine if any such convention existed at all? Chief Justice Laskin, Mr Justice Willard Estey, and Mr Justice William McIntyre drew the logical conclusion. In a joint dissent in the *Patriation Reference*, they pointed out that: "The degree of provincial participation in constitutional amendments has been a subject of lasting controversy in Canadian political life for generations. It cannot be asserted, in our opinion, that any view on this subject has become so clear and so broadly accepted as to constitute a constitutional convention." With reference to the creative conclusion of the majority that an unspecified, but substantial, degree of provincial consent is required by convention, the dissenters held: "It is unrealistic in the extreme to say that the convention has emerged."

On one point in the *Patriation Reference*, the entire Court was agreed: The opinion of the majority on the existence of a convention governing provincial consent to constitutional amendments had no legal authority. Nonetheless, with this ruling, the majority changed the political dimensions of the patriation debate so decisively that Trudeau was forced to engage in another strenuous round of negotiations with the provinces with a view to obtaining broader support for a revised patriation package. In this effort, Trudeau largely succeeded. At a meeting of first ministers on 5 November 1981, he obtained the consent of all provinces, except Quebec, to a compromise that provided for patriation of the Constitution and enactment of the Canadian Charter of Rights and Freedoms. In due course, the Parliament at Westminster formally incorporated this political agreement into the Canada Act, 1982, which Queen Elizabeth II signed into law on 17 April 1982.

Meanwhile, the Government of Quebec went back to the courts, seeking a ruling that Quebec was entitled to a constitutional veto over patriation on the ground that without Quebec, there could be no "substantial degree" of provincial consent to amendments affecting the provinces as required by the Supreme Court of Canada because Quebec is not only the second most populous, but also the only predominantly French-speaking, province in the country. In a ruling on 6 December 1982, the Supreme Court of Canada rejected this argument.[26] In this instance, Laskin, Dickson, and the entire Court agreed that Quebec did not have a conventional power of veto over constitutional amendments affecting the powers of the provinces.

Thus ended the patriation controversy. However, the question remains: Should the Supreme Court of Canada have responded to the questions posed by the dissenting provinces on the existence of a non-legal, political convention governing constitutional amendments? Hogg does not think so. He points out that the Court had refused in the past to respond to questions that were not suitable for judicial determination and should have done so again in these patriation rulings.[27] He maintains: "The convention questions in the *Patriation Reference* and *Quebec Veto Reference* raised no legal issues, and the answers could not lead to any legal consequences ... In my view, the Court, which is not an elected body, and which is not politically accountable for its actions, should have confined itself to answering the legal question, and should not have gone beyond the legal question to exert any further influence over the negotiations."[28]

Hogg is not the only legal scholar to take this view. Trudeau, a former law professor at the University of Montreal, also objected to the intrusion by the Supreme Court of Canada into the politics of the patriation process. At the time of the Court's ruling on the issue in 1981, he felt constrained as prime minister to keep his criticism of the findings of the majority of the Court to himself. It was not until close to ten years later that he finally spoke out. The occasion was an address on 21 March 1991 to a packed audience at Convocation Hall of the University of Toronto to commemorate the opening of the Bora Laskin Law Library. With Dickson sitting in the front row, Trudeau subjected the judgment of the majority in the *Patriation Reference* to a withering critique. He argued that the majority's invention of a requirement of a "substantial degree" of provincial consent to constitutional amendments was so vague that it could not be a constitutional convention. In a direct reference to Dickson and his like-minded colleagues, he charged: "There seems to be little doubt that the majority judges had set their minds to delivering a judgment that would force the federal and provincial governments to seek political compromise.

No doubt believing in good faith that a political agreement would be better for Canada than unilateral legal patriation, they blatantly manipulated the evidence before them so as to arrive at the desired result. They then wrote a judgment which tried to lend a fig-leaf of legality to their preconceived conclusion."[29]

Dickson was deeply wounded by Trudeau's conclusion.[30] Yet his conclusion fits the facts. During oral argument on the *Patriation Reference*, members of the Court had asked counsel for the provinces whether something less than unanimous provincial consent to constitutional amendments affecting the provinces would suffice. In a biography of Dickson, Mr Justice Robert Sharpe and Professor Kent Roach relate: "The point was of particular concern to Dickson, who characteristically was searching for a compromise and who pressed the lawyers several times during oral argument for some 'middle position.' On this crucial point, Saskatchewan broke with the dissenting provinces and won the day with the majority. Saskatchewan's counsel, Ken Lysyk, himself a constitutional scholar, argued that it was unnecessary to specify the degree of provincial consent required ... This offered Dickson and the other judges in the majority the middle ground they were looking for."[31]

What could be clearer? Instead of crafting a legally principled ruling, the Court majority sought, and imposed, a political compromise. Trudeau never got over this gross judicial violation of the separation of legislative and judicial powers. In his Convocation Hall address, he lauded the judicial restraint practised by Laskin, Estey, and McIntyre in the *Patriation Reference*. "It seemed to me that Canadians had a right to expect a legal decision from their Supreme Court, rather than some well-meaning admonitions about what was politically proper,"[32] he said, adding: "The minority's more strictly legal approach lends itself far less to political manipulation of the courts than does the majority's. By refusing to go beyond its role as interpreter of the law, the minority avoided the temptation to which the majority succumbed, that of trying to act as political arbiter at a time of political crisis. While there are no doubt differing views of how well the court performed this role in the *Patriation Reference*, it is not a role to which a court of law striving to remain above the day-to-day currents of political life should aspire."[33]

Trudeau decried the political consequences of the Court's ruling in the *Patriation Reference*, insisting that it gave Quebec "a lever to pry itself out of the Canadian constitutional family."[34] He surmised that if the minority's view had prevailed over the majority's, "I believe that Canada's future would have been more assured."[35] Dickson disagreed. Following Trudeau's speech, he argued that the majority's opinion had salvaged the patriation project. He surmised that Trudeau's unilateral approach to constitutional change might well have been rejected by the Parliament at Westminster. In a 1992 interview, he said: "I hesitate to think what might have happened if our judgment had gone the opposite way."[36]

Such judicial presumption is hard to credit. Had Dickson spoken with Prime Minister Margaret Thatcher in 1982 about the patriation process? Why did he think he was in a better position than Trudeau to judge the reaction of the Parliament at Westminster to a unilateral federal request for constitutional change? It never seems to occur to unelected judicial activists like Dickson that they lack the information and experience necessary to make sound political decisions on key issues of public policy.

Given the controversy provoked by the political decision of the majority in the *Patriation Reference,* one might have supposed that the Supreme Court of Canada would practice greater restraint thereafter in dealing with the threat of Quebec separatism. This has not been the case. In *Quebec Secession Reference,* 1996 SCC, the Court committed an even more egregious intrusion into constitutional politics. Following the shocking result of the Quebec referendum on 30 October 1995, in which the separatist government of Quebec came within one-half of one percentage point of obtaining a virtual mandate to issue a unilateral declaration of Quebec independence, the Chrétien government tried to clarify the issues surrounding Quebec separatism by referring the following questions to the Supreme Court of Canada: "1. Under the Constitution of Canada, can the National Assembly, legislature or government of Quebec effect the secession of Quebec from Canada unilaterally? 2. Does international law give the National Assembly, legislature or government of Quebec the right to effect the secession of Quebec from Canada unilaterally?" On 20 August 1998 Chief Justice Lamer, Madam Justice McLachlin (as she then was), and the rest of the Court answered both questions in the negative. In anonymous reasons, the Court declared: "There is no right, under the Constitution or at international law, to unilateral secession."

This finding settled the only legal issues before the Court. It should also have ended the ruling. Instead, as in the case of the *Patriation Reference,* the Court went on to intrude into matters of political judgment. It stated:

> The Constitution is not a straitjacket. Even a brief review of our constitutional history demonstrates periods of momentous and dramatic change. Our democratic institutions necessarily accommodate a continuous process of discussion and evolution, which is reflected in the constitutional right of each par-

ticipant in the federation to initiate constitutional change. This right implies a reciprocal duty on the other participants to engage in discussions to address any legitimate initiative to change the constitutional order. While it is true that some attempts at constitutional amendment in recent years have faltered, a clear majority vote in Quebec on a clear question in favour of secession would confer democratic legitimacy on the secession initiative which all of the other participants in Confederation would have to recognize.

With this statement, the activist judges on the Supreme Court of Canada plunged into the hottest political controversy of the day. In affirming that the federal and provincial governments would have to recognize the legitimacy of a secession initiative backed by a clear majority vote on a clear question in Quebec, the Court was clearly expressing not a legal but a political opinion. In support of this opinion, the Court cited "four fundamental and organizing principles of the Constitution which are relevant to addressing the question before us (although this enumeration is by no means exhaustive): federalism; democracy; constitutionalism and the rule of law; and respect for minorities." The Court held that these four organizing principles are "clearly implicit in the very nature of a Constitution" but "are not explicitly made part of the Constitution by any written provision, other than in some respects by the oblique reference in the preamble to the Constitution Act, 1867." The pertinent section of the preamble to the Constitution Act, 1867, states that "the Provinces of Canada, Nova Scotia, and New Brunswick have expressed their Desire to be federally united into One Dominion under the Crown of the United Kingdom of Great Britain and Ireland, with a Constitution similar in Principle to that of the United Kingdom." On the basis of these words, the Court claimed that the four organizing principles that it outlined for the first time in the *Quebec Secession Reference* are in some respects, "explicitly made part of the Constitution." And the Court further claimed that the preamble "invites the courts to turn those principles into the premises of a constitutional argument that culminates in the filling of gaps in the express terms of the constitutional text." One of these gaps is the lack of any reference in the express terms of the Constitution of Canada Act to secession. Therefore, the Court propounded an obligation upon the federal and provincial governments to recognize the legitimacy of a secession initiative backed by a clear majority of voters responding to a clear question in a Quebec referendum.

Greg Craven, professor of government and constitutional law at Curtin University in Perth, Australia, has subjected this ruling to a devastating critique in a paper entitled "The Quebec Secession Reference: The Law of Politics or the Politics of Law?" He observes: "One thing which must immediately strike Australian readers of the Supreme Court's opinion is that it is a fundamentally political document. By this is meant not merely that it more closely resembles in style of argumentation a policy speech (or possibly a heavily political sermon) than it does a traditional, legally reasoned judgement – which clearly is the case – but that the various considerations, arguments and justifications which the Court brings forward in support of its position almost invariably call to political, social and cultural values, rather than to strictly legal considerations."[37]

Craven takes particular exception to the discovery by the Court that the Constitution of Canada harbours at least four judicially enforceable organizing principles denominated federalism, democracy, constitutionalism and the rule of law, and protection for minorities. He observes that none of these principles "may be directly derived, at least in such broad and conceptual terms, directly from the text of the Canadian Constitution, or from any conventional process of constitutional interpretation. Rightly or wrongly, the Court seems less engaged in the construction of the Constitution of Canada, than in divining the entrails of the Canadian polity." Furthermore, he notes that these four organizing principles "are so inherently vague that they conceivably could be applied in the future so as to mean virtually anything ... In effect, the potential of the secession reference is to equip the Canadian Supreme Court with four vast subject matters of constitutional morality upon which it conceivably could legislate with much the same freedom as the Canadian parliament legislating upon a subject matter within its competence."

In Craven's opinion, judges are singularly ill-equipped to legislate. He points out:

> Their typical mode of decision-making, adjudication as between litigating parties, is utterly unsuited to the development of general policies applying across society and based on multifarious non-legal considerations. Their experience in dealing with neatly packaged evidence ill suits them to the task of sifting through the multiplicity of factors and material that typically will inform the making of a major policy decision. They have no experience in designing or even foreseeing the systems necessary to translate a policy decision into reality. All in all, it is scarcely possible to imagine a group of individuals less obviously suited to the formulation of policy than Her Majesty's Judges, with the notable exception of legal academics.[38]

Craven wryly adds: "I am sometimes amused when supporters of judicial activism querulously ask me who would be better at policy formulation than judges? The obvious answer to this is an elected Parliament composed of members who at the very least are legitimate, and certainly are both reasonably socially diverse and experienced in the art of government."[39] In short, Craven is a democrat. On the whole, he prefers the operations of a parliamentary democracy to the rule of unelected judges. He observes:

> Perhaps the saddest aspect of this whole sad debate over the capacity of judges to make effective legal policy is the genuine hurt evident on the part of many judges when their deficiencies in this direction are the subject of public comment. After all, no-one is denying the intelligence of the judges, which is undoubted. No-one questions their mastery of the law which is, after all, their field of peculiar expertise. No-one disputes their integrity in the discharge of their judicial functions. All that is being maintained is their incapacity in a field entirely outside their experience and expertise. For judges to resent charges of policy ineptitude is a little like a physicist being irked at not being recognised as a concert violinist.[40]

Regardless, our activist judges on the Supreme Court of Canada think that they are best qualified to supervise and direct the process of legislation and public policy in Canada. In the *Quebec Secession Reference* as in so many other cases in recent years, they have violated the most fundamental principle of democracy: the separation of legislative, executive, and judicial powers. Instead of upholding the law and the Constitution as originally enacted and understood, they legislate. And in so doing, they undermine the very democracy and the rule of law that, as judges, they are supposed to safeguard and affirm.

6

Escalating Judicial Attack on Christians

In the David B. Goodman Memorial Lecture delivered at the University of Toronto Faculty of Law in November 1985, Madam Justice Bertha Wilson drew a distinction between judicial activism and judicial restraint. She said:

> Those judges who advocate judicial restraint have a proper concern over their lack of accountability to the public and tend to think that any significant change in the law should be made by the duly elected representatives of the people. However, while constitutional principles may favour the exercise of judicial restraint, moral considerations may impel a judge in the opposite direction. All judges would like to think that their decisions, as well as constituting a proper application of legal principle, reflect current notions of what is right and fair. The difficulty, however, is to determine what current notions of justice and fairness are.[1]

On this last point, the learned judge was undoubtedly correct: It is difficult to determine what passes for "current notions of justice and fairness." This is one of the reasons why restrained judges leave legislating to elected legislators. In contrast, activist Supreme Court justices like Wilson presume to bring the law into conformity with "current notions of justice and fairness" as they see it. Chief Justice Lamer gave a striking illustration of this penchant for judicial legislation in his reasons for dissent in *Rodriguez v. British Columbia (Attorney General)*, 1993 SCC, a case that was brought before the Court by a woman suffering from amyotrophic lateral sclerosis who claimed that the ban on assisted suicide in section 241(b) of the Criminal Code violated her

Charter rights to freedom and equality because she would no longer be able to commit suicide after losing control of her limbs. In his dissenting opinion, Lamer stated: "Can the right to choose at issue here, that is the right to choose suicide, be described as an advantage of which the appellant is being deprived? In my opinion, the Court should answer this question without reference to the philosophical and theological considerations fuelling the debate on the morality of suicide or euthanasia. It should consider the question before it from a legal perspective ... while keeping in mind that the Charter has established the essentially secular nature of Canadian society."

Like many contemporary judicial pronouncements, this statement has a ring of postmodern deconstruction. The preamble to the Charter plainly declares: "Canada is founded upon principles that recognize the supremacy of God and the rule of law." The pretence that the Charter has established "the essentially secular nature of Canadian society" is a fabrication of activist judges bent on trying to justify their disposition to change the law and the Constitution to conform to their secular values.

Having set aside philosophical and religious considerations in *Rodriquez*, Lamer held that the ban on assisted suicide in the Criminal Code violates the equality rights of the physically handicapped in section 15 of the Charter "since it prevents persons physically unable to end their lives unassisted from choosing suicide when that option is in principle available to other members of the public. This inequality is moreover imposed on persons unable to end their lives unassisted solely because of a physical disability, a personal characteristic which is among the grounds of discrimination listed in s. 15(1) of the Charter." Chief Justice McLachlin and Justice L'Heureux-Dubé rejected this reasoning while advancing the argument that the ban on assisted suicide in the Criminal Code violates the right of handicapped persons to "life, liberty and security of the person" as guaranteed in section 7 of the Charter. Not to be outdone, Justice Cory took the view that in enacting the ban on assisted suicide, Parliament had violated the rights guaranteed in both sections 7 and 15 of the Charter. Together, these four dissenters in *Rodriquez* came within one vote of having the Supreme Court of Canada endorse the perverse notion that despite the guarantee of the right to life in section 7 of the Charter, Canadians have the right to death by assisted suicide.

Law professors Robert Hawkins and Robert Martin are not persuaded by Justice Wilson's attempt to defend her disposition to update the law in accordance with her understanding of current notions of what is right and fair. They point out that, in arguing for a flexible and contextual approach to interpretation of the law and the Charter, she was really arguing for the freedom to decide cases in accordance with her own preferences. We argue that she believed the Charter had turned the Court into a political body, a kind of unaccountable legislature. The Court's role was to constitutionalize the content that judges gave to rights; the Court's method was to elevate judicial value preferences into law; the Court's membership was to represent the different social groups with whom they shared common characteristics.

Justice Wilson's philosophy of judicial review demanded that judges be constrained only by their personal opinions. It is a philosophy which has nothing to do with principle, nothing to do with the rule of law and nothing to do with democracy. It turns the Court into an organ of naked power, and contravenes both the letter and the spirit of the Charter.[2]

THE COURTS VERSUS THE PEOPLE: THE *SURREY* CASE

The inclination of activist judges to change the law to accord with their value preferences is evident in a series of rulings that eradicated Christianity from the public schools. The process began with *Zylberberg v. Sudbury Board of Education (Director)*, 1988 OCA, when the Ontario Court of Appeal overturned a longstanding policy of the Ontario government that mandated recitations of the Lord's Prayer and Scripture readings during opening religious exercises in the public schools for all students except those who were exempted by their parents. The Court held that this regulation infringed the freedom of conscience and religion guaranteed by section 2(a) of the Charter. In the opinion of the Court, "The recitation of the Lord's Prayer, which is a Christian prayer, and the reading of Scriptures from the Christian Bible impose Christian observances upon non-Christian pupils and religious observances on non-believers." The provision for exempting non-Christian students from class during these religious exercises was not good enough for the Court. It argued that "the exemption provision imposes a penalty on pupils from religious minorities who utilize it by stigmatizing them as non-conformists and setting them apart from their fellow students who are members of the dominant religion." On this basis, the Court flouted the will of the Ontario Legislature by striking down the longstanding regulation.

Two years after *Zylberberg*, the Ontario Court of Appeal dealt with the religious studies curriculum of the Elgin County Board of Education in *Canadian Civil Liberties Assn. v. Ontario (Minister of Education)*, 1990 OCA. In this case, the democratically elected local school board had adopted a curriculum that mandated Christian indoctrination for all students except those whose parents objected. Once again, the Court overturned this government-approved policy on the ground that affirming the truth of the Christian faith in the public schools violates the right to freedom of religion guaranteed in the Charter because it "amounts to the imposition of majoritarian religious beliefs on minorities." In compliance with this ruling, the Ontario Ministry of Education issued a policy memorandum forbidding all religious indoctrination in all public schools.

Judicially mandated secularism has had an especially severe impact on the Sturgeon Creek Alternative Program, a school established by the Fort Francis-Rainy River public school board to serve the local Mennonite community. In an account of this school, Lois Sweet reports:

> In 1990, some of what staff and students were teaching and learning on a daily basis was suddenly illegal. The government of NDP premier Bob Rae declared that public schools could no longer include any religious content in their curriculums. The school was ordered to cut out any reference to the Bible in classes. There were to be no more Christian posters on the walls. No more opening religious exercises. So the students closed their Bibles and stopped praying in the classroom.
>
> Today, the students continue to both pray and study the Bible. But they do so by stepping next door to the Mennonite Church. And they do so outside school hours.[3]

Enrolment in this school was entirely voluntary. Any student who might have been offended by expressions of Christian faith in the classroom could have chosen to shun this Mennonite school for one of the regular, non-Christian, public schools within the Fort Francis-Rainy River system. What could justify a virtually court-ordered, government-mandated policy so sweeping as to forbid religious indoctrination even in a school set aside specifically for students of a particular religious faith?

Manohar Singh Bal, a parent of an Ontario public school child, put this question to the Ontario Superior Court of Justice in an action funded by the Multifaith Coalition for Equity in Education, an association of Sikh, Hindu, Muslim, and conservative Christian parents. Bal argued that the banishment of religious indoctrination from schools like the Sturgeon Creek Alternative Program violates the Charter guarantees of freedom of religion and equality of treatment for parents who prefer schools that uphold a particular religious faith. In *Bal v. Ontario (Attorney General),* 1994 ONSGD, Mr Justice Warren Winkler of the Ontario Superior Court of Justice rejected this claim. He held that the Elgin County decision "signified the end of an era of majoritarian

Christian influence, and marked the beginning of a period of secularism in education, based on an awareness of a changing societal fabric and Charter protection for minority rights to freedom of religion."

How is this so? Who signalled the end of an era of majoritarian Christian influence and the beginning of a period of secularism in education in Ontario? As usual in the Charter era, it was appointed judges, not elected representatives of the people, who presumed to make this momentous change in law and public policy. In unilaterally barring recitations of the Lord's Prayer and Scripture readings in the public schools, provincial courts of appeal have purported to uphold the Canadian Charter of Rights and Freedoms, yet there is no evidence that the legislators who enacted the Charter understood that the guarantee of freedom of religion in section 2 would prohibit Christian exercises in the public schools. Nonetheless, have honourable members in the legislatures of Ontario and other provinces objected to this naked exercise of raw judicial power in banning God from the classroom? Not at all. As usual, they have meekly acquiesced. In compliance with the courts, the provinces have suppressed all religious exercises in the public schools. Such is the sorry state of Canadian democracy in the Charter era.

In *Chamberlain v. School District No. 36*, 2002 SCC 86, the Supreme Court of Canada did not just uphold the ban on Christian teaching in the public schools: It imposed an alternative ideology. At issue in this case was a resolution adopted by the School Board for District 36 of Surrey, British Columbia, on 24 April 1997 in relation to three books that depict children with same-sex parents: *Asha's Mums; Belinda's Bouquet;* and *One Dad, Two Dads, Brown Dad, Blue Dads.*[4] The resolution held that these books are not suitable for use as recommended learning resources in the Surrey schools. James Chamberlain, a kindergarten teacher within the Surrey School District, objected to this decision. He is a member of Gay and Lesbian Educators (GALE) of British Columbia, a voluntary association of university professors, teachers, counsellors, child care workers, and administrators affiliated with the province's schools and universities.[5] GALE BC affirms that its "primary focus is to advocate for change in the educational system which will result in a positive environment for lesbians, gays and bisexuals in education, whether they are students, parents, teachers, or administrators." To this end, the organization states that "GALE BC is committed to having information on glbt [gay, lesbian, bisexual, and transgendered] people included in the curriculum, pre-school through post-secondary."[6]

With the backing of four other petitioners, Chamberlain went to court, seeking to have the three-books resolution quashed on the ground that it violated the equality rights of gays and lesbians in section 15 of the Charter as well as the requirements in section 76 of the 1996 British Columbia School Act that: "(1) All schools must be conducted on strictly secular and non-sectarian principles" and "(2) The highest morality must be inculcated, but no religious dogma or creed is to be taught in a school or Provincial school." Chamberlain's case came before Madam Justice Mary Saunders of the British Columbia Supreme Court. In affidavits supporting the three-books resolution, a Roman Catholic priest, an observant Muslim, and several Protestants stated that by the lights of their respective faiths, the practice of homosexuality is sinful. Likewise, a leader of the Guru Nanak Sikh Gurdwara Society testified: "In the Sikh faith, homosexuality is considered a moral and social sin which we are instructed to resist." A leader of the Verdic Hinkhu Society told the court: "The three books display a lifestyle which we, as Hindhus, believe is immoral." Counsel for the Surrey School Board cited this testimony as evidence of widespread support among local leaders of various religions for the decision of the board to restrict use of the three gay pride books.

The tactic backfired. In a ruling on 16 December 1998, Saunders held that by giving weight to the opinion of religious leaders, the School Board had violated the provision in section 76(1) of the School Act that all schools must be conducted on strictly secular principles. She said: "In the education setting, the term secular excludes religion or religious belief. Combining the word 'secular' with the words 'strictly' and 'principles' (in s. 76(1)), and considering the history of schools in British Columbia as being beyond overt church or religious intervention or influence, I conclude that the words 'conducted on strictly secular ... principles' precludes [*sic*] a decision significantly influenced by religious considerations. This interpretation is consistent with the increasingly pluralistic nature of modern British Columbia and accords with the obligation to give statutory provisions a fair, large and liberal interpretation."

Saunders's interpretation of the term "secular" in the School Act as precluding decisions significantly influenced by religious considerations was unprecedented. Ian Benson, executive director of the Centre for Cultural Renewal in Ottawa, has observed that this unique definition of the meaning of secular in Canadian law "leads to the paradoxical result that a religious person could not run for any elected office or, if elected, could not function in a secular manner, ... while using their religious beliefs or their conscience informed by a religious belief. This nonsensical result shows that [Saunders's] approach to 'secular' is, at the very least, shallow and erroneous."[7]

In effect, Saunders decreed that Christians, Jews, Muslims, Sikhs, and Hindus are no longer qualified to serve on a public school board in pluralist British Columbia unless they are willing to forgo their religious understanding of the difference between what is right and what is wrong. Saunders noted that at least one member of the Board of Trustees for the Surrey School District "has campaigned for several years to promote a greater role for religion in governance of the community, including on the issue of homosexuality." In Saunders's view, such behaviour is illegal: "I conclude that by giving significant weight to personal or parental concern that the books would conflict with religious views, the Board made a decision significantly influenced by religious considerations, contrary to the requirement in s. 76(1) that schools be 'conducted on strictly secular ... principles.'"

Saunders also held that in adopting the three-books resolution, the School Board had failed to uphold the "highest morality" as required in the School Act. She said: "Affidavits placed before the court by the School Board depose that some religions or churches with adherents in the community hold that homosexual activity is wrong. Yet in considering the highest morality as those words are used in the School Act, it is appropriate to consider the values embodied in the Charter of Rights and Freedoms and import them into the moral standard that must be applied ... Recent cases under s. 15 of the Charter of Rights and Freedoms state that s. 15 protects equality rights for those of a homosexual orientation: *Egan v. Canada*, [1995 SCC]; *Vriend v. Alberta*, [1998 SCC]."

Theologically orthodox Christians and Jews hold that God is the supreme moral authority. Saunders gives precedence to the Supreme Court of Canada. She contends that for the purposes of public policy, Christians and Jews must renounce the divine moral law in favour of whatever alternative values our secular lawmakers on the Supreme Court of Canada prefer to read into the Charter.

How can a law that bars school board trustees from allowing their religious beliefs to have any significant influence over their decisions comport with the guarantee of freedom of religion in the Charter? Saunders explained that in her view: "Freedom of religion includes freedom from religion." In support of this doctrine, she recalled that in striking down the federal Lord's Day Act in *R. v. Big M Drug Mart Ltd.*, 1985 SCC, Chief Justice Dickson stated: "Religious belief and practice are historically prototypical and, in many ways, paradigmatic of conscientiously-held [*sic*] beliefs and manifestations and are therefore protected by the Charter. Equally protected, are expressions of non-belief and refusals to participate in religious practice." Therefore, Saunders concluded that the guarantee of freedom of religion in the Charter sanctions a law that imposes freedom from religion in the public schools. And on this basis, she quashed the decision of the

Surrey School Board to disapprove of the three gay pride books for classroom use on the ground that the opposition of many Surrey trustees and parents to the promotion of lesbian and gay lifestyles to kindergarten and grade 1 children was significantly influenced by religion.

The Surrey School Board appealed this astounding ruling. On 20 September 2000 a three-judge panel of the British Columbia Court of Appeal unanimously reversed Saunders's judgment,[8] but upon a further appeal by Chamberlain, the Surrey Board ultimately lost the case on 20 December 2002, when the Supreme Court of Canada settled the matter by siding in a seven-to-two ruling with Saunders.[9] Writing for the majority of the Supreme Court, Chief Justice McLachlin acknowledged that in deciding whether to accept or reject the three books, the Surrey Board had "to balance the interests of different groups, such as parents with widely differing moral outlooks, and children from many types of families." McLachlin conceded: "On this aspect, the Board has considerable expertise. As elected representatives, it is their job to bring community views into the educational decision-making process. The Board is better placed to understand community concerns than the court." True enough, yet McLachlin then held that the democratic authority of the board in enacting the three-books resolution counts for little because "the decision of whether to approve the three books has a human rights dimension. The Board must decide whether to accommodate certain parents' concerns about the books at the risk of trumping a broader tolerance program and denying certain children the chance to have their families accorded equal recognition and respect in the public school system. Courts are well placed to resolve human rights issues."

Consider the scope of this audacious claim to judicial authority over human rights. All laws that impinge upon individual freedom have a human rights dimension. By McLachlin's formulation, the Supreme Court of Canada presumes to pass judgment upon the wisdom of all these laws and to strike down any of them that do not uphold human rights in a manner that suits the policy preferences of a majority of the Court. McLachlin cited no legal or constitutional authority for this unilateral assertion of judicial power.

To the contrary, McLachlin virtually conceded that the Supreme Court of Canada had no legal basis for overriding the decision of the Surrey Board. She said: "It is true that the issue does not involve the strict application of legal rules or the interpretation of the law." Quite so. But given the absence of any clear authority in law, the Court should not have undertaken to interfere with the decision of the board. The overriding concern of judges in a democracy should be to uphold legal rules and interpret the law. If a dispute does not involve the strict application of legal rules, judges should have nothing to do with the matter. They should defer to the judgment of the proper legislative, executive, or private authority.

As it is, having conceded that the issue in *Surrey* did not involve the strict application of legal rules, McLachlin argued that in adopting the three-books resolution, the Surrey School Board had violated "the principles of secularism and tolerance in s. 76 of the *School Act.*" Recall that section 76 of the *School Act* simply states: "(1) All schools must be conducted on strictly secular and non-sectarian principles" and "(2) The highest morality must be inculcated, but no religious dogma or creed is to be taught in a school or Provincial school." There is no reference to tolerance in this or any other section of the School Act. McLachlin read a requirement of tolerance into the Act on her own and then accused the Surrey School Board and its superintendent of practising intolerance by refusing to approve the three books. In support of this allegation, she said: "Instead of proceeding on the basis of respect for all types of families, the Superintendent and the Board proceeded on an exclusionary philosophy. They acted on the concern of certain parents about the morality of same-sex relationships, without considering the interest of same-sex parented families and the children who belong to them in receiving equal recognition and respect in the school system. The Board was not permitted to reject the books simply because certain parents found the relationships depicted in them controversial or objectionable."

There was no basis in law for such a conclusion. Nothing in section 76 of the School Act indicates that a school board must not reject kindergarten books depicting same-sex parents on the ground that certain parents object to such relationships. McLachlin relied upon the statement in the preamble of the School Act that "it is the goal of a democratic society to ensure that all its members receive an education that enables them to become personally fulfilled and publicly useful." She also took note of a ministerial directive that "all students have the right to a learning environment that is gender equitable ... and incorporates a consideration of social class, culture, ethnicity, religion, sexual orientation, and age." On the flimsy basis of such statements as guides to the interpretation of section 7 of the School Act, she concluded:

> In summary, the Act's requirement of strict secularism means that the Board must conduct its deliberations on all matters, including the approval of supplementary resources, in a manner that respects the views of all members of the school community. It cannot prefer the religious views of some people in

its district to the views of other segments of the community. Nor can it appeal to views that deny the equal validity of the lawful lifestyles of some in the school community. The Board must act in a way that promotes respect and tolerance for all the diverse groups that it represents and serves.

Let us suppose that some sexual swinger were to ask a school board to approve a book that favourably depicts a so-called open marriage with a multitude of sexual partners moving in and out of the home to gratify the lusts of the husband and wife. While there might be nothing illegal about such sexual promiscuity, a district school board might well find that the vast majority of parents in the community would have serious moral and religious objections to having the book approved for use in the public schools. Yet the board could not lawfully reject a book that favourably depicts sexual swingers for classroom use because McLachlin has decreed that a board "cannot prefer the religious views of some people in its district to the views of other segments of the community. Nor can it appeal to views that deny the equal validity of the lawful lifestyles of some in the school community."

By such reasoning, McLachlin and a majority of the Supreme Court of Canada struck down the decision of the Surrey School Board to reject the three books depicting same-sex parents as recommended learning resources for five- and six-year-old children in kindergarten and grade 1. In doing so, the Court manifestly failed to uphold the School Act as enacted and originally understood by the legislators and the people of British Columbia. Instead, the activist judges on Canada's top court distorted the law to conform to their own ideological preferences in favour of having grade-school children indoctrinated in the acceptability of families headed by same-sex parents.

In a dissenting judgment joined by Mr Justice Michel Bastarache, Mr Justice Charles Gonthier rejected the opinion of the majority on all key points. Gonthier wrote:

I respectfully disagree that the School Act, R.S.B.C. 1996, c. 412, and the relevant ministerial directives demand that all family types, rather than a diversity, be represented and, more importantly, that the three specific books at issue be approved for general classroom use by the School Board despite the fact that the Minister declined to approve them for province-wide use. I am of the view that the decision was intra vires the School Board under the School Act and was clearly reasonable. The practice of approving or not approving books is clearly within the purview of the School Board's authority, the decision is consistent with a proper understanding of s. 76 of that Act (i.e. the decision accords with a correct understanding of "strictly secular and non-sectarian principles" and does not offend the requirement that "[t]he highest morality must be inculcated"), the considerations taken into account by the School Board were appropriate, and the decision is respectful of ss. 2(a), 2(b) and 15 of the Charter.

In plain language, Gonthier and Bastarache held that in refusing to designate the three books as recommended learning resources for kindergarten and grade 1, the Surrey School Board had made a reasonable decision in compliance with the provisions of the School Act and the guarantees in the Charter of freedom of conscience and religion in section 2(a); freedom of thought belief, opinion, and expression in section 2(b); and equality rights in section 15. "In my view," wrote Gonthier, "the relationship between s. 2 and s. 15 of the *Charter*, in a truly free society, must permit persons who respect the fundamental and inherent dignity of others and who do not discriminate, to still disagree with others and even disapprove of the conduct or beliefs of others."

Gonthier maintained that people can believe that homosexual behaviour is immoral without condoning unfair discrimination against homosexuals. He said: "In the case at bar, there is, in my view, no evidence that the parents who felt that the three books were inappropriate for five- and six-year-old children fostered discrimination against persons in any way. Many persons, religious and not, justify this distinction by drawing a line ... between beliefs held about persons and beliefs held about the conduct of persons." He then asked:

> If many Canadians, as a result of deeply held religious or non-religious beliefs or opinions, draw such a line and commit to such a distinction in their daily lives, must the law obliterate it because of the allegation that acts of discrimination against persons are born from the view held by some that certain persons' conduct is immoral or inappropriate? Does a commitment to eradicating the potential for future instances of discrimination require that religious persons or others be forced to abandon their views regarding the immorality of certain conduct? Can s. 15 be used to eliminate beliefs, whether popular or unpopular? In a society committed to liberal values and robust pluralism, the answer to all of these questions must be in the negative.

In short, Gonthier upheld the traditional understanding of freedom of thought, belief, opinion, and expression in a democracy. He insisted in his dissent that there is "nothing in *Vriend v. Alberta* ... or the existing s. 15 case law that speaks to a constitutionally enforced inability of Canadian citizens to morally disapprove of homosexual behaviour or relationships." He stressed: "It is a feeble notion of pluralism that transforms 'tolerance' into 'mandated approval or acceptance.'"

Yet this very feeble notion of pluralism and democracy has been embraced by a majority of the Court. In effect, McLachlin held in *Surrey* that while school board trustees are free to believe in private that homosexual behaviour is sinful and wrong, they must not act on this belief as trustees to the extent of disapproving three books for classroom use that favourably depict families headed by a same-sex couple. From a democratic viewpoint, the best that can be said for McLachlin's judgment in *Surrey* is that she stopped just short of endorsing Justice Saunders's draconian edict that public school boards must refrain from making any decision that is "significantly influenced by religious considerations." In McLachlin's opinion: "A requirement of secularism implies that, although the Board is indeed free to address the religious concerns of parents, it must be sure to do so in a manner that gives equal recognition and respect to other members of the community. Religious views that deny equal recognition and respect to the members of a minority group cannot be used to exclude the concerns of the minority group. This is fair to both groups, as it ensures that each group is given as much recognition as it can consistently demand while giving the same recognition to others."

Within Canada theologically orthodox Christians are in a minority, as are gay-rights activists. When the clashing viewpoints of these two minorities collide, McLachlin maintains that the gay-rights ideology must prevail. "This," she insists, "is fair to both groups." Faithful Catholics and Evangelical Christians might beg to differ. From their perspective, there is nothing at all fair about the judgment of the Supreme Court of Canada in *Surrey*. It constitutes an unprecedented attack on the democratic rights of all parents who uphold the traditional teaching of the Christian Church on the sinfulness of homosexual behaviour. The Court has decreed that even if the overwhelming majority of parents within a school district believe that homosexual behaviour is unhealthy and immoral, the democratically elected school board trustees for that district must endorse materials for classroom use that are plainly intended to persuade children in kindergarten and grade 1 that there is nothing abnormal or wrong about families headed by homosexual couples.

THE *TRINITY WESTERN* PRECEDENT

While the *Surrey schools* case was underway, disagreement over the meaning of freedom of religion as guaranteed in section 2 of the Charter featured prominently in another West Coast dispute, this one between Trinity Western University (TWU) and the British Columbia College of Teachers (BCCT).[10] The case centred on the refusal of the college to approve a full education program at TWU on the ground that students attending the university are required to uphold the discriminatory view that all sexual relations outside of marriage, including homosexual sexual relations, are sinful. In an eight-to-one ruling on 17 May 2001, the Supreme Court of Canada held that by refusing to accredit a full education program at TWU, the college had violated the right of students at the university to freedom of religion. Guy Saffold, Trinity Western vice president, announced that the university was "profoundly grateful" for the decision, hailing it as "in the best interests of every citizen in this country."[11] The dean of Humanities and Social Sciences, Bob Burkinshaw, said that he was "very pleased, grateful to God, and humbled by this decision."[12] Gary Walsh, president of the Evangelical Fellowship of Canada, was no less enthusiastic. He opined: "This will put to rest the fears of other religiously-based colleges and seminaries that are worried that their students will face discrimination upon graduation."[13] Even the Canadian Conference of Catholic Bishops saluted the ruling, lauding it as "a strong affirmation and much needed reminder that freedom of religion is a fundamental human right and public freedom that is guaranteed by the Canadian Charter of Rights and Freedoms. It confirms that it is wrong to stereotype people with religious beliefs as intolerant or to suggest that students of religious institutions are unqualified to work in the public sector."[14]

Was such enthusiasm warranted? Did the Supreme Court of Canada really give a ringing endorsement to the traditional principles of freedom of religion in the *Trinity Western* decision? Can TWU graduates rest secure in the knowledge that the Supreme Court of Canada has upheld their constitutional right to affirm and act upon their religious beliefs while teaching in the public schools?

The answer on all counts is "no." With the *Trinity Western* judgment, the Supreme Court of Canada dealt another blow against freedom of religion. Instead of praising this decision, defenders of religious freedom should ponder how a case involving an attack upon the most elementary principles of religious freedom should ever have come before the courts in the first place.

TWU is an affiliate of the Evangelical Free Church of Canada. The BCCT took exception to a university regulation advising that in accepting an invitation to join the university community, all students and faculty must agree to uphold the university's standards of conduct, including the following:

> REFRAIN FROM PRACTICES THAT ARE BIBLICALLY CONDEMNED. These include but are not limited to drunkenness (Eph. 5:18), swearing or use of

profane language (Eph. 4:29, 5:4; Jas 3:1–12), harassment (Jn 13:34–35; Rom. 12:9–21; Eph. 4:31), all forms of dishonesty including cheating and stealing, (Prov. 12:22; Col. 3:9; Eph. 4:28), abortion (Ex. 20:13; Ps. 139:13–16), involvement in the occult (Acts 19:19; Gal. 5:19), and sexual sins including premarital sex, adultery, homosexual behaviour, and viewing of pornography (I Cor. 6:12–20; Eph. 4:17–24; 1 Thess. 4:3–8; Rom. 2:26–27; 1 Tim. 1:9–10). Furthermore married members of the community agree to maintain the sanctity of marriage and to take every positive step possible to avoid divorce.[15]

When TWU applied to the BCCT for approval of a complete teacher education program in 1995, the Council of the BCCT rejected the application on the ground that the university "appears to follow discriminatory practices that public institutions are, by law, not allowed to follow." In a subsequent statement, the college elaborated: "Both the Canadian Human Rights Act and the B.C. Human Rights Act prohibit discrimination on the ground of sexual orientation. The Charter of Rights and the Human Rights Acts express the values which represent the public interest. Labelling homosexual behaviour as sinful has the effect of excluding persons whose sexual orientation is gay or lesbian. The Council believes and is supported by law in the belief that sexual orientation is no more separable from a person than colour. Persons of homosexual orientation, like persons of colour, are entitled to protection and freedom from discrimination under the law."

The BCCT further explained that the councillors who reviewed the Trinity Western application were concerned that the particular worldview promoted by the university with reference to homosexual behaviour "may have a detrimental effect in the learning environment of public schools. A teacher's ability to support all children regardless of race, colour, religion or sexual orientation with a respectful and non-judgemental relationship is considered by the College to be essential to the practice of the profession." By implication, the BCCT held that no one who upholds the historic teaching of the Christian church on the sinfulness of homosexuality can be permitted to teach in the public schools of British Columbia.

Did the college have reason to believe that such a rule is mandated by judicial interpretation of the guarantee of equality rights in section 15 of the Canadian Charter of Rights and Freedoms? Yes, indeed. The Supreme Court of Canada first spelled out its views on the inherent nature of sexual orientation in *Canada (Attorney General) v. Ward,* 1993 SCC, a case that related to a contested refugee claim by a man from Northern Ireland. The dispute in *Ward* had nothing to do with homosexuality, yet Justice La Forest went out of his way in an obiter dicta to declare that sexual orientation is "an innate or unchangeable characteristic" like race, sex, colour, gender, and linguistic background.[16] La Forest did not cite any medical evidence to support this contention. Two years later in his *Egan* ruling, he expressed a more nuanced view: "I have no difficulty accepting the appellants' contention that whether or not sexual orientation is based on biological or physiological factors, which may be a matter of some controversy, it is a deeply personal characteristic that is either unchangeable or changeable only at unacceptable personal costs." Again, La Forest cited no scientific evidence to support this conclusion. Yet on the basis of his unsubstantiated assertion of medical fact, he and his colleagues on the Court unanimously declared in *Egan* that sexual orientation "falls within the ambit of s. 15 protection as being analogous to the enumerated grounds."

Among medical authorities on homosexuality, there is no consensus on the immutability of sexual orientation. Dr Satinover and his colleagues at the National Association for Research and Therapy of Homosexuality (NARTH) contend that taking up a gay, lesbian, or bisexual lifestyle is a willed choice subject to change.[17] They repudiate the popular notion that homosexual behaviour is genetically determined. In *Homosexuality and the Politics of Truth*, Dr Satinover argues that although some people are genetically prone to homosexuality just as others are to alcoholism, there is no evidence that homosexuality is mostly genetic.[18] He writes: "Of interest in comparing alcoholism to homosexuality is the fact that alcoholism is estimated to be between 50 per cent and 60 per cent heritable; homosexuality to be less than 50 per cent even by activists, probably considerably less. This even greater risk for alcoholism does not lead to the conclusion, however, that alcoholics are not responsible for controlling, changing, or stopping the behaviour."[19]

Perhaps the best evidence of the mutability of sexual orientation has come from an unusual source – Dr Robert Spitzer, professor of psychiatry and chief of biometrics at Columbia University. He is a self-described "Jewish, atheist, secular humanist" who led the taskforce in the 1970s that recommended the deletion of homosexuality from the official list of mental disorders in the diagnostic manual of the American Psychiatric Association.[20] In an address to the annual meeting of the American Psychiatric Association on 9 May 2001, Dr Spitzer described a study that he supervised of 143 men and 57 women who had undergone a significant shift from homosexual to heterosexual attraction that had lasted for at least five years. While the men in this sample reported that they had rarely or never felt any opposite-sex attraction prior to beginning the process of change, the women reported a less extreme commitment to a homosexual orientation. Nonetheless, after undergoing therapy, 66 per cent of the men and 44 per cent of the women indicated that they had managed to maintain a "loving and emotionally satisfying heterosexual relationship" for at least the previous year.[21]

The findings came as quite a surprise to Dr Spitzer. He confided: "Like most psychiatrists, I thought that homosexual behaviour could be resisted, but that no one could really change their sexual orientation. I now believe that's untrue – some people can and do change."[22] While acknowledging that some homosexuals have been harmed by failed attempts to change their sexual orientation through therapy, Dr Spitzer reported that many of the subjects in his study were despondent, and even suicidal, for the opposite reason – "precisely because they had previously thought there was no hope for them, and they had been told by many mental health professionals that there was no hope for them, they had to just learn to live with their homosexual feelings."[23] Dr Spitzer concluded: "Contrary to conventioned [*sic*] wisdom, some highly motivated individuals, using a variety of change efforts, can make substantial change in multiple indicators of sexual orientation, and achieve good heterosexual functioning."[24]

Typically, the Supreme Court of Canada has shown no awareness of the debate within the medical community over the treatment of homosexual promiscuity as a sexual addiction. The Court has dismissed the testimony of hundreds of practising homosexuals who have changed their sexual orientation. It dogmatically insists that homosexuals cannot change their sexual orientation except at unacceptable personal costs. And on the basis of this misinformed and disputed premise, the Court has repeatedly held in *Egan, Vriend,* and other cases that: "Persons of homosexual orientation, like persons of colour, are entitled to protection and freedom from discrimination under the law" by virtue of section 15 of the Charter.

Clearly, then, the BCCT has reason to claim that its belief "that sexual orientation is no more separable from a person than colour" is supported by the Supreme Court of Canada, if not by medical science. Moreover, unlike the Charter, the British Columbia Human Rights Code explicitly includes sexual orientation in section 8 as a prohibited ground for discrimination in the provision of a public service by both private groups and persons. However, section 41 of this same Code stipulates that a nonprofit charitable, educational, or religious institution can give preference to members of a group identified by religion, political belief, or any of six other specified grounds without running afoul of the Code. On this and other grounds, Trinity Western successfully appealed the ruling of the BCCT Council to the British Columbia Supreme Court. On 11 September 1997 Mr Justice W.H. Davies directed the council to grant conditional approval to the TWU teacher training program.[25] In his reasons for judgment, Davies noted that over the preceding seven years, numerous TWU graduates had taken a final year of teacher training at Simon Fraser University and had gone on to teach in the public schools, yet none had ever been accused of discriminating against homosexuals. In Davies's opinion, council ignored this evidence and had no other basis for refusing to approve a full teacher education program at TWU.

Upon further appeal by the college, the British Columbia Court of Appeal upheld Davies's ruling in a two-to-one judgment on 30 December 1998. In written reasons for the majority, Mr Justice Michael Goldie held that the college had no lawful authority to consider the views of TWU graduates on the practice of homosexuality. In his view, the college could evaluate only the knowledge and skills of potential teachers as mandated by section 4 of the Teaching Profession Act. He wrote: "There is no reference in s. 4 to the regulatory role of Council which was invoked in the examination of TWU's application. Nothing expressly required Council to employ its views of Charter values and human rights legislation in the case at bar."

As an exercise in strict construction, Goldie's argument was unassailable but plainly contrary to the free-wheeling style of interpretation preferred by the Supreme Court of Canada. In a dissenting opinion, his colleague Madam Justice Anne Rowles reflected the prevailing judicial mood by endorsing the larger and more liberal interpretation of section 4 advanced by the college. And upon further appeal, the Supreme Court of Canada unanimously concurred with Rowles. In joint reasons for the majority of the Supreme Court of Canada in *Trinity Western*, Justices Frank Iacobucci and Michel Bastarache stated:

> We agree with Rowles J.A. that "it is clear from the terms 'professional responsibility and competence of its members' that the College can consider the effect of public school teacher education programs on the competence and professional responsibility of their graduates" ... The power to establish standards provided for in s. 4 of the Act must be interpreted in light of the general purpose of the statute and in particular, the need to ensure that "the fulfilment of public functions is undertaken in a manner that does not undermine public trust and confidence ..."[26] Schools are meant to develop civic virtue and responsible citizenship, to educate in an environment free of bias, prejudice and intolerance. It would not be correct, in this context, to limit the scope of s. 4 to a determination of skills and knowledge.

On one point, there was unanimous agreement among all the judges who considered this case: There is no evidence to indicate that graduates of the TWU education program are likely to discriminate against students on the basis of sexual orientation. But Rowles took the view that no such evidence is necessary. In her opinion, the publicly professed views on homosexuality expressed by students at TWU were discriminatory enough to disqualify all TWU graduates from teaching in the public schools. She wrote:

> In coming to this conclusion, I have considered TWU's argument, supported by the intervenors [British Columbia Civil Liberties Association and British Columbia Catholic Civil Rights League], that the Community Standards only condemn homosexual behaviour while at TWU, and do not condemn homosexual persons generally, and therefore do not discriminate or promote discrimination against homosexual persons. While the submissions of TWU and the intervenors convince me that the Free Church and the Catholic Church distinguish between the condemnation of homosexual behaviour and the condemnation of homosexual persons, I am not convinced such a distinction is supportable within human rights law.

Justice L'Heureux-Dubé of the Supreme Court of Canada took the same view. In a dissenting opinion in *Trinity Western,* she maintained: "In this case, the undeniable fact is that TWU students sign their names to a discriminatory document." And why is the document discriminatory? Because it directs students that they must "refrain from practices that are biblically condemned." With this argument, L'Heureux-Dubé implied as an undeniable fact that the Bible is a discriminatory document. One wonders why on this basis, she would not propose to ban the Bible outright.

The statement of community standards at TWU not only condemns immoral behaviour as designated in the Bible, but also admonishes that "all students are responsible to: – OBEY JESUS' COMMANDMENT TO HIS DISCIPLES ... ECHOED BY THE APOSTLE PAUL ... TO LOVE ONE ANOTHER. In general this involves showing respect for all people regardless of race or gender and regard for human life at all stages. It includes making a habit of edifying others, showing compassion, demonstrating unselfishness, and displaying patience."[27] Yet not even this affirmation of an overriding obligation to show respect, compassion, unselfishness, and patience for all people mollified L'Heureux-Dubé. Echoing Rowles, she wrote:

> I am dismayed that at various points in the history of this case the argument has been made that one can separate condemnation of the "sexual sin" of "homosexual behaviour" from intolerance of those with homosexual or bisexual orientations. This position alleges that one can love the sinner, but condemn the sin. But, in the words of the intervenor EGALE "requiring

someone not to act in accordance with their identity is harmful and cruel. It destroys the human spirit. Pressure to change their behaviour and deny their sexual identity has proved tremendously damaging to young persons seeking to come to terms with their sexual orientation" ... The status/conduct or identity/practice distinction for homosexuals and bisexuals should be soundly rejected.

Likewise, L'Heureux-Dubé endorsed Rowles's contention that: "Human rights law states that certain practices cannot be separated from identity, such that condemnation of the practice is a condemnation of the person." Rowles explained:

For example, condemnation of someone's religious practice central to his or her religious faith would be discrimination against the person on the grounds of religion. Human rights jurisprudence accepts that homosexual behaviour is as central to the personal identity of gays and lesbians as religious practices are to the religious identity of the faithful. The unanimous decision of the Supreme Court [in *Egan v. Canada*], that sexual orientation is an analogous ground of discrimination, recognized the degree to which sexual orientation is a personal trait and not simply a behavioural choice ...

Even if the Community Standards [at TWU] are understood only to condemn homosexual behaviour and not people, the condemnation is still a harmful one. It is an insidious type of harm because it requires people to deny, condemn, or conceal a part of their own identity.

Note the sweeping implications of this interpretation of the law on equality rights for homosexuals. It is not just the Catholic Church and the Evangelical Free Church of Canada that affirm the practice of homosexuality to be sinful and wrong: Virtually every other Evangelical Protestant and Orthodox church upholds this same view. And so does Orthodox Judaism. Such considerations were of no account to Rowles. She insisted: "The fact that anti-homosexual attitudes and beliefs are often endorsed by some of our most venerated institutions cannot lessen the seriousness of the discrimination. In fact, the pervasiveness of anti-homosexual attitudes in our society points to the need to identify and address it. Failure to do so risks implicitly condoning and perpetuating homophobic discrimination."

In *Vriend* the Supreme Court of Canada listed several reasons for lamenting the omission of sexual orientation from Alberta's human rights legislation. The Court opined: "Perhaps most important is the psychological harm which may ensue from this state of affairs. Fear of discrimination will logically lead to concealment of true identity and this must be harmful to personal confidence and self-esteem." By analogy, L'Heureux-Dubé and Rowles held that a school teacher cannot lawfully state in a public school that sexual intercourse outside of marriage is sinful and wrong because such a statement would be apt to wound the self-esteem of any homosexual or bisexual student who happens to be in attendance. Is it at least permissible for a public school teacher to express such a view outside the classroom provided that he or she does not refer to the sinfulness of homosexual conduct inside a public school? L'Heureux-Dubé and Rowles do not think so. For authority, they cited the judgment of the Supreme Court of Canada in *Ross v. New Brunswick School District No. 15*, 1996 SCC.

At issue in this case was the ruling of the New Brunswick Human Rights Tribunal that School District No. 15 must remove Malcolm Ross from the classroom for repeatedly and publicly expressing racist and discriminatory comments against Jews during his off-duty time. The board of inquiry found no evidence that Ross had ever expressed his anti-Semitic views in class. Nonetheless, the board held that the school district had violated the ban on discrimination on the basis of religion and ancestry in section 5(1)(b) of the New Brunswick Human Rights Code by allowing a notorious anti-Semite like Ross to go on teaching. Both the Court of Queen's Bench and the Court of Appeal for New Brunswick struck down the order of the board of inquiry on the ground that removing Ross from the classroom for expressing anti-Semitic opinions during his free time violated the guarantee of freedom of expression in section 2 of the Charter in a way that could not be justified in a free and democratic society as permitted by section 1 of the Charter.

Upon further appeal, the Supreme Court of Canada unanimously reversed these judgments. In reasons written by Justice La Forest, the Court held: "By their conduct, teachers as 'medium' must be perceived to uphold the values, beliefs and knowledge sought to be transmitted by the school system. The conduct of a teacher is evaluated on the basis of his or her position, rather than whether the conduct occurs within the classroom or beyond." L'Heureux-Dubé argued that the same goes for teachers in training at Trinity Western: "Whether or not TWU students' signatures on the Community Standards contract reflect their true beliefs, it is not patently unreasonable for the BCCT to treat their public expressions of discrimination as potentially affecting the public school communities in which TWU graduates wish to teach." L'Heureux-Dubé added: "Without the existence of supportive classroom environments, homosexual and bisexual students will be forced to remain invisible and reluctant to approach their teachers. They will be victims of identity erasure, forced to endure what Prof. Kathleen Lahey has called 'a "spiral of silence" in which lesbians and gays modify their behaviour to avoid the impact of prejudice.'" As L'Heureux-Dubé noted, Lahey made this statement in testimony before the board of inquiry in *Brillinger v. Brockie.*

What about the right of students at TWU to freedom of expression as guaranteed by section 2(b) of the Charter? L'Heureux-Dubé and Rowles both contended that the decision of the BCCT to deny automatic certification as public school teachers to students who had signed TWU's Community Standards contract constituted a reasonable and demonstrably justifiable restriction on freedom of expression for the purpose of attaining the pressing and substantial objective of assuring a supportive classroom environment for homosexual students. In support of this position, L'Heureux-Dubé noted that the Supreme Court of Canada stated in *Ross*: "There can be no doubt that the attempt to foster equality, respect and tolerance in the Canadian educational system is a laudable goal." She also recalled that in commenting upon the evils of child pornography in *R. v. Sharpe*, 2001 SCC 2, she, Bastarache, and Gonthier affirmed: "Because of their physical, mental, and emotional immaturity, children are one of the most vulnerable groups in society." According to L'Heureux-Dubé, it follows that just as vulnerable children should be protected from anti-Semitic teachers and child pornography, so, too, are they entitled under the Charter to protection from public school teachers who uphold the traditional teaching of the Christian church on the sinfulness of gay sex.

While L'Heureux-Dubé and Rowles were both writing in dissent in *Trinity Western,* this can be of small comfort to freedom-loving Canadians. Given the inclination of the Supreme Court of Canada to adopt ever more radical interpretations of the Canadian Charter of Rights and Freedoms, it is portentous that two such senior appeals court judges have manifested such antipathy for the rights of theologically orthodox Christians and Jews.

As it is, eight of the nine judges on Canada's Supreme Court ruled in *Trinity Western* that the BCCT erred in rejecting TWU's proposed education program. Writing for the majority, Iacobucci and Bastarache stated: "It is important to note that this is a private institution that is exempted, in part, from the British Columbia human rights legislation and to which the Charter does not apply. To state that the voluntary adoption of a code of conduct based on a person's own religious beliefs, in a private institution, is sufficient to engage [equality rights in] s. 15 would be inconsistent with freedom of conscience and religion, which co-exist with the right to equality."

Iacobucci and Bastarache also pointed out that "if TWU's Community Standards could be sufficient in themselves to justify denying accreditation, it is difficult to see how the same logic would not result in the denial of accreditation to members of a particular church." Neither L'Heureux-Dubé nor Rowles addressed this point, but the implication of their position is clear: No member of a church, synagogue, mosque, or other organization that regards the practice of homosexuality as wrong should be allowed to teach in a public school. However, while stopping short of adopting so extreme a position, the majority of the Supreme Court of Canada drew a sharp distinction between belief and actions, saying:

> The proper place to draw the line in cases like the one at bar is generally between belief and conduct. The freedom to hold beliefs is broader than the freedom to act on them. Absent concrete evidence that training teachers at TWU fosters discrimination in the public schools of B.C., the freedom of individuals to adhere to certain religious beliefs while at TWU should be respected. The BCCT, rightfully, does not require public universities with teacher education programs to screen out applicants who hold sexist, racist or homophobic beliefs. For better or for worse, tolerance of divergent beliefs is a hallmark of a democratic society.

Consider some of the implications of the distinction drawn by the Court between the freedom to hold beliefs and the right to act upon them. In light of the *Trinity Western* judgment, can a teacher in a public school safely assume that he or she can legally refer students to www.freetobeme.com – a youth-oriented website that helps youngsters to resist the temptation to act on homosexual feelings? Surely not. FreeToBeMe is sponsored by New Directions for Life Ministries, a Canadian-based organization that aims to "work specifically with men and women who choose to leave homosexuality while respecting those who make other choices." In line with the reasoning in *Trinity Western,* the Supreme Court of Canada is all too likely to rule that a teacher has no right under the Charter to refer a young student to any counselling service that might help him or her to avoid taking up a potentially lethal homosexual lifestyle.

In a commentary in the *Globe and Mail* on 31 May 2001, Ian Hunter examined the Court's distinction in *Trinity Western* between belief and conduct. He stated:

> In essence, the Supreme Court has ruled that there is a right to believe what you want as long as you never communicate those beliefs or attempt to put them into practice. Trinity Western ought not to be celebrating such a Lilliputian view of religious freedom.
>
> If I may paraphrase the university's victory in words that might still have a certain resonance among its own faculty and students: You are free to be

hearers of The Word but not doers; you may render unto God when on campus but only to Caesar off campus. By their deeds no one shall know them.

Iain Benson disagreed with this stark interpretation of the import of the *Trinity Western* ruling. In response to Hunter's article, he said:

> My respectful view is that Prof. Ian Hunter has seriously mischaracterized the result of this decision ... He minimizes the main holding and draws a very negative conclusion from vague suggestions and undeveloped analysis elsewhere in the decision. I do not think this is wise or accurate.
>
> The fact is that the court does not define what constitutes valid religious expression and what constitutes "discrimination" in the case. They do, admittedly, leave open the interpretation that Prof. Hunter mentions, but they certainly don't conclude on the matter and I would doubt very much if that is where they would go.[28]

Hunter and Benson are two of Canada's leading constitutional lawyers. Their inability to agree on the potentially dire implications of the *Trinity Western* ruling underlines the most alarming aspect of this affair: There are no longer any "rules fixed and announced beforehand" defining the limits of religious liberty in Canada. In this vital respect, the rule of law has been destroyed by the Supreme Court of Canada. Instead of upholding the traditional principles of the common law and pre-Charter judicial precedents governing freedom of religion, the Court has invoked the Charter as an excuse for defining new laws on the limits of religious liberty. Hunter is pessimistic about the outcome. Benson thinks that it is wise to be sanguine. Thanks to the proclivity of the Supreme Court of Canada to flout precedents and change the law, no one can now have any sure or certain idea of the legal limits circumscribing the freedom of Canadians to act upon their honestly held, religious convictions.

Meanwhile, reasons for the sanguinity counselled by Benson have been getting ever harder to discern. In *Hall (Litigation guardian of) v. Powers*, 2002 OSCJ, Mr Justice Robert McKinnon of the Ontario Superior Court of Justice cited the declaration of the Supreme Court of Canada in *Trinity Western* that the "freedom to hold beliefs is broader than the freedom to act on them" as justification for issuing the interlocutory injunction that compelled the principal of the Monsignor John Pereyma Catholic Secondary School in Oshawa, Ontario, to allow a seventeen-year-old student, Mark Hall, to attend a high school prom with his homosexual boyfriend as a date. McKinnon stated: "At the heart of the *Trinity Western* decision lies a distinction between holding a discriminatory view and actively discriminating against someone. In

Canada we are permitted to hold views that are in conflict with public policy, but we are not permitted to act upon discriminatory views in prescribed fields of endeavour when the result is discriminatory treatment of others." In the context of the *Hall* case, McKinnon suggested that the principal "could have counselled Mark on his Church's teachings about the sinful nature of all premarital sexual activity (heterosexual or homosexual) and about the sinful nature of homosexual genital contact." But in the opinion of McKinnon, neither the principal nor members of the Catholic School Board had any right under the Constitution to act upon their understanding of Catholic doctrine by refusing to allow a seventeen-year-old student to bring a homosexual date to a high school dance.

THE *KEMPLING* CASE

For Chris Kempling, this is an issue of more than just academic interest: His livelihood as a high school teacher in Quesnel, British Columbia, is at stake. On 9 May 2002 the British Columbia College of Teachers suspended his teaching licence for one month because he had expressed his honestly held views on homosexuality in an article and a series of letters to the editor in the Quesnel *Cariboo Observer*. Kempling appealed the ruling on the ground that it violated his rights to freedom of thought, belief, opinion, and expression in section 2 of the Canadian Charter of Rights and Freedoms. In a judgment on 3 February 2004, Mr Justice Ronald Holmes of the British Columbia Supreme Court rejected the appeal.[29]

Holmes acknowledged that Kempling "has been a BCCT member since 1980, with a long and unblemished teaching career, and a notable record of community service." At the time of the controversy with the BCCT, Kempling served as the voluntary head of the Quesnel Community Health Council. What could this model citizen and teacher have written in his local newspaper to warrant suspension of his teaching licence? Holmes charged: "The appellant consistently associated homosexuals with immorality, abnormality, perversion, and promiscuity. Examples of such statements include: 'Thus my main concern with giving same sex couples legal rights in child custody issues is due to the obvious instability and short term nature of gay relationships ... My second concern is how can children develop a concept of normal sexuality, when their prime care-givers have rejected the other gender entirely?'"

Kempling argued that only discriminatory actions, not speech, can count as unprofessional conduct within the meaning of the law. Justice Holmes disagreed. He pointed out that under the rubric of "discriminatory publication," section 7(1) of the British Columbia Human Rights Code bans any statement that is likely to expose a group or class of persons to contempt because of their sexual orientation. Note the general implications of this finding: Holmes implies that it is a human rights offence for anyone, not just teachers, to lament sexual promiscuity among homosexuals in a letter to the editor of a newspaper.

In the *Trinity Western* ruling, Iacobucci and Bastarache advised: "Discriminatory conduct by a public school teacher when on duty should always be subject to disciplinary proceedings. This Court has held, however, that greater tolerance must be shown with respect to off-duty conduct. Yet disciplinary measures can still be taken when discriminatory off-duty conduct poisons the school environment." In the *Kempling* case, the BCCT cited no evidence that Kempling's letters to the editor and commentary on homosexuality in the Quesnel *Cariboo Observer* had created a poisoned environment within the Quesnel District High School. But that, too, was of no account to Justice Holmes. He said: "In my view, the appellant's published writings were harmful to the public school system ... because of their discriminatory content." As for Kempling's right to freedom of expression under section 2 of the Charter, Holmes stated as his view that the Charter does not protect "the appellant's right to express ... strictly personally-held, discriminatory views with the authority of or in the capacity of a public school teacher/counsellor."

Kempling appealed this ruling and lost again.[30] In a unanimous judgment on 13 June 2005, a three-judge panel of the Court of Appeal for British Columbia held that "it is clear that many of Mr. Kempling's published statements were discriminatory." As an example, the Court of Appeal cited the following assertion by Kempling: "Gay people are seriously at risk, not because of heterosexual attitudes, but because of their sexual behaviour, and I challenge the gay community to show some real evidence that they are trying to protect their own community members by making an attempt to promote monogamous, long lasting relationships and to combat sexual addictions [10 August 1997, *Quesnel Cariboo Observer*]."

Note that the British Columbia Court of Appeal has branded this statement "discriminatory," yet it is undoubtedly true that many, if not most, gay people are seriously at risk because of their sexual behaviour. On 23 May 2005 the *New Yorker* reported in an article in its "Fact" section that: "After years of living in constant fear of AIDS, many gay men have chosen to resume sexual practices that are almost guaranteed to make them sick. In New York City, the rate of syphilis has increased by more than four hundred per cent in the past five years. Gay men account for virtually the entire rise."[31] This alarming development is not confined to New York City. Referring to the United States as a whole, the article added: "Over the past several years, nearly every indicator of risky sexual activity has risen in the gay community. Perhaps for the first time since the beginning of the AIDS epidemic, the number of men who say they use condoms regularly is below 50 per cent; after many years of decline, the number of new HIV diagnoses among gay men increased every year between 2000 and 2003, while remaining stable in the rest of the population."

Ironically, on 14 June 2005, the day after the ruling of the Court of Appeal in *Kempling*, the *National Post* published an article by Todd Klinck, a gay man, who reported that in Toronto, too, "safer sex practices are going out of fashion in gay casual sex circles."[32] Klinck pinned much of the blame on widespread abuse of methamphetamine (popularly known as crystal) among gay men. Klinck related:

> In the last few years, I've been to bathhouses several dozen times. Crystal is everywhere. And in almost every encounter I had, the body language of my partners assumed there would be no condoms. When I brought the issue up, many guys left the room, saying they "only" have sex "raw."
>
> It has gotten to the point where to "bareback" has become a verb. There are bareback Web sites, bareback chatrooms and a huge trend on gay Internet meeting spots toward a type of sex called "PnP" (Party and Play), which is an acronym that almost always translates to mean "sex while doing crystal meth."[33]

Like Kempling, Klink observed that gays are seriously at risk because of their sexual behaviour. He cited the case of a high school friend who confided that he had become HIV positive because of crystal. Klinck wrote: "He said it 'made him do things he wouldn't normally do.' Crystal sends people on an insatiable and obsessive quest for as much sex with as many people as possible, sometimes for days at a time, and almost always bareback."[34]

Klinck has been no less vivid than Kempling in describing drug abuse and promiscuous behaviour among gay men. Yet Klinck runs no risk of getting hauled before a human rights tribunal on charges of publishing something that is "likely to expose a person or group or class of persons to ... contempt because of ... the sexual orientation ... of that person or that group or class of persons."[35] Why not? Because Klinck approves of such behaviour. He states: "I am not against all forms of drug use, and I am definitely not against promiscuity. Party drugs such as Ecstasy, Special K (ketamine), cocaine, amongst others, have their risks, but can sometimes be used in moderation without destroying one's life. But crystal methamphetamine is a different creature, one with a horrendous track record for causing severe addiction, permanent brain damage, paranoia and violence ... While the gay community has had considerable success at getting publicity and support for same-sex marriage, we are less public about our uglier problems."[36]

Meanwhile, Kempling's legal problems have multiplied. He got into trouble with the Quesnel District School Board again in January 2004 as a result of an interview with the Canadian Broadcasting Corporation (CBC) in which he discussed the therapy that he offers through his private counselling practise to homosexuals who wish to change their sexual orientation.[37] In response, the board sent him a disciplinary letter charging him with violating a board directive issued in May 2003 that bars him from making any more public comments on any same-sex issue. Kempling refused to back down. On 12 January 2005 he wrote another letter to the editor of the *Cariboo Observer*, in which he expressed opposition on behalf of the Christian Heritage Party (CHP) to the Martin government's bill on same-sex marriage.[38] On 4 April 2005 Ed Napier, the superintendent for the Quesnel School District, notified Kempling that his teaching licence would be suspended for an additional three months because of this letter. Kempling was planning at the time to run for Parliament on behalf of the CHP. He pointed out that in ordering him to refrain from making any public comments on a homosexual issue, the board had inhibited his political career, impeded his private counselling business, and cost him over $25,000 in lost wages and income. He plans to appeal to the British Columbia Human Rights Commission on the ground that in subjecting him to a gag order and suspension, the school superintendent violated his rights to freedom of thought, belief, opinion, and association under the Charter as well as the provision in section 13(1) of the British Columbia Human Rights Code that: "A person must not ... refuse to employ or refuse to continue to employ a person ... because of the ... political belief ... of that person." Counsel for the school board will no doubt argue that the board can lawfully suspend Kempling by virtue of the equality rights of homosexuals in section 15 of the Charter as well as the provision in section 13(4) of the provincial Human Rights Code that allows an employer to refuse to employ a person on the basis of the person's political belief if the refusal is based on a "bona fide occupational requirement."

In the *Reference re Same-Sex Marriage*, 2004 SCC 79, the Supreme Court of Canada was asked, "Does the Freedom of Religion Guaranteed by Section 2(a) of the Charter Protect Religious Officials From Being Compelled to Perform Same-Sex Marriages Contrary to Their Religious Beliefs?" The Court, in a unanimous and anonymously written response, stated: "If a promulgated statute were to enact compulsion, we conclude that such compulsion would almost certainly run afoul of the Charter guarantee of freedom of religion, given the expansive protection afforded to religion by s. 2(a) of the Charter." This is staggering: How can anyone take this assertion seriously? If the Supreme Court of Canada has afforded expansive protection to religion through its interpretation of the guarantee of freedom of religion in section 2(a) of the Charter, how is it that human rights tribunals and the courts have harassed and persecuted numerous Christians over the past ten years for nothing other than the honest expression of their religious convictions? Mayor Dianne Haskett, Scott Brockie, Hugh Owens, Bill Whatcott, and Bill Kempling are just some of the more notable victims. If freedom of religion still enjoys broad legal protection in Canada, how could an official of the Canada Customs and Revenue Agency have dared in June 2004 to threaten to revoke the charitable status of the Roman Catholic Diocese of Calgary if Bishop Fred Henry did not withdraw a pastoral letter that criticized Prime Minister Martin for professing to uphold the Catholic faith while flouting the teaching of the Church on vital moral issues like abortion and gay marriage?[39] In the cases of King's University College and Trinity Western University, the Supreme Court of Canada has itself constricted the freedom of religion that the staff and students at these Christian universities enjoyed prior to the Charter.

In the *Reference re Same-Sex Marriage,* the Court noted that in addition to the performance of same-sex marriages by ministers of religion, "concerns were raised about the compulsory use of sacred places for the celebration of such marriages and about being compelled to otherwise assist in the celebration of same-sex marriages. The reasoning that leads us to conclude that the guarantee of freedom of religion protects against the compulsory celebration of same-sex marriages, suggests that the same would hold for these concerns." Is this so? Why, then, just a few weeks later, did the British Columbia Human Rights Tribunal proceed with hearings into a complaint by a lesbian couple in Coquitlam who charged that a local chapter of the Knights of Columbus had violated their constitutional right not to be discriminated against on the basis of their sexual orientation by refusing to rent them a hall for a same-sex wedding?[40]

On 14 December 2004 Justice Minister Irwin Cotler assured the Commons that both ministers of religion and secular marriage commissioners who have religious objections to "same-sex marriage" are legally entitled to refuse to marry same-sex couples. He said: "The Supreme Court decision is clear. The Charter is clear. Freedom of religion is protected and people who are not religious officials are also protected with respect to their religious beliefs." Is this so? In short order, the Governments of British Columbia, Manitoba, Newfoundland, and Saskatchewan all advised their civil marriage commissioners that they must, willy-nilly, conduct same-sex weddings. When Saskatchewan Justice Minister Frank Quennell was asked what might happen to Christian marriage commissioners who refuse on religious grounds to perform same-sex marriages, Quennell said: "We'd have to investigate the circumstances and potentially remove their power to perform civil marriages because they weren't willing to administer the law as it stands."[41] He also warned that the Saskatchewan Human Rights Commission could place further sanctions on a Christian marriage commissioner who refused on religious grounds to perform a same-sex marriage if a spurned same-sex couple filed a complaint.

Who is right: Justice Minister Cotler or the justice ministers of British Columbia, Manitoba, Newfoundland, and Saskatchewan? No one knows. In this as in so many other cases, there are no longer any clear legal rules fixed and announced beforehand to safeguard Canadians. Undaunted, Orville Nichols, a marriage commissioner in Regina with more than twenty-three years of experience, refused to obey Quennell's directive that he must either agree to perform same-sex weddings or resign his post. Nichols is a Baptist who objects on religious grounds to joining same-sex couples in marriage. In a complaint filed with the Saskatchewan Human Rights Commission on 5 February 2005, he argued that Quennell's order violated his right to freedom of conscience and religion as guaranteed in the Saskatchewan Human Rights Code and the Canadian Charter of Rights and Freedoms.[42] However, a few weeks later, two homosexuals whom Nichols had refused to marry targeted him for a human rights complaint on the ground that he had violated their equality rights in the Saskatchewan Code and the Canadian Charter. Not surprisingly, the commission was quick to take up this latter complaint. Early in July 2005, it summoned Nichols to appear for a hearing into the matter.[43]

Nichols has resolved with the assistance of his son-in-law, who is a lawyer, to take his fight for fundamental human rights all the way, if necessary, to the Supreme Court of Canada. Asked what he would do if he were to end up losing on all appeals and face a court order requiring him to apologize to the homosexual complainants for refusing to marry them, Nichols insisted that he would defy the court. "I'll go to jail," he vowed. "I will not apologize to them for turning them down for something I do not believe is right. I will not go against any of my personal beliefs. I mean if I did I could not live with myself."[44] Meanwhile, Kempling also faces a stark choice: According to the British Columbia Court of Appeal, he must give up his career as a teacher in the public schools unless he is willing to forgo any more public expressions of his Christian convictions on the sinfulness of homosexual behaviour. And let there be no mistaking the implications of this finding: The same choice is impending for elementary and secondary school teachers all across Canada. And they are not alone. The Evangelical Fellowship of Canada has warned that the *Kempling* precedent suggests that all professionals – be they teachers, lawyers, doctors, accountants, or dentists – could be subjected to a judicially enforced ban on practising their profession for speaking out on the politically incorrect side of the debate over same-sex marriage.[45] Not even Roman Catholic priests feel safe anymore. In testimony before the Senate Committee on Legal and Constitutional Affairs on 13 July 2005, Marc Cardinal Ouellet, the primate of Canada, said: "A kind of climate is developing in which people no longer dare say what they think. Even from the pulpit, we feel threatened if we recall the sexual morality of the Church. That is also part of religious freedom. Even in our churches, these words are troubling, and we feel accused of homophobia, hatred or of hurting homosexuals."[46]

The British Columbia Court of Appeal was dismissive of Kempling's claim that the BCCT had violated his right to freedom of religion as guaranteed in section 2 of the Charter by suspending him for the honest expression of his Christian convictions. Citing the dictum of the Supreme Court of Canada in *Trinity Western* that "the freedom to hold beliefs is broader than the freedom to act on them," the Court asserted: "There is no evidence that establishes that his ability to practice his religion would in any way be compromised by his being restricted from making discriminating public statements about homosexuals."

In short, the Court of Appeal for British Columbia agrees with what Hunter said about *Trinity Western*: "In essence, the Supreme Court has ruled that there is a right to believe what you want as long as you never communicate those beliefs or attempt to put them into practice. You are free to be hearers of The Word but not doers; you may render unto God when [in Church] but only to Caesar [out of Church]. By their deeds no one shall know them."

7

The Chief Justice Defends Judicial Supremacy

In several articles and speeches, Chief Justice Beverley McLachlin has strayed deep into the political arena to defend the Supreme Court of Canada from charges of subverting the legislative process and undermining the rule of law. For example, in June 1999 she pointed out in an article published in the magazine *Policy Options* that the dispute over judicial activism "often reduces itself to a debate about whether one likes or does not like a particular judicial decision."[1] On this point, there is no disputing: Some critics of the courts seem to think that all objectionable judicial decisions stem from judicial activism and that all praiseworthy judgments are the products of judicial restraint. This conception of the nature of judicial activism and judicial restraint is mistaken. As we have seen, judicial activism denotes in precise legal parlance the disposition of unelected judges to invalidate the political decisions of elected legislators in enacting the laws and the Constitution, whereas judicial restraint consists in a determination of the judiciary to uphold the laws and the Constitution as originally enacted and understood.[2] Judgments stemming from judicial activism do not necessarily lead to unfair or unjust outcomes. And the same goes for the converse: In some cases, judicial activism has led to a result that the average person would consider far fairer and more agreeable than the outcome of judicial restraint.

Consider the controversial judgment of the Court of Appeal for British Columbia in *Trociuk v. British Columbia (Attorney General)*, 2001 BCCA 368. The appellant in this case, Darrel Trociuk, began living together with his girlfriend, Reni Ernst, in June 1993. In August 1994 she moved out of the home, but they continued to have consensual sexual relations. In the following year, Ernst became pregnant with triplets, and subsequent DNA testing confirmed that Trociuk is the father.

While still pregnant in November 1995, Ernst moved back in with Trociuk. Three weeks later, she was confined to hospital in a "high risk situation." Trociuk regularly visited Ernst in the hospital, brought her meals, occasionally slept over with her in the hospital, and was present throughout the birthing process on 29 January 1996. Trociuk asked Ernst to register his children with his surname. She refused to do so, although she did not contest his paternity. Instead, she gave the children only her surname and listed the father as "unacknowledged" on the birth-registration form. In March 1996 she moved out of Trociuk's home and took the children with her.

On 15 May 1997 Ernst obtained a court order requiring Trociuk to make support payments to her for the children. He fulfilled this obligation. Still, Ernst refused his pleas to change the names of the children to bear at least his surname and her surname in hyphenated form. As a last resort, he appealed to the courts. In a sworn affidavit, Ernst agreed that Trociuk was "a self-employed, hard-working Canadian citizen," who "has never abused the children, never abused RE [Ernst] and has never missed a support payment for the children." Nonetheless, both the Supreme Court and Court of Appeal for British Columbia rejected his name-change petition on the ground that a 1987 amendment to the province's Vital Statistics Act had given mothers an unfettered right to name their children. In fact, under the terms of this law, no fathers – married or unmarried – were entitled to have their surname included in the names given to their children.

Madam Justice Prowse of the British Columbia Court of Appeal made clear in her dissenting opinion in *Trociuk* that she regarded the treatment of fathers under the Vital Statistics Act as patently unfair. She also held that it was contrary to the ban on discrimination on the basis of sex in section 15 of the Canadian Charter of Rights and Freedoms. As a remedy, Prowse said that she would order the director of Vital Statistics for British Columbia to change the surname of the children on the birth registration to Ernst-Trociuk. And for the protection of other fathers, she also suggested that the Court should amend the Vital Statistics Act by reading in a show-cause procedure giving the father a right to challenge the refusal of the mother to acknowledge him in the naming of his children on the ground that her refusal is unreasonable.

Here we have a quintessential example of judicial activism properly understood: Instead of upholding the law as written and intended by elected representatives of the people in the Legislature, Prowse invoked the guarantee of equality rights in section 15 of the Charter as an excuse for changing the law to accord with her idea of what is just, fair, reasonable, and appropriate. In contrast, Justices Mary Newbury and Mary Southin upheld the plain words and meaning of the law in their joint judgment for the Court in *Trociuk*. In reasons for the majority, Southin reviewed the history of family law legislation in British Columbia that had led to the 1987 Vital Statistics Act. She concluded:

> To end this recital of the shift in legislative values in this Province since its founding, I infer, not only from the changes to these statutes, but also from changes to the Family Relations Act since it was first enacted in 1978 (S.B.C. 1978, c. 20), that the legislature of British Columbia no longer considers that marriage, in the classic sense of a union carried out according to usages prescribed by law of one man and one woman, a union which conferred a status with concomitant rights on the parties, their issue and their kin, is a social institution of paramount or, indeed, any importance. Whether the people of British Columbia generally understand that this is what the legislature has accomplished, whether by accident or design, is an interesting question.
>
> Whether this legislative policy is a good thing or a bad thing is not for a judge to say.

As for the Charter, Southin said: "The word 'discrimination' as it is used in the Charter must take something of its breadth, although I would not presume to say how much, from the world of the framers of the Charter. Would they have thought that this complaint of the appellant was a complaint of 'discrimination'?" Having answered this question in the negative, Southin rejected Trociuk's appeal. With the support of Newbury, she upheld both the law and the Charter as originally understood by elected representatives of the people in the legislative branch of government. All judges should consistently exercise such judicial restraint. They should all respect the separation of powers between the legislative and judicial branches of government.

Consider, however, the ultimate outcome of this case. In a ruling on 6 June 2003 the Supreme Court of Canada unanimously overturned the decision of Southin and Newbury in *Trociuk*.[3] Madam Justice Marie Deschamps served notice in her reasons for judgment for the Supreme Court of Canada that the British Columbia Legislature would have one year to come up with a suitable amendment to the

Vital Statistics Act that would allow a father to appeal a decision to exclude his surname from the surname given to his children. Specifically, Deschamps suggested: "The legislature could provide that a judge in chambers would alone determine whether a father has been justifiably excluded, based solely on affidavit evidence." In this way, a judge could decide on the basis of sworn affidavits alone that a father is not entitled to have his surname given to his children because he had abused the mother. There would be no need for the mother to confront the father in court. Deschamps warned in her conclusion that if the Legislature failed to come up with an amendment to the Vital Statistics Act within the one-year deadline set by the Court, the relevant existing provisions of the Act would be invalidated by the Court's unilateral judicial decree.

Note that all the judges who dealt with this case agreed that the discrimination against married fathers in the British Columbia Vital Statistics Act was manifestly unfair and unjust. The differences of opinion among these judges centred on how the law should be changed. While the judicial activists on the Supreme Court of Canada presumed to supervise and direct this process, the practitioners of judicial restraint in the British Columbia courts left it entirely up to the Legislature of British Columbia to decide if this bad and unjust law warranted amendment.

Clearly, *Trociuk* demonstrates what McLachlin suggested in *Policy Options*: Judicial activism does not always result in unfair and unpopular outcomes. Having made this obvious point in her article, McLachlin proceeded to demolish another straw man: the notion that restrained judges never change the law. She wrote: "Some people equate judicial activism with any judicial decision that changes the law."[4] To explain the falsehood of this supposition, she added:

> The venerable tradition of developing the law through an accumulation of precedent lies at the heart of our legal system, and is the lifeblood of a socially responsible body of law. New circumstances are brought before the courts. In applying the law, be it a previous case or a provision of the Charter, judges examine the law and the circumstances to see whether the old law should apply or whether it now seems unjust to do so. If a careful analysis reveals that the old law no longer reflects what is considered to be fair and appropriate, it is modified. This involves changing the law. But if changing the law is judicial activism, then judicial activism is neither new nor undesirable.[5]

Here, McLachlin muddles the distinction between incremental and radical change in the law. While restrained judges make no more than marginal adjustments to adapt established legal principles to the facts of a particular case, activist judges are not loathe to commit major breaks with precedent for the purpose of changing the law to accord with their personal ideological preferences. This is a key difference between judicial activism and judicial restraint. McLachlin should understand this point. In *Watkins v. Olafson*, 1989 SCC, she wrote:

> There are sound reasons supporting ... judicial reluctance to dramatically recast established rules of law. The court may not be in the best position to assess the deficiencies of the existing law, much less problems which may be associated with the changes it might make. The court has before it a single case; major changes in the law should be predicated on a wider view of how the rule will operate in the broad generality of cases. Moreover, the court may not be in a position to appreciate fully the economic and policy issues underlying the choice it is asked to make. Major changes to the law often involve devising subsidiary rules and procedures relevant to their implementation, a task which is better accomplished through consultation between courts and practitioners than by judicial decree. Finally, and perhaps most importantly, there is the long-established principle that in a constitutional democracy it is the legislature, as the elected branch of government, which should assume the major responsibility for law reform.

Quite so. McLachlin added: "Considerations such as these suggest that major revisions of the law are best left to the legislature. Where the matter is one of a small extension of existing rules to meet the exigencies of a new case and the consequences of the change are readily assessable, judges can and should vary existing principles. But where the revision is major and its ramifications complex, the courts must proceed with great caution."

This last assertion is debatable. Practitioners of judicial restraint insist that the courts should not proceed with "great caution" in making major changes in the law: They should proceed not to make these changes at all. Unelected judges should leave legislating to elected legislators. But has the Supreme Court of Canada been reluctant to engineer major changes in the law? McLachlin thinks so. In her *Policy Options* article, she stated:

> Judges, it is said, are too eager to overturn laws, too ready to strike statutes down, too apt to "rewrite" laws enacted by Parliament and the legislatures. I note at the outset that there is not much hard evidence that judges are inappropriately activist, whatever that many mean. A recent study by Prof. Patrick Monahan of Osgoode Hall Law School concludes on the basis of considerable

statistical analysis that the Supreme Court of Canada, far from being activist, as many have charged, is rather inclined to be judicially conservative and deferential to the elected arms of government. The same study suggests that it is very hard to find instances of the Court "rewriting" laws. Given the absence of any contrary studies of similar depth, this should at least give the critics pause.[6]

In the study cited by the chief justice, Monahan found that between 1996 and 1998, the Supreme Court of Canada had invalidated statutes in only twelve of ninety-eight pertinent cases. On this basis, he concluded that justices of the Supreme Court of Canada are not activist. He wrote: "If anything, they could be faulted in some cases for not being active enough ... When you look at the overall record, it's difficult to see where the court is usurping the role of the legislature."[7] Really? In arriving at this conclusion, Monahan did not take into account the 1997 *Feeney* decision because the Court did not invalidate a statute in this case. This is true, but *Feeney* overturned a longstanding rule of the common law that the Court had consistently upheld prior to the Charter. By any reasonable standard, *Feeney* is no less an instance of judicial law making than the Court's 1998 ruling in *Vriend,* which rewrote the Alberta Human Rights Act. Besides, with the one ruling in *M. v. H.* that redefined "spouse" to include same-sex couples, the Supreme Court of Canada undermined literally hundreds of federal and provincial statutes. Ted Morton and Rainer Knopff observe: "A single blockbuster case like this renders denials of judicial activism problematic."[8]

McLachlin allowed in her *Policy Options* article that: "Radical changes of the law can be considered 'activist' by definition. However, this does not get us any closer to answering the question of whether the Charter has made judges activist. We are left with many difficulties. The first problem is whether the fact that a change is radical necessarily means it is bad. Was it necessarily bad that the Privy Council in 1929 ruled that the word 'persons' included women, thereby opening public life and the professions to women? The change was radical, but most would argue, desirable and long overdue."

McLachlin is referring to the judgment of the Judicial Committee of the Privy Council in *Edwards v. Canada (A.G.),* 1929 JCPC, the so-called Persons Case. At the instigation of Henrietta Muir Edwards and four other Alberta women dubbed the "Famous Five," the Liberal government of Prime Minister Mackenzie King asked the Supreme Court of Canada: "Are women eligible for appointment to the Senate of Canada?" In a unanimous response on 24 April 1928, the Supreme

Court of Canada said "no."[9] McLachlin has observed that this ruling was

> consistent with a cautious, positivist, textual approach to the Constitution. The Court, although conceding that women were obviously persons in the everyday sense of the word, held that they were not qualified persons for purposes of the provisions governing appointments to the Senate. Its analysis focused on the state of the common law at the time of Confederation, 60 years earlier, and the intention of the framers of the BNA [British North America] Act. After all, at the time of Confederation no one imagined women would serve in the Senate, so how could it be said that the drafters of the Constitution intended the word "persons" to include the feminine gender?[10]

Indeed, for the judges of the Supreme Court of Canada who ruled in *Edwards*, the intended meaning of the word "persons" by the drafters of the Constitution was the decisive consideration. Chief Justice Frances Anglin underlined this point in his reasons for the Court:

> In considering this matter we are, of course, in no wise concerned with the desirability or the undesirability of the presence of women in the Senate, nor with any political aspect of the question submitted. Our whole duty is to construe, to the best of our ability, the relevant provisions of the B.N.A. Act, 1867, and upon that construction to base our answer.
>
> Passed in the year 1867, the various provisions of the B.N.A. Act ... bear today the same construction which the courts would, if then required to pass upon them, have given to them when they were first enacted. If the phrase "qualified persons" in s. 24 includes women today, it has so included them since 1867.

Anglin added: "In deciding the question before us, we have to construe not merely the words of the Act of Parliament but the intent of the legislature." He recalled that in 1867, women had no legal right to sit in the House of Commons or to vote in federal elections. Moreover, in 1867 women did not yet have the right to vote or to serve in any legislative body in any English-speaking country. Anglin also pointed out that "never from 1867 to the present time has any woman ever sat in the Senate of Canada, nor has any suggestion of women's eligibility for appointment to that House until quite recently been publicly made." Citing this evidence as a guide to the proper interpretation of the text of section 24, he concluded: "Women are not eligible for appointment by the Governor General to the Senate of Canada under Section 24 of the British North America Act, 1867, because they are not 'qualified persons' within the meaning of that section." The entire Court, which included Justice Duff, concurred.

However, in a sensational judgment on 18 October 1929, the law lords on the Judicial Committee of the Privy Council reversed the Supreme Court of Canada. In doing so, their Lordships also reversed the rulings of English Courts in likewise holding that women are ineligible to hold public office. In reasons for judgment on behalf of the Judicial Committee, Viscount Sankey stated: "Their Lordships are of [the] opinion that the word 'persons' in s. 24 does include women, and that women are eligible to be summoned to and become members of the Senate of Canada." In an attempt to adorn this ruling with a patina of legality, Sankey advanced some textual arguments for his interpretation of section 24 but stopped well short of claiming that the Fathers of Confederation understood that through the adoption of section 24, they were authorizing women to serve in the Senate. To justify flouting the original understanding of the drafters of the Constitution, Sankey contended: "The British North America Act planted in Canada a living tree capable of growth and expansion within its natural limits." By implication, he held that just as a living tree must adapt to changes in its environment, so must the Constitution adjust to the assertion of women's rights. "The exclusion of women from all public offices is a relic of days more barbarous than ours," he wrote. "From 1916 to 1922 various Dominion and provincial Acts were passed to admit women to the franchise and to the right to sit as members in both Dominion and provincial legislative bodies. At the present time women are entitled to vote and to be candidates: (1) At all Dominion elections on the same basis as men; (2) At all provincial elections save in the province of Quebec." On the basis of this nonlegal analysis, he concluded that section 24 of the British North America Act, 1867, should now be interpreted as allowing women to serve in the Senate.

Chief Justice McLachlin's claim that this Privy Council judgment had the effect of "thereby opening public life and the professions to women" is plainly incorrect. As Sankey noted, the elected chambers of Parliament and all but one of the provincial legislatures of Canada had been opened up to women prior to his ruling in *Edwards*. Three of the Famous Five – Nellie McClung, Louise McKinney, and Irene Parlby – had served in the Alberta Legislature. In 1916 the leader of the group, Emily Murphy, was appointed to serve as a magistrate in Alberta, the first in the British Empire. In sum, public life and the professions had, to a large extent, already been opened up to women in Canada well before the judgment of the Privy Council in *Edwards*.

Granted, giving women the right to serve in the Senate was a significant additional victory for equality between the sexes. At a Famous Five breakfast meeting in Ottawa on 17 October 2000, the featured speaker, Chief Justice McLachlin, commended the Privy Council for having found in *Edwards* "that women were indeed persons and qualified to be appointed to the Senate." She added: "It was a great day, not only for women but for Canadian law. In his judgment, Viscount Sankey coined the phrase that has been the animating premise of our constitutional law ever since. 'The British North America Act planted in Canada a living tree capable of growth and expansion within its natural limits,' he pronounced. Canadian constitutional law would never be the same. To this day, when we interpret our Constitution we look at what its words mean in the context of the society in which we now live. We try to give life and meaning to the text in the real world."[11]

To some extent, the "living tree" metaphor makes sense: The Constitution of Canada cannot be subjected to a fixed and frozen interpretation. The courts are necessarily involved in constantly revising the interpretations of old legislative enactments to take into account unforeseen changes in the social and economic environment. Thus in the *Radio Reference*, 1932 JCPC, the Privy Council was asked to determine whether Parliament or the provincial legislatures have constitutional jurisdiction over radio transmissions. In 1867 the Fathers of Confederation had not foreseen the development of radios or any form of long-distant wireless communication. The closest reference to something like radio transmissions in the Constitution is the provision in section 92(10) that gives Parliament exclusive jurisdiction over "Telegraphs, and other [interprovincial] Works and Undertakings." By analogy, the Privy Council allocated exclusive jurisdiction over radio communications to Parliament. In this way, through a reasonable interpretation of the plain words of the law as originally understood, their lordships allowed the Constitution of Canada to grow and adapt to the unanticipated development of radio communications.

Lord Sankey's ruling in *Edwards* was fundamentally different. Instead of upholding the original understanding of section 24 of the British North America Act, he effectually amended the Constitution through interpretation so as to update the law as he saw fit. In an article published in *The Canadian Bar Review* in 1937, Arthur Berriedale Keith, an eminent constitutional authority at the University of Edinburgh, took exception to this high-handed and, at the time, unusual judicial manoeuvre. Keith observed that Sankey's ruling in *Edwards* "has never carried much conviction for those who hold that the convenience of avoiding an amendment of the Canadian constitution should not have been allowed to produce a situation wholly foreign to the minds of those who framed the constitution of Canada."[12] In contrast, McLachlin lauds the *Edwards* ruling. With reference to this judgment, she acknowledges: "The law was altered, indeed fundamentally reversed."[13] But this is fine with her and other judicial activists: They do not understand that such naked judicial law making is entirely inappropriate, illegitimate, and unconstitutional.

Of the Privy Council's ruling in *Edwards*, McLachlin argued: "An amendment to the British North America Act of 1867 could have made clear that women could be appointed to the Senate, but that would have taken years, even had the political will been there. And it was not."[14] Is this right? Given that women were already entitled to serve in the House of Commons and the legislatures of eight of the nine provinces, it is far from clear that these legislatures would have been unwilling in 1929 to support a constitutional amendment admitting women to the Senate if the Privy Council had exercised the restraint exhibited by the Supreme Court of Canada in upholding the original understanding of section 24. Furthermore, given the strength of the women's movement in the 1930s, it is also far from evident that it would have taken years for the elected legislators of Canada and Britain to get such a manifestly fair and reasonable amendment adopted. Regardless, even if McLachlin were right that an amendment allowing women to serve in the Senate would not have been quickly and overwhelming approved in the 1930s, she would still have no justification for drawing the undemocratic conclusion that the unelected law lords on the Privy Council were right in *Edwards* to take it upon themselves to amend the Constitution of Canada through judicial interpretation.

Consider the similar issue confronted by the Supreme Court of the United States in *Minor v. Happersett*, 1874. At issue in this case was the right of women to vote in federal elections. As originally enacted, the Constitution of the United States authorized each of the states to determine which of its citizens could vote in both state and federal contests. In 1870 Congress and the states qualified this power by ratifying the Fifteenth Amendment, which states: "The right of citizens of the United States to vote shall not be denied or abridged by the United States, or by any State, on account of race, color, or previous condition of servitude." Women are conspicuously missing from this amendment. At the time, they did not have the right to vote in any state or federal election. This did not sit well with Virginia Minor, a married woman resident in the State of Missouri. In 1873 she went to court seeking an order that the exclusion of women from the electoral franchise in the Constitution of the State of Missouri violated the rights of women to the equal protection of the laws and to the due process of law as guaranteed to all citizens in the Fifth and Fourteenth Amendments to the Constitution of the United States. The case ended up in the United States Supreme Court, where the judgment of the Court was delivered by Chief Justice Morrison Waite. Following a detailed analysis of the history and text of the United States Constitution in relation to voting rights, he concluded that women had never had a right to vote under the Constitution of the United States. "Our province is to decide what the law is, not to declare what it should be," said Chief Justice Waite. "We have given this case the careful consideration its importance demands. If the law is wrong, it ought to be changed; but the power for that is not with us."

Waite's restrained judgment left the task of changing the Constitution where it belongs – in the political and legislative arenas. For the suffragettes, the ensuing battle was long and difficult. Not until 1918 did they persuade President Woodrow Wilson to propose the Nineteenth Amendment to the United States Constitution, guaranteeing women the right to vote in all states. The amendment was duly approved by a two-thirds vote in both houses of Congress, ratified by three-quarters of the states, and finally promulgated on 26 August 1920.

In *Edwards*, Chief Justice Anglin displayed the kind of judicial restraint manifest by Chief Justice Waite in *Minor v. Happersett*. Both of these chief justices upheld the plain words of the law as originally understood: They did not twist the words of the Constitution to conform with their ideas of constitutional reform. Today – in the United States no less than in Canada – most Supreme Court judges prefer a more creative and activist approach to constitutional interpretation. They have abandoned judicial restraint. Like McLachlin, they scorn the "cautious, positivist, textual approach to the Constitution" that was the hallmark of their restrained predecessors.

Let us suppose that in January 2004 Prime Minister Paul Martin had asked a restrained judge in the mould of Chief Justice Anglin whether the government's draft legislation on same-sex marriage came within the exclusive authority of Parliament over "Marriage and Divorce" as conferred by section 91(26) of the Constitution Act, 1867. There can be no doubt about the answer. Any restrained judge would have held that the word "marriage" as used in section 91(26) is a constitutionally entrenched term that refers to the legal definition of marriage at the time of Confederation as the voluntary union for life of one man and one woman. And such a judge would therefore have found that Parliament has no authority under the Constitution to enact same-sex marriage into law.

Senator Anne Cools, Liberal Member of Parliament Roger Galloway, and Robert Leurer, a lawyer for the Government of Alberta, put this argument to the Supreme Court of Canada in submissions relating to the *Reference re Same-Sex Marriage*, 2004 SCC 79. Once again, McLachlin and her colleagues on the Court disdainfully rejected a restrained approach to constitutional interpretation. In a unanimous and unsigned judgment, they acknowledged that the legal meaning of marriage at the time of Confederation was authoritatively defined by Lord Penzance in *Hyde v. Hyde*, 1866: "I conceive that marriage, as understood in Christendom, may for this purpose be defined as the voluntary union for life of one man and one woman, to the exclusion of all others." In 2004 the Supreme Court of Canada dismissed this definition of marriage as outmoded. "The reference to 'Christendom' is telling," the Court argued. "*Hyde* spoke to a society of shared social values where marriage and religion were thought to be inseparable," whereas today, "marriage, from the perspective of the state, is a civil institution." Therefore, the Court concluded that the definition of the term marriage in the Constitution must be updated. The Court said: "The 'frozen concepts' reasoning [that would uphold the original understanding of marriage enshrined in section 91(26)] runs contrary to one of the most fundamental principles of Canadian constitutional interpretation: that our Constitution is a living tree which, by way of progressive interpretation, accommodates and addresses the realities of modern life."

Here we have it again: The hoariest of constitutional clichés – the Constitution as a living tree – trotted out by the Supreme Court of Canada to rationalize an act of judicial legislation. In this vein, the Court argued: "A large and liberal, or progressive, interpretation ensures the continued relevance and, indeed, legitimacy of Canada's constituting document. By way of progressive interpretation our Constitution succeeds in its ambitious enterprise, that of structuring the exercise of power by the organs of the state in times vastly different from those in which it was crafted. For instance, Parliament's legislative competence in respect of telephones was recognized on the basis of its authority over interprovincial 'undertakings' in s. 92(10)(a) even though the telephone had yet to be invented in 1867: *Toronto Corporation v. Bell Telephone Co. of Canada*, [1905] A.C. 52 (P.C.)."

This argument will obviously not do. As we have seen, section 91(10) of the Constitution confers specific authority on Parliament over "Telegraphs, and other Works and Undertakings" that link one province with another. In *Toronto Corporation v. Bell Telephone Co. of Canada*, the Judicial Committee of the Privy Council held that telephones come within federal jurisdiction because they comprise a form of communication analogous to the telegraph. Therefore, it stands to reason that if the telephone had been invented in 1867, the Fathers of Confederation would have included it along with the telegraph in section 91(10).

What, however, about same-sex marriage? In 1867, sodomy was a criminal offence. The concept of same-sex marriage was inconceivable. On this basis, a restrained judge would have concluded that same-sex marriage does not come within the original understanding of marriage in section 91(26) of the Constitution of Canada Act, 1867, and that same-sex marriage cannot therefore be legalized in Canada except by means of a constitutional amendment that is duly approved by elected representatives of the people in the legislative branch of government. No restrained judge who upholds the separation of legislative and judicial powers would have presumed to impose same-sex marriage on Canadians by means of a unilateral judicial decree.

In both Canada and the United States, there are still some appeal court judges who practise judicial restraint in the classical manner exemplified by Anglin and Waite. These principled jurists still insist that the courts should uphold the original meaning of the laws and the Constitution. A prime proponent of this viewpoint is Mr Justice Antonin Scalia of the United States Supreme Court. He unabashedly describes himself as a "textualist" of the old school.[15] In a lecture at Princeton University in 1995, he explained: "What I look for in the Constitution is precisely what I look for in a statute: the original meaning of the text."[16] He observed: "The ascendant school of constitutional interpretation affirms the existence of what is called the 'Living Constitution,' a body of law that (unlike normal statutes) grows and changes from age to age, in order to meet the needs of a changing society. And it is the judges who determine those needs and 'find' that changing law."[17] Scalia rejects this approach. He said:

> Perhaps the most glaring defect of Living Constitutionalism ... is that there is no agreement, and no chance of agreement, upon what is to be the guiding principle of the evolution ... What is it that the judge must consult to determine when, and in what direction, evolution has occurred? Is it the will of the majority, discerned from newspapers, radio talk shows, public opinion polls, and chats at the country club? Is it the philosophy of Hume, or of John Rawls,

or of John Stuart Mill, or of Aristotle? As soon as the discussion goes beyond the issue of whether the Constitution is static, the evolutionists divide into as many camps as there are individual views of the good, the true, and the beautiful. I think that is inevitably so, which means that evolutionism is simply not a practicable constitutional philosophy.[18]

Scalia maintains that evolutionalism as an approach to constitutional interpretation is also undemocratic. He observed: "Seventy-five years ago, we believed firmly enough in a rock-solid, unchanging Constitution that we felt it necessary to adopt the Nineteenth Amendment to give women the vote ... Who can doubt that, if the issue had been deferred until today, the Constitution would be (formally) unamended, and the courts would be the chosen instrumentality of change?"[19]

While Scalia upholds democracy and the rule of law, McLachlin lauds the Judicial Committee of the Privy Council for having amended the Constitution of Canada in *Edwards*. She acknowledges: "The change was radical," but she insists "most would argue, desirable and long overdue."[20] With this statement, she confuses the desirability of an innovation in the law with the propriety of having the judiciary change the law. Even if 99 per cent of the people of Canada had agreed in 1929 that women should have a constitutional right to serve in the Senate, the decision of the Privy Council to write such a provision retroactively into the British North America Act, 1867, was illegitimate. Judges have no constitutional authority to make sudden and radical changes in the law, no matter how desirable those changes might be. In a democracy, it is always wrong for appointed judges to encroach upon the law-making authority of elected legislators. Judges have a duty to uphold established legal principles. They should never undertake to second-guess the wisdom of laws that Parliament and the provincial legislatures have enacted within their respective jurisdictions under the Constitution. Quite simply, appointed judges should not set themselves up as the ultimate authorities on appropriate public policies. They should not usurp the authority of elected legislators to amend the laws and the Constitution.

What, however, has the Supreme Court of Canada done since the Canadian Charter of Rights and Freedoms came into effect in 1982? It has assumed the right to change the law and dictate national policies on abortion and euthanasia, on lesbian and gay rights, on Aboriginal land claims and fishing rights, on the admission of refugees and immigrants to Canada – the list gets ever longer. Our judges-cum-politicians on the Supreme Court of Canada have laid down new rules governing the hot pursuit of murderers by the police. They have changed the rules on eligibility for spousal benefits under the Old Age Security Act. They have mandated translation services in the nation's hospitals and imposed two-tiered medicine on the Province of Quebec.

In *Operation Dismantle v. The Queen*, 1985 SCC, the Supreme Court of Canada even presumed to pass judgment on a key issue of national security. At issue was the decision by the federal Cabinet to permit the United States to test cruise missiles in Canada. An array of protestors led by Operation Dismantle Inc., the National Action Committee on the Status of Women, and the Canadian Union of Public Employees sought a court injunction to forbid the testing of cruise missiles over remote parts of Canada, claiming that the proposal "poses a threat to the lives and security of Canadians by increasing the risk of nuclear conflict and thereby violates the right to life, liberty and security of the person" as guaranteed in section 7 of the Charter. Mr Justice Gerald Le Dain of the Federal Court of Appeal took the restrained view that the case centred on a nonjusticiable issue of public policy that fell within the jurisdictions of the legislative and executive branches of government, not the courts. In support of this opinion, he cited the judgment under British law of Lord Radcliffe in *Chandler v. Director of Public Prosecutions*, 1962 HLUK, a case concerning the nuclear weapons policies of the Government of the United Kingdom. Lord Radcliffe stated: "The more one looks at it, the plainer it becomes, I think, that the question whether it is in the true interests of this country to acquire, retain or house nuclear armaments depends on an infinity of considerations, military and diplomatic, technical, psychological and moral, and of decisions, tentative or final, which are themselves part assessments of fact and part expectations and hopes. I do not think that there is anything amiss with a legal ruling that does not make this issue a matter for judge or jury."

No such considerations inhibited the activist judges on the Supreme Court of Canada. In *Operation Dismantle* they rejected the argument that it is inappropriate in principle for the courts to second-guess the wisdom of a Cabinet decision on such a vital question of public policy. While the Court decided, in the end, to refuse to grant the injunction sought by Operation Dismantle and the other petitioners, it did so only on the ground that the appellants could not prove their case. In reasons for the Court, Chief Justice Dickson stated: "I have no doubt that disputes of a political or foreign policy nature may be properly cognizable by the courts." In a separate, concurring opinion, Justice Wilson rejected what she called "the well-established principle of American constitutional law" that the courts should not deal with "political questions" that relate to the nonjudicial discretion of the legislative or executive branches of government to make policy determinations. She pointed out that the principle of excluding political questions from judicial review had not been consistently applied by the United States Supreme Court inasmuch as activist judges on the Court had presumed over the previous thirty years to impose policy decisions on political questions of the utmost sensitivity, beginning with the epochal school-desegregation ruling in *Brown v. Board of Education of Topeka,* 1954 USSC. In Wilson's opinion, Canadian courts are obligated to do the same: Under terms of the Charter, they must evaluate the wisdom of legislative and executive policies in the light of constitutional norms. "However unsuited courts may be for the task," she said, "they are called upon all the time to decide questions of principle and policy."

Law professors Hawkins and Martin respond: "In our opinion, if judges are empowered by the Charter to create constitutional norms, as Justice Wilson argues, the judicial function and the legislative function become indistinguishable. Under such circumstances, it no longer makes sense to say that certain kinds of questions are out of bounds to the judiciary simply because their political nature reserves them for the political authorities. Indeed, Justice Wilson's view of the courts' role under the Charter sounds the death knell for the doctrine of separation of powers."[21]

In the face of mounting criticism of judicial activists on the Supreme Court of Canada, Chief Justice McLachlin served up another defence of the Court in an address on 17 June 2003 to the Canadian Club in Toronto. For this occasion, she entitled her speech: "Judging, Politics, and Why They Must Be Kept Separate." It was a timely topic given that just seven days earlier, Chief Justice Roy McMurtry, Mr Justice James MacPherson, and Madam Justice Eileen Gillese of the Ontario Court of Appeal had handed down their unanimous ruling in *Halpern,* which imposed same-sex marriage on the people of Ontario. This same, intensely controversial issue was bound to come before the Supreme Court of Canada, as it did just a few months later in the *Reference re Same-Sex Marriage.* Given this likelihood, one might have supposed that McLachlin would sedulously avoid any reference to *Halpern* in her Canadian Club speech. Instead, she implied support for the Ontario Court's radical ruling. Having noted that it is the standard stock of some editorial pages to claim that "judges are acting more and more like legislators" and that it is therefore appropriate to rethink their manner of appointment, she observed: "Commentaries over the decision of the Court of Appeal of Ontario on the question of same-sex marriages pick up the first theme, while the nomination of a new judge to the Supreme Court of Canada will doubtless reactivate the second."[22] She added:

> Let us turn first to the charge that judges are usurping the legislative power of Parliament and the legislatures. To put it simply, it displays misunderstanding of what judges do. The reality comes down to this: Parliament and the legislatures are the supreme arbitrators of the social course of the nation, subject only to the constraints imposed by the constitution and its traditions. The courts, by contrast, are the interpreters of the law and the constitution. Drafting, debating, and passing laws are essentially political activities. Interpreting the laws and the constitution are essentially legal activities ... The aim of the judicial role ... is to interpret the laws that our common law tradition and the legislators have put in place.[23]

What, however, did the Ontario Court of Appeal do in *Halpern*? Did the Court merely "interpret the laws that our common law tradition and the legislators have put in place"? Decidedly not. For centuries, the common law defined marriage as the lawful union of one man and one woman to the exclusion of all others. In 2000, Parliament incorporated this same definition in section 1.1 of the Modernization of Benefits and Obligations Act. Regardless, in *Halpern* the Ontario Court of Appeal reformulated the common law and statutory definition of marriage to include same-sex couples.[24] Courts in British Columbia, Manitoba, Newfoundland, Nova Scotia, Saskatchwan, Quebec, and the Yukon have done the same. In effect, all of these appeal courts have legislated a new law from the bench that mandates the imposition of same-sex marriages on Canadians.

In *Winnipeg Child and Family Services (Northwest Area) v. G. (D.F.)*, 1997 SCC, Chief Justice McLachlin held: "As a general rule, judicial change is confined to incremental change based largely on the mechanism of extending an existing principle to new circumstances; courts will not extend the common law where the revision is major and its ramifications complex." By this reasoning, McLachlin should be unalterably opposed to the judicial reformulation of the common law definition of marriage to accommodate same-sex couples. A more major and far-reaching change to the common law is difficult to imagine. Yet in the *Reference re Same-Sex Marriage*, she and her colleagues on the Supreme Court of Canada declared that the government's draft bill to extend marriage for civil purposes to couples of the same sex "points unequivocally to a purpose which, far from violating the *Charter*, flows from it."

Naturally, Svend Robinson has lauded the judicial discovery that the Constitution requires same-sex marriage. In a commentary published in the *Globe and Mail* on 24 June 2003, he maintained: "Those who argue that the courts are usurping the power of elected representatives are misreading our Constitution. Remember, it was judges who ordered Canadian politicians to treat women as 'persons' in law."[25] Note the irony of this argument: Here we have Robinson, a democratic socialist, commending their lordships, the judges on the Judicial Committee of the Privy Council, for presuming in *Edwards* to order around our democratically elected Canadian politicians. And on the basis of this quasi-colonial precedent, Robinson contends that members of the Supreme Court of Canada are entitled to order around Canada's elected legislators. In his *Globe* article, Robinson particularly commended the decision of the Supreme Court of Canada in *Egan* to read sexual orientation into section 15. He defended this high-handed act of judicial legislation on the ground that during parliamentary deliberations on section 15, "then-justice minister Jean Chrétien agreed to leave open-ended the grounds of discrimination in that key section to future judges to include new grounds."[26] Robinson was alluding to an exchange at a hearing of the Special Joint Committee of the Senate and the House of Commons on the Constitution on 16 January 1981, when he asked Chrétien whether the Supreme Court of Canada could interpret section 15 to exclude discrimination on the grounds of sexual orientation. Chrétien replied: "That will be for the court to decide. It is open-ended."[27]

However, this is not all that Chrétien had to say on the subject. When, two weeks later on 29 January 1981, Robinson tried to remove any doubt on this point by moving an amendment to the Charter to include sexual orientation as one of the explicitly enumerated grounds of prohibited discrimination in section 15, Chrétien, together with all other Liberals and the Conservatives on the committee, rejected this amendment. Of the twenty-four parliamentarians who took part in the vote, only two New Democrats – Robinson and Lorne Nystrom – supported the motion. Chrétien left the Joint Committee in no doubt about the position of the Trudeau government. He said: "I am not here as a judge to determine what sexual orientation means. It is because of the problem of the definition of these words that we do not think they should be in the Constitution."[28]

Robinson's final argument in defence of *Egan* was that an all-party committee of the Commons had unanimously recommended in 1985 that Parliament should amend the Canadian Human Rights Act to include sexual orientation as a prohibited ground of discrimination.

Parliament never acted on this recommendation. Robinson contends: "It is only because elected representatives failed to respect the Charter that judges were forced to step in."[29]

How is this so? Parliament refrained in 1985 from amending the Canadian Human Rights Act to include sexual orientation as a prohibited ground of discrimination, so Robinson says that judges on the Supreme Court of Canada were "forced" to step in and amend section 15 of the Charter on their own. But no one forced these activist judges to do any such thing. They had a choice: They could have upheld the Charter as originally enacted and understood. Instead, they arbitrarily chose in *Egan* to amend the Charter through interpretation to include equality rights for homosexuals under section 15.

This is not to say that the Chrétien Liberals were innocent in the *Egan* affair. Quite the contrary. Acting under the instructions of Justice Minister Allan Rock, counsel for the attorney general of Canada agreed with the argument advanced by counsel for the appellants in *Egan* that the Court should read sexual orientation as an analogous ground of discrimination into section 15. This directive from the attorney general was improper. Cabinet ministers are no less obligated than Supreme Court judges to uphold the law and the Constitution. Still, the Supreme Court of Canada was mainly at fault in *Egan:* It should have rejected the advice of the attorney general and upheld the original understanding of the scope of section 15 of the Charter. Parliament had made its position clear in 1981 by deliberately excluding sexual orientation as one of the enumerated grounds of prohibited discrimination in section 15. Moreover, when the Charter was proclaimed in 1982, neither Canada nor any of the provinces, except Quebec, had a law on the books banning discrimination on the basis of sexual orientation. Parliament had excluded sexual orientation from the original Canadian Human Rights Act of 1977. The Ontario Legislature had done the same in adopting the Ontario Human Rights Code of 1962 and in rejecting an amendment to the Code on 1 December 1981 that would have included sexual orientation as a prohibited ground of discrimination.[30]

The Supreme Court of Canada chose in *Egan* to ignore these unambiguous indications of the original understanding of the scope of section 15. Instead, abetted by the Chrétien Cabinet, the Court broke the law and violated the Constitution by reading sexual orientation into section 15 of the Charter. The people of Canada and their elected representatives never had an opportunity to discuss and debate, let alone to vote upon and approve, this momentous change in the law. The Supreme Court of Canada imposed on Canadian society the inclusion of sexual orientation as a constitutionally prohibited ground for discrimination.

This, then, is the best that Robinson can do to defend arbitrary judicial decisions on gay rights like *Egan* and *Halpern*. On the basis of a single, off-the-cuff remark by Chrétien, he contends that Parliament and the provincial legislatures mandated activist judges on the Supreme Court of Canada to read whatever they want into section 15 of the Charter. McLachlin defends the hardly less plausible notion that in *Edwards* their lordships on the Judicial Committee of the Privy Council gave the courts of Canada free rein to amend the Constitution through interpretation. Consider, however, the precise words of Lord Sankey's dictum: "The British North America Act planted in Canada a living tree capable of growth and expansion within its natural limits." How can any reasonable person regard the judicial imposition of same-sex marriage as an example of growth and expansion of the Constitution within its natural limits?

In "Democracy, Judging and Bertha Wilson," Hawkins and Martin recall that Justice Wilson warned against the judicial misuse of the "living tree" metaphor in an address on 12 April 1988 entitled "The Making of a Constitution." She said: "As Canadian judges we are appointed, not elected, officials. There would be something deeply illegitimate about our forays into judicial review of legislation if all there was to them was a desire to substitute our own personal values for those of our duly elected representatives."[31] True enough. She added:

> We cannot placidly assume that by some mysterious process we, the judges, have been given access to the true answers to fundamental social and political dilemmas. If anything, the converse may be true ...
>
> While things are slowly changing, it cannot be said that judges in Canada are broadly representative of the general public. There is, therefore, no plausible justification for us to substitute our personal values and our moral choices for those of the elected legislature. The metaphor of the living tree is a harmless one so long as it is used merely to suggest that a constitution must adapt and grow to meet modern realities. It could, however, become dangerous and antidemocratic if it were used to justify the shaping of the constitution according to the personal values of individual judges.[32]

A more cogent summary of the case against judicial activism is difficult to imagine. However, as Hawkins and Martin acidly note: "The difficulty is that this does not reflect Justice Wilson's practice."[33] Just two and a half months prior to this speech, she had handed down her judgment in *Morgentaler*, in which she struck down the abortion restrictions in the Criminal Code on the ground that in her personal view, a baby in the womb has no legal right to life prior to the second trimester.

McLachlin insisted in her address to the Canadian Club that interpreting the law and the Constitution "is high-level, specialized, intellectual work." She added: "Contrary to popular myth, judges do not pluck meanings from the air according to their political stripe. The image of the judicial cowboy riding amok through the carefully planted legislative garden is just that, an image – and a distorted one at that ... Unlike politicians, judges do not have agendas."[34] Is this right? If judges do not have agendas, why, just a few days after the *Halpern* ruling, did a bevy of judges led by Ontario Chief Justice Roy McMurtry, Justice MacPherson, and retired Justice L'Heureux-Dubé show up at the annual "Pride Week reception and forum" convened by the Law Society of Upper Canada? There, they received the accolades of gay rights activists for their contributions to changing the common law definition of marriage?[35] A smiling McMurtry commemorated the event by having his picture taken between two of Canada's most prominent gay rights activists, Kevin Bourassa and Joe Varnell. On 14 January 2001 Bourassa and Varnell generated headlines across Canada by pledging their troth to each other in a simulacrum of a marriage ceremony at the Metropolitan Community Church in Toronto.[36]

In defence of judges who invoke the Charter as justification for striking down laws that have been duly enacted by Parliament and the provincial legislatures, McLachlin claimed in her Canadian Club address that the "notion that Parliamentary democracy resides only in majority rule is both false and dangerous. It is false because, as we have seen, the power of elected officers is necessarily limited by the law in a constitutional democracy. And it is dangerous. It offers no protection against the tyranny of the majority and it overlooks the need to accommodate and validate minoritarian views essential to long-term democratic stability."[37] Here we come to the nub of the dispute over judicial activism: McLachlin subscribes to the authoritarian view that unelected judges are better qualified than elected legislators not only to interpret and uphold the laws, but also to enact and amend laws affecting minority rights.

POLITICAL SAFEGUARDS FOR MINORITY RIGHTS

Activist judges invariably insist that their disposition to overturn the popular will as enshrined in democratically enacted laws and the Constitution is necessary to thwart the tyranny of the majority. That majorities can sometimes act tyrannically is beyond dispute. Alexis de Tocqueville underlined this threat in his classic study *Democracy in America*.[38] Based on his observations of the United States during an extensive visit in the 1830s, he concluded that the authority "entrusted to members of the legal profession, and the influence which these individuals exercise in the Government, is the most powerful existing security against the excesses of democracy." Nonetheless, de Tocqueville was far from a proponent of judicial activism. On the contrary, he commended the judicial restraint that was characteristic of British and United States judges in the nineteenth century. He wrote: "The English and the Americans have retained the law of precedents; that is to say, they continue to found their legal opinions and the decisions of their courts upon the opinions and decisions of their predecessors. In the mind of an English or American lawyer a taste and a reverence for what is old is almost always united with a love of regular and lawful proceedings." De Tocqueville held that these tradition-bound lawyers could be counted upon to curb the occasional propensity of a majority to violate the human rights and fundamental freedoms enshrined in the common law. He wrote: "When the American people is intoxicated by passion, or carried away by the impetuosity of its ideas, it is checked and stopped by the almost invisible influence of its legal counsellors, who secretly oppose their aristocratic propensities to its democratic instincts, their superstitious attachment to what is antique to its love of novelty."[39]

Today's judicial activists bear no resemblance to these lawyers of old. Far from harbouring a superstitious attachment to what is antique, most appeal court judges in Canada and the United States have embraced such novelties as the legalization of same-sex marriage. Under the pretence of checking the tyranny of the majority, today's activist judges have taken to imposing something close to a tyranny of their own. They bear no resemblance to the restrained judges observed by de Tocqueville who respected the strict separation of legislative and judicial powers. He remarked: "Armed with the power of declaring the laws to be unconstitutional, the American magistrate perpetually interferes in political affairs. He cannot force the people to make laws, but at least he can oblige them not to disobey their own enactments and not to be inconsistent with themselves."[40] In contrast, today's activist judges habitually ignore the enactments of the people and have taken it upon themselves to change the shape of the law.

Like De Tocqueville, the framers of the United States Constitution were aware that a tyrannical majority could seize power in a representative democracy. However, in "The Federalist No. 10,"[41] Madison observed that the danger that a majority might act tyrannically is less severe in a large and diverse federation than in a small and cohesive direct democracy. He explained: "Extend the sphere and you take in a greater variety of parties and interests; you will make it less probable that a majority of the whole will have a common motive to invade the rights of other citizens; or if such a common motive exists, it will be more difficult ... to act in unison." Madison also had confidence that a tyranny of the majority would be thwarted by the sense of fairness of the people of the United States: "If it be asked, what is to restrain the House of Representatives from making legal discriminations in favour of themselves and a particular class of the society? I answer: the genius of the whole system; the nature of just and constitutional laws; and above all, the vigilant and manly spirit which actuates the people of America – a spirit which nourishes freedom, and in return is nourished by it."[42]

Sir John A. MacDonald was no less confident that the vigilant and manly spirit of the Canadian people could be counted on to uphold the rights of minorities enshrined in the politically binding conventions of the Constitution. During debate in the Legislative Assembly of Canada on the proposed British North America Act, 1867, he predicted: "We will enjoy here that which is the great test of constitutional freedom – we will have the rights of the minority respected. In all countries the rights of the majority take care of themselves, but it is only in countries like England, enjoying constitutional liberty, and safe from the tyranny of a single despot or of an unbridled democracy, that the rights of minorities are regarded."[43] And what is it about the Constitution of Canada and Britain that prevents the abuse of minority rights? MacDonald's colleague Sir Richard Cartwright explained:

> That constitution ... while it does not require the possession of those lofty, impracticable virtues which most republican institutions demand from their votaries, does nevertheless presuppose a reasonable amount of discretion at the hands of those who are entrusted with the carrying out of its details. And, sir, though it is true that it does recognize the calm, deliberate, just decision of the majority – and the calm, deliberate decision is almost always just – as final in the last resort, it does still so abound with safeguards – with latent checks of all kinds – checks established, many of them, more by custom and usage than by positive law – as to make it all but impossible for any majority, however strong, to perpetrate any gross act of injustice on a minority, so long as that minority could command but one or two resolute representatives on the floor of parliament.[44]

History bore out the confidence of MacDonald, Cartwright, and other Fathers of Confederation: For more than a hundred years, the Parliament of Canada respected the rights of minorities, although the Constitution of Canada included nothing comparable to the United States Bill of Rights. Granted, Parliament did commit some undeniable excesses such as authorizing the unduly harsh treatment of Japanese Canadians during the Second World War. Nonetheless, by any international comparison, Canada had an exemplary human rights record prior to the Charter. In the *Constitutional Law of Canada*, Peter Hogg sums up:

> Despite the lack of a bill of rights (for most of its history), Canada, like the United Kingdom, Australia and New Zealand, has a good record of respect for civil liberties. Tolerance of political and religious dissent, and of racial and linguistic minorities, freedom of movement, control of police powers and fair and open trials are among the criteria by which a nation's record is judged. Canada's record, while far from perfect, seems to be much better than that of most of the countries of the world, although nearly all countries have bills of rights in their constitutions. The basic reason for this has very little to do with the contents of Canada's (or any other country's) constitutional law. It is to be found in the democratic character of Canada's political institutions, supported by long traditions of free elections, opposition parties and a free press. Democracy is without doubt the most important safeguard of civil liberties.[45]

What about the role of the Charter? Does it now constitute the principle guardian of civil liberties in Canada? Professor Hogg thinks not. He argues: "The Charter will never become the main safeguard of civil liberties in Canada. The main safeguards will continue to be the democratic character of Canadian political institutions, the independence of the judiciary and a legal tradition of respect for civil liberties. The Charter is no substitute for any of these things, and would be ineffective if any of these things disappeared. This is demonstrated by the fact that in many countries with bills of rights in their constitutions the civil liberties which are purportedly guaranteed do not exist in practice."[46]

While activist judges insist that they are upholding minority rights, Professor Monahan has argued that these judges are actually undermining Canada's exemplary human rights record. He noted: "Rule by judiciary supposes that the only way to deter oppression is to impose external restraints on the political process. But because such external restraints deny the competence of citizens to arrive at informed ethical judgments, they undermine the very process of reflection and self-criticism which might lead to a more mature collective morality. Elitist politics breeds only a mob; to produce citizens, one needs democracy."[47]

This argument is altogether persuasive, yet Monahan has criticized the 1995 *Egan* decision of the Supreme Court of Canada for not going far enough toward extending spousal benefits to homosexual couples.[48] Monahan cannot have it both ways. If he believes that democracy is preferable to rule by judiciary, he should repudiate all decisions like *Egan* in which activist judges impose constraints on the political process by amending the Constitution.

Notwithstanding the pretensions of judges like McLachlin, there is no evidence to suggest that judicial oversight of the law-making process is necessary to safeguard minorities from the tyranny of the majority. In *Democracy and Its Critics*, Robert Dahl has observed:

> To demonstrate that a judiciary with the power to negate laws passed by the national legislature is essential to the protection of fundamental rights in democratic orders would require showing one of two things. Either the democratic countries in which courts lack such powers are not really democratic or at any rate are not as democratic as the United States or in these countries fundamental rights are less well protected than in the United States. No one has shown that countries like the Netherlands and New Zealand, which lack judicial review, or Norway and Sweden, where it is exercised rarely and in highly restrained fashion, or Switzerland, where it can be applied only to cantonal legislation, are less democratic than the United States, nor, I think, could one reasonably do so.[49]

Perhaps something could be said for judicial activism if the application of the abstract rights of the Charter to specific cases were subject to just one true interpretation that only judges can grasp. But this is obviously not the case. In a treatise entitled *Law and Disagreement*, law professor Jeremy Waldron of Columbia University points out that despite broad support for the kind of basic rights and fundamental freedoms listed in documents like the Canadian Charter of Rights and Freedoms and the United States Bill of Rights, people of good will, including learned judges, frequently disagree on the application of these abstract and general rights to concrete and specific issues like abortion, the licensing of firearms, or the use of corporal punishment in publicly funded schools. He notes:

> It is not a case of there being some of us who are in possession of the truth about rights – a truth which our opponents wilfully or irrationally fail to acknowledge because they are blinded by ignorance, prejudice or interest. The issues that rights implicate are much too complicated to permit or require

> that sort of explanation. They are simply hard questions – matters on which reasonable people differ. They are important questions, to be sure, and people are properly ferocious and indignant in defence of the answers they take to be correct. But it is a mistake to think that the more important the question, the more straightforward or obvious the answer.[50]

Time and again, judges on the Supreme Court of Canada have not been able to agree among themselves on the application of Charter rights to issues like search warrants, voting rights for prisoners, pornography laws, and so on. In the appalling 1988 *Morgentaler* ruling on abortion, only seven judges heard the case for the Supreme Court of Canada, yet they split no fewer than four ways. Given, then, that judges, like other people, can in good faith reasonably differ over the nature of rights and their application to specific policies, how should these disagreements be settled? Waldron is a democrat. He prefers to have disputes over the scope of rights resolved by elected representatives of the people rather than by "a nine man junta clad in black robes and surrounded by law clerks."[51] He explains:

> When citizens or their representatives disagree about what rights we have or what those rights entail, it seems something of an insult to say that this is not something they are to be permitted to sort out by majoritarian processes, but that the issue is to be assigned instead for final determination to a small group of judges. It is particularly insulting when they discover that the judges disagree among themselves along exactly the same lines as the citizens and representatives do, and that the judges make their decisions, too, in the courtroom by majority-voting. The citizens may well feel that if disagreements on these matters are to be settled by counting heads, then it is their heads or those of their accountable representatives that should be counted.[52]

McLachlin takes the elitist position: She insists that unelected judges, not elected legislators, are best qualified to spell out the specific implications of the general human rights listed in the Charter. On this basis, she has backed quasi-legislative enactments of the Supreme Court of Canada like *Egan*, in which the Court read sexual orientation into section 15 of the Charter, and *Vriend*, in which the Court did the same to the Alberta Human Rights, Citizenship, and Multiculturalism Act. In *Vriend*, Justice Iacobucci acknowledged in his reasons for judgment that the exclusion of sexual orientation from the Alberta Human Rights Act was "a conscious and deliberate legislative choice." He also conceded that: "In carrying out their duties, courts are not to second-guess legislatures and the executives; they are not to make value judgments on what they regard as the proper policy choice; this is for the other branches. Rather, the courts are to uphold the Constitution and have been expressly invited to perform that role by the Constitution itself." But what did McLachlin and her colleagues on the Supreme Court of Canada actually do in *Egan* and *Vriend*? First, they second-guessed the wisdom of Parliament in deliberately excluding "sexual orientation" from the prohibited grounds of discrimination in section 15 of the Charter, and then they second-guessed the wisdom of the Alberta Legislature in deliberately excluding sexual orientation as a prohibited ground for discrimination in Alberta's human rights code.

Most appeal court judges in Canada are like McLachlin and Iacobucci in that they pay only lip service to the separation of legislative and judicial powers. The late Mr Justice John McClung of the Alberta Court of Appeal was a conspicuous exception. He was a leader among the small but staunch band of principled Canadian judges in the Charter era who have remained committed to upholding the laws and the Constitution as originally understood. In his reasons for judgment in *Vriend* for the Alberta Court of Appeal,[53] McClung observed: "Rightly or wrongly, the electors of the Province of Alberta, speaking through their parliamentary representatives, have declared that homosexuality (I assume that the term 'sexual orientation' defends nothing more) is not to be included in the protected categories of the IRPA [Alberta's human rights code]." McClung insisted that it is not up to the courts to change this law. He said:

> In my view, "judicial legislation" should never be undertaken where, after inspection of the background of the statute, it must be concluded that the "omission" was a step that had been weighed and deliberately declined by the legislating body in whose jurisdiction it lay. This must be so whatever the private concerns of the reviewing judge ...
>
> Justice according to Canada's constitution is best advanced when the courts listen to the wishes of the people along with the hortatories of the Charter. The vast majority of Canadians obey the laws that are imposed upon them by their chosen representatives. In short, they keep to the statutes and they are entitled to expect that their judges will do so too. They do not want their judges to redesign them when those statutes are written in perfectly understandable words of daily French or English usage.

To illustrate this point, McClung sarcastically noted how in *Egan* "the word 'spouse', a simple word of long usage and one which clearly connotes the continuance of a marital relationship, had been judge-pummelled in bursts of adaptation that would have gladdened

Procrustes. Another example is *M. v. H.*" He added: "Even the Charter was written in 'small, old words' so all Canadians could understand and therefore relate to its declarations. Canadians want a constitution that serves according to their own expectation of its purposes and result, and distrust one that is laid upon them by untranslatable processes of judicial carpentry."

The Supreme Court of Canada was not impressed by McClung's trenchant criticism. Iacobucci argued: "The process by which the Alberta legislature decided to exclude sexual orientation from the IRPA was inconsistent with democratic principles. Both the trial judge and all judges in the Court of Appeal agreed that the exclusion of sexual orientation from the IRPA was a conscious and deliberate legislative choice. While McClung J.A. relies on this fact as a reason for the courts not to intervene, the theories of judicial review developed by several authors ... suggest the opposite conclusion."

In support of this viewpoint, Iacobucci cited *Constitutional Law in Theory and Practice* by David Beatty, a professor in the Faculty of Law at the University of Toronto. In this textbook, Beatty commends the Supreme Court of Canada for having creatively interpreted the Charter without regard for the original understanding of its provisions. He enthuses: "Even when there was some evidence of a common understanding of what a particular [Charter] right or freedom was intended to protect, the Court did not feel bound to give effect to it."[54]

Nonetheless, Beatty claims the Court has continued to uphold the rule of law. He acknowledges:

> If the judges are not governed by rules of law – if the rule of law has no definite, determinate meaning that can distinguish laws that are constitutionally valid from those that are not – judicial review should have no place in a society that claims a liberal-democratic pedigree. It would be completely at odds with our tradition of popular sovereignty and personal autonomy to allow decisions about the most controversial and fundamental questions of the day to be made by a small, elite group of unelected officials. If judges were free to decide cases and the limits of legal authority according to their own (considered) views about law, morality, and the state, judicial review would be as much an agent of as a check against arbitrary and autocratic rule. As the critics point out, much more effective – and democratic – solutions could be fashioned in the political domain.[55]

With activist judges flouting common law rules, striking down statutory enactments, and ignoring the original legislative understanding of the Charter, how can Beatty maintain that the courts are still upholding the rule of law rather than imposing their own views from the bench? His answer is to redefine the meaning of the rule of law. In Beatty "Newspeak,"[56] every rule of constitutional law can be reduced to the application of two fundamental legal principles, rationality and proportionality. He holds that for a law to pass the rationality test, supporters of the provision must demonstrate that "no alternative policies or instruments were available that would have allowed them to accomplish their purposes in a way that displayed more respect for the freedom of individuals or the sovereignty of other governments."[57] Correspondingly, for a law to survive the proportionality test, it must be evident that "the public interest or purpose of the law is of sufficient importance that it offsets (justifies) whatever limitation or restriction it imposes on individuals or groups or other orders of government."[58]

Beatty concedes that the application of these two vague principles of constitutional interpretation to particular cases is complicated by differences in predominant values and cultures from one society to another:

> What is well proportioned and evenly balanced in one society may appear to be quite distorted and skewed in another.
>
> When judges and courts disagree on whether a law should be upheld as being constitutional in such circumstances, it is not because of the indeterminacy or subjectivity of the law. Everyone is agreed on what principles control the outcome of the case and what the content of those rules are. The divergences occur because of different perceptions that judges may take of the relevant factual (evidentiary) material and the legal and cultural background against which the principles are applied. The importance of tranquillity and civility in Japanese society, or of foetal life in the Irish Republic, for example, may justify laws restricting street demonstrations and door-to-door canvassing in Japan and abortions in Ireland, even though they might be struck down in other societies, such as Canada and Denmark, where these interests and activities have been valued quite differently.[59]

Having made this argument, Beatty proceeds a few pages later in his book to commend the judgment of the European Court of Human Rights in *Dudgeon v. United Kingdom*, 1981, which struck down the sodomy law in force in Northern Ireland. Beatty writes:

> Once the Court had compared the law in Northern Ireland with those in force in the other free and democratic societies in Europe and elsewhere, its

supporters could not defend it on the basis of preventing some social harm or securing some public good. The only ground on which it could be justified was the offence it gave to those who regard all homosexual behaviour as salacious and immoral. While not denying that behaviour of this kind gives offence to people of various moral and religious views, the judges in Strasbourg – like most of my students – had little difficulty in seeing that, in relative terms, this harm is neither qualitatively nor quantitatively nearly as significant to the lives of those who experience it as the injuries suffered by those who are prevented from making what is a very intimate and personal choice for themselves.[60]

Where is the consistency in these arguments? First, Beatty says that courts might have justification for upholding abortion restrictions in the Irish Republic, but not in Canada, because the Irish have greater respect for the lives of babies in the womb than do Canadians. Yet he then argues that the European Court of Human Rights was right to strike down the sodomy law in Northern Ireland despite the antipathy of the Irish people for the practice of sodomy. Given these obvious contradictions, how can anyone suppose that the strict application of Beatty's two principles of constitutional interpretation would be sufficient to uphold the rule of law by providing the courts with a definite and determinate means of distinguishing laws that are constitutionally valid from those that are not?

It is a telling commentary on the quality of analysis provided by the Supreme Court of Canada that Iacobucci could do no better in *Vriend* than cite the kind of implausible arguments advanced by Beatty as justification for the Court's decision to read homosexual rights into Alberta's human rights code. The Court's resolve to do so over the express and repeated unwillingness of the Alberta Legislature was patently undemocratic. Yet Iacobucci thinks otherwise. In defence of his *Vriend* ruling, he argued: "In my view, a democracy requires that legislators take into account the interests of majorities and minorities alike, all of whom will be affected by the decisions they make. Where the interests of a minority have been denied consideration, especially where that group has historically been the target of prejudice and discrimination, I believe that judicial intervention is warranted to correct a democratic process that has acted improperly."

In *Vriend*, McClung arrived at precisely the opposite conclusion. He upheld the basic democratic principle that it is up to elected legislators, not appointed judges, to enact laws and determine public policies. He understood that a judge should not presume to overturn or amend a law on the ground that in enacting the law, elected legislators failed to give adequate consideration to the interests of a minority. Rather, judges should unfailingly uphold laws that have been duly enacted in conformity with the original understanding of the provisions of the Constitution. Thus, if some provincial legislature were to enact a law banning theologically orthodox Christians and Jews from teaching in the public schools, the courts should strike down this law on the ground that it violates the original understanding of the freedom of conscience and religion guaranteed in section 2(a) of the Charter. By the same token, the Supreme Court of Canada should have refrained in *Egan* from reading sexual orientation into section 15 of the Charter because it is clear from the legislative history of the Charter that this ruling contradicted the express intentions of Canada's elected representatives in Parliament and the provincial legislatures.

THE COURT'S FUNDAMENTAL ERROR: *R v. SHARPE*

On 13 January 1999 Mr Justice Duncan Shaw of the British Columbia Supreme Court created a national scandal with his ruling in *R. v. Sharpe*, 1999 BCSC.[61] Few judgments have done more to underline the excesses of judicial activism. The accused in this case, John Robin Sharpe, was sixty-five years old and a resident of Surrey, British Columbia. He admitted to possessing an array of salacious materials that included books, manuscripts, stories, photographs, and a set of computer discs entitled *Sam Paloc's Flogging, Fun and Fortitude: A Collection of Kiddie Kink Classics.* Judge Shaw noted in his reasons for judgment in *Sharpe* that: "Many of the seized photographs are of nude boys displaying their genitals or anal regions." Sharpe's sordid collection also included "a sketch of a nude boy obviously under the age of 18 (and probably under the age of 14) with an erect penis."[62] Police duly charged Sharpe with possession of child pornography contrary to section 163.1(4) of the Criminal Code. However, Judge Shaw struck down this law and threw out the charge on the ground that all Canadians, including pedophiles, have a right to possess child pornography by virtue of the guarantee of freedom of expression in section 2(b) of the Charter. The ruling made headlines throughout the country. Most commentators could not fathom the untranslatable process of judicial carpentry that prompted Shaw to assert that freedom of expression includes the right to possess the most degrading child pornography.

Yet the fault lay not with Shaw. He was only following precedents set by the Supreme Court of Canada on the interpretation of freedom of expression in section 2 of the Charter. Moreover, upon appeal, every member of both the British Columbia Court of Appeal and the Supreme Court of Canada who dealt with this case took the same view as Shaw: They all agreed that the guarantee of freedom of expression in section 2 of the Charter confers upon degenerates like Sharpe the right to possess the most disgusting and repellent child pornography. How can this be? There is nothing in either the plain language or the legislative history of the Charter to indicate that Canada's elected legislators intended such a bizarre interpretation of section 2.

The language of section 2 is straightforward. It states: "Everyone has the following fundamental freedoms: a) freedom of conscience and religion; b) freedom of thought, belief, opinion and expression, including freedom of the press and other media of communication." These are historic freedoms. They have long been enshrined in the common law, and they have always been hedged about by legally defined restrictions relating to such matters as libel, slander, sedition, and various forms of fraudulent communication. In *R. v. Keegstra*, 1998 SCC, the Supreme Court of Canada acknowledged that "pre-Charter jurisprudence used freedom of expression primarily in relation to political expression." This was in accord with the general understanding of the meaning of freedom of expression. Therefore, this is the meaning that a restrained court, respecting the separation of legislative and judicial powers, should have read into the guarantee of freedom of expression in section 2 of the Charter.

Consider the approach taken by the United States Supreme Court to interpretation of the similar guarantee in the First Amendment to the Constitution of the United States that: "Congress shall make no law ... abridging the freedom of speech, or of the press." In *Roth v. United States*, 1957 USSC, the Court dealt specifically with the issue of obscenity in relation to the guarantee of freedom of the press in the First Amendment. Mr Justice William Brennan began his reasons for the Court by reviewing the legislative history of the First Amendment. Among other considerations, he noted that when the provision came into effect in 1792, every state had a law designating blasphemy and/or profanity as statutory crimes. Consequently, he concluded that the unconditional phrasing of the First Amendment was "not intended to protect every utterance." Instead, Justice Brennan found:

> The protection given speech and press was fashioned to assure unfettered interchange of ideas for the bringing about of political and social changes desired by the people ... All ideas having even the slightest redeeming social importance – unorthodox ideas, controversial ideas, even ideas hateful to the

prevailing climate of opinion – have the full protection of the guaranties, unless excludable because they encroach upon the limited area of more important interests. But implicit in the history of the First Amendment is the rejection of obscenity as utterly without redeeming social importance. This rejection for that reason is mirrored in the universal judgment that obscenity should be restrained, reflected in the international agreement of over 50 nations, in the obscenity laws of all of the 48 States, and in the 20 obscenity laws enacted by the Congress from 1842 to 1956.

Earlier, in *Chaplinsky v. New Hampshire,* 1942 USSC, the United States Supreme Court affirmed: "There are certain well-defined and narrowly limited classes of speech, the prevention and punishment of which have never been thought to raise any Constitutional problem. These include the lewd and obscene ... It has been well observed that such utterances are no essential part of any exposition of ideas, and are of such slight social value as a step to truth that any benefit that may be derived from them is clearly outweighed by the social interest in order and morality." In conformity with this precedent, the United States Supreme Court has upheld a state law prohibiting any person from viewing or possessing child pornography "that constitutes lewd exhibition or focuses on genitals."[63]

With these judgments, the United States Supreme Court has upheld the original understanding of the guarantee of freedom of speech and of the press in the First Amendment. Justice Brennan and his likeminded colleagues have refrained from imposing their own views on the requirements of a just law on obscenity. The Supreme Court of Canada, for its part, has rejected such a restrained approach to the interpretation of section 2 of the Charter. In *Irwin Toy,* 1989 SCC, Chief Justice Dickson paid no heed to the historical facts that when the Charter came into effect in 1982, the Parliament of Canada and the legislatures of the provinces all had statutes in effect that constricted freedom of expression in relation to such matters as libel, slander, and fraud on the provincial level, and pornography, sedition, and incitement to violence on the federal level. Despite the existence of all these laws as guides to the original understanding of the guarantee of freedom of expression in the Charter, Dickson resolved entirely on his own authority to declare on behalf of the Court that: "Freedom of expression was entrenched in our Constitution ... so as to ensure that everyone can manifest their [*sic*] thoughts, opinions, beliefs, indeed all expressions of the heart and mind, however unpopular, distasteful or contrary to the mainstream." Dickson had no legal justification for this sweeping assertion. He could cite no evidence that Parliament and the provincial legislatures understood that section 2 of the Charter would confer upon Canadians the right to indulge in virtually any manner of expression. Yet, on the basis of his arbitrary interpretation of section 2 in *Irwin Toy*, the Supreme Court of Canada has gone on in other cases to specify that the right to freedom of expression in Canada includes the right to commit such excesses as hate propaganda,[64] defamatory libel,[65] obscenity,[66] and even lap dancing.[67] In one case, Dickson went so far as to declare: "In my view, the scope of freedom of expression does extend to the activity of communication for the purpose of engaging in prostitution."[68] The mind boggles.

Granted, the Supreme Court of Canada has also held that the alleged rights of Canadians to solicit prostitutes, disseminate hate propaganda, defame respectable citizens, and indulge in lap dancing and other obscene performances are subject to reasonable and demonstrably justified limits defined by law as specified in section 1 of the Charter. Note, however, that the proportionality tests that Dickson devised out of whole cloth in *Oakes* for the interpretation of section 1 are not clearly defined rules of law but vaguely delimited standards for subjective judgment. In applying these proportionality tests to a law limiting Charter rights, the Court is not upholding abstract legal principles but second-guessing the wisdom of Parliament in enacting the law. In essence, the Court is not adjudicating but legislating under the guise of interpreting and applying the Charter.

There was nothing inevitable about this judicial encroachment upon legislative powers. In *Irwin Toy* the Supreme Court of Canada could have followed its own pre-Charter precedents, which defined freedom of expression primarily in relation to political speech. By taking this approach, the Court would have upheld the provisions on obscenity and the solicitation of prostitutes in the Criminal Code on the ground that there is no reason to believe that Parliament and the provincial legislatures understood that the guarantee of freedom of expression in section 2(b) of the Charter covered these perverse forms of expression. Had the Court applied such a clear and principled interpretation to section 2(b), there would have been no necessity for the Court to evaluate laws on obscenity, lap dancing, hate propaganda, defamatory libel, and solicitation for the purposes of prostitution under the subjective, nonlegal terms laid out by Dickson in *Oakes* for the interpretation of section 1 of the Charter. In all such cases, members of the Court would have upheld the traditional separation of legislative and judicial powers by deferring to the wisdom of Parliament in enacting the law, instead of changing the law to accord with the judges' subjective policy preferences.

In *Constitutional Law of Canada*, Professor Peter Hogg has observed that the Supreme Court of Canada chose to define Charter rights broadly in conjunction with a relaxed standard for justification under section 1, although it was open to the Court to adopt a narrow interpretation of rights while applying a stringent standard for section 1 exceptions. Hogg argued in favour of the latter approach:

> If we assume that the outcomes of cases will be much the same under either approach, the second approach is surely preferable, because it will reduce the volume of litigation and limit the policy-making role of the courts. If the scope of the guaranteed rights is wide, and the standard of justification is relaxed, then a large number of Charter challenges will come before the courts, and will fall to be determined under s. 1. Since s. 1 requires that the policy of the legislation be balanced against the policy of the Charter, and since it is difficult to maintain meaningful standards to constrain the balancing process, judicial review will become even more unpredictable than it is now.[69]

Events have fully born out this prediction. Most judges on the Supreme Court of Canada have shown no disposition to uphold the original meaning of the rights of the Charter. They have preferred a sweeping approach that has provoked a flood of Charter appeals. Time and again, the Court has presumed to evaluate the wisdom of the laws enacted by elected representatives of the people in Parliament and the provincial legislatures on the most sensitive political issues. Yet even the most activist judges of the Supreme Court of Canada maintain that they are simply upholding the law and the Charter. This argument is not persuasive. While Professor Ian Hunter predicted in 1981 that most judges on the Supreme Court of Canada would take an activist approach to interpretation of the Charter, he insists that there was nothing inevitable or legitimate about this manner of interpretation. He avers that "under the Charter, the Court could have – and should have – developed a doctrine of judicial self-restraint, as the U.S. Supreme Court has done on occasion. Instead, the Supreme Court of Canada leapt at the opportunity to substitute its will for that of Parliament on the most contentious and divisive social issues."[70]

Dean Patrick Monahan of Osgoode Hall Law School is generally sympathetic to the approach taken by the Supreme Court of Canada to interpretation of the Charter, yet he candidly rejects the Court's claim "that its function under the Charter is a peculiarly legal and not a political one."[71] Monahan observes: "The story hasn't convinced anyone. Instead of arguments aimed at differentiating its function from that of the legislature, the Court has offered only bare and hollow assertion."[72] Monahan contends: "Even a cursory analysis of the language and structure of the Charter indicates that most Charter litigation may well turn on the issue of the 'wisdom' of legislative choices. In part, this is a product of the abstract and generalized nature of the rights protected by the Charter. The very process of defining the content of the rights protected by the Charter seems inherently political. Many of these rights – most notably the right to 'equality' and 'liberty' – contain little or no substantive criteria; they resemble blank slates on which the judiciary can scrawl the imagery of their choice."[73]

John T. Saywell has expressed much the same view in *The Lawmakers: Judicial Power and the Shaping of Canadian Federalism.* He holds that enactment of the Charter gave the Supreme Court of Canada a "mandate ... to fashion the law relating to rights and freedoms."[74] In the absence of any precedents for interpretation of the Charter, Saywell argues, "the court had a clean slate on which to write its constitutional prescriptions."[75] Yet this claim is patently untrue. The 1960 Canadian Bill of Rights declares in section 1 that Canadians are entitled to an array of rights and freedoms, such as "(c) freedom of religion; (d) freedom of speech; (e) freedom of assembly and association; and (f) freedom of the press." Yet the Supreme Court of Canada did not treat these generalized rights as so many blank slates. Rather, in conformity with the canons of judicial restraint, the Court took the view expressed in 1993 by Mr Justice Ritchie in *Robertson and Rosetanni* that "the *Canadian Bill of Rights* is not concerned with 'human rights and fundamental freedoms' in any abstract sense, but rather with such 'rights and freedoms' as they existed in Canada immediately before the statute was enacted."

When the Charter came fully into effect in 1985, the members of the Supreme Court of Canada had the same choice: They could have looked to existing statute laws, common law precedents, and the legislative history of the Charter for interpretive guidance. Alternatively, they could have regarded the rights and freedoms of the Charter as so many blank slates on which they, the judges, are entitled to scrawl the imagery of their choice. With rare exceptions, members of the Supreme Court of Canada have chosen this latter course. The great majority of justices on Canada's top court, including Chief Justices Dickson, Lamer, and McLachlin, have wilfully treated the rights and freedoms of the Charter as clean slates to be written upon by themselves. Monahan notes the consequences:

> Having given content to these open-ended rights, the judiciary must then "balance" these rights against considerations of general welfare under s. 1.

This process of "interest balancing" seems just another way of asking the fundamental legislative question: "is this worth what it costs?" The process of balancing individual interests against collective interests is a calculation which would have already been made by the legislature when it passed the statute under review. Since the legislature passed the statute, it must have calculated that the interests to be served outweighed those to be sacrificed. Section 1 of the Charter appears to invite the Court to assess and to second-guess the "wisdom" of the balance struck by the legislature.[76]

Note the tentativeness of this last assertion: Section 1 of the Charter "appears to invite the Court" to assess and second-guess the "wisdom" of the balance struck in policies adopted by the Legislature. Monahan cites no evidence to support this speculation, and for good reason: There is no such evidence. There is no reason to believe that Parliament and the provincial legislatures intended that the Charter would result in a wholesale surrender of their legislative authority to the courts.

The judges of the Supreme Court of Canada have taken it upon themselves to violate the separation of legislative and judicial powers under the Constitution. And the same goes for many judges on the United States Supreme Court. They, too, have taken to treating historically defined rights as blank slates on which the judiciary can wilfully countermand the decisions of legislators in balancing the interests of some people against others. Stephen B. Presser, a professor of law at Northwestern University, has pointed out that the disposition of a majority of the United States Supreme Court to adopt interest balancing as an explicit mode of interpreting constitutional rights dates from the late 1930s and early 1940s. He bluntly affirms: "It is a jurisprudential approach that emerged when the Supreme Court abandoned the rule of law."[77]

In abandoning judicial restraint and the rule of law, the Supreme Court of the United States, like its Canadian counterpart, has assumed the authority to supervise and direct the legislative process. The framers of the United States Constitution did not anticipate such a judicial seizure of power. Their views on the proper separation of legislative and judicial powers was spelled out in *The Federalist Papers*, a collection of polemical essays published in 1788–89 that were variously written by Alexander Hamilton, John Jay, and James Madison to persuade the people of New York State to ratify the proposed Constitution. "For more than 200 years," writes Presser, "the best guide to understanding the original intention of the Constitution's framers has been *The Federalist Papers*."[78] In "Federalist No. 78," Hamilton endorsed Montesquieu's affirmation that "there is no liberty, if the power of judging be not separated from the legislative and executive powers." Therefore, Hamilton explained, the courts of the United States will have authority to uphold the law only within the limits of the Constitution. He acknowledged: "Some perplexity respecting the rights of the courts to pronounce legislative acts void, because contrary to the Constitution, has arisen from an imagination that the doctrine would imply a superiority of the judiciary to the legislative power. It is urged that the authority which can declare the acts of another void, must necessarily be superior to the one whose acts may be declared void."[79] Hamilton rejected this argument. He wrote:

> The courts were designed to be an intermediate body between the people and the legislature, in order, among other things, to keep the latter within the limits assigned to their authority. The interpretation of the laws is the proper and peculiar province of the courts. A constitution is, in fact, and must be regarded by the judges, as a fundamental law. It therefore belongs to them to ascertain its meaning, as well as the meaning of any particular act proceeding from the legislative body. If there should happen to be an irreconcilable variance between the two, that which has the superior obligation and validity ought, of course, to be preferred; or, in other words, the Constitution ought to be preferred to the statute, the intention of the people to the intention of their agents.
>
> Nor does this conclusion by any means suppose a superiority of the judicial to the legislative power. It only supposes that the power of the people is superior to both; and that where the will of the legislature, declared in its statutes, stands in opposition to that of the people, declared in the Constitution, the judges ought to be governed by the latter rather than the former. They ought to regulate their decisions by the fundamental laws, rather than by those which are not fundamental.[80]

Note Hamilton's key argument: Judges are not to impose their own views on the application of the abstract and generalized terms of the Constitution to concrete and specific issues: Rather, they should uphold as best they can the will of the people as originally declared in the Constitution. Professor Presser underlines the implications of this restrained approach to constitutional interpretation:

> For Hamilton's theory of the judiciary as the expositor and enforcer of the popular will to make any sense, then, two important corollaries must follow. Not only must the judiciary only enforce the will of the people when it engages in constitutional interpretation, but (1) it must be able to discern the popular will as expressed in the document, and (2) there must be a clear original

understanding – the popular will must have a single correct meaning. The search for the popular will, as expressed in the Constitution, is the only valid means of constitutional interpretation. If there are correct answers to constitutional questions – and if there are not, then the rule of law itself makes no sense – there can be only one meaning for the Constitution. Constitutional adjudication, then, is nothing more nor less than the search for the single correct expression of the popular will inherent in the document. There must be right answers to constitutional questions, and they are to be sought in the original understanding of the words and phrases ratified by the people in convention.[81]

If Chief Justice McLachlin upheld the orthodox approach to judicial interpretation of a federal Constitution as expounded by Alexander Hamilton and applied by Justice Brennan in *Roth*, how would she have decided the *Sharpe* case? First, she would have undertaken to determine the popular will inherent in section 2 of the Charter by conducting a legislative review of the provision, and, in doing so, she would have found that when the Charter came into effect in 1982, Parliament and the provincial legislatures all had numerous statutes in effect limiting freedom of expression. On this basis, she would have rejected the manifestly erroneous and entirely unprecedented, all-embracing interpretation of the guarantee of freedom of expression in section 2 that was wrongly pronounced by the Dickson Court in *Irwin Toy*. In the context of the *Sharpe* case, McLachlin would also have taken particular note of the fact that when the Charter was proclaimed in 1982, the Criminal Code provided in section 159(1), now section 163(1), that: "Every one commits an offence who ... makes, prints, publishes, distributes, circulates, or has in his possession for the purpose of publication, distribution or circulation any obscene written matter, picture, model, phonograph record or other thing whatever." In conformity with this evidence of the popular will inherent in the Charter, she would have repudiated the absurd notion that the guarantee of freedom of expression in section 2 confers upon Canadians the right to express themselves through the possession of child pornography. And she would have upheld the existing ban on the possession of child pornography in section 163(1) of the Criminal Code as entirely compatible with the original understanding of section 2 of the Charter.

As it is, McLachlin did not take a restrained approach to interpretation of the Constitution in her *Sharpe* ruling. She failed to uphold the popular will as originally enshrined in the Charter. Instead, like Dickson, she affirmed the ridiculous notion that the guarantee of freedom of expression in section 2 is so all-encompassing as to include the right to possess child pornography. Then, in a clear violation of the separation of legislative and judicial powers under the Constitution, she and a majority of her colleagues on the Supreme Court of Canada amended the ban on the possession of child pornography in the Criminal Code by decreeing that perverts have a right under the guarantee of freedom of expression in section 2 of the Charter to make and possess for their private use the most repugnant and degrading forms of child pornography.

THE CHARTER MAKES US DO IT

Such conduct is typical of activist judges like McLachlin. In *Sharpe,* as in *Egan, Vriend, Halpern* and so many other crucial cases, these unelected, appeal court judges have fundamentally altered the law and the Constitution through interpretation. "Don't blame us," these judicial autocrats are wont to say, "the Charter makes us do it." Like Hunter, law professors Hawkins and Martin beg to differ. In the course of a thorough review of the legislative history of the Charter, Hawkins and Martin demonstrate that:

> the legislators who entrenched the Charter in the Constitution had no intention of abandoning the doctrine of parliamentary supremacy in favour of a doctrine of aggressive judicial review. They never intended to pass the legislative torch. Instead, the Charter was a typically Canadian compromise, a deal struck after a very politicized negotiation in which it was decided that rights would be protected by the Constitution, but in such a way as to respect, to the greatest degree possible, the supremacy of Parliament. There was to be judicial review, but a fair reading of the historical record shows that it was intended to be careful and restrained judicial review.[82]

Regardless, few appeal court judges uphold the orthodox, restrained approach to constitutional interpretation advocated by Hawkins, Hunter, and Martin. Over the past thirty years, a succession of Liberal and Progressive Conservative prime ministers have stacked the courts with activist judges. Granted, there have been some noteworthy exceptions like Mr Justice John McClung of the Alberta Court of Appeal, Mr Justice Francis Muldoon of the Federal Court Trial Division, and Mr Justice George Finlayson of the Ontario Court of Appeal. Madam Justice Mary Southin of the British Columbia Court of Appeal has also stood out among the small band of restrained judges in the Charter era who still uphold the separation of legislative and judicial powers under the Constitution. In an extraordinary aside in *R. v. M.S.*, 1996 BCCA, she commented on the chaos created by unrestrained judicial misinterpretation of the Charter. The appellant in this case was a Vancouver man who had fathered two children with his adult daughter. Consequently, he was charged with violating the ban on incest in section 155 of the Criminal Code, found guilty at trial, and sentenced to five years in prison. Upon appeal, counsel for the father asked the Court to strike down the ban on incest in the Criminal Code on the ground that it violates the rights of incestuous men to life, liberty, and security of the person as guaranteed in section 7 of the Charter. Mr Justice Ian Donald of the British Columbia Court of Appeal refuted this argument at length. In a concurring opinion, Justice Southin succinctly stated:

> It is regrettable – nay, it may be said to be ludicrous – that our legal system should have become so encumbered by the advent of the Canadian Charter of Rights and Freedoms and the authorities on the reach of s. 7 that my colleague has been obliged to expend his talents and his energy on such an exercise. He ought to have been able to say to the appellant, and had he been able to do so I would have concurred without further ado: "Incest was a crime in the Maritime provinces before confederation. By virtue of The British North America Act, (as it then was called); it continued a crime in those provinces. In 1892, Parliament made it a crime throughout the whole of Canada. It had become a capital crime in Scotland as early as 1567. It was a capital crime in England from 1650–1660. It became a crime, although not a capital crime, in England again on 1st January, 1909. Who are we to say that the legislators who enacted these statutes did not know what they were doing? Take your arguments to Parliament."

Note that Justice Southin laments not so much the advent of the Charter as how it has been interpreted. In case after case, the Supreme Court of Canada has signalled that virtually every traditional legal rule is open to moral and legal challenge under the Charter. In *R. v. M.S.*, Justice Southin recalled that in 1978 the Law Reform Commission of Canada had recommended the decriminalization of incest between consenting adults. She speculated: "It may be that the question will become a matter of debate here and the crime of incest will suffer the same fate as the crime of the 'detestable and abominable vice of buggery.' But it is no more the proper business of the judiciary, which has no collective claim to moral wisdom, to bring about that fate than it is the proper business of Parliament to try a man for murder."

As it is, Parliament would not presume to intrude upon the powers of the judiciary by trying a man for murder, yet the Supreme Court of Canada has no compunction about systematically intruding upon the powers of the legislative branch of government by presuming to change rather than uphold the law and the Constitution as written and originally understood. In so doing, the Court has gravely compromised the rule of law. Prior to enactment of the Charter and the onset of judicial activism, Canadians who had access to expert counsel could know their legal rights with a fair degree of certainty. Today, that is no longer the case. Activist judges predominate. They routinely flout rules fixed and announced beforehand. Like vacillating politicians, they lurch from one arbitrary ruling to another. Their only fixed rule of interpretation is that the end result must accord with the judge's peculiar notions of justice, regardless of common law rules, judicial precedents, and the plain language of ordinary statutes, human rights codes, and the Constitution.

In short, we now have something close to chaos in our courts of appeal. Leading constitutional scholars can no longer predict when the Supreme Court of Canada is likely to uphold or abandon basic constitutional principles. At a conference convened at Osgoode Hall Law School in April 1998 to mark the sixteenth anniversary of the Charter, Robert Hubbard, a senior counsel for the federal Department of Justice, lamented: "Every time I go to the Supreme Court of Canada, I haven't a clue what will happen. The only trend I have seen is no trend. Flipping a coin is not a bad way to proceed: At least you have a 50-per-cent chance of winning."[83] Osgoode Hall law professor Jamie Cameron was no less bewildered. He decried the baffling disposition of the Supreme Court of Canada to defer to Parliament on some questions while altering the law on other issues that had no bearing upon the case at hand. "There is a lack of any principle to explain patterns of activism or deference in the past year," he said. "I can't make heads nor tails of them from one case to another."[84]

Judicial disarray in the United States is just as bad, and for the same reason: Judges have supplanted the rule of law with the arbitrary imposition of their own views on the requirements of justice. Steven D. Smith, a professor of constitutional law at the University of Colorado, relates:

> A friend who has been teaching a course on constitutional law for a couple of decades and has achieved a national reputation confided recently that he plans to stop teaching the course; there just isn't any integrity to the subject, and it becomes almost a degrading experience to have to teach, say, equal protection doctrine and pretend that the Court's decisions are the product of any sort of coherent thinking. Students in constitutional law courses increasingly echo the Critical Legal Studies slogan from the last decade: It's all "just politics." One student wrote on an exam in one of my courses: "The only essential

skill needed to understand the Supreme Court's constitutional decisions is the ability to count to five." In this atmosphere, mandarin moral philosophy bequeathed to us by our elders come to seem no longer elegantly erudite, but instead weirdly comic.[85]

Sir William Blackstone would not be amused. While allowing that judges should temper law with their personal understanding of the requirements of equity, he warned: "The liberty of considering all cases in an equitable light must not be indulged too far, lest thereby we destroy all law, and leave the decision of every question entirely in the breast of the judge. And law, without equity, though hard and disagreeable, is much more desirable for the public good, than equity without law; which would make every judge a legislator, and introduce most infinite confusion; as there would then be almost as many different rules of action laid down in our courts, as there are differences of capacity and sentiment in the human mind."[86]

Our judicial lawmakers on the Supreme Court of Canada disregard Blackstone. Instead of upholding the law, they routinely impose their understanding of the requirements of equity. In so doing, they have compromised the rule of law and introduced most infinite confusion into the courts.

8

Reviving Parliamentary Democracy

Conor Gearty is a law professor and director of the Centre for the Study of Human Rights at the London School of Economics. On 11 December 2000 he generated a rousing debate with a provocative lecture entitled "What Are Judges For?" in which he discussed the changing role of the judiciary brought on by the British Human Rights Act, 1998, which incorporated the European Convention on Human Rights into the domestic law of Britain. Gearty contended that Parliament should hold appeal court judges accountable for their interpretations of the vague provisions of this Act. Members of the British judicial establishment were outraged. Gearty relates: "I was delighted to hear my views described as 'insane' by a retired judge on BBC radio."[1]

Gearty is not alone in underlining the revolutionary implications of the British Human Rights Act. Professor K.D. Ewing of King's College, London, likewise contends that the Act has engineered "an unprecedented transfer of political power from the executive and legislature to the judiciary, and a fundamental re-structuring of our 'political constitution'. As such it is unquestionably the most significant formal redistribution of political power in this country since 1911, and perhaps since 1688 when the Bill of Rights proclaimed loudly that proceedings in Parliament ought not to be questioned or impeached in any court or any other place."[2]

Yet compared to the Canadian Charter of Rights and Freedoms, the British Human Rights Act is a model of legislative restraint.[3] While both enactments incorporate similar legal rights and fundamental freedoms into law, the British Act, unlike the Canadian Charter, confers no formal authority on the judiciary to strike down or amend legislation. Section 4 of the British Act provides that even if the courts declare that a provision in a statute or a government regulation is "incompatible with a Convention right," this declaration "does not affect the validity, continuing operation or enforcement of the provision in respect of which it is given."[4] However, the Act includes a fast-track procedure that empowers the government to ask Parliament to circumvent the normal rules of procedure for the purpose of quickly approving legislation that eliminates a judicially declared incompatibility between a statute law and a Convention right.[5] Lord Woolf, the Lord Chief Justice of England and Wales, welcomed this provision in the law. Asked in an interview on the British Broadcasting Corporation (BBC) how often Parliament might invoke this fast-track procedure to remedy a declaration of incompatibility by the courts, he responded: "My own feeling is that Parliament will always do so because Parliament wants our law to be in accord with the Convention."[6] Lord Irvine, then the Lord Chancellor, agreed, although he allowed: "It is possible that there will be cases when [Parliament] will not want to do so."[7]

If Woolf and Irvine are right, section 4 of the British Human Rights Act confers upon the courts essentially the same de facto powers to strike down or amend laws that Canadian courts have under the Charter because the Parliament at Westminster will be no less willing than the Parliament of Canada to take direction from the judiciary on how the abstract principles of human rights and fundamental freedoms should be translated into public policy. Moreover, unlike the Canadian Charter, the British Act formally confers upon the courts the authority to disregard their own precedents governing the nature and scope of human rights in Britain. In section 2(1) the Act stipulates: "A court or tribunal determining a question which has arisen in connection with a Convention right must take into account any ... judgment, decision, declaration or advisory opinion of the European Court of Human Rights ... whenever made or given, so far as, in the opinion of the court or tribunal, it is relevant to the proceedings in which that question has arisen." In this way, British judges have been given much the same free rein that Canadian judicial activists have assumed to redefine the content and application of human rights. Ewing warns: "We have something much closer to a distinctive British Bill of Rights than is sometimes imagined: not perhaps in terms of the structure of the rights themselves; but certainly in terms of their interpretation and application, with British judges having the same unfettered ... discretion as their counterparts in Canada and elsewhere."[8]

Is it right that the judiciary should have such unfettered power? Should ultimate responsibility for translating the abstract principles of a bill of rights into precise laws for particular purposes rest with appointed judges? Gearty doesn't think so. He said:

> Let us envisage an abstract spectrum of judicial types. On the extreme left (no political point intended) is the strict constructionist whose only job is to work out the meaning of the words deployed by the legislature and then to give effect to them. There is no common law to interpret, only statutes together with a civil and (perhaps) a Criminal Code. Then in the centre is the judge who engages in statutory interpretation in a rather more creative way and who has full autonomy in a particular legislative field, described as the common law. Finally on the extreme right (again no subliminal message intended) is the judge as overt law maker, whose origins as an adjudicator have long been transcended by his or her overriding responsibility both to make and to oversee the making of general rules for the public good ...
>
> I may be irretrievably nostalgic or a true revolutionary (I am not sure which it is – perhaps both) but I have a strong hankering for a very limited judicial function, somewhere well to the left of the spectrum I have described, in other words a society in which broadly speaking the rules are made by representatives, interpreted by the courts and enforced if needs be by the executive arm.[9]

Prior to the Human Rights Act, British judges straddled the middle of this left-right judicial spectrum. Like their Canadian counterparts, they were responsible for gradually adapting the common law and the interpretation of statute laws to changing social circumstances. Gearty noted that the "legislative" function of the courts was "well camouflaged and in the main (with one or two exceptions of course) timidly deployed. But what no one could have expected was that the legislative branch itself would invite the judiciary to exercise legislative power of a far more general and pervasive nature than has ever hitherto been countenanced. This is the effect of the Human Rights Act."[10] Gearty marvels that there has been no outcry from the British people. He observes: "If such a power were given to any other branch or sub-branch of the State, and certainly if it were given to the executive, the legal community would be up in arms, conferences would be held, papers issued, deploring this unprecedented 'Henry VIII clause', as the cognoscenti would call it. But because it is the judges we seem to assume it must be all right."[11]

So far, British judges have proven to be hardly less eager than their Canadian colleagues to formulate "huge issues of policy" as "legal rules of general application." Given the judicial determination to take on this overtly political role, what other constitutional changes are in order? Gearty offers several suggestions.

CONFIRMATION HEARINGS

In Britain as in Canada, judges are appointed essentially on the sole recommendation of the prime minister, who is free to accept or reject the confidential advice of legal experts on the qualifications of the candidate. There was little controversy over this secretive procedure for filling vacancies in the courts as long as judges set their personal political opinions aside for the purpose of upholding the law as enacted and defined by judicial precedents. However, now that many judges have taken to legislating from the bench, there have been many calls for reform of the appointment process. Gearty is one of those who maintains that a committee of Parliament should be authorized to subject judicial nominees to the kind of open confirmation hearings held by the Judiciary Committee of the United States Senate. Many judges and lawyers recoil at this prospect. They recall how Democrats on this committee subjected Judge Robert Bork to an ideological grilling in 1987, before rejecting his nomination to the United States Supreme Court. Bork is a former professor in the Yale Law School and a leading advocate of judicial restraint. His Democrat critics were fearful that he would try to reverse the unprincipled decisions on abortion, school prayers, and other sensitive issues that activist judges on the United States Supreme Court have handed down over the past forty years.

In 1991, Democrats on the Senate Judiciary Committee next concentrated their ire on Judge Clarence Thomas, another eminent apostle of judicial restraint. These hearings descended into scandal when Anita Hill accused Thomas of sexual harassment. He survived the ordeal, his nomination was approved, and he has gone on to serve with distinction on the United States Supreme Court.

Despite these unseemly precedents, Gearty insists that Parliament should have a voice in the selection of judges. He points out that "there are not nearly so many controversial candidacies in the United States as is widely believed and the main ones we know about – those involving Robert Bork and Clarence Thomas – were rightly controversial in my view. United States federal judges have in the main drawn a degree of comfort from their confirmation hearings, feeling that it has given them at least a degree of democratic legitimacy in relation to their subsequent judicial work."[12]

Justice La Forest takes much the same view.[13] In an interview with *The Hill Times* shortly before his retirement from the Supreme Court of Canada in September 1997, he said: "The thing about which I am a bit of a heretic is that I think we should have a vetting process of some kind" for appointments to the Supreme Court of Canada.[14] Like Gearty, La Forest discounted the risk that this procedure would subject judicial appointees to the kind of rough political treatment meted out to Thomas. In La Forest's judgment, the United States senators who cross-examined Thomas had good reason to probe his views on sexual harassment. "I think that the attitude of a judge about that sort of issue is important," said La Forest. "So the vetting process may have been painful, it may have been unpleasant, but I think it is important for the people to know what kind of person they are getting."[15]

Chief Justice McLachlin disagrees. She sees nothing wrong either with the behaviour of current judges or with how they are appointed. In her address to the Canadian Club in Toronto in June 2003, she said:

> The independent, apolitical nature of the judicial role suggests that it would be misguided to appoint judges in a manner that gives more weight to partisan politics. In this debate, the most important question should always be the following: What kind of judges do we want? To me, the sole concern should be to appoint individuals who embody the most valuable qualities of impartiality, empathy and wisdom. From where I sit, the current judiciary in Canada meets the highest standards in this respect. A reform of our appointments process would certainly be welcome if it enables us to improve on this excellent record. That is the standard against which proposals for reform must be assessed. Most would agree that in terms of product, the present process seems to work well. Why, one might ask, fix the system if it isn't broken? Or to borrow a figure of speech I recently ran across – "Why open up that Pandora's Box when you don't know what kind of Trojan horse might come out of it?"[16]

Ironically, with this statement, McLachlin has demonstrated the need for closer political scrutiny of judicial appointments. In the pre-Charter era, no chief justice would have made such a speech. At that time, there was no need to do so. As a strictly adjudicative body, the Supreme Court of Canada commanded virtually universal public respect. All judges strove to maintain their reputation for independence and impartiality by rigorously avoiding public comment outside the courtroom on partisan issues. Activist judges like McLachlin neglect such restraint. In October 2002 Paul Martin had endorsed the idea of having judicial nominees vetted by a parliamentary committee.[17] McLachlin must have known about this speech, yet she had no compunction about repudiating Martin's proposed reform eight months later in her Canadian Club address. Roger Gallaway, parliamentary secretary for democratic reform in Martin's government, was not pleased. In an address at Sir Wilfrid Laurier University on 29 January 2004, he admonished McLachlin and other sitting judges to "remember their proper roles, one of which is to avoid comment on political or parliamentary affairs."[18] Gallaway argued that the proposal to "subject prospective appointments to an open, public hearing, simply is an acknowledgment that Canadians have a right or opportunity to know something about these people who exercise their Charter interpretations on a more regular basis." He reminded his audience that the courts are "the creation of Parliament and subject to it." He added: "What is obvious is the courts, but particularly the Supreme Court, have assumed a position of power which challenges the doctrine of the supremacy of Parliament ... The role of the courts in 'discerning rights' is, among a growing cross-section of Canadians, an issue which is unsettling. The power of the courts themselves, dictated by the courts, are by some believed to be exaggerated."[19]

As it is, McLachlin is not the only chief justice of Canada to have spoken out against parliamentary scrutiny of judicial nominees. In an address to the Faculty of Law of the University of Toronto on 6 February 1998, Chief Justice Lamer likewise opposed the idea. He pointed out that the views expressed by nominees to a parliamentary committee would not be a reliable guide to their behaviour on the bench. To illustrate the point, Lamer confided: "Had you asked me at a hearing if I was for or against [abortion], I would have said against."[20] Why, then, did he back the decision of the Supreme Court of Canada in *Morgentaler,* 1988, to strike down the restrictions on abortion in the Criminal Code? Lamer explained: "My reasoning is that unless you have a vast majority of people think something is criminal, you should not make it a crime."[21] Note his rationale: Lamer made no reference to the current state of public opinion on abortion in his reasons for judgment in *Morgentaler,* 1988. The conclusion is inescapable: His ostensibly legal reasons for judgment in that case were just a fig leaf to disguise his essentially political decision to strike down the country's abortion law.

Be that as it may, Lamer is right about the limited utility of confirmation hearings. The procedure could not lend even the thinnest patina of democratic legitimacy to judicial law making. Even if the nominations of Lamer and McLachlin had been carefully reviewed by a committee of parliamentarians, there could be nothing democratic about their presumption to impose changes in the laws and the Constitution by means of unprincipled judicial decisions.

ADVICE ON PUBLIC POLICY FOR THE COURTS

Gearty notes that British judges lack not only the legitimacy to legislate, but also the information necessary for sound policy making. To help judges fulfil their new law-making role, he argues that the Parliament at Westminster should "work out what is the best way of getting the full facts before a court so that when it makes a ruling on the law under the Human Rights Act, it does so explicitly acknowledging its legislative character and with a clear understanding of its widespread implications."[22] In Gearty's opinion, it is no longer sufficient for the courts to rely on lawyers' submissions and occasional briefs prepared by a friend of the court. "How can the court be sure that an amicus brief that has been filed is authoritative?" he asks. "How can it choose between amicus briefs if there is a conflict?" Gearty submits that

> the Court of Appeal, the appellate committee and the judicial committee should have appointed to them a "public interest officer" with a small team of officials, whose job it is to prepare reports on the effects of possible rulings not just on the law but on the wider public and on society as a whole ... The advantage of a "public interest statement" filed by a court officer would be that it would take such huge issues out of the narrow and artificial confines of the adversarial process, and it would also – an additional advantage I would say – open up the process to persons other than lawyers.[23]

There is much to be said for this proposal. If the Supreme Court of Canada had been able to draw upon the advice of a public interest officer, it might perhaps have avoided its disastrous judgment in *R. v. Askov*, 1990 SCC. The appellants in this case – one Elijah Anton Askov and three criminal associates – had been variously charged with conspiracy to commit extortion, possession of a prohibited weapon (a sawed-off shotgun), pointing a firearm, assault with a weapon, and criminal negligence in the operation of a motor vehicle. A preliminary hearing in the case was completed on 21 September 1984, but a trial for the four accused did not get underway until 2 September 1986 in the Ontario Judicial District of Peel because of a backlog of cases clogging the courts. Counsel for the defence moved to stay the proceedings on the grounds that the nearly two-year delay in bringing the case to trial violated the rights of the accused "to be tried within a reasonable time" as guaranteed in section 11(b) of the Charter.

The trial judge granted this defence motion. In effect, he declared that the four accused could not be prosecuted because they had been required to wait an unreasonable time for the trial to begin. In 1987 the Ontario Court of Appeal overturned this ruling on the grounds that the delay in bringing the case to trial had not been due to any misconduct by the Crown and that there was no evidence that the delay had caused any actual prejudice to the accused.

Three years later, the Supreme Court of Canada reversed this judgment and agreed with the trial judge that a delay of twenty-three months from the time Askov was committed to trial until his trial took place was unreasonable and unconstitutional. Prior to adoption of the Charter, this issue would never have arisen. The courts would have deferred to the judgment of the legislative branch of government on the length of a reasonable delay between committal and trial. In *Askov*, the Supreme Court of Canada took over this responsibility. In reasons for judgment on behalf of the Court, Mr Justice Peter Cory cited a comparative study of trial delays by Professor Carl Baar, director of the Judicial Administration Program at Brock University. Cory took particular note of Baar's claim that: "If Canadian courts were required to set cases for trial within six months, they could almost universally do so. No Provincial Court in Canada is normally setting cases for trial or preliminary hearing more than six months after first appearance. Of the five provinces with county courts, only one location in one province routinely sets criminal cases for trial more than six months after committal: Ontario's Peel County Court in Brampton. That court has set trial dates a full ten months ahead, perhaps the longest delay in Canada."

Justice Cory also cited Baar's evidence that average waiting times between remission for trial and trial in various other jurisdictions in Canada and the United States were substantially less than in the judicial district of Peel. On this basis, Cory concluded: "Making a very rough comparison and more than doubling the longest waiting period to make every allowance for the special circumstances in Peel would indicate that a period of delay in a range of some six to eight months between committal and trial might be deemed to be the outside limit of what is reasonable." With this statement, the Supreme Court of Canada created a new law on trial delays that was unknown to the common law and the statute laws of Canada. The immediate result was to let Askov and his associates off scot-free on all charges. Cory described this outcome as "most unfortunate and regrettable." He added: "There can be no doubt that it would be in the best interest of society to proceed with the trial of those who are charged with posing such a serious threat to the community. Yet, that trial can only be undertaken if the Charter right to trial within a reasonable time has not been infringed. In this case that right has been grievously infringed and the sad result is that a stay of proceedings must be entered."

Cory also acknowledged that his ruling would result in a stay of proceedings for any accused who experiences a delay of more than eight months between committal and trial. He said: "Fortunately, Prof. Baar's work indicates that most regions of this country are operating within reasonable and acceptable time limits with the result that such relief will be infrequently granted."

This conclusion soon proved to be wrong – calamitously wrong. In *Charter Politics*, Knopff and Morton report: "In Ontario, 43,640 charges were stayed, dismissed, or withdrawn on the basis of *Askov* by mid-1991. These included at least one charge of manslaughter, 817 'extreme assault' offences (e.g., assault with a weapon, assault on a police officer, or assault causing bodily harm), 290 sexual assault charges, 402 lesser sex offences, and 11,623 charges of impaired driving."[24]

None of these considerations swayed Chief Justice Lamer. Seven years after the *Askov* ruling, he still defended the decision, saying: "Of course, there was a price society had to pay to get this moving. In some provinces, the criminal justice system was not a very high priority. There ain't many votes in that. I think *Askov* was a smack on the hand. It said: 'We do mean business. Clean up your act.' It is cruel and unusual punishment to come have to wait two or three years to get your trial."[25]

At least Justice Cory is contrite about his role in the worst law-enforcement setback in Canadian history. Scarcely ten months after his ruling in *Askov*, he confessed in an address to the Advanced Legal Studies Conference in Cambridge, England, that he was "shocked" by the results.[26] Professor Ian Hunter has pointed out that this confession "indicated how perilously out of touch with reality the Supreme Court of Canada is."[27]

In the context of the *Askov* case, a public interest officer might well have discovered with just a few phone calls that, regardless of what Professor Baar thought, the imposition of a court-ordered limit of eight months between a preliminary hearing and the beginning of a trial would allow thousands of violent criminals to escape justice. Given this information, it is inconceivable that a majority of the Court would have endorsed the *Askov* ruling.

Advice from an independent public interest officer might also have saved the Supreme Court of Canada from its disruptive and embarrassing ruling in *R. v. Marshall*, 17 September 1999 SCC. In this case, the appellant, Donald Marshall, Jr., a Mi'kmaq, had been charged with selling eels without a licence, fishing without a licence, and fishing during the closed season with illegal nets. While admitting that he had caught and sold eels as charged, he claimed that he was exempt from federal fisheries regulations by virtue of an eighteenth-century treaty that granted the Mi'kmaq the right to catch and sell fish. The trial judge rejected this argument and convicted Marshall. The Nova Scotia Court of Appeal upheld the conviction. Upon further appeal, the Supreme Court of Canada agreed that the Mi'kmaq were exempt from federal fisheries regulations and acquitted Marshall.

East Coast lobster fishermen reacted with immediate alarm. Many feared that they would soon lose their livelihoods if Mi'kmaq started scooping up out-of-season lobster. Tensions rose and violence flared between Natives and non-Natives in East Coast fishing ports. On Sunday, 3 October 1999, the situation got so out of hand that normally law-abiding fishermen in Burnt Church, New Brunswick, engaged in one of the worst race-riots in Canadian history. While Royal Canadian Mounted Police officers looked on, an enraged mob of non-Native fishermen destroyed thousands of lobster traps placed by Natives in the Bay of Fundy. In retaliation, a mob of Natives burned two trucks owned by non-Natives on a public wharf. Later that night, an enraged Native rammed a pickup truck into the garage of a non-Native fisherman. In the ensuing melee, one Native ended up in the hospital. By good fortune, no one was killed.[28]

Newfoundland premier Brian Tobin blamed the *Marshall* decision of the Supreme Court of Canada for the tragedy. "The court has a responsibility to make themselves aware of how the fishery works," he said. "And if there is anarchy today, and there is a measure of anarchy in New Brunswick, in Nova Scotia, the Supreme Court of Canada has to take responsibility for that."[29] Tobin's criticism was on target but for the wrong reason. He should have understood that unlike legislators, judges have few means of assessing the potential impact of changes in the law. If Herb Dhaliwal, the federal fisheries minister at the time of the *Marshall* ruling, had got it into his head to give Mi'kmaq an exemption from the conservation rules in federal fisheries regulations, experts within his ministry would surely have warned him that such an ill-considered measure would provoke a strong reaction from non-Native lobster fishermen, especially as they had only recently been subjected to tighter conservation rules by the fisheries ministry in an attempt to prevent an outright collapse in the declining lobster catch.[30] Furthermore, if Dhaliwal had scorned this warning, he could not have proceeded without Cabinet and parliamentary approval. And it is inconceivable that Parliament would have sanctioned such a momentous change in the law without calling expert witnesses, holding public hearings, and engaging in a prolonged public debate.

As it is, the Supreme Court of Canada did not have access to advice from a public interest officer or conservation experts in the fisheries department. Neither did the Court solicit expert counsel from any other source on the social and economic impact of exempting Mi'kmaq from federal conservation rules. In typical judicial fashion, the Court deliberated in secret and sprung its ruling on the public with no advance warning. Even Dhaliwal was left completely in the dark. Nonetheless, defenders of the Court insist that the activist judges who adopted this ruling were not to blame for the resulting anarchy because they simply upheld the law in *R. v. Marshall* as set out in a 1760 treaty between the Crown and the Mi'kmaq. This argument is unpersuasive. The key paragraph at issue in the treaty states only that the Mi'kmaq "will not Traffick, Barter or Exchange any Commodities in any manner but with such persons or the managers of such Truck houses as shall be appointed or Established by His Majesty's Governor at Lunenbourg or Elsewhere in Nova Scotia or Accadia." Both the trial judge and the Nova Scotia Court of Appeal ruled that there is nothing in the plain language or history of this treaty to support the Mi'kmaq's claim that they are exempt from federal conservation rules. Even Chief Justice McLachlin agreed with the lower courts on this point. In a dissenting opinion supported by Mr Justice Charles Gonthier in *Marshall,* she flatly asserted: "There is no existing right to trade in the Treaties of 1760–61 that exempts the [Mi'kmaq] appellant from the federal fisheries regulations." Regardless, under the pretext of upholding these 1760–61 treaties, a majority of the activist judges on the Supreme Court of Canada decreed that Mi'kmaq can hunt and fish for profit out of season. In formulating this legal rule, these judges usurped the law-making powers of Parliament: They did not uphold the law but changed it. And in so doing, they provoked one of the worst race riots in the history of Atlantic Canada.

Devising effective new laws of general application that can ameliorate, if not solve, the kind of deeply rooted social problems that afflict many Native communities throughout Canada is an immensely complex undertaking that is bound to task the collective wisdom and political skills of all the legislators and policy experts available to the federal and provincial governments. Yet time and again, the Supreme Court of Canada has presumed to direct this task of legal and social reform. In *Marshall, Delgamuukw,*[31] *Sparrow,*[32] and several other cases relating to the rights of Canada's Native peoples, the Court has aimed to right the wrongs of the historical treatment of Canada's Aboriginals by creating special legal rights and privileges for them. Correspondingly, in the *Egan, Vriend,* and *M. v. H.* rulings, the Court undertook to remedy the disadvantages facing homosexual, bisexual, and transgendered men and women by amending section 15 of the Charter, revising Alberta's human rights code, and directing both Parliament and the provincial legislatures to change literally hundreds of other laws to the end that gay and lesbian couples shall have essentially the same rights and privileges in law as common law, heterosexual couples.

A small public interest office might suffice for the comparatively restrained courts of Britain but would be wholly incapable of supplying the policy information required by Canada's aggressively activist judges. Under the colour of interpreting the Charter, the Supreme Court of Canada has reduced Parliament and the provincial legislatures to filling in the details of broad policies set by the Court in virtually all major areas from the structure of medicare to refugee processing, Aboriginal rights, the testing of cruise missiles, the definition of reasonable police procedures, and the obligation of hospitals to provide patients with translation services. To rule wisely on all these issues, the Supreme Court of Canada would need the advice not just of a small public interest office, but of the entire legislative and executive branches of government.

HOLDING JUDGES ACCOUNTABLE TO PARLIAMENT

To avoid conflict between Parliament and the courts on issues of public policy, Gearty concludes that appellate court judges should be required from time to time to give an account of their policy preferences to Parliament. If the British Human Rights Act is to work, he says:

> Judges will have to be prepared to meet with Parliament – perhaps with (a new) human rights committee – to explain in general terms what is happening in the courts under the Human Rights Act and to defend – not specific decisions but general policy developments – to that body ... Of course all this will be very new for the judges. But it surely flows from the enactment of the Human Rights Act in what is still a highly democratic culture. Far from being antagonistic about such developments, the judges should welcome them, as part of that dialogue with the other branches of government for which many have so long argued.[33]

The Supreme Court of Canada maintains that it has already established a dialogue between Parliament and the courts. In *Vriend*, Justice Iacobucci suggested that "the Charter has given rise to a more dynamic interaction among the branches of governance. This interaction has been aptly described as a 'dialogue' by some (see e.g. Hogg and Bushell).[34] In reviewing legislative enactments and executive decisions to ensure constitutional validity, the courts speak to the legislative and executive branches. As has been pointed out, most of the legislation held not to pass constitutional muster has been followed by new legislation designed to accomplish similar objectives ... By doing this, the legislature responds to the courts; hence the dialogue among the branches."

How ironical that Iacobucci should have served up this discourse on dialogue in *Vriend*, a case in which the Court manifestly renounced dialogue with the Alberta Legislature in favour of a monologue whereby the Court unilaterally inserted gay rights into Alberta's human rights code. In other instances, the Court has given legislators some leeway, but the resulting exchange can hardly be called a genuine dialogue. Professor Morton has observed: "Obeying orders is not exactly what most of us consider a dialogue. If I go to a restaurant, order a sandwich, and the waiter brings me the sandwich I ordered, I would not count this as a 'dialogue.' Yet this is how the concept is used in Hogg and Thornton's 1997 study.[35] They count as dialogue any legislative response to the judicial nullification of a statue. If a government repeals the offending legislation or amends it according to specifications laid out by the Court, this is 'dialogue.' No wonder they found a two-thirds incidence of dialogue!"[36]

In a jointly delivered judgment in *R. v. Mills*, 1999 SCC, Chief Justice McLachlin and Justice Iacobucci allowed that: "The courts do not hold a monopoly on the protection and promotion of rights and freedoms. Parliament also plays a role in this regard and is often able to act as a significant ally for vulnerable groups ... While it is the role of the courts to specify constitutional standards, there may be a range of permissible regimes that can meet these standards." While it is reassuring that McLachlin and Iacobucci concede that Parliament is still often able to act as a significant ally of vulnerable groups within limits determined by the courts, who is the boss in this arrangement? The Supreme Court of Canada, of course. While Gearty envisions a meaningful dialogue between appeal courts and Parliament, the Supreme Court of Canada prefers a master-servant relationship between judicial overseers and legislative vassals.

Regardless, Gearty's proposal for policy discussions between members of Parliament and judges is impractical. Even if most judges were willing to engage in such a dialogue, they could not spare the time. While parliamentary committees routinely devote weeks or months to gathering information at public hearings across Canada on a single issue of public policy, the Supreme Court of Canada typically devotes no more than a few days to oral arguments on the most complicated cases. For the momentous *M. v. H.*, *Askov*, and *Marshall* cases, the Court reserved just one day for oral arguments, heard testimony only from fellow lawyers, retired for several months to ponder the complex policy questions at issue, and then released a decision with no advance warning to either elected legislators or the interested public. This manner of law making by legislatively incompetent judges is guaranteed to produce ever more misconceived decisions like *Askov*, *Marshall*, *Egan*, *Vriend*, *Halpern*, and *Chaoulli*.

THE NOTWITHSTANDING CLAUSE: A DEAD LETTER?

Over the past forty years, the United States Supreme Court has been hardly less disposed than its Canadian counterpart to change, instead of uphold, the laws and the Constitution as originally understood. The

Founders of the United States Constitution did not anticipate such a development. Judge Bork relates: "Thinking of the Court as a minor institution, they provided no safeguards against its assumption of powers not legitimately its own and its consistent abuse of those powers. Congress and the President check and balance one another, but neither of them can stop the Court's adventures in making and enforcing left-wing policy."[37]

In Bork's opinion, half-measures will not suffice to restore the United States Constitution:

> There appears to be only one means by which the federal courts, including the Supreme Court, can be brought back to constitutional legitimacy. That would be a constitutional amendment making any federal or state court decision subject to being over-ruled by a majority vote of each House of Congress. The mere suggestion of such a remedy is certain to bring down cries that this would endanger our freedoms. To the contrary, as already noted, it is the courts that are not merely endangering our freedoms but actually depriving us of them, particularly our most precious freedom, the freedom to govern ourselves democratically unless the Constitution actually says otherwise. The United Kingdom has developed and retained freedom without judicial review.[38]

In Canada a limited version of the kind of constitutional authority recommended by Bork for checking the judicial subversion of legislative and executive powers is already available to our legislators. Section 33(1) of the Charter provides: "Parliament or the legislature of a province may expressly declare in an Act of Parliament or of the legislature, as the case may be, that the Act or a provision thereof shall operate notwithstanding a provision included in s. 2 or ss. 7 to 15 of this Charter." Section 33 further provides that for these declarations to remain in effect, they must be renewed at least every five years.

Note that the notwithstanding clause applies only to sections 2 and 7 to 15 of the Charter. It does not apply to judicial rulings on such matters as official languages in sections 16 to 22 of the Charter, minority language educational rights in section 23, the preservation and enhancement of the multicultural heritage of Canadians in section 27, the provision in section 28 that the rights and freedoms of the Charter are guaranteed equally to male and female persons, or the rights of Aboriginal peoples in section 35.

Justice Binnie noted in his reasons for judgment in *Marshall* that: "Until enactment of the Constitution Act, 1982, the treaty rights of aboriginal peoples could be overridden by competent legislation as easily as could the rights and liberties of other inhabitants." Today, Parliament can do nothing to counter an extravagant interpretation by the Supreme Court of Canada of a 1760 peace treaty between the Crown and the Mi'kmaq, short of initiating a constitutional amendment to section 35 of the Constitution Act, 1982, which would require the approval of at least two-thirds of the provinces having half the population of all the provinces. Thanks to the adoption of the Constitution Act, 1982, appointed judges on the Supreme Court of Canada, rather than elected representatives of the people in Parliament, have the final say on the meaning and extent of Aboriginal treaty rights in Canada.

This point has eluded many commentators, including Elsie Wayne, the former deputy leader of the Progressive Conservative Party and member of Parliament for Saint John. In the aftermath of the Burnt Church riots in 1999, she urged the Chrétien government to circumvent the *Marshall* ruling by invoking section 33 of the Charter. "They should use the notwithstanding clause and suspend that ruling for five years," said Wayne. "I know that's a big step, but something has to be done because this has become a real mess."[39] The fallout from the *Marshall* ruling remains a real mess, but as Wayne soon found out, the remedy that she proposed is not available to Parliament. There is nothing that the elected representatives of the people of Canada can do to change or extinguish the hunting, fishing, gathering, and trading rights that the Supreme Court of Canada conferred on the Mi'kmaq, short of amending the Constitution.

Granted, in numerous instances, Parliament and the provincial legislatures could have invoked the notwithstanding clause to overturn a judicial intrusion into the legislative process, but with the exception of the Quebec National Assembly, they have rarely done so. From the beginning, the prospect of legislative recourse to the notwithstanding clause has provoked considerable controversy. New Brunswick premier Richard Hatfield pledged to a gathering of first ministers on the Constitution: "I want to give you an undertaking that I will do everything possible to urge the legislature of New Brunswick not to use that opportunity, consistent with my firm view that if we are going to have rights, they must be shared by all Canadians, regardless of where they live."[40]

Premier Allan Blakeney of Saskatchewan was one of the few first ministers who defended section 33 as essential to upholding the democratic powers of the legislative branch of government. He contended that the Charter "protects the interests of individual Canadians, yet in several vital areas allows Parliament and legislatures to override a court decision which might affect the basic social institutions of a province or region, and this is fully consistent with the sort of argument we have put forward that we need to balance the protection of rights with the existence of our institutions which have served us so well for so many centuries."[41] Manitoba Premier Sterling Lyon and Alberta Premier

Peter Lougheed also insisted upon the democratic override in section 33 as a condition for approval of the Charter. Lougheed later recalled: "We needed to have the supremacy of the legislatures over the courts ... We did not [want] to be in a position where public policy was being dictated or determined by non-elected people."[42]

Prime Minister Pierre Trudeau maintained in his memoirs that he agreed to the notwithstanding clause in the Charter only as a means of reaching the compromise agreement that led to enactment of the Constitution Act of 1982. He wrote: "I would have much preferred not to have included the notwithstanding clause that limited the charter of rights. But I certainly prefer to have a charter with a notwithstanding clause than no charter at all."[43]

Nonetheless, Trudeau also stated that he did not have much concern about legislative misuse of the notwithstanding clause. In a 1981 radio interview, he said: "I must be honest and say that I don't fear the notwithstanding clause very much. It can be abused as anything can, but the history of the Canadian Bill of Rights Diefenbaker had adopted in 1960 – it has a notwithstanding clause and it hasn't caused any great scandal. So I don't think the notwithstanding clause deters [*sic*] very significantly from the excellence of the Charter ... It is a way that the legislatures, federal and provincial, have of ensuring that the last word is held by the elected representatives of the people rather than by the courts."[44]

Section 2 of the Canadian Bill of Rights provides: "Every law of Canada shall, unless it is expressly declared by an Act of the Parliament of Canada that it shall operate notwithstanding the Canadian Bill of Rights, be so construed and applied as not to abrogate, abridge or infringe or to authorize the abrogation, abridgment or infringement of any of the rights or freedoms herein recognized and declared." Trudeau invoked this notwithstanding clause in the Bill of Rights in the 1970 Public Order Temporary Measures Act, emergency legislation that Parliament adopted after agents of the Front de Libération du Québec (FLQ) had kidnapped and murdered Quebec vice premier and labour minister Pierre Laporte.

Joe Clarke has accused Trudeau of misrepresentation in professing to have unalterably opposed the notwithstanding clause of the Charter. While serving as secretary of state for external affairs in 1990, Clarke recalled:

> Let us not forget that Mr. Trudeau also entrenched the notwithstanding clause, which permits legislatures to override everything from freedom of religion to the right not to be discriminated against on the basis of race, national or ethnic origin, color, religion, age or mental or physical disability.

While he is now saying someone made him do it, he was not a reluctant bridesmaid, as revealed by the secret undertaking he made in a letter sent to Cardinal Carter on Dec. 21, 1981: "Should a court decide at some future date that sections 7 (the right of women to security of the person) or 15 (equality rights) establish a right to abortion on demand, Parliament will continue to legislate on the matter by overriding the court's decision and the specific charter right."[45]

Like Trudeau, Jean Chrétien also initially contemplated at least some use of the notwithstanding clause of the Charter. As the minister of justice in the Trudeau Cabinet, he told the Commons during debate on adoption of the Charter on 20 November 1981: "What the Premiers and Prime Minister agreed to is a safety valve which is unlikely ever to be used except in non-controversial circumstances by Parliament or legislatures to override certain sections of the Charter. The purpose of an override clause is to provide the flexibility that is required to ensure that legislatures rather than judges have the final say on important matters of public policy."

On this last point, several constitutional scholars concur. For example, in 1988 Peter Russell, a professor of political science at the University of Toronto, hailed the notwithstanding clause of the Charter as a brilliant innovation. "This element of the Charter expresses the unique Canadian blend of British and American constitutionalism," he wrote. "It may prove to be Canada's most significant contribution to the constitutional statecraft of liberal democracy. By permitting legislative review of judicial review, the override removes much of the anti-democratic sting from judicial activism."[46] A similar view has been expressed by Peter McCormick, a professor of political science at the University of Lethbridge. While lauding the judicial activism of the Supreme Court of Canada in the Charter era, he, like Russell, is troubled by the democratic implications of law making by the courts. In McCormick's view: "The courts do not have a monopoly on the interpretation of the Charter. They are not infallible."[47] Referring to the Supreme Court of Canada, he added:

> Under the pre-Laskin style of decision-making, the Court's main function was the mechanical application of formal rules to the extraction of meaning from legal texts, guided by the past decision of their own, but, also and particularly, of the English courts. If this had unfortunate practical consequences, the fault lay not with the people who interpreted the words but with the people who had drafted them. This was a narrow technical task, and the professionals could rightly demand that we acknowledge and defer to their proficiency. But applying to the very general terms of the Charter a purposive analysis guided

by concern for the context and for policy consequences is a horse of a different colour. It means that the Courts deserve a lower level of deference – which is not to say that they deserve no deference at all.[48]

As McCormick acknowledges, restrained judges in the pre-Charter era were entitled to complete independence from political interference because they essentially upheld existing laws and rarely, if ever, challenged the wisdom of enactments by the legislative branch of government. But now that activist judges on the Supreme Court of Canada routinely amend laws from the bench, it has become necessary to assure some judicial accountability. He says: "The challenge is to find the balance, to find the way of making judicial independence fully congruent with majority rule, so that we protect the judges who are making the decisions that involve principled but unpopular applications of the law, but not the judges who make decisions based on their own biases and prejudices."[49]

The problem with this formulation is that judicial activism is inherently unprincipled. Instead of upholding established principles in existing laws, activist judges misuse their power to create new and sometimes radically different laws. Referring to the United States Supreme Court, Judge Bork observes:

It is impossible for a Court that views itself as a political and cultural institution as much as a legal institution to make reasoned decisions whose principles it will adhere to in the future. The Court will change the Constitution as politics and culture change. The reasons given in one opinion are often little indication of what will happen in the next case. Since a cultural Court acts without guidance from the historic Constitution, the Justices could produce a coherent jurisprudence of individual rights only if they could construct and agree upon a systematic moral philosophy. Moral philosophers have been unable to agree on such a philosophy; it is preposterous to suppose that a committee of lawyers could. One result is that the Court's opinions, when it is engaged in the enterprise of creating rights, defy logical parsing. The decisions are diktats embedded in lofty but irrelevant rhetoric.[50]

McCormick has failed to grasp the distinction between political pronouncements by the Supreme Court of Canada and reasoned legal opinions. He writes: "If the Court has an Achilles heel, it lies in the fact that 'purposive interpretation' with a strong emphasis on contextualism and policy implications sometimes looks as if 'the Court is holding legislation valid or invalid on the basis of standards which it is making up as it goes along.'"[51] To illustrate the point, McCormick cites the contradiction between La Forest's ruling in *Egan*, 1995 SCC, which upheld the denial of pension benefits to same-sex couples in federal law, and the ruling by Cory and Iacobucci in *M. v. H.*, 1999 SCC, which declared that the denial of benefits to same-sex couples in Ontario law was unconstitutional. McCormick rhetorically asked: "Why did the Court turn around so abruptly?"[52] He gave the obvious answer:

> It was less that the two situations were massively different (indeed, La Forest's rhetoric on the family probably fits better with *M v. H*) than that the personnel [of the Supreme Court of Canada] had changed and the Court's centre of gravity had changed with it.
>
> Given such rapid evolution of doctrine, legislators must feel that they are shooting at hidden targets without knowing if the targets have been moved since the last time the lights were on. Even if you approve the Court's ruling in any individual case, this mutability might make you a little nervous. If you disapprove, it tends to make you angry.[53]

Given the disposition of the Supreme Court of Canada to hand down decisions with policy consequences, McCormick holds that the traditional constraints on judicial misconduct will no longer suffice. He contends: "What we need is a mechanism that will allow other actors into the debate." [54] The notwithstanding clause of the Charter was intended to provide just such a mechanism, but so far, it has not worked out. In McCormick's view, "it has become something of a constitutional dead letter."[55]

Indeed, Parliament has never invoked the notwithstanding clause, and among the provincial legislatures, only the Quebec National Assembly has made extensive use of the provision. In June 1982 the separatist Parti Québécois government of Quebec prompted the Legislature to invoke section 33 to shelter every Quebec law from Charter review by the courts.[56] After regaining provincial power in 1985, the Quebec Liberals allowed this blanket use of the notwithstanding clause to lapse, but they invoked section 33 in twelve other cases, including, most controversially, Bill C-178, the legislation enacted in 1988 that prohibited the use of English on outdoor commercial signs.[57] Most recently, on 4 May 2005 Quebec education minister Jean-Marc Fournier announced plans to extend invocation of the notwithstanding clause in the Quebec Education Act for an additional three years from July 2005 to August 2008 so that the government can continue to fund Catholic and Protestant schools during this period despite any perception by the courts that this arrangement is incompatible with the guarantee of freedom of religion in section 2(a) of the Charter.[58]

Only one other province has ever properly invoked the notwithstanding clause of the Charter: The Blakeney government of

Saskatchewan used it in 1984 to prevent the courts from interfering with a back-to-work law in a dairy strike. In 2000 the Legislature of Alberta declared that the traditional definition of "marriage" as between a man and a woman in the provincial Marriage Act shall apply notwithstanding the provisions in sections 2 and 7 to 15 of the Charter. However, this invocation of the notwithstanding clause was of no legal consequence because the definition of marriage is a subject matter that comes within the exclusive jurisdiction of Parliament by virtue of section 91(26) of the Constitution Act, 1867. Therefore, only Parliament, not a provincial legislature, can use the notwithstanding clause to prevent the courts from redefining marriage. Regardless, after some vacillation, Premier Ralph Klein consented on 17 March 2005 to renewal of the merely symbolic notwithstanding clause in the Alberta Marriage Act for another five years as a means of sending a political signal to Parliament that the Alberta Legislature remains steadfast in its support for the traditional definition of marriage in Canadian law.[59]

While serving as the New Democratic Party attorney general of British Columbia in 1998, Ujjal Dosanjh (currently the Liberal health minister in the Martin government), called upon the Parliament of Canada to enact legislation to assure that trials for sexual and violence offences will proceed, notwithstanding any judicially perceived conflict with the right "to be tried within a reasonable time" as guaranteed in section 11(b) of the Charter.[60] Dosanjh was prompted to make this suggestion by the scandalous case of a former public school teacher, Ian Cocker, who had been convicted on several charges of sexual assault of three minors and sentenced to fourteen months imprisonment. Cocker appealed the conviction on the ground that he had been subjected to an unreasonable delay of more than seventeen months between the laying of charges and the beginning of his trial. In *R. v. Cocker,* 1997 BCCA, the British Columbia Court of Appeal agreed with this argument, overturned Cocker's conviction, and, in effect, quashed the charges against him, despite having found "that the right of the accused to a fair trial has not been affected by the delay." With as many as 40,000 criminal cases clogging the overcrowded courts of British Columbia, Dosanjh feared that many more violent offenders and sexual predators could go free because they could not be brought to trial within the arbitrary limits set by the Supreme Court of Canada eight years earlier in its *Askov* ruling. Dosanjh lamented: "We don't live in an ideal world where we have resources coming out of our ears to throw at these things."[61]

Other prominent federal Liberals have also dissented from the doctrinal opposition of their party to invocation of the notwithstanding provision of the Constitution. For example, following the terrorist attacks on Manhattan and the Pentagon on 11 September 2001, Tom Kent, former policy secretary to Prime Minister Lester Pearson and deputy minister of immigration in the 1960s, called for use of the notwithstanding clause to toughen up the scandal-ridden process for screening refugee claimants in Canada. In an article published in *Policy Insights* on 1 October 2001, he observed that anyone who arrives in Canada and makes a refugee claim, no matter how transparently bogus, is entitled to free legal counsel and one appeal after another as the case winds through the system.[62] Kent pointed out that these "appeals to stay in Canada can be dragged out for years," giving fraudulent refugee claimants ample time to set down roots in Canada. They make friends; some get married and have children. "The humanitarian case against deportation becomes stronger with every legal delay," Kent observed. "And from time to time, as the administrative burden of unfinished cases mounts, the government devises some kind of amnesty to allow many of the applicants to stay without further proceedings."

Immigration Minister Elinor Caplan claimed that the Immigration and Refugee Protection Act, which was then before the Senate, would fix the system. Kent begged to differ. He derided the Act as "a classic of its political kind: If you can't fix on a definite policy, perhaps fiddling with process and procedure will cover your nakedness. Such wishful thinking comes easily to governments that are politically insecure. In this case, however, it is our peaceable society that will be made insecure by failure to fit immigration policy to the times. The danger is heightened in the aftermath of the terrorist attacks on Wall Street and the Pentagon."[63]

Kent traced the inability of immigration officials to summarily deport bogus refugee claimants and potential terrorists to the ruling by the Supreme Court of Canada in *Singh v. the Queen*, 1985. "The Constitution as such is not the obstacle," he said. "Its makers, including Mr. Chrétien, surely never intended it to apply to non-Canadians. They made, according to the Court's finding, a mistake in wording. It can be corrected: not, with the urgency required, by a constitutional amendment, but by use of the 'notwithstanding' provision that was included in order to retain the sovereignty of Parliament." Specifically, Kent called on Parliament to invoke section 33 of the Charter to enact a law "that confines the legal protections of the Charter to persons whose residence in Canada is legally sanctioned." The federal Liberals have rejected this sensible proposal. Rather than stand up to the Supreme Court of Canada, they prefer to stick with a defective refugee system – a system, Kent warns, that is so wide open to abuse that it affords "an easy entry for people, including those with terrorist intentions."[64]

In June 2001 similar concerns were expressed in an open letter to Prime Minister Jean Chrétien by several other leading immigration authorities, including Charles M. Campbell, former president of the British Columbia Liberal Party and vice chair of the Immigration Appeal Board; Martin Collacott, former director general for security services in the Department of Foreign Affairs; and Jack Manion, another former deputy minister of immigration. In this letter, Campbell, Collacott, Manion, and the others charged that the *Singh* ruling has saddled Canada with "the most time-consuming and expensive refugee determination system in the world" with the result that Canada has "become a magnet not only for tens of thousands of persons who are simply seeking better economic opportunities, but also for criminals and terrorists who are fugitives from justice in their own countries. Because Charter protection is now available to everyone on our territory, it is also now almost impossible to remove serious criminals and terrorists, along with many others who should not be allowed to remain here."[65] Like Kent, these experts urged: "The application of the Charter to those who have no right of residency here needs to be re-examined as a matter of urgency. The relevant sections should henceforth apply only to Canadian citizens and legal permanent residents of Canada. This could be achieved by amending the Charter or invoking the notwithstanding clause."[66]

More than a few Liberal backbenchers in Parliament have also contemplated invocation of the notwithstanding clause. In reaction to the ruling by the British Columbia Court of Appeal in *Sharpe,* which struck down the ban on the possession of child pornography in the Criminal Code on the ground that it allegedly violated the rights of pedophiles to freedom of expression as guaranteed in section 2(b) of the Charter, some seventy Liberal backbenchers and senators signed a letter to Chrétien urging the introduction of strong new child pornography legislation as soon as possible. The letter stated: "We ask that you consider the use of the notwithstanding clause or other equivalent effective measures to send a clear message that Canada's Charter of Rights will never again be used to defend the sexual abuse of children."[67] On 2 February 2000 the Reform Party advanced this same suggestion in the form of a resolution in the Commons. While the motion got solid support from all the opposition parties, it was defeated on a vote of 143 to 129, as all but four dissident Liberals backed the government's disposition to take no action pending a ruling in the case by the Supreme Court of Canada.[68]

Nonetheless, Justice Minister Anne McLellan did not rule out use of the notwithstanding clause in dealing with this issue. Speaking in the Commons on 2 February 1999, she said: "Before we take such a serious step as invoking s. 33 of the charter, we have a duty to ensure that other mechanisms for addressing the situation have been tried and have failed. This principle applies even in the most difficult circumstances, even when we are faced such as we are today with a decision that has so very clearly elicited the concern of Canadians from coast to coast to coast."[69] Premiers Peter Lougheed of Alberta and Allan Blakeney of Saskatchewan forthrightly stated that Parliament should invoke the notwithstanding clause if Shaw's ruling were upheld on appeal to the Supreme Court of Canada. "If you are going to have a charter of rights, you are going to have to have a safety valve," Lougheed said. "It should be used when the elected legislatures believe that judge-made law is not in accordance with the citizens and I'm glad we have it." [70] Similarly, Blakeney said that judicial activism is becoming a "modestly growing problem," particularly for Westerners and rural Canadians, who object to the "courts using the charter of rights to reinforce a more liberal, non-restrictive approach to lifestyle issues."[71]

While this controversy was ongoing, McCormick speculated that the Supreme Court of Canada "may very well go along" with the British Columbia Court of Appeal in striking down entirely the ban on the possession of child pornography in the Criminal Code.[72] He asked: "Could this be the Charter straw that breaks the back of public support? Could we then expect moves to tame the Court by invoking the notwithstanding clause, amending the Charter, or opening up the appointments process? I believe the answer is 'almost certainly not.' This is the Court that tackled the abortion issue, the most divisive issue in Western industrialized societies in the late 20th century, and came away without a scratch ... This is the Court that took on Alberta's Ralph Klein over gay rights. This is the Court that has found the marriage laws of most provinces unconstitutional."[73]

As it turned out, the Supreme Court of Canada mollified much of the public by striking a compromise in *Sharpe* that only amended the law on the possession of child pornography instead of following the British Columbia Court of Appeal in abolishing the law altogether. Nonetheless, in the aftermath of the controversy over the *Sharpe* rulings, a substantial number of Canadians finally began to question the disposition of the courts to second-guess the wisdom of Parliament and the provincial legislatures in enacting laws on the most sensitive political issues. In a poll conducted for CTV and the *Globe and Mail* in November 1999, Ipsos-Reid asked a sample of 1,000 Canadians if they agreed or disagreed with the statement "Judges in Canada have too much power." Twenty-one per cent responded "strongly agree," 24 per cent "somewhat agree," 33 per cent "somewhat disagree," and 18 per cent "strongly disagree." The remaining 4 per cent either did not know or declined to answer the question.[74] In a subsequent poll in January 2001, Ipsos-Reid found that 50 per cent of respondents felt that judgments of the Supreme Court of Canada "are sometimes influenced by partisan politics," 18 per cent agreed that "Partisan politics almost always play a role in Supreme Court decisions," while only 26 per cent believed that the Court was rarely or never influenced by partisan politics. Yet in this same poll, 89 per cent of the respondents said that they retained a "great deal" or "fair amount" of respect for justices of the Supreme Court of Canada.[75]

Two years later, Ipsos-Reid conducted another poll on this issue for CTV and the *Globe and Mail.* This time, respondents were asked if they agreed or disagreed with the statement "It should be up to Parliament and Provincial legislatures, not the courts, to make laws in Canada." No fewer than 71 per cent said they agreed. In this same survey, respondents were also asked whether they agreed or disagreed with the statement "Judges in Canada have too much power." In response, 54 per cent agreed, and 44 per cent disagreed.

It is noteworthy that this last opinion survey took place in the aftermath of the 2003 gay marriage ruling by the Ontario Court of Appeal in *Halpern,* which overturned the express wishes of Parliament stated just three years earlier in the Modernization of Benefits and Obligations Act that marriage shall remain "the lawful union of one man and one woman to the exclusion of all others." Prompted by the *Halpern* ruling, the leader of the Opposition in Parliament, Stephen Harper, introduced a motion in the Commons on behalf of the Canadian Alliance on 17 September 2003 stating: "That, in the opinion of this House, it is necessary, in light of public debate around recent court decisions, to reaffirm that marriage is and should remain the union of one man and one woman to the exclusion of all others, and that Parliament take all necessary steps within the jurisdiction of the Parliament of Canada to preserve this definition of marriage in Canada." This motion was virtually identical to the resolution adopted by the Commons on 8 June 1999 in response to the controversial ruling of the Supreme Court of Canada in *M. v. H.,* which granted spousal benefits to same-sex couples. Most Liberals, including Justice Minister Martin Cauchon, voted for this earlier resolution.[76] Yet just four years later, Cauchon told the House:

> Like most members, like most Canadians, the definition of marriage that [*sic*] the union of one man and one woman to the exclusion of all others is the one I grew up with, the one I learned from my parents. However let me remind members of parliament that our attachment to long cherished traditions and

conventions is not the only, or even the best, measure of what is just or what is right.

There was a time in Canada, not all that long ago, when it was considered perfectly acceptable that women could not vote. There was a time when women were not even legally defined as persons.

There was a time when immigrants were denied the right to vote, when they were turned away from our shores, when visible minorities were denied access to their rightful opportunities for employment.[77]

Harper was incensed by this line of argument. He said:

Unfortunately for the Liberals, the view that being for traditional marriage is analogous to some kind of racist or ethnocentric agenda is, unfortunately, not just a slur in this case against political opponents, as they are all too willing to do. It is an attack on the traditional beliefs of every single culture and faith that has come to this country.

Whether we are talking about Britain, France, Europe, China, India, Asia or Africa, just name it, all of us came here to build a future that would respect the values and traditions of our ancestors and build a future for our children and families. One of those things was based on our traditional institutions like marriage. For the Liberals or anyone in the Liberal Party to equate the traditional definition of marriage with segregation and apartheid is vile and disgusting.

Harper also minced no words about the inappropriateness of the judicial rulings that imposed gay marriage on Canadians. He reminded the House that in 1982, Parliament had deliberately excluded sexual orientation as analogous to race and ethnicity in the Canadian Charter of Rights and Freedoms. Sexual orientation, he said, "was not included, not because of some kind of accident or oversight, but deliberately and explicitly by all sides of the House of Commons." Regardless, the Supreme Court of Canada proceeded to read sexual orientation into the Charter in *Egan* and a string of other cases. Harper derided these rulings as unconstitutional. He said: "I would point out that an amendment to the constitution by the courts is not a power of the courts under our constitution. Something the House will have to address at some point in time is where its powers begin and where those of the courts end."

In contrast to Harper, Prime Minister Chrétien and his Cabinet colleagues bowed down to the Ontario Court of Appeal. Instead of appealing the *Halpern* ruling, they asked the Supreme Court of Canada in July 2003 for an opinion on the constitutionality of a draft bill on gay marriage stating: "1. Marriage, for civil purposes, is the lawful union of two persons to the exclusion of all others. 2. Nothing in this Act affects the freedom of officials of religious groups to refuse to perform marriages that are not in accordance with their religious beliefs." Paul Martin, who was to take over as prime minister from Jean Chrétien a few months later on 12 December 2003, went along with this Liberal manoeuvre. He agreed to asking the Supreme Court of Canada for an advanced opinion on the constitutionality of gay marriage, despite his promise during his leadership campaign to eliminate the "democratic deficit" in the House of Commons that has eroded the influence of most elected legislators over the determination of public policy. "Where is Mr. Democratic Deficit, Mr. Fix the Democratic Deficit?" mocked Harper in the Commons. "All of a sudden his position is whatever the courts say that is fine with him."[78] In response to Harper, Justice Minister Cauchon took the same line as Martin. "Let me be clear," said Cauchon. "A vote in favour of the Alliance motion means a vote to use the notwithstanding clause. The Government of Canada has never invoked this clause to override the charter rights of a minority. I believe this would set a dangerous precedent."[79] Nonetheless, no fewer than fifty-two Liberal backbenchers voted in favour of the Canadian Alliance resolution. They supported this motion, despite Cauchon's warning that it implied use of the notwithstanding clause to prevent the courts from overturning the traditional definition of marriage as the voluntary union of one man and one woman to the exclusion of all others.[80] Clearly, the notwithstanding clause of the Charter can no longer be written off as something of a constitutional dead letter: It is very much a live option for elected legislators in Parliament and the provincial legislatures who are determined to overcome the judicial usurpation of legislative authority.

Nonetheless, Prime Minister Paul Martin remains steadfast in his opposition to any use of the notwithstanding clause. During the 2004 federal election, he vowed in a press conference that he would never ask Parliament to invoke this constitutional authority: "We have got to ensure that minority rights are protected when challenged by the majority," he said. "The only way you can do this is to have a Charter of Rights which is ultimately interpreted by the Supreme Court of Canada."[81] In contrast, Harper insisted that "the notwithstanding clause is a legitimate part of the constitution and can be applied. I think it should always be applied prudently, but my hope would be that we don't get into that situation."[82] During a national leaders' debate on 16 June 2004, Martin challenged Harper: "Would you use the notwithstanding clause on the case of a woman's right to choose? Will you protect it?"[83] Harper responded: "I will not have legislation limiting a woman's right to choose. I have said that. But let me ... talk about an example where the notwithstanding clause might be appropriate. We've had repeated ... court decisions limiting our ability to stop child pornography. If I can't do it through ordinary legislation, I will do that to protect the rights of children."[84] Martin repudiated this argument. Throughout the campaign, he stuck to his position that: "The Government of Canada has never used the notwithstanding clause and if you're prepared to use the notwithstanding clause then what you're saying essentially is that in fact minority rights can be subjected to the will of the majority. That is not the kind of country that I believe in, nor do I think it is the kind of country that Canadians believe in."[85] It matters not to Martin that the Fathers of Confederation placed their trust in the willingness of the majority in Canada to fulfil their duty to uphold legitimate minority rights. This is simply not the kind of country that Martin believes in.

However, on the issue of the notwithstanding clause, Martin does not seem to know his own mind. In the same press conference in which he rebuked Harper for defending use of this constitutional provision, he pledged: "Never, never will I allow the rights of women to be removed by going back to the past. I believe that the situation in Canada is a free choice for women. They have to decide for themselves."[86] What, then, would Martin do if the Supreme Court of Canada were to outlaw at least the horrors of dilation and extraction (D&X) abortions – a commonly used procedure for aborting a baby after the sixteenth week of a pregnancy? In *Stenberg v. Carhart,* 2000 USSC, Mr Justice Stephen Breyer of the United States Supreme Court quoted a statement by the American College of Obstetricians and Gynecologists that describes a D&X abortion as typically entailing "breech extraction of the body excepting the head and the partial evacuation of the intracranial contents of a living fetus to effect vaginal delivery of a dead but otherwise intact fetus." In Canada, there is no law to prevent an unscrupulous physician from performing a D&X abortion at the mother's request on a perfectly healthy baby in the womb because the Supreme Court of Canada ordained in *R. v. Sullivan,* 1991 SCC, that no baby in the womb – not even, in the Court's words, "a living child partially born" – has any right to life under the laws or the Constitution of Canada. But given that the Supreme Court of Canada no longer has any reluctance to overturn its own precedents, it is not inconceivable that a majority of the Court might some day decide to reverse *Sullivan,* at least to the extent of outlawing D&X abortions on healthy babies. If so, what would Martin do? Either he would have to allow the courts to impose at least this minimal restriction on abortion or he would have to invoke the notwithstanding clause of the Constitution to override the Court's decision. Martin cannot have it both ways: He cannot promise to forgo all use of the notwithstanding clause while pledging that he will never, never allow any restriction on a woman's right to choose abortion.

Martin is a Catholic. In his private life, he upholds the teachings of the Catholic Church on the right to life and the meaning of marriage. But as a legislator, he takes the view that a right is a right only if the Supreme Court of Canada says so. Thus on the abortion issue, he says: "I'm a legislator. I believe that women should have the right to choose."[87] As a legislator, Martin spent years upholding marriage as the voluntary union for life of one man and one woman, but shortly after the Ontario Court of Appeal reformulated the common law definition of marriage in *Halpern* as "the voluntary union for life of two persons to the exclusion of all others," he reversed course and came out in favour of gay marriage. He explained: "I am a practising Catholic and I have responsibilities as a legislator and those responsibilities must take in a wider perspective."[88] What would Martin do if the Supreme Court of Canada came out in favour of polygamy or incest? Would he still kowtow to the arbitrary will of the Court?

A related question was put to Martin in an interview on CBC Radio on 18 December 2003: Would he invoke the notwithstanding clause if the Supreme Court ruled that churches must perform gay marriages? Martin replied: "Oh yes, I would. I would look at it if it was a question of affirming a right."[89] Apparently, Martin agrees that there are occasions when elected representatives of the people in Parliament should use their constitutional authority to override an egregious interpretation of the Charter by the Supreme Court of Canada. Only as a matter of political expediency, not principle, has he ruled out use of the notwithstanding clause to uphold the sanctity of human life and the natural family.

In defending Bill C-38, the legislation that proposed to enact same-sex marriage into law, Martin told the Commons on 16 February 2004: "I believe in and I will fight for a Canada that respects the foresight and the vision of those who created and entrenched the charter." Is this so? Those who created and entrenched the Charter rejected sexual orientation as a prohibited ground of discrimination in section 15 and included the notwithstanding clause in section 33. Yet Martin proceeded as usual in this speech to repudiate both of these initiatives. Instead of upholding the foresight and vision of the elected legislators who enacted the Charter, he championed the trendy views on same-sex marriage that currently hold sway among the appointed judges on the Supreme Court of Canada. "The debate here today is not about whether to change the definition of marriage," he said. "It has been changed. The debate comes down to whether we should override a right that is now in place. The debate comes down to the charter, the protection of minority rights, and whether the federal government should invoke the notwithstanding clause." Martin then issued a challenge to Harper: "There is one question that demands an answer, a straight answer, from those who would seek to lead this nation and its people. It is a simple question. Will the notwithstanding clause be used to overturn the definition of civil marriage and deny Canadians a right that is guaranteed under the charter?"

Harper refused to take the bait. In response to Martin, he pointed out that in *Reference re Same-Sex Marriage,* the Court had explicitly refused to express an opinion on the constitutionality of the opposite-sex requirement for marriage for civil purposes as established by the common law on the ground that: "The government has stated its intention to address the issue of same-sex marriage by introducing legislation regardless of our opinion on this question." In this way, the Court batted the controversial issue back to Parliament, where responsibility for changing the law and amending the Constitution properly belongs. Harper welcomed this aspect of the Court's decision. He said: "In short, we have every reason to believe if the House moved to bring in a reasonable, democratic, compromise solution, one which defined in statute that marriage remains the union of one man and one woman to the exclusion of all others, which extended equal rights and benefits to couples living in other forms of unions, and which fully protected freedom of religion to the extent possible under federal law, that the Supreme Court of Canada would honour such a decision by Parliament."

On this point, the great majority of law professors disagree with Harper and side with Martin. In an open letter to Harper published in the *Globe and Mail* on 25 January 2005, 134 of these professors opined: "If Parliament were to adopt your proposal and define marriage to exclude same sex couples, this legislation would very quickly end up in court, and be struck down as unconstitutional."[90] In sum, these law professors insisted that the Supreme Court of Canada would strike down any legislation passed by Parliament that reaffirmed the traditional opposite-sex definition of marriage. The professors accused Harper of political chicanery, saying:

> The fact that you want Parliament to enact clearly unconstitutional legislation and adopt the traditional definition of marriage without using the notwithstanding clause leads us to suspect that you are playing politics with the Supreme Court and the Charter. The use of the notwithstanding clause would have to be justified to Canadians, who overwhelmingly support the Charter. Not using the notwithstanding clause therefore protects opponents of same sex marriage from political controversy. And if the Supreme Court judgment

struck down the opposite sex definition of marriage, opponents of same sex marriage would blame the Court for challenging Parliament's will.

That last point is surely correct: Canadians who repudiate the concept of same-sex marriage would be outraged if the Supreme Court of Canada were to strike down an act of Parliament reaffirming the traditional definition of marriage as the voluntary union of one man and one woman to the exclusion of all others. The law professors conceded that "the Charter allows Parliament to have the last word on many issues of fundamental rights, through the notwithstanding clause. Frankly," they added, "we do not think this is an appropriate case for the use of this extraordinary provision." Of course not. These professors have embraced what Professor Robert Martin aptly calls "the orthodoxy" – that is, a closed mindset that holds sway within the mass media, the universities, and the judiciary.[91] "The pervasiveness of the orthodoxy is such that Canada gives every appearance of being a de facto one-party state," writes Martin. "All political parties in Canada today promote a politics which combines social radicalism and a return to nineteenth century economics."[92] Apart from Martin's debatable reference to nineteenth-century economics, there can be no doubt that he is right about the social radicalism of the orthodoxy. Under Harper, even the Conservative Party of Canada has embraced the ideology of gay rights to the extent of advocating equal rights and benefits in law for same-sex and opposite-sex couples. Just a few years ago, this idea would have been universally condemned as an extremist exercise in social radicalism. Today, it is the orthodox position. In the debate over same-sex marriage, all Harper and the Conservatives are essentially proposing is to preserve the traditional definition of marriage in name only. Even this is too much for 134 law professors. Like most proponents of the orthodoxy, they will settle for nothing less than equal marriage for same-sex and opposite-sex couples.

The law professors admonished Harper: "You should either invoke the use of the notwithstanding clause, and justify this decision to Canadians, or concede that same-sex marriage is now part of Canada's legal landscape. If you intend to override Canadians' constitutional rights, you at least owe it to them to say this openly and directly." This challenge misstates the entire controversy: Harper and other defenders of heterosexual marriage are resolved not to override the constitutional rights of Canadians but to defend those rights from judicial attack. To this end, they insist that the courts should uphold the traditional definition of marriage as enshrined in the common law and section 92(16) of the Constitution of Canada.

As it is, the Martin government's bill on same-sex marriage was approved by Parliament and proclaimed into law on 20 July 2005. Meanwhile, Harper is standing by the commitment in the 2005 policy declaration of the Conservative Party that "A Conservative Government will support legislation defining marriage as the union of one man and one woman."[93] Let us suppose, then, that the Conservatives eventually gain power and persuade Parliament to enact legislation redefining marriage once again as the union of one man and one woman to the exclusion of all others. If the Supreme Court of Canada were then to strike down the law as the 134 law professors speculate, the Conservatives would have an ideal opportunity to call another election to seek a mandate from the Canadian people to invoke the notwithstanding clause of the Constitution to prevent the Court from imposing legalized same-sex marriage.

Would the Conservatives take advantage of such an opportunity? Let us hope so. Nothing less than an epochal confrontation between Parliament and the Supreme Court of Canada can persuade activist judges and their abettors in the academy that unelected judges should stick to judging and allow elected legislators to do the law making.

PROBING THE LIMITS OF PUBLIC TOLERANCE

Some would argue that Parliament and the provincial legislatures should simply abolish the Charter as a means of curbing the subversion of democracy by the courts. There is much to be said for this argument. By any international comparison, Canada had an excellent human rights record prior to the Charter. The Charter was not, is not, and never will be necessary to safeguard the rights and freedoms of Canadians. However, the same 1982 Constitution Act that entrenched the Charter in the Constitution also saddled the country with a deadlock-prone constitutional amendment formula that makes it all but impossible for Parliament and the provincial legislatures to get rid of the Charter. Regardless, abolishing the Charter would not be sufficient to curb the excesses of the judiciary.

As we have seen, judicial activism in Canada preceded the Charter. It was in the pre-Charter *Carswell* case that Chief Justice Bora Laskin proposed to flout the Legislature of Manitoba by amending the province's trespass law through judicial interpretation. Just as Justice Dickson upheld the original understanding of this trespass law in *Carswell,* he could have, and should have, upheld the Charter as originally enacted and understood in his 1986 judgment in *Oakes.* Instead, he and most of his colleagues on the Supreme Court of Canada have chosen to interpret the Charter as a licence for the Court to flout its own precedents as well as the original understanding of statute laws and the Constitution. There was nothing inevitable about this development. Prior to enactment of the Charter, the Supreme Court of Canada had dealt with about thirty cases that bore directly on the 1969 Canadian Bill of Rights. In only one of these cases did the Court strike down a provision in a federal statute on grounds of incompatibility with the Bill. In an article published in the *McGill Law Journal* in 1982, law professor Berend Hovius noted: "This cautious approach was not dictated by either the status or wording of the Bill. Rather, it was the result of an underlying philosophy of government adopted by a majority of the judges on the Court, a philosophy which holds that an elected legislature is the only appropriate forum for policy formation."[94] Hovius surmised: "To the extent that the judges continue to accept that philosophy, the case law on the Bill may foreshadow the Court's interpretation and application of the Charter."[95]

What, however, happened? Soon after the Charter was adopted, most judges on the Supreme Court of Canada abandoned judicial restraint. They renounced the philosophy that an elected legislature is the only appropriate forum for policy formulation. In the process, they undermined the rule of law and circumvented the democratic process. In *Final Appeal: Decision-Making in Canadian Courts of Appeal*, Professors Ian Greene, Carl Baar, Peter McCormick, George Szablowski, and Martin Thomas observe: "It was most certainly the case prior to the Charter that nearly all Canadian judges resisted a law-making role for the courts, and many denied its possibility altogether. Instead, they espoused the legal positivist school of thought that good judges merely interpret the law."[96] How do Canadian judges conceive of their role today? Greene and his colleagues put this question to eighty-nine appeal court judges in Canada. Only twenty-six (29 per cent) reported that they still see themselves fundamentally as law interpreters. Half the respondents felt that the courts had moved closer to the law-making side of the continuum since the Charter came into effect.[97] Greene and his colleagues relate: "We asked the judges whether they thought the Charter had created a 'crisis of legitimacy' for the courts – a phrase which was used by some judges in the mid-1980s to describe their fears about judges becoming involved in lawmaking through high-profile Charter of Rights cases. The judges were evenly split on this issue, with 33 of 73 thinking that such a crisis existed (45 per cent), and 32 saying that there was no crisis; the remainder were neutral."[98]

This is a reassuring finding: At least half the judges understood that the disposition of activist judges on the Supreme Court of Canada to usurp the legislative authority of elected representatives of the people has created a crisis of legitimacy for the courts. What will it take to persuade the other half? Why cannot all judges appreciate that the law-making supremacy of the legislative branch of government is no less essential to democracy than the independence of the judiciary? If judges insist upon indulging in politically controversial law making, they cannot reasonably expect to retain public respect for judicial independence. Professor Craven explains:

> That respect is based on a communal perception that judges operate above and beyond the despised field of politics, and genuinely are engaged in the resolution of disputes according to law.
>
> This is why judges traditionally have enjoyed an enormously high respect within the community, while politicians have ranked slightly above tiger snakes. Were the population to come to the view that the highest officers of our judiciary are, at least in a constitutional context, little more than highly specialised political operatives, judicial respect would decline dramatically.[99]

To safeguard the constitutional authority of the courts, judges – most especially those sitting on senior appellate courts – have no choice but to revert to the traditional practice of judicial restraint. They should heed the warnings of authorities like Craven:

> While an element of activism may be accepted in the context of the common law, it should there be confined to a slow, cautious progress, mindful of precedent and the limitations of judicial method. In relation to statutory and constitutional interpretation, judicial activism is entirely illicit and must be stigmatised as such.
>
> Unless we fully appreciate the inability of the judges to make the key contribution to complex policy debates, and the truly appalling constitutional consequences that will follow from any attempt on their part to do so, we run the risk of destroying both the independence of our judiciary and the separation of powers.[100]

Lord Irvine, the Lord High Chancellor of Great Britain, took the same view. In an address to a preparatory conference on a bill of rights for the United Kingdom at University College, London, in 1997, he warned:

> Incorporating basic human rights into our domestic law will be a major new departure. It will offer new challenges. What is critical is that the form of incorporation sits comfortably with our United Kingdom institutions. It must not disturb the supremacy of Parliament. It should not put the judges in a position where they are seen as at odds with Parliament. That would be a recipe for

conflict and mutual recrimination. It is vital that the courts should not become involved in a process of policy evaluation which goes far beyond its allotted constitutional role. In a democratic society, compromises between competing interests must be resolved by Parliament – or if Parliament so decides, by Ministers.[101]

During second reading of the British Human Rights Act, 1998, Home Secretary Jack Straw made the same point:

> The sovereignty of Parliament must be paramount. By that, I mean that Parliament must be competent to make any law on any matter of its choosing. In enacting legislation, Parliament is making decisions about important matters of public policy. The authority to make those decisions derives from a democratic mandate. Members of this place possess such a mandate because they are elected, accountable and representative.
>
> To allow the courts to set aside Acts of Parliament would confer on the judiciary a power that it does not possess, and which could draw it into serious conflict with Parliament. As the Lord Chief Justice said on Second Reading in another place, the courts and the senior judiciary do not want such a power.[102]

Alas, the same cannot be said about the courts and the senior judiciary in Canada. Instead of upholding the sovereignty of Parliament and the provincial legislatures within their respective spheres of constitutional jurisdiction, the majority of judges on the Supreme Court of Canada routinely usurp the authority of elected representatives of the people to enact laws and determine public policy. Like all activist judges, Mr Justice Frank Iacobucci resents this charge. In reasons for judgment in *Vriend v. Alberta*, 1998 SCC, he admitted that the Court was amending Alberta's human rights code in defiance of the express will of the elected representatives of the people of Alberta, yet he lamented: "It seems that hardly a day goes by without some comment or criticism to the effect that, under the Charter, courts are wrongfully usurping the role of the legislatures. I believe this allegation misunderstands what took place and what was intended when our country adopted the Charter in 1981–82. When the Charter was introduced, Canada went, in the words of former Chief Justice Brian Dickson, from a system of parliamentary supremacy to constitutional supremacy."

Like Dickson, Iacobucci has no appreciation for the distinction between constitutional supremacy and judicial supremacy – between the rule of law and the rule of judges. In the not so distant past, virtually all Canadian judges agreed with Alexander Hamilton that "where the will of the legislature, declared in its statutes, stands in opposition to that of the people, declared in the Constitution, the judges ought to be governed by the latter rather than the former." Today, the Supreme Court of Canada is packed with activist judges who are given to substituting their own will for the will of the people. To justify the exercise of judicial supremacy, these judges have persuaded themselves that only they can protect the vulnerable from a tyrannical majority. Yet there is nothing in the historical record of civil liberties in Canada, the United States, and elsewhere to support such judicial hubris.

Abraham Lincoln was a champion of democracy. He opposed judicial rule. In his first inaugural address, he said: "The candid citizen must confess that if the policy of the Government upon vital questions affecting the whole people is to be irrevocably fixed by decisions of the Supreme Court, the instant they are made in ordinary litigation between parties in personal actions, the people will have ceased to be their own rulers." Consider the implications for Canadians: Now that the policy of the federal and provincial governments upon vital questions is routinely fixed by the Supreme Court, we, the Canadian people, must candidly confess that we have ceased to be our own rulers. With the infamous *Dred Scott* ruling, the United States Supreme Court thwarted the policy of Congress to curtail slavery. In opposing this arrogant assertion of judicial supremacy, Lincoln did not mount any elaborate defence of constitutional democracy. He simply asked two basic questions that Canadians should urgently ponder: "Why should there not be a patient confidence in the ultimate justice of the people? Is there any better or equal hope in the world?"

Notes

PREFACE

1 See *The Queen v. Drybones,* 1970 SCC.

INTRODUCTION

1 For the facts relating to this case, see the judgment of the Supreme Court of Canada in *Vriend v. Alberta,* 1998 SCC. The T-shirt provocation is reported in "Courts Reject Traditional Values: Vriend and Rosenberg," *REALity,* May/June 1998.
2 See Rae, *From Protest to Power,* 251–3.
3 See *House of Commons Debates,* 8 June 1999.
4 Department of Justice, "Backgrounder."
5 See "Gay Widows Win Pension Case," *Canadian Press,* 26 November 2004.
6 See Mandel, *The Charter of Rights.*
7 See Martin, *The Most Dangerous Branch.*
8 See Vancouver Rape Relief Society, "Vancouver Rape Relief Seeks BC Supreme Court Appeal."
9 See *Nixon v. Rape Relief Society,* 2002 BCHRT 1.
10 See *M.L. v. Maison des Jeunes,* 1998 QHRT.
11 Ibid.
12 Following Rivet's precedent, judges and human rights adjudicators now invariably refer to preoperative male-to-female transsexuals as females. To avoid confusion, I will refer to a male-to-female transsexual as a male unless he has completed sex reassignment surgery as a female.

13 See *Sheridan v. Sanctuary Investments Ltd. dba "B.J.'s Lounge,"* 1999 BCHRT.

14 See *Mamela v. Vancouver Lesbian Connection,* 1999 BCHRT.

15 See "Transsexual 'Always a Woman' Lawyer Says," *Vancouver Sun,* 23 February 2001.

16 See *Ontario Human Rights Commission v. Scott Brockie,* 2002 OSCJDC.

17 See *Hudler* v. *London (City),* 1997 OBI.

18 For a perceptive analysis of this case, see Cauchi, "A Catholic Lawyer."

19 See "Calgary Bishop Defiant about Gay Marriage Views," *Canadian Press,* 31 March 2005.

20 See "Official: Bible 'Exposes Homosexuals to Hatred,'" *WorldNetDaily,* 22 June 2001.

21 "Charte des droits et libértés," *Le Devoir,* 2 October 2000, my translation from the French: "Pour moi, Pierre Elliott Trudeau n'a pas commencé, il n'a pas terminé, parce que ce n'est jamais fini la protection des droits et libertés de la personne, mais il a fait une contribution énorme dans l'implantation de ce que j'appelle une culture des droits et libertés de la personne au Canada. Et j'espère qu'il y a quelqu'un là-bas pour prendre sa relève là-dessus. Parce qu'une charte, ce n'est pas tout. On peut faire ce qu'on en veut. Regardez ce que l'ex-URSS a fait de la sienne."

22 See Johnson, *A History of the Modern,* 275–7.

23 Orwell, *Nineteen Eighty-Four,* 5–6.

24 Hunter, *Three Faces of the Law,* 74.

25 Hunter, "Liberty and Equality," 8. Professor Hunter wryly adds: "It should be (but is not) superfluous to point out to human rights commissions that one may defend John Ross Taylor's right to free speech without endorsing his views."

26 For an account of this injunction and its impact, see *A.G. Ontario v. Dieleman,* 1994 OCJ.

27 Borovoy, *The New Anti-Liberals,* 141.

28 Ibid.

29 See "A Test of Free Speech?" *Ottawa Citizen,* 31 January 1999.

30 For information on Linda Gibbons, see Truscott, *Alone.*

31 See "Linda Gibbons: Prisoner of Conscience," http://www.lifesite.net/gibbons/index.html.

32 Bartlett, *Familiar Quotations,* 824.

CHAPTER ONE

1 For a summary of the facts of the *Nixon* case, see the reasons for judgment by Heather MacNaughton of the British Columbia Human Rights Tribunal in *Nixon v. Rape Relief Society,* 2002 BCHRT 1.

2 See Vancouver Rape Relief Society, "Transcripts."

3 See *Nixon v. Rape Relief Society*, 2002 BCHRT 1.
4 Ibid.
5 MacNaughton explained in her *Nixon* ruling that "Transgendered is an umbrella term describing individuals on a spectrum with varying degrees of gender identity mix. It includes cross-dressers and transvestites, at one end of the spectrum, and transsexuals at the other end of the spectrum. Transsexuals experience the most intense level of gender identity dissonance."
6 Hogg, *Constitutional Law of Canada*, 798.
7 Ibid.
8 For a detailed account of the emergence of judicial activism in Canada, see McCormick, *Supreme At Last.*
9 The chief justice of the Supreme Court of Canada used to sit on the Judicial Committee of the Privy Council. Appeals from the Supreme Court of Canada to this body were abolished by a federal statute in 1949. See ibid., 7.
10 de Secondat, *The Spirit of Laws.*
11 Blackstone, *Commentaries*, 259.
12 Katz, "Introduction to Book 1," iii.
13 Ibid.
14 Blackstone, *Commentaries*, 149.
15 Bacon, "Of Judicature."
16 Ibid.
17 Blackstone, *Commentaries*, 73.
18 Ibid., 68–9.
19 Ibid., 69.
20 Black, *Black's Law Dictionary*, 1261.
21 Blackstone, *Commentaries*, 69–70.
22 Ibid., 70.
23 Cardozo, *The Nature of the Judicial Process*, 24.
24 Ibid., 25.
25 Dicey, *Introduction to the Study of the Law of the Constitution*, 110.
26 Hayek, *The Road to Serfdom*, 72.
27 Corry and Hodgetts, *Democratic Government and Politics.* Hodgetts, a specialist in public administration, joined Corry as coauthor of the revised, third edition in 1959.
28 Corry and Hodgetts, *Democratic Government and Politics*, 93–4.
29 Ibid., 104.
30 See ibid., 94, 104.
31 Ibid., 429–30.
32 Blackstone, *Commentaries*, 59.
33 Ibid.
34 Ibid., 60–1.

35 Driedger, *The Construction of Statutes*, 87.
36 *Peters v. the Queen,* 1971 SCC.
37 See Hogg, *Constitutional Law of Canada*, 770.
38 Ibid.
39 Black, *Black's Law Dictionary*, 967.
40 Corry and Hodgetts, *Democratic Government and Politics*, 414.
41 See *Minutes,* 29 January 1981. The two dissenters were Robinson and his NDP colleague Lorne Nystrom.
42 For an account of the impact that the Women's Legal Education and Action Fund (LEAF) and other interest groups have had on the equality rights jurisprudence of the Supreme Court of Canada, see Morton and Knopff, *The Charter Revolution*; Brodie, *Friends of the Court*; and Manfredi, *Feminist Activism in the Supreme Court.*
43 British Columbia Human Rights Commission, "Human Rights for the Next Millennium."
44 "Centre Right to Reject Transsexual, Rebick Says," *National Post,* 19 December 2000.
45 Ibid.
46 Ibid.
47 See "Transsexual Wins Rights Ruling over Rejection As Rape Counsellor," *Vancouver Sun,* 18 January 2002.
48 Vancouver Rape Relief Society, "Vancouver Rape Relief Seeks BC Supreme Court Appeal."
49 See *Vancouver Rape Relief Society v. Nixon et al.*, 2003 BCSC 1936.
50 See *Law v. Canada (Minister of Employment and Immigration),* 1999 SCC 497.
51 Vancouver Rape Relief Society, "BC Supreme Court Overrules BC Human Rights Tribunal."
52 See "M to F Not a Woman: Judge," *Xtra! West,* 8 January 2004.
53 Ibid.
54 Ibid.
55 Hayek, *The Road to Serfdom,* 72.

CHAPTER TWO

1 Unless otherwise indicated, the facts of this case are drawn from the ruling of the Ontario human rights board of inquiry in *Hudler v. London (City),* 1997 OBI.
2 *Oliver v. Hamilton (City),* 1995 OBI.
3 Ibid.
4 The Human Rights Tribunal of Ontario, which replaced the province's human rights boards of inquiry in 2003, retains the powers conferred in section 41(1) of the Code.

5 Quoted in *Hudler v. London (City),* 1997 OBI, *Factum of Mayor Dianne Haskett,* 1–2.

6 *Hudler v. London (City),* 1997 OBI, *Brief Filed by the Corporation of the City of London,* 2.

7 *Alta. Statutes, Re (Alta. Press),* 1938 SCC.

8 Paragraph 77(c) refers to the request by the Ontario Human Rights Commission that the board order, "c. that the City of London and London City Council make a statement of recognition that the Lesbian and Gay and Bisexual Communities are integral and important communities within the City of London."

9 See *Brief Filed by the Corporation of the City of London,* 10– 11.

10 "Mayor Ponders Appeal of Discrimination Ruling," *London Free Press,* 10 October 1997.

11 "Council Won't Appeal HALO Rights Ruling," *London Free Press,* 21 October 1997.

12 Haskett, "Text of the City Hall Statement."

13 Ibid.

14 Ibid.

15 "Haskett Should Stay on the Job," *London Free Press,* 22 October 1997.

16 "Like It or Not, Proclamations Are an Issue," *London Free Press,* 16 October 1997.

17 Herman Goodden, "Human Rights: Haskett Has the Makings of a Mayor for All Seasons," *London Free Press,* 27 August 1997.

18 Bolt, *A Man for All Seasons,* 95.

19 Goodden, "Human Rights."

20 Robert Butcher, "Speaker's Corner: Morality Inherent in a Public Life," *London Free Press,* 28 October 1997.

21 Ibid.

22 Bolt, *A Man for All Seasons,* 12.

23 Feldthusen, "Debate." Feldthusen is currently dean of the Faculty of Common Law at the University of Ottawa.

24 Ibid.

25 See "Battle Raging for Mayor's Chair: Pro-Hopcroft Rally Slams Haskett Stand," *London Free Press,* 8 November 1997.

26 "Citizens for Grant Hopcroft," *London Free Press,* 8 November 1997.

27 Haskett, "Text of the Election Rally."

28 Technically, of course, it was not the Ontario Human Rights Commission but the human rights board of inquiry that released its decision shortly before the election.

29 The facts of this case are drawn from the judgment of the British Columbia Human Rights Tribunal in *Okanagan Rainbow Coalition v. City of Kelowna,* 2000 BCHRT, capitals in the original.

30 See "Human Rights Tribunal Slams Kelowna Mayor for Fiddling with Gay Pride Proclamation," *Canadian Press,* 23 March 2000.

31 Ibid.

CHAPTER THREE

1 Feldthusen, "Debate."

2 For the facts of the Brockie case, see the judgment of Ontario Superior Court of Justice, Divisional Court, in *Ontario Human Rights Commission v. Scott Brockie,* 2002 OSCDC, and the ruling of the Ontario board of inquiry in *Ray Brillinger and the Canadian Lesbian and Gay Archives v. Scott Brockie and Imaging Excellence Inc.,* 2000 OBI.

3 See Tompkins, "2000 CLGA Annual General Meeting."

4 "Human Rights Not What They Should Be," *London Free Press,* 8 October 1998.

5 "Code Delicately Balances Responsibility," *London Free Press,* 15 October 1998.

6 "Imprecise Wording," *London Free Press,* 3 November 1998.

7 "Canadian Christians in Crisis," *CBN News,* 9 December 1999.

8 "If there is a home-grown jurisprudential 'superstar' to whom citation practices lead us, then that person was former chief justice Duff." McCormick, *Supreme At Last,* 27. Duff is the only puisne, or nonchief, judge of the Supreme Court of Canada to have been appointed to the Judicial Committee of the Privy Council.

9 See ibid., 121.

10 Not the University of Western Ontario as misstated by MacNaughton in *Brillinger,* 2.

11 Cited in Riordan, *The First Stone,* 21.

12 Division of Mission in Canada, *In God's Image ... Male and Female,* 67.

13 Ibid., 98.

14 Division of Mission in Canada, *Draft Statement on Human Sexuality,* 66.

15 "Chronology of Marriage and Equality Rights in the United Church of Canada," *The United Church of Canada,* 9 May 2004, http://www.united-church.ca/moderator/short/2003/1008d.shtm.

16 "Controversial Resolutions on Sexuality Approved," *The United Church of Canada,* 19 August 2000, http://www.united-church.ca/gc37/news/1902.shtm.

17 "Council Tells Federal Government to Legalize Same-Sex Marriages," *The United Church of Canada,* 13 August 2003, http://www.united-church.ca/gc38/news/1403.shtm.

18 Romans 1:26–33.

19 See Scroggs, *The New Testament and Homosexuality,* 115–18.

20 See Countryman, *Dirt, Greed and Sex,* 122–3. Boswell advanced this same argument in *Christianity, Social Tolerance and Homosexuality.*
21 Schmidt, *Straight and Narrow?* 99.
22 Comstock, *Gay Theology without Apology,* 11.
23 Ibid., 4.
24 Ibid., 47.
25 Ibid., 99.
26 "Revelation and Homosexual Experience," *Christianity Today,* 11 November 1996.
27 Canadian Conference of Catholic Bishops, *Catechism of the Catholic Church,* para. 2357.
28 Quoted in Satinover, *Homosexuality,* 215.
29 Schmidt, *Straight and Narrow?* 14–15.
30 Ibid., 174.
31 Satinover, *Homosexuality,* 142.
32 These facts and an array of supporting data are reported in Michael et al., *Sex in America.*
33 See Satinover, *Homosexuality,* 51.
34 Ibid.
35 Ibid.
36 See Hogg et al., "Modelling the Impact of HIV Disease."
37 Brownlie was vice president of the archives.
38 James 1:22.
39 For an account of these events, see the ruling of the Saskatchewan human rights board of inquiry in *Gens Hellquist, Jason Roy and Jeff Dodds v. Hugh Owens and Sterling Newspapers Company, Operating as The StarPhoenix,* 2001 SBI.
40 See "Say It Isn't Hate Literature," *Alberta Report,* 25 December 1995.
41 Ibid.
42 Ibid.
43 "Saskatchewan Human Rights Commission a Legal Fiasco," *REALity,* September/October 1999.
44 See "Printer Defends 'Act of Conscience,'" *Christian Week,* 8 January 2002.
45 See "Saskatchewan Human Rights Commission a Legal Fiasco," *REALity,* September/October 1999.
46 See "Church Leaders Demand Right to Express Opinion," *Canadian Press,* 27 August 1999.
47 See "Saskatchewan Human Rights Commission a Legal Fiasco," *REALity,* September/October 1999.
48 See "Laws Can't Deny Free Speech: Religious Leaders," *Saskatoon StarPhoenix,* 27 August 1999.

49 Ibid.
50 Ibid.
51 See Leviticus 20:7–12 and 14–16.
52 Personal communication with the author, 2 May 2003.
53 Ibid.
54 Ibid.
55 Ibid.
56 "Laws Can't Deny Free Speech: Religious Leaders," *Saskatoon StarPhoenix*, 27 August 1999.
57 Ibid.
58 Personal communication with the author, 2 May 2003.
59 See *Wallace, Komar, Taylor, Hamre v. William G. Whatcott*, 2005 SHRT.
60 The quotations are drawn from Pandila's summary of Pudrycky's testimony.
61 See "Hate Crimes Unit Investigates Anti-Gay Flyers," *Edmonton Journal*, 8 June 2005.
62 See "Anti-Gay Crusader Whatcott Fined for 'Offensive' Flyers," *Saskatoon StarPhoenix*, 14 May 2005.
63 See "Whatcott Won't Obey Human Rights Order," *CBC News*, 17 May 2005, http://sask.cbc.ca/regional/servlet/ View?filename=whatcott050517.

CHAPTER FOUR

1 See "And Justice for All?" *World Magazine*, 10 January 1998.
2 Then named the Seattle Human Rights Department.
3 "Seattle Admits That Activist Was Wronged," *Seattle Times*, 10 September 1997.
4 Ibid.
5 See "Both Sides Appeal Civil-Rights Case," *Seattle Times*, 31 October 1997.
6 Ibid.
7 "Eliminate Rights Laws Enforced in a Discriminatory Manner," *Seattle Times*, 21 September 1997.
8 *Sheridan v. Sanctuary Investments Ltd. dba "B.J.'s Lounge,"* 1999 BCHRT.
9 *Shields v. Cameron*, 1993 BCCHR.
10 "Promoting Equality: A New Vision, Final Report of the Canadian Human Rights Act Review Panel," 23 June 2000, http://canada.justice.gc.ca/chra/en/toc.html.
11 Specifically, the federal tribunal cited *M.L. and the Quebec Human Rights Commission v. Maison des Jeunes*, 1998 QHRT; *Sheridan v. Sanctuary Investments Ltd. dba "B.J.'s Lounge,"* 1999 BCHRT; *Ferris v. Office and Technical Employees Union, Local 15*, 1999 BCHRT; and *Mamela v. Vancouver Lesbian Connection*, 1999 BCHRT.

12 For the facts of this case, see *Kavanagh v. Attorney General of Canada,* 2001 CHRT.
13 "Convict Allowed to Have Sex Change Surgery," *Canadian Press,* 21 November 1999.
14 See *Canada (Attorney General) v. Canada (Human Rights Commission),* 2003 FCTD 89.
15 The tribunal observed in a footnote to its ruling: "Sex reassignment surgery is covered by provincial health care plans in Alberta, Saskatchewan, Manitoba, Newfoundland and British Columbia. Ontario and the Maritime provinces do not pay for surgery. Québec's Medicare program will fund sex reassignment surgery, provided the surgery is carried out in a public hospital. There are, however, no public hospitals performing sex reassignment surgery in Canada."
16 Ontario Public Health Association, "Trans Health Project." The Ontario Public Health Association (OPHA) indicates in the Preface to this paper that it was submitted by "The Public Health Alliance for Lesbian, Gay, Bisexual, Transsexual, Transgendered, Two-spirit(ed), Intersexed, Queer and Questioning Equity, an OPHA workgroup."
17 See findlay, "Transsexuals in Canadian Prisons."
18 See *Canada (Attorney General) v. Canada (Human Rights Commission),* 2003 FCTD 89.
19 See McHugh, "Surgical Sex."
20 Ibid.
21 See Egale Canada, "Egale Launches Campaign to Restore Funding of SRS."
22 Ibid.
23 Michelle Josef has placed a copy of her notice of constitutional question online at http://www.lilithitsnotfair.com/notice.html.
24 For an account of Justine Blainey's battle against all-male hockey leagues, see the judgment of the Ontario Court of Appeal in *Blainey v. Ontario Hockey Association,* 1986 OCA.
25 Keene, *Human Rights in Ontario,* 194.
26 "Rise of Women's Hockey," *LCS Hockey,* 1996, http://www.merceishockey.de/damen/dameneishockey/riseofwomenshockey.htm.
27 See *Blainey v. Ontario Hockey Association,* 1987 OBI.
28 See Loney, *The Pursuit of Division.*
29 Monahan, *Storming the Pink Palace,* 222.
30 Ibid., 224.
31 See "Anti-Racism Groups Angered by Cartoon," *National Post,* 27 July 2001.
32 See "The Employment Equity Conundrum," *London Free Press,* 31 July 2001.
33 See Public Service Commission, "Employment Equity."

34 See Public Service Commission, "Equity Group Definitions."
35 See "Reverse Discrimination Threatens Integrity of Universities," *London Free Press,* 20 September 1994.
36 See Carter, *Reflections of an Affirmative Action Baby.*
37 See Sowell, *The Economics and Politics of Race.*
38 See the views on reverse discrimination expressed in the dissenting judgment by Justice Clarence Thomas in *Grutter v. Bollinger,* USSC 2003.
39 Ian Hunter, "Liberty and Equality," 9–10.
40 Martin, "Debate."
41 For the facts of this case, see *Entrop v. Imperial Oil Ltd.,* 2000 OCA.
42 Backhouse is currently Distinguished University Professor in the Faculty of Law at the University of Ottawa.
43 This Act was replaced by the Controlled Drugs and Substances Act (1996).
44 *Entrop v. Imperial Oil,* 2000 OCA.
45 See *Canadian Civil Liberties Association v. Toronto Dominion Bank,* 1998 FCA.
46 See Canadian Human Rights Commission, "Policy on Alcohol and Drug Testing."
47 Martin, "Debate."
48 *Ontario Human Rights Commission v. Simpson Sears Ltd.,* 1985 SCC.
49 See Ontario Human Rights Commission, *Annual Report: 2003–2004,* 3.
50 See Canadian Human Rights Commission, *Annual Report 2004,* 3.
51 For the background to this case, see *Ford Motor Co. of Canada v. Ontario (Human Rights Commission),* 2001 OCA.
52 The reference is to *Seneca College of Applied Arts and Technology v. Bhadauria,* 1981 SCC.
53 The quotation is from Backhouse's ruling for the Ontario human rights board of inquiry in *Naraine v. Ford Motor Co.,* 25 July 1996 OBI.
54 Ontario Human Rights Code Review Task force, *Achieving Equality,* Appendix 1.
55 Ibid., 2.
56 Ibid., 94.
57 Quoted in ibid., 94.
58 Ibid.
59 Ibid., 96.
60 Ibid., 129.
61 Ibid., 130.
62 Ibid., 136.
63 Ibid.
64 Ibid., 138.
65 Ibid., 146.
66 Ibid.

67 Ibid., 150.
68 Ibid.
69 Ibid., 151.
70 Ibid., 135.
71 Ontario Human Rights Commission, *Annual Report: 1996–1997*, 8.
72 Sowell, *Civil Rights: Rhetoric or Reality?*, 53.
73 Ibid., 90.
74 Loney, *The Pursuit of Division*, 332.
75 "The Right to Be Wrong," *Forbes Magazine*, 17 June 1996.
76 Sowell, *A Conflict of Visions*, 185–6.
77 See Debates of the British Columbia Legislative Assembly, 23 October 2002.
78 See British Columbia Human Rights Tribunal, *Annual Report: 2003–04*, 2–3. The current chair of the tribunal is Heather MacNaughton, the adjudicator in the *Brockie* and *Nixon* cases.
79 Jefferson's inaugural presidential address, http://www.yale.edu/lawweb/avalon/presiden/inaug/jefinau1.htm.
80 Martin, "Debate." The operating budget for the Ontario Human Rights Commission during 1999–2000 was $11,657,277.
81 de Tocqueville, *Democracy in America*.
82 Hunter, "Liberty and Equality," 22–3.

CHAPTER FIVE

1 See Presser, *Recapturing the Constitution*, 162.
2 The quotation is from Olsen v. Nebraska ex rel. Western Reference & Bond Assn., 1941 USSC.
3 Tremblay, "Section 7 of the Charter," 254.
4 Quoted by Justice William McIntyre, dissenting in *Morgentaler*, 1988.
5 Knopff and Morton, *Charter Politics*, 267.
6 See "Waiting Your Turn: Hospital Waiting Lists in Canada," *The Fraser Institute*, 2004, http://www.fraserinstitute.ca/shared/readmore.asp?sNav=pb&id=705.
7 Benson and Miller, "Now Hear This."
8 Senator Cools joined the Conservative Party on 8 June 2004.
9 See *Debates of the Senate*, 20 November 1997.
10 Ibid.
11 Friedland, "Judicial Independence and Accountability."
12 "Justice's Letter to Minister Inappropriate," *London Free Press*, 6 January 2001.
13 See Department of Justice, "Minister of Justice Responds to the 1999 Quadrennial Commission on Judicial Compensation and Benefits."
14 See *House of Commons Debates*, 12 March 2001.

15 Dicey, *Introduction to the Study of the Law of the Constitution*, 3–4.
16 Ibid., 39.
17 The Lord Chancellor is the British equivalent of the Canadian minister of justice and also serves as the Speaker of the House of Lords and head of the judiciary.
18 "How the Charter Has Helped Antonio Lamer Turn His Dubious Ideals into the Law of the Land," *Alberta Report*, 21 September 1998.
19 See McLellan's address on second reading of Bill C-36 in *House of Commons Debates*, 16 October 2001.
20 See "30 Drafters, Many Charter Experts Later," *National Post*, 16 October 2001.
21 For information on Ahmed Ressam, see the series of reports published by the *Seattle Times* as "The Terrorist Within: The Story Behind One Man's Holy War against America," *Seattle Times*, 23 June-7 July 2002.
22 See *Suresh v. Canada (Minister of Citizenship and Immigration)*, 2002 SCC 1.
23 In July 2005 Ressam was sentenced to twenty-two years in prison. The United States government is appealing the sentence. See "Longer Term Sought for Ressam," *Seattle Times*, 27 August 2005.
24 For a summary of the patriation controversy, see Sharpe and Roach, *Brian Dickson*, 268–81.
25 *Reference re the Amendment of the Constitution of Canada*, 1981 SCC.
26 *Re Objection by Quebec to Resolution to Amend the Constitution (1982)*, 1982 SCC.
27 Hogg, *Constitutional Law of Canada*, 20.
28 Ibid., 20–1.
29 Trudeau, *Against the Current*, 256.
30 See Sharpe and Roach, *Brian Dickson*, 272.
31 Ibid.
32 Trudeau, *Against the Current*, 256.
33 Ibid., 258.
34 Ibid., 259.
35 Ibid., 247.
36 Sharpe and Roach, *Brian Dickson*, 280.
37 Craven "The Quebec Secession Reference."
38 Craven "Reflections on Judicial Activism."
39 Ibid.
40 Ibid.

CHAPTER SIX

1 Quoted in Hawkins and Martin, "Democracy, Judging and Bertha Wilson," 23–4. Hawkins is president of the University of Regina and a former law professor at the University of Western Ontario. Martin is a

professor in the Faculty of Law at the University of Western Ontario.

2 Hawkins and Martin, "Democracy, Judging and Bertha Wilson," 57.
3 See Sweet, "The Fourth 'R'."
4 For the background on the *Surrey* case, see *Chamberlain v. Surrey School District #36,* BCSC 1998.
5 See "About GALE," *GALE BC,* http://www.galebc.org/about.htm
6 Ibid.
7 Benson, "Notes towards a (Re)definition of the 'Secular,'" 536– 7.
8 See *Chamberlain v. Surrey School District #36,* 2000 BCCA.
9 *Chamberlain v. Surrey School District No. 36,* 2002 SCC 86.
10 The facts of this case are summarized in Trinity Western University v. British Columbia College of Teachers, 2001 SCC 31.
11 "Trinity Western Is Cheering the Supreme Court's Affirmation of Its Right to Teach Its Creed," *Globe and Mail,* 31 May 2001.
12 Ibid.
13 Evangelical Fellowship of Canada, "EFC Pleased with Outcome in Trinity Western University Case."
14 Canadian Conference of Catholic Bishops, "CCCB Statement Re Supreme Court Decision in the Trinity Western University Case."
15 Capitals in the original.
16 La Forest's inclusion of "sex" and "gender" in this list of supposedly unchangeable characteristics is curious given the number of homosexuals who have undergone sex reassignment surgery.
17 See the resources listed on the NARTH website at http://www.narth.com.
18 Satinover, *Homosexuality,* 97–117.
19 Ibid., 96.
20 See "Some Gays Can Go Straight, Study Says," *ABC News,* 9 May 2001.
21 See Spitzer, "Can Some Gay Men and Lesbians Change Their Sexual Orientation?"
22 See NARTH, "Prominent Psychiatrist Announces New Study Results."
23 "Some Gays Can Go Straight, Study Says," *ABC News,* 9 May 2001.
24 NARTH, "Historic Gay Advocate Now Believes Change Is Possible."
25 See *Trinity Western University and Donna Gail Lindquist Petitioners (Respondents) AND: The British Columbia College of Teachers Respondent,* 1997 BCSC.
26 This quotation is from the judgment of the Court in *Ross v. New Brunswick School District No. 15,* 1996 SCC.
27 Capitals in the original.
28 Iain Benson made these remarks in a letter to Henry Friesen at hfriesen@bond.net. Benson concluded: "I think Ian Hunter has, with respect to his usual analysis, done the wider community a disservice in this article. Please feel free to circulate this personal assessment of mine to whomever you think might be interested."

29 See *Kempling v. The British Columbia College of Teachers,* 2004 BCSC 133.
30 See *Kempling v. British Columbia College of Teachers,* 2005 BCCA 327.
31 Specter, "Higher Risk: Crystal Meth, the Internet, and Dangerous Choices about AIDS."
32 See Todd Klinck, "The Party Drug That Kills," *National Post,* 14 June 2005.
33 Ibid.
34 Ibid.
35 Section 7 of the British Columbia Human Rights Code.
36 Todd Klinck, "The Party Drug That Kills," *National Post,* 14 June 2005.
37 See "Teacher's Rights Complaint against SD 28 Will Proceed," *Cariboo Observer,* 23 March 2005.
38 See "Anti-Gay Teacher under Suspension," *Vancouver Province,* 6 April 2005.
39 See "Ten Questions for Paul Martin: Tax Minister's Visit Calls for More Answers," *Calgary Herald,* 27 September 2004.
40 See "Same-Sex Couple Argue Knights of Columbus Hall Discriminated against Them," *Vancouver Sun,* 26 January 2005.
41 See "Commissioner Will Refuse," *Regina Leader Post,* 5 January 2005.
42 See "Second Saskatchewan Marriage Commissioner Files Human Rights Complaint," *Lifesite News,* 3 February 2005.
43 See "Marriage Commissioner Ready for Human Rights Fight," *Saskatoon StarPhoenix,* 14 July 2005.
44 Personal communication with the author, 25 July 2005.
45 See "Kempling Decision Very Disappointing," *Evangelical Fellowship of Canada,* 13 June 2005.
46 *Proceedings,* 23 July 2005.

CHAPTER SEVEN

1 McLachlin, "Courts, Legislatures and Executives," 45.
2 See Hogg, *Constitutional Law of Canada,* 798.
3 See Trociuk v. British Columbia (Attorney General), 2003 SCC 34.
4 McLachlin, "Courts, Legislatures and Executives," 45.
5 Ibid.
6 Ibid. Monahan is currently the dean of Osgoode Hall Law School.
7 See "Top Court Judges Shy Away from Rewriting Laws," *National Post,* 9 April 1999.
8 Morton and Knopff, *The Charter Revolution,* 20.
9 See *Re British North American Act 1867 (UK) Section 24,* 1928 SCC.
10 See McLachlin, "Remarks."
11 Ibid.
12 Keith, "The Privy Council Decisions," 192.

13 McLachlin, "Courts, Legislatures and Executives," 43.
14 McLachlin, "Remarks."
15 See Scalia "Common-Law Courts in a Civil-Law System."
16 Ibid.
17 Ibid.
18 Ibid.
19 Ibid.
20 McLachlin, "Remarks."
21 Hawkins and Martin, "Democracy, Judging and Bertha Wilson," 18– 19.
22 McLachlin, "The Judiciary's Distinctive Role."
23 Ibid.
24 See Barbeau v. British Columbia (Attorney General), 2003 BCCA 251.
25 Svend Robinson, "Do I Take This Man?" *Globe and Mail,* 24 June 2003.
26 Ibid.
27 *Minutes,* 16 January 1981.
28 *Minutes,* 29 January 1981.
29 Robinson, "Do I Take This Man?" *Globe and Mail,* 24 June 2003.
30 See National Gay Rights Coalition, "Human Rights."
31 Quoted in Hawkins and Martin "Democracy, Judging and Bertha Wilson," 12,
32 Ibid.
33 Ibid.
34 McLachlin, "The Judiciary's Distinctive Role," 7.
35 See Equal Marriage for Same-Sex Couples, "The Law Society of Upper Canada: Celebrating Justice."
36 See "Same Sex Couples Exchange Vows," *Canadian Press,* 16 January 2001.
37 McLachlin, "The Judiciary's Distinctive Role," 5.
38 de Tocqueville, *Democracy in America.*
39 Ibid.
40 Ibid.
41 See "The Federalist No. 10," in Hamilton, Jay, and Madison, *The Federalist Papers.*
42 Ibid.
43 Quoted in Asjzenstat et al., *Canada's Founding Debates,* 206.
44 Ibid., 19.
45 Hogg, *Constitutional Law of Canada,* 767.
46 Ibid., 796.
47 Monahan, *The Charter,* 138.
48 See "Courts and the Media for Social Change," *The Fraser Institute: On Balance* 9, no. 9 (1996): http://oldfraser.lexi.net/publications/onbalance/1996/9–9.
49 Dahl, *Democracy and Its Critics,* 189.

50 Waldron, *Law and Disagreement*, 12.
51 Waldron used this colourful phrase in an address to a conference on "Constitutionalism in the Charter Era" held at the University of Western Ontario on 12 September 2003.
52 Waldron, *Law and Disagreement*, 15.
53 *Vriend v. Alberta*, ACA 1996.
54 Beatty, *Constitutional Law in Theory and Practice*, 65.
55 Ibid. 15.
56 For an explanation of the principles of Newspeak, see Orwell, *Nineteen Eighty-Four*, 312–26.
57 Beatty, *Constitutional Law in Theory and Practice*, 16.
58 Ibid., 15.
59 Ibid., 145.
60 Ibid., 153–4.
61 See Leishman, "Our Judges Are Activist Only When It Suits Them."
62 This quotation is from the reasons for judgment of Chief Justice Allan McEachern of the British Columbia Court of Appeal in *R. v. Sharpe*, 1999 BCCA.
63 See *Osborne v. Ohio*, 1990 USCC.
64 See *R. v. Keegstra*, 1990 SCC.
65 See *R. v. Lucas*, 1998 SCC.
66 See *R. v. Butler*, 1992 SCC.
67 See R. v. Pelletier, 1999 SCC.
68 See *Reference re ss. 193 and 195.1(1)(c) of the Criminal Code (Man.)*, 1990 SCC.
69 Hogg, *Constitutional Law of Canada*, 813.
70 Hunter, *Three Faces of the Law*, 46.
71 Monahan, *The Charter*, 56.
72 Ibid.
73 Ibid., 53.
74 Saywell, *The Lawmakers*, 275.
75 Ibid.
76 Monahan, *The Charter*, 56.
77 Presser, *Recapturing the Constitution*, 50.
78 Ibid., 77.
79 "The Federalist No. 78," in Hamilton, Jay, and Madison, *The Federalist Papers*.
80 Ibid.
81 Presser, *Recapturing the Constitution*, 82.
82 Hawkins and Martin "Democracy, Judging and Bertha Wilson," 29.
83 "Legal Experts Slam Top Court's Charter Decisions," *Globe and Mail*, 18 April 1998.
84 Ibid.

85 Smith, "The Constitution of Babel," 27.
86 Blackstone, *Commentaries*, 62.

CHAPTER EIGHT

1 Personal communication with the author, 15 December 2000.
2 Ewing, "The Human Rights Act," 79.
3 For an appraisal of the British Human Rights Act, 1998, see Malleson, "A British Bill of Rights."
4 See the British Human Rights Act, 1998, c. 42, s. 4.
5 See mainly section 10 and schedule 2 of the Act.
6 See "Rights Act Shifts Balance of Power to Judges," *Daily Telegraph* (London), 2 October 2000.
7 Quoted in ibid.
8 Ewing, "The Human Rights Act," 86.
9 Gearty, "What Are Judges For?"
10 Ibid.
11 Ibid.
12 Ibid.
13 Morton and Knopff, *The Charter Revolution,* 17.
14 See "Public Review of Judges Good Idea, Says Retired Supreme Court Justice," *The Hill Times,* 1 September 1997.
15 Ibid.
16 McLachlin, "The Judiciary's Distinctive Role," 7.
17 See "MPs Will Vet Top-Court Nominees, Liberal Says," *Globe and Mail,* 30 January 2004.
18 Ibid.
19 Ibid.
20 "Lamer Opens Pandora's Box of Public Opinion," *The Interim,* April 1998.
21 Ibid.
22 Gearty, "What Are Judges For?"
23 Ibid.
24 Knopff and Morton, *Charter Politics,* 218.
25 See "Lamer Worries about Public Backlash: Angry Reaction Could Affect Judges' Decisions, Chief Justice Says," *Globe and Mail,* 6 February 1999.
26 See Hunter, *Three Faces of the Law,* 47.
27 Ibid.
28 See "Violence Erupts in N.B. As Natives' Lobster Traps Cut," *National Post,* 4 October 1999.
29 See "Local Lobster Fishers Join Tense Rebellion," *St John Times Globe,* 1 October 1999.
30 See Fisheries and Oceans Canada, "Highlights of the 1999 Lobster Management Measures."

31 *Delgamuukw v. British Columbia,* 1997 SCC.
32 *R. v. Sparrow,* 1990 SCC
33 Gearty, "What Are Judges For?"
34 The reference is to Hogg and Bushell, "The Charter Dialogue."
35 Thornton is Bushell's married name.
36 Morton, "Dialogue or Monologue," 23.
37 Bork, *Slouching toward Gomorrah,* 109.
38 Ibid., 117.
39 "Quash Court Decision on Natives: MP," *St John Times Globe,* 19 October 1999.
40 Quoted in Johansen and Rosen, "The Notwithstanding Clause."
41 Ibid.
42 Quoted in Morton, "Can Judicial Supremacy Be Stopped?"
43 Trudeau, *Memoirs,* 328.
44 Quoted in Johansen and Rosen, "The Notwithstanding Clause."
45 See "Trudeau Left Canada 'a Ticking Time Bomb,'" *Globe and Mail,* 20 March 1990.
46 Russell, "The Supreme Court and the Charter," 226.
47 McCormick, *Supreme At Last,* 174.
48 Ibid., 174–5.
49 Ibid., 173.
50 Bork, *Slouching toward Gomorrah,* 109.
51 McCormick, *Supreme At Last,* 173. The subquote in this passage is from Weiler, *In the Last Resort,* 173. Weiler is a professor of law at Harvard University.
52 McCormick, *Supreme At Last,* 174.
53 Ibid.
54 Ibid., 175.
55 Ibid.
56 See Hogg, *Constitutional Law of Canada,* 892–3.
57 See ibid., 893.
58 See Ministère de l'Èducation, "La mise en place."
59 See "Klein Vows to Renew Law That Defends Marriage," *Canadian Press,* 19 March 2005.
60 See "Charter Too Soft," *Globe and Mail,* 6 February 1998.
61 Ibid.
62 Kent, "Immigration Now."
63 Ibid.
64 Ibid.
65 See "Canada Must Stand On Guard: An Open Letter to Jean Chretien," *Globe and Mail,* 6 June 2001.
66 Ibid.

67 See "Parliament Fails to Correct the Courts, and Pedophilia's Path to Acceptance Is Open," *Alberta Report*, 15 February 1999.
68 See "4 Maverick MPs Ignore Liberal Line Over Porn Motion," *National Post*, 3 February 1999.
69 *House of Commons Debates*, 2 February 1999.
70 See "Ex-premiers Call for Use of Charter's 'Safety Valve,'" *National Post*, 1 March 1999.
71 Ibid.
72 McCormick, *Supreme At Last*, 168.
73 Ibid., 168–9.
74 Ipsos-Reid, "The Power of Judges," 23 November 1999.
75 Ipsos-Reid, "Canadian Supreme Decisions: Public's View of the Supreme Court," 4 July 2001.
76 Cauchon served as justice minister in the Chrétien government from 15 January 2002 to 11 December 2003.
77 *House of Commons Debates*, 16 September 2003.
78 Ibid.
79 Ibid.
80 See "Marriage Divides the House," *Globe and Mail*, 17 September 2003.
81 See "Minority Rights At Risk under Tories: Martin," *Globe and Mail*, 7 June 2004.
82 See "Old Issues Continue to Haunt Harper," *Globe and Mail*, 3 June 2004.
83 See "Election 2004 Federal Leaders Debate Excerpts on Life and Family Issues," *LifeSite Special Report*, 15 June 2004.
84 Ibid.
85 See "Minority Rights At Risk under Tories: Martin," *Globe and Mail*, 7 June 2004.
86 Ibid.
87 See "'Catholic' Canadian Prime Minister Martin Says He Supports 'Right to Choose' Abortion," *LifeSite News*, 1 June 2004.
88 See "Martin Has Same View As PM," *Calgary Herald*, 2 August 2003.
89 See "The Leaders, on the Record," *CBC News*, http://www.cbc.ca/canadavotes/analysiscommentary/ontherecord.html.
90 A copy of this letter is available at http://www.law.utoronto.ca/samesexletter.html.
91 See Martin, *The Most Dangerous Branch*, 9.
92 Ibid.
93 "*Conservative Party of Canada: Policy Declaration,*" 19 March 2005, http://www.conservative.ca/media/20050319–POLICY%20DECLARATION.pdf.
94 Hovius, "The Legacy of the Supreme Court," 31.
95 Ibid.

96 Greene et al., *Final Appeal*, 188.
97 Ibid., 187.
98 Ibid.
99 Craven, "Reflections on Judicial Activism."
100 Ibid.
101 Irvine of Lairg, "Keynote Address."
102 House of Commons Debates, 16 February 1998.

Bibliography

Asjzenstat, Janet, et al., eds. *Canada's Founding Debates.* Toronto: University of Toronto Press, 1999.

Bacon, Sir Francis. "Of Judicature." *Essays.* 1601. http://www.authorama.com/essays-of-francis-bacon-56.html.Bartlett, John. *Familiar Quotations.* Toronto: Little, Brown, 1980.

Beatty, David. *Constitutional Law in Theory and Practice.* Toronto: University of Toronto Press, 1995.

Benson, Iain T. "Notes towards a (Re)definition of the 'Secular.'" *UBC Law Review* 33 (2000): 536–7.

– and Brad Miller. "Now Hear This: The Supreme Court of Canada on Equality Rights." *Lex View* 14 (1997): http://www.centreforrenewal.ca/lex-14.html.

Black, Henry Campbell. *Black's Law Dictionary.* 5th ed. St Paul, MN: West Publishing, 1979.Blackstone, William. *Commentaries on the Laws of England.* Chicago: University of Chicago Press, 1979.Bolt, Robert. *A Man for All Seasons.* Agincourt: Book Society of Canada, 1960.Bork, Robert. *Slouching toward Gomorrah: Modern Liberalism and American Decline.* New York: Regan Books, 1996.

Borovoy, A. Alan. *The New Anti-Liberals.* Toronto: Canadian Scholars' Press, 1999.Boswell, James. *Christianity, Social Tolerance and Homosexuality.* New Haven: Yale University Press, 1980.

British Columbia Human Rights Commission. "Human Rights for the Next Millennium: Recommended BC Human Rights Codes Amendments for British Columbians by British Columbians." 19 January 1998. http://www.bchrc.gov. bc.ca/home.htm. British Columbia Human Rights

Tribunal. *Annual Report: 2003–04*. http://www.bchrt.bc.ca/reports/Annual_Report_2003–2004.pdf.

Brodie, Ian. *Friends of the Court: The Privileging of Interest Group Litigants in Canada*. Albany: State University of New York Press, 2002.

Canadian Conference of Catholic Bishops. *Catechism of the Catholic Church*. Ottawa: Publications Service, Canadian Conference of Catholic Bishops, 1994.

– "CCCB Statement Re Supreme Court Decision in the Trin[i]ty Western University Case." 17 May 2001. http://www.cccb.ca/PublicStatements.htm?CD=&ID=827.

Canadian Human Rights Commission. *Annual Report 2004*. Ottawa: Ministry of Public Works, 2005.

– "Policy on Alcohol and Drug Testing." 2002. http://www.chrc-ccdp.ca/legislation_policies/alcohol_drug_testing-en.asp.

Cardozo, Benjamin. *The Nature of the Judicial Process*. New Haven: Yale University Press, 1921.

Carter, Stephen L. *Reflections of an Affirmative Action Baby*. New York: Basic Books, 1991.

Cauchi, Geoff. "A Catholic Lawyer Takes a Look at the *Marc Hall* Case." In Alphonse de Valk, ed., *Judicial Activism: A Threat to Democracy and Religion*, 70–111. Toronto: Life Ethics Information Centre, 2003.

Comstock, Gary. *Gay Theology without Apology*. New York: Pilgrim, 1993.Corry, J.A., and J.E. Hodgetts. *Democratic Government and Politics*. Toronto: University of Toronto Press, 1959.Countryman, L. William. *Dirt, Greed and Sex*. Philadelphia: Fortress, 1988.

Craven, Greg. "The Quebec Secession Reference: The Law of Politics or the Politics of Law?" *Murdoch University Electronic Journal of Law* 6, no. 1 (March 1999): http://www.murdoch.edu.au/elaw/issues/v6n1/craven61_text.html.

– "Reflections on Judicial Activism: More in Sorrow Than in Anger." *Notes for an Address to the Samuel Griffith Society – Ninth Conference*. 1997. http://www.samuelgriffith.org.au/papers/html/volume9/v9chap9.h tm.

Dahl, Robert A. *Democracy and Its Critics*. New Haven: Yale University Press, 1989.

Department of Justice Canada. "Backgrounder: Modernization of Benefits and Obligations." 11 February 2000. http://canada.justice.gc.ca/en/news/nr/2000/doc_25021.html.—. "Minister of Justice Responds to the 1999 Quadrennial Commission on Judicial Compensation and Benefits." 13 December 2000. http://canada.justice.gc.ca/en/news/nr/2000/doc_25776.html.de Secondat, Charles, Baron de Montesquieu. *The Spirit of Laws*. 1752. Trans. Thomas Nugent. Rev. J.V. Prichard. http://www.constitution.org/cm/sol.htm.

de Tocqueville, Alexis. *Democracy in America*. Vol. 2. Trans. Henry Reeve. http://www.gutenberg.net/etext/816.

Dicey, A.V. *Introduction to the Study of the Law of the Constitution.* London: Macmillan, 1915.

Division of Mission in Canada. *Draft Statement on Human Sexuality.* Toronto: United Church of Canada, 1984.

– *In God's Image ... Male and Female.* Toronto: United Church of Canada, 1980.

Driedger, Elmer. *The Construction of Statutes.* Toronto: Butterworths, 1983.

Egale Canada. "Egale Launches Campaign to Restore Funding of SRS." 1 October 2004. http://www.egale.ca/index.asp?lang=E&menu=34&item=1091.

Equal Marriage for Same-Sex Couples. "The Law Society of Upper Canada: Celebrating Justice." 3 July 2003. http://www.samesexmarriage.ca/legal/law_society.htm.

Evangelical Fellowship of Canada. "EFC Pleased with Outcome in Trinity Western University Case." 17 May 2001. http://www.evangelicalfellowship.ca/media/pr_viewer.asp?Press_ Release_ID=77.

– "Kempling Decision Very Disappointing." 13 June 2005. http://www.evangelicalfellowship.ca/media/pr_viewer.asp?Press_ Release_ID=228.

Ewing, K.D. "The Human Rights Act and Parliamentary Democracy." *The Modern Law Review* 62, no. 1 (1999): 79–99.

Feldthusen, Bruce. "Debate." *London Free Press,* 3 November 1997.

findlay, barbara. "Transsexuals in Canadian Prisons: An Equality Analysis." 2000. http://64.233.167.104/search?q=cache:yT6V2DCTyKkJ:www.barbaraf indlay.com/articles/45.pdf+dickey+clarke+institute+%22sex+reas signment+surgery%22&hl=en.

Fisheries and Oceans Canada. "Highlights of the 1999 Lobster Management Measures." 28 April 1999. http://www.mar.dfo-mpo.gc.ca/communications/maritimes/news99e/m99014.htm.

Friedland, Martin. "Judicial Independence and Accountability in Canada." 10 May 2001. http://www.courts.gov.bc.ca/1701/1701%20Papers/Friedland.htm.

Gearty, Conor. "What Are Judges For?" *Law School Archive, King College London School of Law,* 11 December 2000. http://www.kcl.ac.uk/depsta/law/events/00_01/gearty_lecture/lect ure.pdf.

Greene, Ian, et al. *Final Appeal: Decision-Making in Canadian Courts of Appeal.* Toronto: Lorimer, 1998.

Hamilton, Alexander, John Jay, and James Madison. *The Federalist Papers.* http://thomas.loc.gov/home/histdox/fedpapers.html.

Haskett, Dianne. "Text of the City Hall Statement by London Mayor Dianne Haskett." 21 October 1997.

– "Text of the Election Rally Address by London Mayor Dianne Haskett." 10 November 1997.

Hawkins, Robert, and Robert Martin. "Democracy, Judging and Bertha Wilson." *McGill Law Journal* 41, no. 1 (1995): 1–58.

Hayek, Friedrich. *The Road to Serfdom.* Chicago: University of Chicago Press, 1944.

Hogg, Peter. *Constitutional Law of Canada.* Toronto: Carswell, 1992.

– and Allison Bushell. "The Charter Dialogue between Courts and Legislatures: Or Perhaps the Charter of Rights Isn't Such a Bad Thing After All." *Osgoode Hall Law Journal* 35, no. 1 (1997): 75–124.

Hogg, R.S., et al. "Modelling the Impact of HIV Disease on Mortality in Gay and Bisexual Men." *International Journal of Epidemiology* 26, no. 3 (1997): 657–61.Hovius, Berend. "The Legacy of the Supreme Court of Canada's Approach to the Canadian Bill of Rights: Prospects for the Charter." *McGill Law Journal* 28, no. 1 (1982): http://www.scc-csc.gc.ca/aboutcourt/judges/speeches/famousfive_e.asp.

Hunter, Ian. "Liberty and Equality: A Tale of Two Codes." *McGill Law Journal* 29, no. 1 (1983): 3–23.

– *Three Faces of the Law: A Christian Perspective.* Mississauga: Work Research Foundation, 1996.

Ipsos-Reid, "The Power of Judges," 23 November 1999. http://www.ipsos-na.com/news/pressrelease.cfm?id=604.

– "Canadian Supreme Decisions: Public's View of the Supreme Court," 4 July 2001. http://www.ipsos-na.com/news/pressrelease.cfm?id=1257.

Irvine of Lairg, Lord. "Keynote Address to the Conference on a Bill of Rights for the United Kingdom." University College, London, 4 July 1997. http://www.lcd.gov.uk/speeches/1997/speechfr.htm.

Johansen, David, and Philip Rosen. "The Notwithstanding Clause of the Constitution." Library of Parliament, Parliamentary Research Branch, February 1989. http://www.parl.gc.ca/information/library/PRBpubs/bp194-e.htm.

Johnson, Paul. *A History of the Modern: From 1917 to the 1990s.* London: Weidenfeld and Nicolson, 1991.

Katz, Stanley. "Introduction to Book 1." In William Blackstone, *Commentaries on the Laws of England,* iii-xii. Chicago: University of Chicago Press, 1979.

Keene, Judith. *Human Rights in Ontario.* Toronto: Carswell, 1992.

Keith, Arthur Berriedale. "The Privy Council Decisions: A Comment from Great Britain." *The Canadian Bar Review* 15 (1937): 428– 35.

Kent, Tom. "Immigration Now: How to Regain Control and Use It Well." *Policy Insight,* October 2001.

Knopff, Rainer, and F.L. Morton. *Charter Politics.* Scarborough: Nelson, 1992.

Landolt, C. Gwendolyn. "Project Justice: Changing Canada's Flawed Political and Judicial Systems." *REALWomen of Canada.* http://www.realwomen ca.com/analyses/analyses_03.htm.

Leishman, Rory. "The Judicial Imposition of 'Gay' Rights." In Alphonse de Valk, ed., *Judicial Activism: A Threat to Democracy and Religion,* 46–57. Toronto: Life Ethics Information Centre, 2003.

– "Judicial Leaps of Logic." *Policy Options,* October 2003.

– "Mad Court Disease." *Touchstone: A Journal of Mere Christianity,* March 2005.
– "Our Judges Are Activist Only When It Suits Them." *Policy Options,* September 1999.
– "Robed Dictators." *The Next City,* October 1998.
Loney, Martin. *The Pursuit of Division: Race, Gender and Preferential Hiring in Canada.* Montreal and Kingston: McGill-Queen's University Press, 1998.
Malleson, Kate. "A British Bill of Rights: Incorporating the European Convention on Human Rights." *IRPP Choices* 5, no. 1 (1999): 31–42.
Mandel, Michael. *The Charter of Rights and the Legalization of Politics in Canada.* 2nd rev. ed. Toronto: Thompson Educational Publishers, 1994.Manfredi, Christopher. *Feminist Activism in the Supreme Court: Legal Mobilization and the Women's Legal Education and Action Fund.* Vancouver: University or British Columbia Press, 2004.
Martin, Robert. "Debate." *London Free Press,* 3 November 1997.
– *The Most Dangerous Branch: How the Supreme Court of Canada Has Undermined Our Law and Our Democracy.* Montreal and Kingston: McGill-Queen's University Press, 2005.
McConnell, W.H. *William R. McIntyre: Paladin of Common Law.* Ottawa: Carleton University Press, 2000.McCormick, Peter. *Supreme At Last: The Evolution of the Supreme Court of Canada.* Toronto: James Lorimer, 2000.McHugh, Paul. "Surgical Sex." *First Things,* November 2004.
McLachlin, Beverley. "Courts, Legislatures and Executives in the Post-Charter Era." *Policy Options,* June 1999.
– "The Judiciary's Distinctive Role in our Constitutional Democracy." *Policy Options,* September 2003.
– "Remarks of the Right Honourable Beverley McLachlin, P.C., Famous Five Breakfast." 17 October 2000. http://www.scc-csc.gc.ca/AboutCourt/judges/speeches/famousfive_e.asp.
Michael, R.T., et al. *Sex in America: A Definitive Study.* Boston: Little, Brown, 1994.
Ministère de l'Èducation, du Loisir et du Sport du Québec. "La mise en place d'un programme d'éthique et de culture religieuse: Une orientation d'avenir pour tous les jeunes du Québec." 4 May 2005. http://www.mels.gouv.qc.ca/lancement/Prog_ethique_cult_reli/fi che_ethique_cult_reli.pdf.
Minutes of the Proceedings and Evidence of the Special Joint Committee of the Senate and the House of Commons on the Constitution. Issue 39, First Session of the Thirty-Second Parliament, 1980–81, 16 January 1981.
Minutes of the Proceedings and Evidence of the Special Joint Committee of the Senate and the House of Commons on the Constitution. Issue 48, First Session of the Thirty-Second Parliament, 1980–81, 29 January 1981.
Monahan, Patrick. *The Charter, Federalism and the Supreme Court of Canada.* Toronto: Carswell, 1987.

– *Storming the Pink Palace.* Toronto: Lester, 1995.

Morton, F.L. "Can Judicial Supremacy Be Stopped? Reconsidering the Notwithstanding Power." *Fraser Forum*, September 2003.

– "Dialogue or Monologue." *Policy Options,* April 1999.

– and Rainer Knopff. *The Charter Revolution and the Court Party.* Peterborough: Broadview, 2000.

National Association for Research and Therapy of Homosexuality (NARTH). "Historic Gay Advocate Now Believes Change Is Possible." http://www.narth.com/docs/spitzer3.html.

– "Prominent Psychiatrist Announces New Study Results: 'Some Gays *Can* Change.'" http://www.narth.com/docs/spitzer2.html.

National Gay Rights Coalition. "Human Rights." http://www.yorku.ca/jspot/5/stand_together/4.

Ontario Human Rights Code Review Task Force. *Achieving Equality: A report on Human Rights Reform.* Ontario: Government of Ontario, 1992.

Ontario Human Rights Commission. *Annual Report: 1996–1997.* Ontario: Ontario Human Rights Commission, 1997.

– *Annual Report: 2003–2004.* Ontario: Ontario Human Rights Commission, 2004.

Ontario Public Health Association. "Trans Health Project." 2003. http://www.opha.on.ca/ppres/2004–06_pp.pdf.

Orwell, George. *Nineteen Eighty-Four.* London: Penguin Books, 1990.

Presser, Stephen B. Recapturing the Constitution: Race, Religion, and Abortion Reconsidered. Washington: Regnery, 1994.

Proceedings of the Standing Senate Committee on Legal and Constitutional Affairs. Issue 21, First Session of the Thirty-Eighth Parliament, 2004–05, 23 July 2005.

Public Service Commission of Canada. "Employment Equity." http://jobs.gc.ca/fswep-fete/manager/equity_e.htm.

– "Equity Group Definitions." http://www.jobs-emplois.gc.ca/menu/usefulinfo_e.htm.

Rae, Bob. *From Protest to Power: Personal Reflections on a Life in Politics.* Toronto: Viking, 1996.

Riordan, Michael. *The First Stone: Homosexuality and the United Church.* Toronto: McClelland and Stewart, 1990.

Russell, Peter. "The Supreme Court and the Charter: A Question of Legitimacy." In David P. Shugarman and Reg Whitaker, eds, *Federalism and Political Community: Essays in Honour of Donald Smiley,* 225–40. Peterborough: Broadview, 1989.

Satinover, Jeffrey. *Homosexuality and the Politics of Truth.* Grand Rapids: Baker Books, 1996.Saywell, John T. *The Lawmakers: Judicial Power and the Shaping of Canadian Federalism.* Toronto: University of Toronto Press, 2002.

Scalia, Antonin. "Common-Law Courts in a Civil-Law System: The Role of

United States Federal Courts in Interpreting the Constitution and Laws." *The Tanner Lectures on Human Values*. Princeton University, 8 and 9 March 1995. http://www.tannerlectures.utah.edu/lectures/scalia97.pdf.

Schmidt, Thomas. *Straight and Narrow? Compassion and Clarity in the Homosexuality Debate*. Downers Grove: InverVarsity Press, 1995.

Scroggs, R. *The New Testament and Homosexuality*. Philadelphia: Fortress, 1983.

Sharpe, Robert J., and Kent Roach. *Brian Dickson: A Judge's Journey*. Toronto: University of Toronto Press, 2003.

Smith, Stephen D. "The Constitution of Babel." *First Things*, January 1998.

Sowell, Thomas. *Civil Rights: Rhetoric or Reality?* New York: William Morrow, 1984.

– *A Conflict of Visions: Ideological Origins of Political Struggles*. New York: William Morrow, 1987.

– *The Economics and Politics of Race: An International Perspective*. New York: William Morrow, 1983.

Specter, Michael. "Higher Risk: Crystal Meth, the Internet, and Dangerous Choices about AIDS." *The New Yorker*, 23 May 2005. http://www.newyorker.com/fact/content/articles/050523fa_fact.

Spitzer, Robert. "Can Some Gay Men and Lesbians Change Their Sexual Orientation? 200 Participants Reporting a Change from Homosexual to Heterosexual Orientation." *Archives of Sexual Behavior* 32, no. 5 (2003): 403–17.

Sweet, Lois. "The Fourth 'R': Religion in Our Classrooms." The Atkinson Charitable Foundation. 1996. http://atkinsonfdn.on.ca/publications/fellowship/sweet.html.

Tompkins, Edward. "2000 CLGA Annual General Meeting: President's Report." Canadian Lesbian and Gay Archives. 8 May 2000. http://www.clga.ca.Tremblay, L. "Section 7 of the Charter: Substantive Due Process?" *University of British Columbia Law Review* 18 (1984): 201–54.

Trudeau, Pierre Elliott. *Against the Current: Selected Writings, 1939–1996*. Toronto: McClelland and Stewart, 1996.

– *Memoirs*. Toronto: McClelland and Stewart, 1993.

Truscott, Gord. *Alone: A Grandmother's Struggle for Life*. Toronto: Campaign Life Coalition, 2000.Vancouver Rape Relief Society. "BC Supreme Court Overrules BC Human Rights Tribunal." 22 December 2003. http://www.rapereliefshelter.bc.ca/issues/nixon/pr_20031219_ju dgement.html.

– "Transcripts, *Rape Relief v. Kimberly Nixon*." 11 December 2000. http://www.rapereliefshelter.bc.ca/issues/nixon/dec112000_nixo n.pdf.

– "Vancouver Rape Relief Seeks BC Supreme Court Appeal of Human Rights Decision in Women-Only Case." 24 June 2002. http://www.rapereliefshelter.bc.ca/issues/knixon_pr_appeal.html.

Waldron, Jeremy. *Law and Disagreement*. Oxford: Clarendon Press, 1999.

Weiler, Paul. *In the Last Resort: A Critical Study of The Supreme Court of Canada*. Toronto: Carswell-Methuen, 1974.

Index